Contemporary French Poetry
Towards a Minor Poetics

LEGENDA

LEGENDA is the Modern Humanities Research Association's book imprint for new research in the Humanities. Founded in 1995 by Malcolm Bowie and others within the University of Oxford, Legenda has always been a collaborative publishing enterprise, directly governed by scholars. The Modern Humanities Research Association (MHRA) joined this collaboration in 1998, became half-owner in 2004, in partnership with Maney Publishing and then Routledge, and has since 2016 been sole owner. Titles range from medieval texts to contemporary cinema and form a widely comparative view of the modern humanities, including works on Arabic, Catalan, English, French, German, Greek, Italian, Portuguese, Russian, Spanish, and Yiddish literature. Editorial boards and committees of more than 60 leading academic specialists work in collaboration with bodies such as the Society for French Studies, the British Comparative Literature Association and the Association of Hispanists of Great Britain & Ireland.

The MHRA encourages and promotes advanced study and research in the field of the modern humanities, especially modern European languages and literature, including English, and also cinema. It aims to break down the barriers between scholars working in different disciplines and to maintain the unity of humanistic scholarship. The Association fulfils this purpose through the publication of journals, bibliographies, monographs, critical editions, and the MHRA Style Guide, and by making grants in support of research. Membership is open to all who work in the Humanities, whether independent or in a University post, and the participation of younger colleagues entering the field is especially welcomed.

ALSO PUBLISHED BY THE ASSOCIATION

Critical Texts
Tudor and Stuart Translations • *New Translations* • *European Translations*
MHRA Library of Medieval Welsh Literature

MHRA Bibliographies
Publications of the Modern Humanities Research Association

The Annual Bibliography of English Language & Literature
Austrian Studies
Modern Language Review
Portuguese Studies
The Slavonic and East European Review
Working Papers in the Humanities
The Yearbook of English Studies

www.mhra.org.uk
www.legendabooks.com

RESEARCH MONOGRAPHS IN FRENCH STUDIES

The *Research Monographs in French Studies* (RMFS) are selected, edited and supported by the Society for French Studies. The series seeks to publish the best new work in all areas of the literature, language, thought, history, politics, culture and film of the French-speaking world and to cover the full chronological range from the medieval period to the present day. Proposals are accepted for monographs of up to 85,000 words, while proposals for 'short' monographs (50,000–60,000 words), a traditional strength of the series, are still welcomed.

Editorial Committee
Diana Knight, University of Nottingham (General Editor)
Robert Blackwood, University of Liverpool
Jane Gilbert, University College London
Katherine Ibbett, Trinity College, Oxford
Shirley Jordan, Newcastle University
Max Silverman, University of Leeds

Advisory Committee
Wendy Ayres-Bennett, Murray Edwards College, Cambridge
Celia Britton, University College London
Ann Jefferson, New College, Oxford
Sarah Kay, New York University
Michael Moriarty, University of Cambridge
Keith Reader, University of Glasgow

PUBLISHED IN THIS SERIES

20. *Selfless Cinema? Ethics and French Documentary* by Sarah Cooper
21. *Poisoned Words: Slander and Satire in Early Modern France* by Emily Butterworth
22. *France/China: Intercultural Imaginings* by Alex Hughes
23. *Biography in Early Modern France 1540–1630* by Katherine MacDonald
24. *Balzac and the Model of Painting* by Diana Knight
25. *Exotic Subversions in Nineteenth-Century French Literature* by Jennifer Yee
26. *The Syllables of Time: Proust and the History of Reading* by Teresa Whitington
27. *Personal Effects: Reading the 'Journal' of Marie Bashkirtseff* by Sonia Wilson
28. *The Choreography of Modernism in France* by Julie Townsend
29. *Voices and Veils* by Anna Kemp
30. *Syntactic Borrowing in Contemporary French*, by Mairi McLaughlin
31. *Dreams of Lovers and Lies of Poets: Poetry, Knowledge, and Desire in the 'Roman de la Rose'* by Sylvia Huot
32. *Maryse Condé and the Space of Literature* by Eva Sansavior
33. *The Livres-Souvenirs of Colette: Genre and the Telling of Time* by Anne Freadman
34. *Furetière's* Roman bourgeois *and the Problem of Exchange* by Craig Moyes
35. *The Subversive Poetics of Alfred Jarry*, by Marieke Dubbelboer
36. *Echo's Voice: The Theatres of Sarraute, Duras, Cixous and Renaude*, by Mary Noonan
37. *Stendhal's Less-Loved Heroines: Fiction, Freedom, and the Female*, by Maria C. Scott
38. *Marie NDiaye: Inhospitable Fictions*, by Shirley Jordan
39. *Dada as Text, Thought and Theory*, by Stephen Forcer
40. *Variation and Change in French Morphosyntax*, by Anna Tristram
41. *Postcolonial Criticism and Representations of African Dictatorship*, by Cécile Bishop
42. *Regarding Manneken Pis: Culture, Celebration and Conflict in Brussels*, by Catherine Emerson
43. *The French Art Novel 1900-1930*, by Katherine Shingler
44. *Accent, Rhythm and Meaning in French Verse*, by Roger Pensom
45. *Baudelaire and Photography: Finding the Painter of Modern Life*, by Timothy Raser
46. *Broken Glass, Broken World: Glass in French Culture in the Aftermath of 1870*, by Hannah Scott
47. *Southern Regional French*, by Damien Mooney
48. *Pascal Quignard: Towards the Vanishing Point*, by Léa Vuong
49. *France, Algeria and the Moving Image*, by Maria Flood
50. *Genet's Genres of Politics*, by Mairéad Hanrahan
51. *Jean-François Vilar: Theatres Of Crime*, by Margaret Atack
52. *Balzac's Love Letters: Correspondence and the Literary Imagination*, by Ewa Szypula
53. *Saints and Monsters in Medieval French and Occitan Literature*, by Huw Grange
54. *Laforgue, Philosophy, and Ideas of Otherness*, by Sam Bootle
55. *Theorizing Medieval Race: Saracen Representations in Old French Literature*, by Victoria Turner

www.rmfs.mhra.org.uk

Contemporary French Poetry

Towards a Minor Poetics

Daisy Sainsbury

LEGENDA

Research Monographs in French Studies 65
Modern Humanities Research Association

2021

Published by Legenda
an imprint of the Modern Humanities Research Association
Salisbury House, Station Road, Cambridge CB1 2LA

ISBN 978-1-78188-842-1 *(HB)*
ISBN 978-1-78188-846-9 *(PB)*

First published 2021

All rights reserved. No part of this publication may be reproduced or disseminated or transmitted in any form or by any means, electronic, mechanical, photocopying, recording or otherwise, or stored in any retrieval system, or otherwise used in any manner whatsoever without written permission of the copyright owner, except in accordance with the provisions of the Copyright, Designs and Patents Act 1988, or under the terms of a licence permitting restricted copying issued in the UK by the Copyright Licensing Agency Ltd, Saffron House, 6–10 Kirby Street, London EC1N 8TS, *England, or in the USA by the Copyright Clearance Center, 222 Rosewood Drive, Danvers MA 01923. Application for the written permission of the copyright owner to reproduce any part of this publication must be made by email to legenda@mhra.org.uk.*

Disclaimer: Statements of fact and opinion contained in this book are those of the author and not of the editors or the Modern Humanities Research Association. The publisher makes no representation, express or implied, in respect of the accuracy of the material in this book and cannot accept any legal responsibility or liability for any errors or omissions that may be made.

Trademark notice: Product or corporate names may be trademarks or registered trademarks, and are used only for identification and explanation without intent to infringe.

© *Modern Humanities Research Association 2021*

Copy-Editor: Charlotte Brown

CONTENTS

	Acknowledgements	ix
	List of Abbreviations	x
1	Minor Literature, Minor Poetry?	1
2	Dominique Fourcade, 'L'Expérience de la poésie'	43
3	Olivier Cadiot, 'La Poésie par d'autres moyens'	81
4	Christophe Tarkos, 'Pour la poésie'	126
	Conclusion	171
	Bibliography	179
	Index	187

ACKNOWLEDGEMENTS

This monograph would never have been possible without the guidance and generosity of my D.Phil. supervisors, Ian Maclachlan and Michael Sheringham. I could not have hoped for two more supportive and inspirational mentors, and it is with feelings of gratitude and regret that this project comes to fruition without Michael being here to see it.

I'd also like to thank my D.Phil. examiners, Nikolaj Lübecker and Eric Robertson, whose insight and advice significantly shaped the development of the book. This project would not have materialised without the generous financial support of the University of Oxford's Zaharoff D.Phil. Scholarship, jointly funded by the Faculty of Medieval and Modern Languages and Lady Margaret Hall, and the Laming Fellowship at The Queen's College, Oxford, which funded my post-doctoral research. I must also thank Edinburgh University Press, publishers of *Paragraph*, for their permission to incorporate material which first appeared in the journal in 2019 in an article entitled 'Towards a Minor Poetry: Reading Twentieth-Century French Poetry with Deleuze-Guattari and Bakhtin', as well as Liverpool University Press, publishers of *Modern Languages Open*, for the permission to incorporate material which first appeared in the article 'Language and Statelessness in the Poetry of Olivier Cadiot' (2019). I am also grateful to Charlotte Brown for her rigorous copy-editing, and to Diana Knight and Graham Nelson at Legenda, whose help and advice in preparing this monograph has been invaluable.

D.S., April 2021

LIST OF ABBREVIATIONS

Works by Gilles Deleuze:
- *CC*   *Critique et clinique*, 1993
- *ECC*   *Essays Critical and Clinical*, 1998

Works by Gilles Deleuze and Félix Guattari:
- *ATP*   *A Thousand Plateaus: Capitalism and Schizophrenia*, 2013
- *K1*   *Kafka: pour une littérature mineure*, 1975
- *K2*   *Kafka: Toward a Minor Literature*, 1986
- *MP*   *Mille plateaux*, 1980

Works by Mikhail Bakhtin:
- *DI*   *The Dialogic Imagination*, 1981

Works by Dominique Fourcade:
- *CD*   *Citizen Do*, 2008
- *CPA*   *Le Ciel pas d'angle*, 1983
- *EJP*   *Est-ce que j'peux placer un mot?*, 2001
- *M*   *Manque*, 2012
- *OU*   *Outrance utterance*, 1990
- *RD*   *Rose-déclic*, 1984
- *SB*   *Son blanc du un*, 1986

Works by Olivier Cadiot:
- *AP1*   *L'Art poétic'*, 1988
- *AP2*   *Art poétic'*, 1999
- *FAF*   *Futur, ancien, fugitif*, 1993

Works by Christophe Tarkos:
- *A*   *Anachronisme*, 2001
- *B*   *Le Baroque*, 2009
- *C*   *Caisses*, 1998
- *E*   *L'Enregistré*, 2014
- *EP*   *Écrits poétiques*, 2008
- *MC*   *Morceaux choisis*, 1995
- *ML*   *Ma langue*, 2000
- *S*   *Le Signe =*, 1999
- *T*   *Le Train*, 1996

All translations from primary and secondary material in French are my own unless otherwise specified.

CHAPTER 1

Minor Literature, Minor Poetry?

In a passage in *Mille plateaux* [A Thousand Plateaus], Gilles Deleuze and Félix Guattari refer to the 'expressions singulières' of the American poet E. E. Cummings ('*he danced his did* ou *they went their came*'), arguing that Cummings offers an example of how, in literature, the atypical stylistic and syntactic variations of an author push language towards its limit, extending it 'vers un en-deçà ou un au-delà de la langue' [towards a near side or a beyond of language].[1] This comment forms part of an analysis, introduced in *Kafka: pour une littérature mineure* [Kafka: Towards a Minor Literature] (1975), developed in *Dialogues* (1977), *Mille plateaux* (1980), *Critique et clinique* [Essays Critical and Clinical] (1993), and elsewhere, which elaborates the notion of a 'minor literature'. Deleuze and Guattari's analysis situates literature within the language system more broadly; they understand this system as a socio-political phenomenon, structured around relations of power, where two opposing forces are at work. On the one hand, there is a 'major' or 'territorialising' impulse, which seeks to suppress the intrinsic variation of language, and to assert, in its place, a homogenous system, characterised by norms and constants. On the other hand, there is a 'minor' or 'deterritorialising' impulse, which serves to resist this former impulse, and to highlight instead the heterogeneous reality of the continuous variation of language. The stylistic variation of certain types of literature present prime examples of the deterritorialisation of a major mode: they disorder language, rendering it agrammatical, strange, and foreign. Thus, in Cummings's example, his subversive use of syntax highlights the homogenising tendency of prescriptive grammar, pointing towards novel possibilities in language, new 'outsides' to the parameters established by a dominant discourse. Deleuze and Guattari call this type of literature 'minor', and argue that it is intrinsically political in so far as it destabilises a major linguistic mode, which is itself a discourse of power.

What Deleuze and Guattari recognised in Cummings and his 'expressions singulières', readers of modern French poetry will also recognise in the experimental poets for whom the limits of language, this 'en-deçà ou au-delà de la langue' have long been the locus of innovation. From Mallarmé, Rimbaud, and Lautréamont in the nineteenth century, a well-documented trajectory has developed, characterised by its tendency towards linguistic experimentation, wherein the normative functioning of major literary and non-literary discourses has been systematically dissected and dismantled. In the twenty-first century, poets such as Dominique Fourcade, Olivier Cadiot, and Christophe Tarkos continuously revise and develop the experiments of their predecessors, working at the forever mutating boundaries of the major/minor divide. They are attentive to how new forms of dominant discourse evolve, in everyday life as in literature, and are alert to how the once-innovative literary practices that previously served to unpick such discourses can in turn crystallise as reproducible models. They offer a striking example of the form of 'littérature mineure' that Deleuze and Guattari describe, while also raising a broader question about poetry's specificity within a Deleuzo-Guattarian analysis. Add to this the philosophers' influence, either direct or indirect, on this strand of experimental practice, and it is perhaps surprising that this subject has not already received more critical attention.

Indeed, while there are a significant number of critical works that read contemporary literature through the lens of Deleuze and Guattari's philosophy, relatively few are focused on poetry. This may well reflect the fact that, despite their reference to E. E. Cummings above, the philosophers primarily consider novelists and playwrights (Kafka, Artaud, Beckett, and Proust, for example). They typically only refer to poetry in its broadest sense, and rarely discuss individual poets. This is particularly true for contemporary poets, who are largely absent from Deleuze and Guattari's writing; the one figure who does appear is Gherasim Luca, but, as Christian Prigent suggests, those references are fleeting and underdeveloped.[2]

In recent years, however, critics have begun to explore the possibilities of reading poetry with Deleuze and Guattari as a conceptual apparatus; given the ongoing centrality of the lyric subject in contemporary criticism, their philosophy is typically harnessed in the study of subjectivity. In one characteristic example, the collective volume *Sens et présence du sujet poétique* [Meaning and Presence of the Poetic Subject] (2006) contains no less than six essays that draw on Deleuze and Guattari to varying degrees in their analysis of contemporary French poetry.[3] Bruno Gelas and Hervé Micolet's *Deleuze et les écrivains* [Deleuze and Writers] (2007) assembles various articles on Deleuze, including a number on poetry by Christian Prigent, Jean-Claude Pinson, and Jérôme Game.[4] Game is the critic who has most systematically applied Deleuze's thinking to the analysis of French poetry. His *Poetic Becomings* (2011) represents, to my knowledge, the only book-length exploration of contemporary French poetry through a Deleuzo-Guattarian lens.[5] Game uses Deleuze and Guattari's philosophy to consider how processes of subjectivation take place on a textual level in the work of four contemporary poets: Christian Prigent, Dominique Fourcade, Olivier Cadiot, and Hubert Lucot. He outlines a passage from subject to subjectivation, elaborating a 'poetics of becoming' whereby 'the poem is no longer determined by its subject or theme; instead, the poem becomes the symbolic plane upon which subjectivation (that is, the production of subjectivity) operates'.[6] In a further notable example, Michael G. Kelly's article on 'deterritorialised' or 'unhoused' writing subjects also employs Deleuze and Guattari's account to conceptualise the processes of subjectivation taking place in four works by Olivier Cadiot, Katalin Molnár, Christian Prigent, and Dominique Fourcade.[7]

However, to date, the possibilities of reading contemporary poets alongside Deleuze and Guattari's extensive discussion of minor literature remain unexamined, even though their account configures many issues, typically studied in isolation elsewhere, that are particularly pertinent to the contemporary field: agrammaticality, style, and the foreign, disordered, and political dimensions of literary language, for example. Likewise, the questions that arise by considering Deleuze and Guattari's account in relation to poetry in particular are yet to be addressed. One of the original starting points for this book was a fleeting reference found in Emmanuel Hocquard's essay 'La Bibliothèque de Trieste' [The Library at Trieste], in which he refers to a certain strand of experimental, contemporary French poetry as 'poésie mineure (au sens deleuzien du terme)' [minor poetry (in the Deleuzian sense of the word)].[8] This reference to a 'poésie mineure' prompts several questions: firstly, how might this particular strand of contemporary poetry be read as minor? More broadly, what constitutes minor poetry, and what would set certain types of poetry apart from others in this regard? A second set of questions arose from Prigent's article, 'Deleuze / "Poésie"', which offers a short but valuable survey of the place afforded to poetry in the philosopher's œuvre. In a passing remark, Prigent evokes the possibility of applying Deleuze's analysis to our understanding of poetic language, when he states that for Deleuze literature 'est un 'devenir-autre de la langue, [...] une ligne [...] qui s'échappe du système dominant' [...]. C'est un procès de 'déterritorialisation' dont le dynamisme excentrique 'trace du réel' [...]. On peut voir là une définition du 'langage poétique' [is a 'becoming-other of language, [...] a line [...] that escapes the dominant system' [...]. It is a process of 'deterritorialisation' whose eccentric dynamism 'traces the real' [...]. We might see here a definition of 'poetic language'].[9] Prigent's comment resonates with a further remark made by Michael G. Kelly in *Strands of Utopia* (2008):

> To envision according to another terminological dyad originating with Deleuze and Guattari, the poetic would thus be that entry into language which serves to 'de-territorialize' all that supposedly dominant forms of language use had served to 'territorialize' — to establish and impose upon the reader-addressee with the self-evidence of power.[10]

This idea that Deleuze and Guattari's notion of deterritorialisation might offer a definition of 'the poetic' or of poetic language itself, poses a number of questions. Given that, according to Deleuze and Guattari, the defining feature of minor literature is that it involves a high coefficient of deterritorialisation, then if Prigent's reflection is true, is any instance of poetic language then an instance of 'littérature mineure'? What is the status of poetry and poetic language in Deleuze and Guattari's analysis, and would minor poetry be distinct in any significant way from minor literature? Such questions necessarily invite a number of broader reflections: what then constitutes poetic language, and how does this relate to or differ from 'ordinary' or other types of language? What is the role of style or syntactic variation in this? What do we make today of the well-trodden claim that poetry can have a political dimension in its very use of language? One of the aims of this book is to investigate what Deleuze and Guattari's analysis might offer to the consideration of these questions.

The Stakes of the Contemporary Field

Dominique Fourcade, Olivier Cadiot, and Christophe Tarkos represent three successive generations of contemporary poetry and, while each is by no means representative of a broader movement or trend, together they represent a cross-section of the variegated practices found in the contemporary field. Deleuze and Guattari's analysis therefore configures differently with their respective projects, as it does with the wider trends and practices at play. In order to understand quite what their account might contribute to the study of contemporary poetry, and vice versa, we need to consider first what the stakes of this field are. What are the key issues that face poetry and its criticism today; what questions are they grappling with?

One of the most widespread ways in which critics have tried to make sense of the contemporary landscape involves dividing the field into two broad groups, marking an extension of two general trends in poetry from across the second half of the twentieth century. This division has been formulated in several ways: some talk about a 'poétique du texte' [poetics of the text] or 'poétique de la lettre' [poetics of the letter], as opposed to a 'poétique du sens' [poetics of meaning] or 'poétique du sujet' [poetics of the subject]. Elsewhere it is described according to Saussure's terminology, with the opposition being made between a 'poétique du signifiant' [poetics of the signifier] and a 'poétique du signifié' [poetics of the signified]. The appellation of 'poètes du signifiant' or 'poètes du texte' assembles a number of movements from across the twentieth century: textualism in the 1960s and 1970s, typically associated with the review *Tel Quel*; the 'modernité négative' [negative modernity] or 'écriture blanche' [white writing] of poets such as Jean Daive, Claude Royet-Journoud, Emmanuel Hocquard, and Anne-Marie Albiach; sound poets such as Bernard Heidsieck and Henri Chopin; and the constraint-based poetry of the Oulipo, for example. Predicated on a Saussurean conception of the language system, a 'poétique du signifiant' renders the poem a self-reflexive and metapoetic space that experiments with meaning, representation, and referentiality, often placing emphasis on the linguistic materiality of the text itself. Following from the experiments with voice of nineteenth-century figures such as Baudelaire, Rimbaud, Lautréamont, and Mallarmé, a certain conception of lyric voice involving, to use David Nowell Smith's phrase, a 'metonymic relation of voice and authorship', is thrown into question.[11] In this traditional conception, the first-person pronoun *je* converges with the poet him- or herself, and, consequently, the lyric *je* often becomes a vehicle for voicing the poet's interior affective or psychological states. The words of the text are thus read as the direct expression of the poet, an approach which is typified by Mikhail Bakhtin's well-known analysis of the monologism of poetic discourse: 'Each word must express the poet's *meaning* directly and without mediation; there must be no distance between the poet and his word'.[12]

Over the last 150 years, the 'poètes du signifiant' or 'poètes du texte' have dismantled this conception of voice, typically associated with Romantic and Surrealist poetry, and with that have often rejected the accompanying significance granted to subjective, emotional experience, the 'cancer romantico-lyrique', as Francis Ponge famously put it. A major part of the destabilising of the lyric *je* was the theoretical re-evaluation of the metonymic relationship that underlies it, a recognition of an 'écart énonciatif' [enunciative gap], where the intrinsic properties of the language system require the divorce between poet and first-person pronoun. As Dominique Rabaté suggests, the way that poets deal with this gap delineates:

> Deux tendances selon que la poétique d'un écrivain va dans le sens d'une fusion de l'écart énonciatif, vers ce qu'il faudra appeler une 'voix' poétique, qui transcende ses manifestations ou les unifie dans le rythme d'un chant; ou qu'à l'inverse l'effort poétique tende vers le maintien de cet écart.[13]
>
> [Two tendencies depending on whether the poetics of a writer is orientated towards a fusion of the enunciative gap, towards what should be called a poetic 'voice' that transcends its manifestations or unifies them in the rhythm of a song; or whether, conversely, the poetic effort tends towards maintaining this gap.]

The distinction is not entirely clear cut, particularly after the 'néo-lyrique' movement shortly to be discussed, but broadly speaking the language-focused poets of the twentieth century align with the latter 'tendance', and the lyric poets with the former.

Resisting the perceived stasis and self-reflexivity of the linguistic turn, the 'poètes du signifié' insist on the importance of the world outside the text, sustaining, to varying degrees, a more traditional conception of lyric voice. This 'poétique du signifié' manifests itself in various ways, from the philosophical or metaphysical inclination of poets such as Yves Bonnefoy, André du Bouchet, and Philippe Jaccottet, to the concern for the everyday in the works of Jacques Réda, Henri Thomas, and Paul de Roux. Following the dominant linguistic focus of the previous decades, the 1980s saw a significant revival of lyricism, which appeared in two distinct forms: firstly, in poetry that reprised a seemingly uncomplicated use of the lyric *je*, and revisited traditional lyric themes in turn; and secondly, in poetry that assessed critically the lyricism of nineteenth-century Romanticism or twentieth-century Surrealism, presenting in its place a 'néo-lyrisme' or 'lyrisme critique'. Championed by figures such as Jean-Michel Maulpoix, Michel Collot, and Jean-Claude Pinson, this second mode was more self-reflexive than its previous incarnations, and set about engaging with the criticisms of lyricism raised by the 'poètes du texte'. Neo-lyricism reprises the lyric voice with a greater consciousness of what this gesture entails; as Maulpoix writes, 'Le lyrisme d'aujourd'hui [...] constitue un espace de quête, d'interpellation et de questionnement' [Lyricism today [...] constitutes a space of research, interrogation and questioning].[14] The question remains as to how novel this new lyric poetry actually is — Jean-Marie Gleize, for example, would brand much of it 'la re-poésie', arguing that it represents a return to old forms in a new guise.[15]

At the beginning of the 1990s, Gleize's elaboration of the notion of 'littéralité' [literality] saw the distinction described above reformulated as a division between 'lyrique' poets on the one hand, and 'littéraliste' poets on the other, a paradigm that has carried particular weight in recent criticism. In *A noir: poésie et littéralité* [A for Black: Poetry and Literality], Gleize describes a 'poésie littéraliste' which involves the rejection of a traditional mode of lyricism, a suspicion of the poetic image, and a grappling with the hopelessness or indeed impossibility of poetry as a genre.[16] Taking up Rimbaud's famous phrase 'littéralement et dans tous les sens' [literally and in all the senses], Gleize's notion of 'littéralité' stresses linguistic materiality or 'le primat de la lettre', a radical realism close to American Objectivism, and a 'neutralisation des images' in poetry (despite the fact that, as Gleize himself concedes, all language is to some degree 'imagé').[17] Jean-Claude Pinson writes that the notion of 'littéralité' 'peut d'abord renvoyer, comme dans l'expression 'sens littéral', à un usage idéalement transparent, dénotatif, du langage, usage qu'on situe traditionnellement aux antipodes du recours littéraire au registre métaphorique. Le littéraire se définit alors par opposition au littéral' [might first refer, as in the expression 'literal sense', to an ideally transparent, denotative use of language, a use that we traditionally identify as being polar opposite to the literary recourse to a metaphoric register. The literary therefore defines itself in opposition to the literal].[18] A principal characteristic of 'littéraliste' poetry is that it attempts to expunge the figures associated with literary language — metaphor, simile, and the image understood in its broadest sense. In Gleize's elaboration of 'littéralité', he discusses two significant and interrelated movements that crystallised in the 1970s and 1980s: 'poésie blanche' and 'poésie négative' (or, more generally, 'modernité négative'). The former derives from Roland Barthes's analysis in *Le Degré zéro de l'écriture* [Writing Degree Zero] (1953) of 'une écriture blanche', that is 'neutre', 'transparente', and 'amodale', characterised by 'un style de l'absence qui est presque une absence idéale du style' [a style of absence which is almost an ideal absence of style].[19] Citing, among other examples, Mallarmé's poetry, Barthes continues, 'l'écriture se réduit alors à une sorte de mode négatif dans lequel les caractères sociaux et mythiques d'un langage s'abolissent au profit d'un état neutre et inerte de la forme' [writing is then reduced to a sort of negative mood in which the social or mythical characters of a language are abolished in favour of a neutral and inert state of form].[20] Subsequently, 'poésie blanche' places emphasis on ellipses and fragments, on the white space of the page, on a stylistic minimalism often described as 'écriture plate' [flat writing], and on silence, negation, absence, and whiteness as thematic motifs. It is associated most immediately with Royet-Journoud, Albiach, Hocquard, and Gleize himself, although, as the essays in the collective volume *Écritures blanches* would suggest, many poets writing during this period could also be evoked: Jean Daive and Dominique Fourcade, for instance.[21]

Involving many of the same poets associated with 'poésie blanche', and closely linked with this former term, 'modernité négative' evokes not an organised literary movement per se, but a broader literary zeitgeist, critical of the once triumphant faith in the power of literature and the revolutionary potential of literary language. The term was coined by Hocquard in 'La Bibliothèque de Trieste', where he gives the following description:

> Pas la *modernité triomphante* de l'avant-guerre, celle des avant-gardes de tous bords, dont on a pu déclarer, à juste titre, qu'elle avait pris fin avec Auschwitz; mais l'autre versant de cette modernité, la *modernité négative* (apophatique) de

l'après-guerre, celle de la suspicion, du doute, des interrogations sur tout et sur elle-même, dont les temps forts en poésie se situent dans les années soixante et soixante-dix.[22]

[Not the *triumphant modernity* of the post-war period, espoused by avant-gardes of all persuasions, which was said, quite rightly, to have ended with Auschwitz; but the other aspect of this modernity, the post-war (apophatic) *negative modernity* of suspicion, doubt, the questioning of everything and of itself, which saw its heyday in poetry in the 1960s and 1970s.]

As Hocquard suggests, negative modernity saw literature rounding upon itself, questioning the value of its practice and the possibilities of its future production. This contributed to the widespread 'crise de poésie' in the latter half of the twentieth century, one of the most well-known formulations of which was Denis Roche's conclusion that 'la poésie est inadmissible, d'ailleurs elle n'existe pas' [poetry is inadmissible, besides, it doesn't exist].[23] As Gleize argues, this crisis has become a constitutive element of the poetic act. Gleize, whose own contribution to this discussion involved leaving '*la* poésie' behind, in favour of a '*post*-poésie', evokes the crisis in the following terms:[24]

'La poésie' n'existe pas, n'existe plus, ce qui ne signifie pas, bien sûr, le tarissement de la pratique poétique, mais simplement que la poésie vit son état de crise, sans doute *de* son état de crise, un état critique et autocritique permanent qui est certainement sa seule définition possible aujourd'hui [...]. La question est ouverte, la poésie est ouverte à ses questions: celle de sa spécificité [...], celle de sa relation à son histoire, à différents moments de son histoire, à l'évaluation de l'héritage (prosodique notamment), celle de sa relation à des traditions autres, à d'autres langues, celle de la validité de l'expérimentation dont elle est le lieu depuis maintenant un bon siècle, celle du lieu de son effectuation [...], celle de sa capacité à dire l'être, ou à en suggérer le manque, celle de son occultation sociale, de ses raisons, celle même, évidemment, de son existence, etc.[25]

['Poetry' does not exist, no longer exists, which doesn't mean, of course, that poetic practice has dried up, but simply that poetry is living its state of crisis, no doubt *from* its state of crisis, a permanent critical and self-critical state which is certainly its only possible definition today [...]. The question is open, poetry is open to its questions: that of its specificity [...]; its relationship to its history, to different moments in its history, to the evaluation of its heritage (notably its prosodic heritage); its relationship to other traditions, to other languages; the validity of the experimentation that it has played host to for more than a century now; the locus of its performance [...]; its capacity to express being, or to suggest the lack of it; its social occultation; its reasons; even its existence, etc.]

As Gleize suggests, if there is one thing that defines French poetry today, it is this state of perpetual self-questioning. Each poet's subsequent response to these questions might situate them on a continuum of 'poésie positive' and 'poésie négative'. In the following chapters, it will become clear that Fourcade, Cadiot, and Tarkos arrive at very different conclusions in this regard, each of them reflecting broader trends in the contemporary field. Fourcade, linked as we saw above with 'poésie blanche', and Cadiot, the most closely associated with 'littéralité', demonstrate many affinities with negative modernity; Tarkos, a generation later, describes the inaugural gesture of his poetry as an affirmative 'yes', which works against the '"non" désespéré' [despairing 'no'] of many of his (slightly older) contemporaries.²⁶ The 'crise de poésie' that Gleize evokes goes hand-in-hand with an interrogation of its own social or political significance. Pursuing the same question as many contemporary poets and critics, in *A quoi bon encore des poètes* (1994) Christian Prigent asks what is the purpose or use of poetry: 'à quoi ça sert?'²⁷ Addressing the role of the poet, he writes: 'Penser ce rôle en termes de génie civil, d'efficacité sociale immédiate, d'"engagement" ne peut plus que faire rire' [Conceiving this role in terms of civil engineering, or immediate social efficiency, or political 'engagement' is just laughable now].²⁸ Here, Prigent epitomises the posture of many avant-garde writers of the 1960s and 1970s (the period in which he began writing), as well as that of many poets publishing today, by looking towards the differential discourse of poetic language for an answer. He sees poetic language as fundamentally opposed to ordinary language 'parce que le découpage étrange, alambiqué, démultiplié de l'écrit "poétique" impose un autre régime du sens (un autre rythme d'apparition, de constitution et de dispersion du sens dans le temps — le temps d'écrire et le temps de lire)' [because the strange, tortuous, augmented splicing of 'poetic' writing imposes another regime of meaning (another rhythm of meaning's formation, constitution and dispersal in time — the time of writing and the time of reading)].²⁹ Following this line of argumentation, poetic language finds its purpose and political potential in so far as it presents an alternative to normative discourses and signifies 'une protestation [...] contre la réduction de la dimension linguistique à celle de la "communication"' [a protest [...] against the reduction of the linguistic dimension to that of 'communication'].³⁰

New lyricists, such as Jean-Claude Pinson, have also addressed the question of the social or political role of poetry. In *Habiter en poète* [Dwelling as a Poet] (1995), Pinson assesses the existential dimensions of poetry as a practice, elaborating the notion of a 'poéthique', or 'poethics'.³¹ He reminds us that, etymologically, 'ethos' conveys the notion of 'dwelling', evoking a way of being, or existing in the world. In a subsequent collection of essays that elaborate this notion, he writes that every great poetic work:

> Est aussi *proposition de monde* — et notamment proposition, une ou plurielle, quant à telle ou telle modalité possible de son habitation. [...] elle pose, plus ou moins obliquement, la question 'poéthique' du comment vivre, la question de la 'vraie vie' toujours absente et toujours recherchée.³²
>
> [Is also a *world proposition* — and notably a proposition, singular or plural, for a given possible modality of its dwelling. [...] it poses, more or less obliquely, the 'poethical' question of how to live, the question of the 'real life' that is still absent and still sought-after.]

These questions around the social, political, or ethical position of poetry, and its place in the world today, continue to be of great significance in contemporary criticism and practice. They are closely linked with a second question that Gleize alludes to in the passage above, where he evokes poetry's 'capacité à dire l'être, ou en suggérer le manque'. In light of the gap produced by the semiotic structure of the linguistic system, between language and the world it designates, poets tend to adopt one of three approaches: i) to accentuate absence ('modernité négative', 'littéralité'); ii) to reaffirm presence, despite acknowledging certain irreducible properties of the linguistic system, by asserting language's capacity to *point towards* presence ('néo-lyrisme'); or, iii) to see any such gap as inconsequential and carry on regardless ('lyrisme'). As we can see from how these various approaches configure onto the contemporary landscape, this issue is intimately bound up in ongoing discussions of lyricism — hence its centrality in critical debate, and hence why it is Deleuze and Guattari's work on subjectivity that has attracted poetry critics thus far.

Cadiot reformulates Gleize's reference to the 'capacité à dire l'être' in the following terms: 'Le lyrisme, c'est bien ça, l'expression des affects importants. Il y a des affects importants. Il y a des choses importantes qui se passent dans la vie. Comment les dire?' [Lyricism is just that: the expression of important affects. There are important affects. There are important things that happen in life. How do we express them?].[33] Cadiot's question gets to the heart of what is at stake in poetry today: we can agree that there are important things to say, how then do we set about saying these things, despite the obstacles posed by the intrinsic properties of poetry as a language-based practice? What place is there for the world outside the text (subjective experience, emotion, politics, the everyday, etc.) in poetry, and what then do we do with description, narrative, and voice? The centrality of these questions reconciles poets from all areas of the contemporary field, 'littéraliste' and 'néo-lyrique' alike.

In the mid-1990s, the publication of two substantial and stand-alone volumes of the *Revue de littérature générale*, edited by Pierre Alferi and Olivier Cadiot, represented an important moment in this discussion. The reviews saw the crystallisation and convergence of a number of different concerns, assembling texts and critical essays from many twentieth-century poets, Fourcade, Cadiot, and Tarkos included. Alferi and Cadiot provided an overall critical framework for the enterprise in the shape of two editorial essays: 'La Mécanique lyrique', which opens the first review, and 'Digest', which concludes the second. Surveying the contemporary landscape, they outline a series of features that unite the poets collected in the volume. Agnès Disson summarises these into six key points: 1) the primacy of grammar and syntax, 2) the blurring of genres, 3) the accumulation of different points of view and perspectives, 4) an emphasis on speed and movement, 5) repetition as a prevalent lyric figure, and 6) humour.[34] Two principal aspects of Alferi and Cadiot's discussion have had particular currency in recent criticism: the notion of a 'mécanique lyrique' and that of the 'OVNI'. In their discussion of 'la mécanique lyrique', they build on Apollinaire's prophetic remark that poets would one day 'machiner la poésie comme on a machiné le monde' [mechanise poetry the way we have mechanised the world], prefiguring the conception of the poem as, alternately, an 'engin' (Francis Ponge), a 'writing machine' (Brion Gysin), or 'a small (or large) machine made of words' (William Carlos Williams).[35] In Alferi and Cadiot's model, poetry is evoked as a machine or mechanism that fabricates texts from a raw linguistic material comprised of 'boules de sensations-pensées-formes' [balls of sensations-thoughts-forms].[36] Using artisanal processes (among which, cut-up and collage, samples and grafts), the text operates as an eclectic motor or engine where subjecthood and lyricism are constructs of the various devices at work. As Eric Lynch points out, the very term 'mécanique lyrique' demonstrates Alferi and Cadiot's desire 'to integrate lyricism within a formalist theory of poetry', and rather than the direct expression of the author, 'lyricism becomes the energy or tension that animates the work and creates a unified ensemble from multiple registers of language'.[37] In this respect, like the 'néo-lyristes', Alferi and Cadiot are attempting to bypass or overcome the stasis of post-lyrical theory (often referred to as the 'Mallarméan impasse' of modern poetry). They work against 'une sorte de vulgate du manque propre à la France littéraire' [a sort of orthodoxy of lack/absence that is specific to French literature], and look for ways to produce lyricism *by other means*.[38] Unconvinced, the neo-lyrical theorist Michel Collot questions the plausibility of producing emotion from a mechanical treatment of language, writing that Alferi and Cadiot's approach maintains a distinction between emotion and language that is illusory. He argues that lyricism becomes possible when the poet treats the signifier 'non comme un simple matériau linguistique mais comme une "matière-émotion"' [not as a simple linguistic material but as an 'emotion-material'].[39] One could reasonably argue that this is precisely what Alferi and Cadiot are suggesting when they talk of handling language as 'boules de sensations-pensées-formes', and this represents just one of the many overlaps in these supposedly oppositional approaches.

The second key aspect of Alferi and Cadiot's discussion is their account of the OVNI, or 'objet verbal non identifié' [unidentified verbal object], a term that, playing on the French for UFO, captures the variegated and generically-unclassifiable literary forms that pervade the contemporary field, leaving the specificity of poetry, its utility, and ultimately its fate as a genre in a state of crisis.[40] Well beyond the longstanding question of the prose/poetry divide, a significant development in twentieth-century poetry has been its extension into different medias and domains. Whether it be performance poetry, sound poetry, or 'la cinépoésie', this extension has brought the question of form to the fore, and has subsequently prompted broader reflections on what constitutes poetry as a genre. For Tarkos, the very tradition of experimental poetry resides in this development. He describes a 'tradition poétique', ushered in by Apollinaire, that is characterised by three fundamental properties: i) the liberation of poetry from traditional versification, ii) an 'anything goes' approach where poetry uses all means at its disposal, and iii) the displacement of the locus of the poem, whereby performances and multimedia experiments take poetry off the page altogether (*E*, 19). Indeed, in Jean-Michel Espitallier's survey of contemporary French poetry, he writes that a key characteristic of current practice is that it 'travaille aux frontières', working at the boundaries of different media.[41] Here, we might think of conceptual poetry, theorised extensively by Kenneth Goldsmith and Marjorie Perloff, which sits at the intersection of textual practice and performance art; forms not traditionally legimitised as poetry, such as rap, slam, and the French *chanson*; as well as the many poets who experiment with new technologies, such as film and the internet.[42] With regard to the former, one thinks of Alferi's 'cinépoèmes' or Anne-James Chaton's 'autoportraits' which combine text with moving image.[43] With regard to the latter, one thinks of Eric Sadin's interactive digital poems, hosted on the internet, which respond to the heterogeneous experiences of language that shape modern life, and experiment with novel forms of engagement with text (text as moving image; text supplemented or replaced by sound; text generated by computer algorithms; text as an interactive phenomenon, involving 'clicking through', scrolling, copy and pasting, and deleting). As Nathalie Wourm and Nina Parish have pointed out, Sadin calls into question certain dimensions of traditional poetic production: the notion of authorship, the role of the reader, the ephemerality or permanence of the text, and its mode of dissemination.[44] His theoretical reflections in *Poésie atomique* and *éc/artS* are significantly influenced by Deleuzian thought, as in the following passage where he describes how contemporary multimedia projects take poetry off the written page:[45]

> If as Deleuze asserts, *minor literature* is that which makes the structuring order of the dominant linguistic regime shake, these projects can then be *perceived* as attempts to initiate a process of *minor poetics*, within the historic superiority attributed to the transparency of the book.[46]

Offering one possible interpretation of what a 'minor poetics' might look like, here Sadin evokes how contemporary poetry's experimentation with different forms and media disrupts a major poetic mode, symbolised, as he would have it, by the book. Collaborative projects, which might involve multiple poets, an interactive reader, or indeed the intervention of sound engineers or computer programmers, challenge traditional notions of poetic production and authorship. Interactive websites, where the reader navigates his or her way through a poem by clicking through hyperlinks, represent an entirely different form of engagement with the text. In each instance, the various experiences that compose the poetic act — how we write, read, or encounter a poem — are called into question.

This formal and media experimentation sees both a disruption of traditional conceptions of poetry and a blurring of distinctions between different art forms. What is clear is that such experiments have radically changed the shape of poetry, raising the question: how do we recognise a poem today?[47] It becomes increasingly difficult to pinpoint what unites, for example, Lamartine's *Méditations poétiques* and Sadin's interactive algorithmic poems, as the last two centuries have seen the dismantling, one by one, of the defining features that once constituted poetry as a genre. The fact that poetry no longer represents a straightforward, easily recognisable form has no doubt compounded this on-going 'crise de poésie'. If poetry is under threat, then its desire to determine its essence and in turn to establish its value as a practice, is all the more pressing. It is perhaps unsurprising then that so many contemporary poets are also literary critics (Gleize, Prigent, Hocquard, Sadin, and so on), who theorise their practice and address such questions directly.[48] Carrie Noland describes this inclination towards self-analysis, writing,

'Perhaps the single most defining characteristic of twentieth- and twenty-first century poetry is, paradoxically, its tendency to place the definition of poetry in question'.[49] For Gleize, contemporary poetry is thus animated by its own identity crisis; the opening lines of *A noir* read as follows: 'Reste pour nous: la poésie. L'ignorance de ce qu'elle est. La faire, l'écrire, "pour savoir". Pour progresser dans cette ignorance. Pour savoir cette ignorance. Pour l'élucider' [What we're left with is poetry. The ignorance of what it is. Doing it, writing it, 'to know'. To progress in this ignorance. To know this ignorance. To elucidate it].[50] As Gleize suggests 'écrire la poésie, c'est l'inventer absolument' [to write poetry is to invent it absolutely]; every act of poetry is subsequently a self-reflexive gesture that ventures an answer to the question 'what is a poem?'[51] It is engaged in a sustained process of becoming-poetry, as it constantly reinvents and redefines its very identity as a genre.

Fourcade, Cadiot, Tarkos

It is against this backdrop that Fourcade, Cadiot, and Tarkos are writing; they reflect three successive generations of contemporary poetic practice, and although none is comprehensively representative of a broader movement or 'tendance', their poetry is nonetheless inflected in various ways by the particular moment in which they were working. Of the three poets, Dominique Fourcade is the oldest; born in 1938, he began publishing poetry in the 1960s. His early writing, such as *Epreuves du pouvoir* [Trials of Power] (1961) and *Lessive du loup* [The Wolf's Washing] (1966), has a lyrical inclination and demonstrates the influence of René Char, a poet whom Fourcade deeply admired. It is not until the 1980s, after a long hiatus from writing, that he returns with a series of books published by P.O.L.: *Le Ciel pas d'angle* [The Unangular Sky] (1983), *Rose-déclic* [Click-Rose] (1984), *Son blanc du un* [White Sound of One] (1986), and *Xbo* (1988). This return marked a distinct change in his poetic project, and he has continued to publish throughout the 1990s until the present day: *Outrance utterance* [Extravagance Utterance] (1990), *IL* [IT] (1994), *Le Sujet monotype* [The Monotype Subject] (1997), *Est-ce que j'peux placer un mot?* [Can I Get a Word In?] (2001), *Sans lasso et sans flash* [Without Lasso and Without Flash] (2005), *En laisse* [On a Leash] (2005), *Eponges modèle 2003* [2003 Model Sponges] (2005), *Citizen Do* [Citizen Do] (2008), and *Manque* [Lack] (2012). The self-referential nature of Fourcade's writing, and its emphasis on the materiality of language, links him to many of the textualist movements of the second half of the twentieth century. The use of the fragment, and the motif of whiteness in, for example, *Son blanc du un*, sees his association with 'poésie blanche'.[52] His interest in the American Objectivists and his on-going dialogue with certain L=A=N=G=U=A=G=E poets, offer a link to the radical realism of Gleize's 'littéralité'. However, there is also a sustained lyrical inclination to his work, and a conceptualisation of poetry as a distinct way of inhabiting the world, that reflects something of his generation and the discussions of neo-lyricism that shaped the field in the 1980s. This unique configuration of features serves to situate him outside the 'lyrisme' and 'littéralité' camps. Chapter 2 will examine the significance of the foreign and mother tongue in his work, exploring his use of actual foreign language within the text, as well as the way he elaborates these notions as a conceptual paradigm for different experiences of literary and non-literary language. It will then consider the significance of the stutter, which disrupts the text rendering it agrammatical, and the notion of disordered language as a further conceptual paradigm. Investigating the poet's self-proclaimed mantra 'tout arrive' [everything happens], and building on Jérôme Game's account of his 'poetics of the rhizome', I explore how Fourcade's rhizomatic, 'toutarrivesque' (*EJP*, 61) poetics privileges variation, simultaneity, plurality, and interconnection, offering clear resonances with Deleuze and Guattari's account of minor literature.[53]

Born in 1956, Olivier Cadiot is a generation younger than Dominique Fourcade, with his earliest works being published by P.O.L. from the late 1980s onwards: *L'Art poétic'* [Art *poétic'*] (1988), *Roméo & Juliette I* [Romeo & Juliet I] (1989), *Futur, ancien, fugitif* [Future, Former, Fugitive] (1993), *Le Colonel des Zouaves* [The Colonel of the Zouaves] (1997), *Retour définitif et durable de l'être aimé* [Definitive and Durable Return of the Loved One] (2002), *Fairy Queen* (2002), *Un nid pour quoi faire* [A Nest to Do What With] (2007), *Un mage en été* [A Magus in Summer] (2010), *Providence* (2015), and *Histoire de la littérature récente* [History of Recent Literature] (2016–17). His work, which includes books of poetry, novels, adaptations of texts as operas and plays, and musical collaborations, has a distinctly heterogeneous, hybrid feel to it. Although he is wary of the label, of the three poets Cadiot is the most closely associated with 'littéralité'. Like many 'littéraliste' poets, we can trace an American influence in his work: Gertrude Stein in his experiments with grammar, and Charles Reznikoff in his use of compositional techniques such as cut-ups and audio-sampling. The sincerity of traditional lyric voice is wholly absent and there is a humorous, detached, and often cynical tone to much of Cadiot's writing. Chapter 3 explores his use of 'ready-made' language, investigating how this intersects with questions of voice, lyricism, and heteroglossia. I argue that his reworking of cut-ups from grammar manuals and dictionaries into stuttered, disordered assemblages, presents a prototypical example of Deleuzo-Guattarian deterritorialisation. Returning to themes of multilingualism and foreign language, the chapter considers how Cadiot engages with various forms of 'langue mineure', particularly through his interest in regional and minority languages. It explores how Cadiot began his literary career writing poetry, but soon abandoned the enterprise to focus on prose. In his explicit rejection of poetry, Cadiot maintains a generic distinction that his formulation of the OVNI in the *Revue de littérature générale* appears to resist. Examining these questions of genre, Chapter 3 pursues the idea that Cadiot's later musical collaborations with Rodolphe Burger present a form of Gleizian post-poetry, marking a continuation of his earlier poetic project outside the poem.

Christophe Tarkos, born in 1963, is the youngest of the three poets. He died in 2004 at the age of forty-one, after years of treatment for what proved to be a fatal brain tumour. He started writing and performing his poetry in the 1990s, publishing his earliest works with various small publishing houses. Among this early work is: *L'Oiseau vole* [The Bird Flies] (1995), *Morceaux choisis* [Selected Pieces] (1995), *Le Train* [The Train] (1996), *Oui* [Yes] (1996), *Processe* [Process] (1997), and

Le Bâton [The Stick] (1998). In the late 1990s, four further texts were published by P.O.L.: *Caisses* [Boxes] (1998), *Le Signe =* [The Sign =] (1999), *PAN* [BANG] (2000), and *Anachronisme* [Anachronism] (2001). P.O.L. subsequently brought out two posthumous collections: *Écrits poétiques* [Poetic Writings] (2008), which collects together his earlier written work, and *L'Enregistré* [Recorded] (2014), which contains a CD, DVD, and transcripts of his performance work. Tarkos's concern for 'la projection *orale*' establishes a link with 'la poésie sonore' and the performance poetry of figures such as Bernard Heidsieck and Jean-Pierre Bobillot.[54] Whether written or performed, his poetry has a stylistic unity to it; the immediate familiarity of the poem's language, which is resolutely 'ordinary' and accessible, is rendered strange and unfamiliar through the vertiginous repetitions and revisions of a central phrase. Alongside a number of poets who began publishing in the 1990s, such as Charles Pennequin and Nathalie Quintane, his poetry sustains the metalinguistic and experimental dimension of earlier textualist poets, but sees a return of the real in the poem. Language is still of primary importance, but the gap between word and world is not maintained with the brutal insistence of certain textualist predecessors. As Chapter 4 will argue, this stems from Tarkos's conception of language as a 'pâte-mot' [word-dough], and his rejection of Saussure's concept of the sign which has significantly defined the way poets across the twentieth century have thought about language and its relationship to the world. In opposition to the 'poésie négative' of the preceding decades, Tarkos elaborates a poetics of presence, where narration, description, and the reinstatement of lyric voice affirm the existence of the real outside the text. Rather than representing a regressive gesture that simply reprises lyric voice in a form of Gleizian 'repoésie', this stems from a fundamental re-evaluation of the binary relationship between language and world. In this broader monistic, continuist conception, we see certain parallels to Collot's notion of language as 'matière-émotion'. Against a backdrop of 'modernité négative' and the 'crise de poésie', Tarkos is quick to assert the value of poetry, and to evoke the revolutionary potential of its language.

As Deleuze and Guattari have formed part of the philosophical and intellectual zeitgeist of the last forty years, an influence — either direct or indirect — can be found in all three poets' work. In a recent collection of interviews, *Poètes français du 21ème siècle: entretiens* [Twenty-first Century French Poets: Interviews] (2017), Nathalie Wourm interrogates a number of contemporary poets about the perceived influence of Deleuze and Guattari's philosophy on their practice. In her introduction, she argues that a deconstructionist tendency, manifested notably in an engagement with the works of Deleuze and Guattari and Jacques Derrida, forms 'une philosophie commune' that groups together the otherwise heterogeneous poetry of Anne Portugal, Jérôme Game, Olivier Cadiot, Anne-James Chaton, Pierre Alferi, Nathalie Quintane, and others.[55] In her interview with Cadiot, the poet acknowledges the influence explicitly: 'Le Deleuze des années 1980 m'a donné de l'énergie. Il a été comme un *coach* pour moi' [The Deleuze of the 1980s energised me. He was like a coach to me].[56] He often uses Deleuzo-Guattarian terminology, such as 'langue mineure' and 'bégaiement', in interviews, and in his musical collaborations with Rodolphe Burger, he samples recordings of Deleuze's lectures on Spinoza at the Université de Vincennes, lectures that he attended in person.[57] We know that Christophe Tarkos read and annotated texts by Deleuze and Guattari, and, as we shall see, the philosophical underpinnings of his *œuvre* demonstrate several parallels with their thinking.[58] In two interviews in 2015, Dominique Fourcade and I discussed at length Deleuze and Guattari's notion of a 'littérature mineure', and, despite taking issue with a perceived lack of nuance in their analysis, Fourcade confirmed their undeniable significance in ways of thinking about literature and literary language today. That said, it is not my intention to demonstrate the influence of Deleuze and Guattari's thought on these poets' work, but rather to use their analysis to explore what the poetic language of Fourcade, Cadiot, and Tarkos does. To do so, we first need to consider Deleuze and Guattari's discussion in greater detail.

Major Language and Minor Literature

Deleuze and Guattari's conception of the language system, on which their analysis of minor literature depends, is elaborated most extensively in the chapter 'Postulats de la linguistique' [Postulates of Linguistics] in *Mille plateaux*. Here, they emphasise how language, rather than being simply a communication system involved in the giving of information, is first and foremost a socio-political system, structured around relationships of power. In their discussion, Deleuze and Guattari develop the notion of a major language, that is language which is 'homogénéisée, centralisée, standardisée, langue de pouvoir, majeure ou dominante' [homogenized, centralized, standardized, a language of power, a major or dominant language] (*MP*, 127; *ATP*, 117). A major language is characterised by standards, norms, rules, and universals that 'territorialise' language, eliminating variation and tending towards homogeneity. These norms will take various forms: grammatical, syntactic, stylistic, phonological, and so on. The 'langue majeure' is often wielded as a sociopolitical tool, used to dominate, control, and reinforce power relationships within society. Various 'major' institutions underpin this; a brief glance at the history of the French language will flag up a range of examples, from the beacon of prescriptive language ideology that is the Académie française, to the widespread imposition of standard French and eradication of regional dialects that went hand in hand with Jules Ferry's educational reforms at the end of the nineteenth century.

Ultimately, a major language is more a language ideology than an attainable reality for a spoken, living language. It is an ideal linguistic state that any given language will tend towards or diverge from, but never fully realise. As Deleuze and Guattari suggest, the reality of the language system is that it is characterised by intrinsic heterogeneity, and it is variation itself that is systematic (*MP*, 118; *ATP*, 108). Any given language, they argue, is already characterised by continuous variation, and by a multitude of languages intrinsic to it; in any one day, an individual will switch between different linguistic codes in his or her multiple social roles, and there are as many linguistic variants as there are facets to one's individual or collective identity (119; 109). Where the 'langue majeure' attempts to deny the heterogeneous reality of the language system, imposing standardising norms and creating a myth of a singular, unified language, we might expect that a 'langue mineure' would do the reverse. However, as Deleuze and Guattari point out, in their desire for political recognition, minor languages (for example patois or regional dialects belonging to a community of minority speakers) tend to impose in turn their own set of homogenising norms and standards, aspiring towards the status of a major language by replicating its structural properties. A 'langue mineure' is thus often 'une langue localement majeure' [a locally major language] (130; 119). Rather than talking about major versus minor languages, Deleuze and Guattari insist instead on using the terms 'majeur' and 'mineur' to qualify two usages or functions of a language:

> Il n'y a donc pas deux sortes de langues, mais deux traitements possibles d'une même langue. Tantôt l'on traite les variables de manière à en extraire des constantes et des rapports constants, tantôt, de manière à les mettre en état de variation continue. (*MP*, 130)

> [There are not, therefore, two kinds of languages but two possible treatments of the same language. Either the variables are treated in such a way as to extract from them constants and constant relations or in such a way as to place them in continuous variation.] (*ATP*, 120)

For Deleuze and Guattari, there are two principal operations on and within language, and true to the sociopolitical dimension of their analysis, they conceptualise these operations in terms of territories. On the one hand, there is a territorialising operation, an 'usage majeur', which constructs a homogenous linguistic territory that suppresses variation and accentuates constants. On the other hand, there is a deterritorialising operation, an 'usage mineur', which seeks to accentuate the heterogeneity and continuous variation that is already inherent in the language system, and to destabilise or deconstruct the territory of the major language. In so doing, an 'usage mineur' involves a movement outside such a territory; it traces a 'ligne de fuite' [line of flight], as Deleuze and Guattari would have it (*MP*, 16; *ATP*, 9). The point at which such a movement fixes, becoming a 'langue mineure', this would constitute a re-territorialisation, the construction of a new territory. Thus, the truly minor usage of the major language is 'le *devenir*-mineur de la langue majeure' [the *becoming*-minor of the major language] (134; 123, my emphasis), a process or movement of deterritorialisation, not its end point.

It is in these terms, using the paradigm of 'territorialisation' and 'deterritorialisation', that Deleuze and Guattari introduce the notion of minor literature in *Kafka: pour une littérature mineure*: 'Une littérature mineure n'est pas celle d'une langue mineure, plutôt celle qu'une minorité fait dans une langue majeure. Mais le premier caractère est de toute façon que la langue y est affectée d'un fort coefficient de déterritorialisation' [A minor literature doesn't come from a minor language; it is rather that which a minority constructs within a major language. But the first characteristic of minor literature in any case is that in it language is affected with a high coefficient of deterritorialization].[59] Minor literature is thus characterised by its deterritorialisation of the major language within the text. In several respects, this notion of 'déterritorialisation' resonates with other ways that critics have sought to conceptualise literature, and poetry in particular. Such accounts offer a similar spatialised conception of the relationship between poetic discourse and language more broadly, envisaging poetry as the exploration of the limits of language, as the probing of the boundaries of conventional expression, or the movement towards a utopic language beyond. For example, in *Wittgenstein's Ladder* (1996), Marjorie Perloff describes the language game of poetry as the '"bumping of one's head" against the limits of language'.[60] This recalls Deleuze and Guattari's account of E. E. Cummings's poetry as occupying a liminal point between language and its outside, 'un en-deçà ou un au-delà de la langue' (*MP*, 126; *ATP*, 116). Discussing the work of another American poet, Gertrude Stein, Perloff writes that, far from being involved in a game of 'information-giving', Stein is instead involved in a 'game of testing the limits of language'.[61] It follows from Wittgenstein's proposition, 'the limits of my language mean the limits of my world', that experimenting with the limits of language represents an attempt to access a reality unattainable through ordinary speech. Experimenting with new linguistic forms entails the possibility of new modes of perception, therefore offering a means of, as Perloff puts it, 'running against the walls of our cage'.[62]

These kinds of spatialised descriptions are prevalent in the discussion of contemporary French poetry; Prigent, for example, evokes the 'dynamisme excentrique' [eccentric dynamism] of contemporary poets, highlighting their linguistic 'excentricité' or their 'voix excentriques'.[63] The term 'excentrique' aligns with the notion of deterritorialisation in so far as it denotes a position outside the centre, where the centre designates the comfort of a mother tongue, the firm ground of a sane mind or the reassuring normality of a major territory. Dominique Rabaté's evocation of poetry's desire to find the way out, to 'chercher la sortie' in language, takes us even closer to Deleuze and Guattari's deterritorialisation by emphasizing the process or movement, rather than the end position:

> A la suite d'Emmanuel Hocquard, il faudrait donc se demander si l'affaire même de la poésie moderne et contemporaine ne consisterait pas justement dans la recherche des façons pour trouver la sortie, mais selon une inflexion ou une clause à mes yeux capitale: trouver la sortie une fois que l'on a renoncé à la possibilité (parce qu'on n'en a pas ou plus les moyens) de se situer dans quelque dehors du langage.[64]

> [Following Emmanuel Hocquard, one should therefore wonder whether the very business of modern and contemporary poetry might not consist precisely of this search for means to find the way out, but with a modulation or stipulation that is, to my eyes, crucial: to find the way out once one has renounced the possibility (because we don't have, or no longer have, the means) to situate oneself in some outside of language.]

Here, Rabaté identifies the bind of experimental poetry: while attempting to find an outside of language, any such experiment must be conducted within the confines of language itself. Deleuze explores the same theme in the preface to *Critique et clinique*:

> L'écrivain, comme dit Proust, invente dans la langue une nouvelle langue, une langue étrangère en quelque sorte. Il met à jour de nouvelles puissances grammaticales ou syntaxiques. Il entraîne la langue hors de ses sillons

coutumiers, il la fait *délirer*. [...] en effet, quand une autre langue se crée dans la langue, c'est le langage tout entier qui tend vers une limite 'asyntaxique', 'agrammaticale', ou qui communique avec son propre dehors.

La limite n'est pas en dehors du langage, elle en est le dehors: elle est faite de visions et d'auditions non-langagières, mais que seul le langage rend possibles. [...] Beckett parlait de 'forer des trous' dans le langage pour voir ou entendre 'ce qui est tapi derrière'. [...]

Ces visions, ces auditions] sont des événements à la frontière du langage.

[Writers, as Proust says, invent a new language within language, a foreign language, as it were. They bring to light new grammatical or syntactic powers. They force language outside its customary furrows, they make it *delirious*. [...] in effect, when another language is created within language, it is language in its entirety that tends toward an 'asyntactic', 'agrammatical' limit, or that communicates with its own outside.

The limit is not outside language, it is the outside *of* language. It is made up of visions and auditions that are not of language, but which language alone makes possible. [...] Beckett spoke of 'drilling holes' in language in order to see or hear 'what was lurking behind'. [...]

[These visions, these auditions] are events at the edge of language.]⁶⁵

Here, Deleuze describes literary language as occupying a liminal space at the boundaries of ordinary language, but tending towards an immanent outside. As he goes on to say, this literary language presents itself as 'une sorte de langue étrangère, qui n'est pas une autre langue, ni un patois retrouvé, mais un devenir-autre de la langue' [a kind of foreign language within language, which is neither another language nor a rediscovered patois, but a becoming-other of language] (*CC*, 15; *ECC*, 5). The distinction is slight but significant: literary language is not the fully-realised creation of another language (which might represent an external beyond or outside of language), but rather a becoming-other, a future-orientated process that takes place within language ('en-deçà') and that points towards a potentialised outside ('au-delà'). This accords with the conception of poetry as a quest for a utopic space of language, by definition always unrealisable, and calls to mind Bernard Noël's phrase: 'la poésie est l'expérience des limites intérieures de l'expression verbale: en touchant ces limites, la poésie touche à la fois l'origine et l'avenir' [poetry is the experience of the limits interior to verbal expression: by touching these limits, poetry touches both the origin and the future].⁶⁶

'Expression atypique'

In *Mille plateaux*, Deleuze and Guattari suggest that deterritorialisation appears with the atypical expression of certain writers:

L'expression atypique constitue une pointe de déterritorialisation de la langue, elle joue le rôle de tenseur, c'est-à-dire fait que la langue tend vers une limite de ses éléments, formes ou notions, vers un en-deçà ou un au-delà de la langue. (*MP*, 126)

[Atypical expression constitutes a cutting edge of deterritorialization of language, it plays the role of tensor; in other words, it causes language to tend toward the limit of its elements, forms, or notions, toward a near side or a beyond of language.] (*ATP*, 116)

Atypical expression acts as a tensor, setting the process of deterritorialisation in motion and highlighting the tensions that are already embedded within a language (*K1*, 41; *K2*, 22). These tensors are stylistic features which undo the familiar expressions of the major language, making language strange and foreign. A marked use of syntax in Cummings's poetry, for example, destabilises the normative function of grammar; Artaud's non-linguistic 'cris-souffles' [cries, gasps] (*K1*, 49; *K2*, 26) point to the conventions of meaning production in ordinary language use. In turn tensors create lines of flight, pointing to new linguistic possibilities, as Zornitsa Dimitrova suggests:

> The tensor shows just what language could also become, what variegated potentialities is it yet capable of unlocking. [...] [The] tensor paves the way to a new becoming of language. It triggers an encounter with what language could be, what forces it could evoke within itself while remaining the same well-known system.[67]

For Deleuze and Guattari, the author's style is the locus for such a process. The stylistic variations that an author carves into the major language trigger its becoming-minor, and in their analysis of authors such as Kafka, Beckett, Artaud, and Luca, they offer several examples. Prigent gives a helpful account of the recurring stylistic characteristics Deleuze and Guattari allude to; he begins by highlighting their emphasis on the decomposition of language (e.g. into phonetic components in Artaud's glossolalia, or in the alliterative and prosodic effects of poetry), which stresses its materiality, and brings language into continuity with music.[68] He subsequently identifies their emphasis on repetition and excess (Beckett's polyptotons or Luca's stuttering).[69] Elsewhere, Deleuze and Guattari evoke a stylistic 'poverty' of certain forms of minor literature, a notable example being the suppression of metaphorical language in Kafka's work (*K1*, 40; *K2*, 23). Here, the linguistic features of minor literature exhibit an unsurprising parallel with 'des langues dites mineures' [so-called minor languages]: 'un appauvrissement, une déperdition des formes, syntaxiques ou lexicales' [an impoverishment, a shedding of syntactical and lexical forms] (*MP*, 131; *ATP*, 121). This 'appauvrissement' is reminiscent of Barthes's conception of 'une écriture blanche'. In *Le Degré zéro de l'écriture*, he writes:

> Cette parole transparente, inaugurée par *L'Etranger* de Camus, accomplit un style de l'absence qui est presque une absence idéale du style; l'écriture se réduit alors à une sorte de mode négatif dans lequel les caractères sociaux ou mythiques d'un langage s'abolissent au profit d'un état neutre et inerte de la forme.
>
> [This transparent form of speech, initiated by Camus's *Outsider*, achieves a style of absence which is almost an ideal absence of style; writing is then reduced to a sort of negative mood in which the social or mythical characters of a language are abolished in favour of a neutral and inert state of form.][70]

Here, Barthes evokes a style that is characterised precisely by an impoverishment or absence of style, a form of writing that strips language of the stylistic conventions of a given literary mode or genre. The connection to Deleuze and Guattari's observations on certain stylistic features of 'littérature mineure' is apparent, and indeed, has already been evoked, albeit obliquely, by Hocquard in 'La Bibliothèque de Trieste', where he describes the 'modernité négative' of contemporary poets (who were significantly influenced by Barthes's 'écriture blanche') as 'cette poésie mineure (au sens deleuzien du terme), cette poésie sans accent poétique' [this minor poetry (in the Deleuzian sense of the word), this poetry without poetic accent].[71]

Agrammaticality

Having stressed that the deterritorialising of language takes place at the level of style, in his later work *Critique et clinique*, Deleuze underlines the significance of syntax:

> Création syntaxique, style, tel est ce devenir de la langue: il n'y a pas de création de mots, il n'y a pas de néologismes qui vaillent en dehors des effets de syntaxe dans lesquels ils se développent. Si bien que la littérature présente déjà deux aspects, dans la mesure où elle opère une décomposition ou une destruction de la langue maternelle, mais aussi l'invention d'une nouvelle langue dans la langue, par création de syntaxes. (*CC*, 15–16)

> [Syntactic creation or style — this is the becoming of language. The creation of words or neologisms is worth nothing apart from the effects of syntax in which they are developed. So literature already presents two aspects: through the creation of syntax, it brings about not only a decomposition or destruction of the maternal language, but also the invention of a new language within language.] (*ECC*, 5)

Throughout their analysis, Deleuze and Guattari oscillate between a literal and a metonymic use of terms such as a 'syntax' and 'grammaticality'. For example, they use the term *agrammaticalité* to describe particular syntactic features of Cummings's or Luca's poetry, but also to evoke more generally the 'expression atypique' of minor literature. In the following passage, they define the scope of the term so that it encompasses not just syntactically or grammatically incorrect forms, but all language use that is atypical and that subverts the rules or conventions of the major language: 'L'agrammaticalité, par exemple, n'est plus un caractère contingent de la parole qui s'opposerait à la grammaticalité de la langue, c'est au contraire le caractère idéal de la ligne qui met les variables grammaticales en état de variation continue' [Agrammaticality, for example, is no longer a contingent characteristic of speech opposed to the grammaticality of language; rather, it is the ideal characteristic of a line placing grammatical variables in a state of continuous variation] (*MP*, 125; *ATP*, 115). We might identify two principal motivations for Deleuze and Guattari's focus on grammar and agrammaticality: firstly, it reflects certain developments in linguistics during the twentieth century whereby grammar, as the fundamental structure of language, comes to stand metonymically for language as a whole. The theory of Universal Grammar elaborated by Noam Chomsky, to whom Deleuze and Guattari allude throughout 'Postulats de la linguistique', as well as the subsequent rise of transformative syntax as a discipline, has placed grammar at the centre of linguistic enquiry, conflating the study of grammar and language so that grammar is increasingly viewed by linguists as the very essence of language.[72] Consequently, agrammaticality is not merely an ancillary stylistic variant, but a form of variation that disrupts the entire structure of language itself. Secondly, grammar represents an element of language that is most immediately bound up with questions of power, regulation, and control. It conveys one very tangible instance of the sociopolitical policing of language, where particular linguistic variables connote levels of education, socioeconomic status, and so on (think: 'I ain't' versus 'I am not', 'me and John' versus 'John and I'). It is both a tool and a symbol of the various forms of power structures that regulate language use and insist on conformity to the standard. Indeed, Deleuze and Guattari begin the chapter 'Postulats de la linguistique' by evoking the grammar classroom and 'la maîtresse d'école' [schoolmistress] (*MP*, 95; *ATP*, 88):

> Les mots ne sont pas des outils; mais on donne aux enfants du langage, des plumes et des cahiers, comme on donne des pelles et des pioches aux ouvriers. Une règle de grammaire est un marqueur de pouvoir, avant d'être un marqueur syntaxique. (*MP*, 96)
>
> [Words are not tools, but we give children language, pens, and notebooks as we give workers shovels and pickaxes. A rule of grammar is a power marker before it is a syntactical marker.] (*ATP*, 88)

Later in the chapter, they expand this reflection:

> Qu'est-ce que la grammaticalité, et le signe S, le symbole catégoriel qui domine les énoncés? C'est un marqueur de pouvoir avant d'être un marqueur syntaxique, et les arbres chomskiens établissent des rapports constants entre variables de pouvoir. Former des phrases grammaticalement correctes est, pour l'individu normal, le préalable de toute soumission aux lois sociales. Nul n'est censé ignorer la grammaticalité, ceux qui l'ignorent relèvent d'institutions spéciales. L'unité d'une langue est d'abord politique. (*MP*, 127–28)
>
> [What is grammaticality, and the sign S, the categorical symbol that dominates statements? It is a power marker before it is a syntactical marker, and Chomsky's trees establish constant relations between power variables. Forming grammatically correct sentences is for the normal individual the prerequisite for any submission to social laws. No one is supposed to be ignorant of grammaticality; those who are belong in special institutions. The unity of language is fundamentally political.] (*ATP*, 117–18)

Consequently, the tension between the grammatical and syntactic variation of style and the imposition of norms and rules that attempt to govern it, is a prime locus for the operation of a major language, and its subsequent subversion within minor literature. The two poets that Deleuze and Guattari evoke to illustrate their discussion, E. E. Cummings and Gherasim Luca, have in common their atypical use of syntax. If we consider the extracts from their poems that appear in Deleuze and Guattari's analysis, both involve the subversion of ordinary syntax, either in discontinuous, truncated phrases, in the omission of parts of speech, or in the slipping around of grammatical categories — from Cummings, 'he danced his did', 'they went their came' (*MP*, 125; *ATP*, 115) and from Luca's quasi-untranslatable 'JE T'AIME PASSIONÉMENT' [I LOVE YOU, PASSIONATELY]:

> Passionné nez passionenem je
> je t'ai je t'aime je
> je je jet je t'ai jetez
> je t'aime passionnem t'aime.
> (*CC*, 139)

The emphasis placed on syntax in Deleuze and Guattari's theory of minor literature is significant, particularly when it is applied to a generation of contemporary poets where grammar and grammaticality are a primary focus. In the introduction to his anthology of contemporary poetry, *Tout le monde se ressemble* [Everyone Is Alike], Emmanuel Hocquard labels the poets collected there (among whom Cadiot, Alferi, Daive, Albiach, and Royet-Journoud) 'poètes grammairiens'.[73] Hocquard has played a prominent role in theorising the significance of grammar in contemporary poetry; in an interview with Stéphane Baquey, he remarked that he likes:

> L'idée d'être des mécaniciens de précision du langage [...]. Je suis aujourd'hui convaincu que nous avons moins besoin d'écrivains, de linguistes ou de philosophes (sauf si ce sont des gens comme Wittgenstein ou Gilles Deleuze [...]) que d'ingénieurs-grammairiens du langage ordinaire, celui avec lequel, dans lequel nous vivons, pensons, communiquons peut-être.[74]
>
> [The idea of being language precision mechanics [...] Nowadays I am convinced that we are less in need of writers, linguists or philosophers (except if they're people like Wittgenstein or Gilles Deleuze [...]) than engineer-grammarians of ordinary language, the language with and in which we live, think, and communicate perhaps.]

The image of the grammatical 'mécanicien' or 'ingénieur' ties in clearly to the poem-as-machine imagery that is widespread among the 'mécanique lyrique' generation, and reveals a tacit homage to Francis Ponge, the self-proclaimed 'technicien [...] du langage' whose anti-lyrical, language-focused poetry saw the affective states of the writer relegated in favour of a 'parti pris des choses' and a 'compte tenu des mots' [taking the side of things; taking words into account].[75] Such images convey how experimenting with grammar constitutes a desire to examine the functioning of language within the text, to 'redécouvrir le squelette de la langue, de faire jouer ses jointures, ses articulations' [rediscover the skeleton of language, play around with its joints and articulations], as Disson says of the poets assembled in the *Revue de littérature générale*.[76] Hocquard's further precision, 'ingénieurs-grammairiens du langage *ordinaire*' (my emphasis), evokes the recent movement away from the perceived obscurity of certain earlier poetic practices, but also contains a reference to Wittgenstein and the school of linguistics that stresses the importance of ordinary language as the object of study. In his reference to the grammar of 'langage ordinaire', Hocquard evokes the distinction between descriptive grammar (the grammatical functioning of actual language use) and prescriptive grammar (a set of grammatical rules, often ideologically motivated, that do not always reflect current usage, but which attempt to regulate it). On this point, Hocquard, like Deleuze and Guattari, identifies this capacity for prescriptive grammar to operate as a monopolising, standardising regulator. In the introduction to *Tout le monde se ressemble*, he writes:

> Nous vivons tous avec l'idée reçue — avant même l'école primaire — que la grammaire (le squelette de la langue), comme la Loi, doit être la même pour tous et qu'elle est immuable. [...] La grammaire dit: 'Tout le monde se ressemble'. Nous la 'respectons' comme un monopole d'Etat, jusque dans les aspects les plus anodins et les plus intimes de notre vie. Ses lois régissent nos manières de parler et d'écrire, de lire et d'écouter.[77]

> [We all live with the received idea — acquired even before primary school — that grammar (the skeleton of language) is immutable, and, like the Law, must be the same for everyone. [...] Grammar says: 'Everyone is alike'. We 'respect' it like a state monopoly, even in the most trivial and private aspects of our lives. Its laws govern our ways of speaking and writing, reading and listening.]

A subversive use of syntax and grammar, the 'minorising' of major grammatical forms, has particular purchase in the discussion of poetry, where syntax has historically been of heightened significance because of the rhythmic, prosodic, and structural constraints of various traditional poetic forms. Poetic discourse involves a greater degree of variation and flexibility in syntax than other literary discourses, and it presents an instance of language use where the grammatical and syntactic properties of the poem are most divergent from those of ordinary language. As a result, the syntactic variation of poetry has often highlighted how the ideological underpinnings of prescriptive grammar — that normative grammar rules facilitate clarity of thought, abide by an internal logic, or allow for a maximal expressive value — are precisely that: ideologies. In this sense, we might pursue the hypothesis that certain constitutive features of poetic language render it a prime locus for the deterritorialising processes of minor literature. The chapters that follow will investigate some of the ways in which Fourcade, Cadiot, and Tarkos experiment with grammatical and syntactic forms and engage with notions of grammaticality and its subversion within the text. Fourcade, for example, uses grammar as a metaphor to describe the structural constraints that shape not only our language, but also the way we live and experience space. Cadiot's cut-ups in *L'Art poétic'* exploit the tension between the grammaticality of their original sources (prescriptive language manuals) and the agrammaticality of their 'usage mineur' in the displaced context of the poem. Tarkos's poetry, which proceeds via minimal, syntactic revisions of resolutely 'ordinary' language, often in polyptotons that displace meaning across different grammatical categories, embeds these slight yet crucial variations into a broader philosophy, where the difference between nouns, verbs, and adjectival attributes takes on a greater significance.

Destroying the Mother Tongue

In the passage above where Deleuze refers to the 'création syntaxique' of minor literature, he evokes a second, significant dimension of his analysis: 'la littérature [...] opère une décomposition ou une destruction de la langue maternelle' [literature [...] operates a decomposition or destruction of the maternal language] (*CC*, 16; *ECC*, 5). Throughout their discussion, Deleuze and Guattari make frequent recourse to 'la langue maternelle' and 'la langue étrangère'. These terms are occasionally used in their literal sense, for example when they point out that many of the 'auteurs mineurs' considered are writing in distinct sociolinguistic situations, sometimes working in a language that is not their mother tongue (for example, Beckett). They argue that the bilingual or multilingual situations of figures such as Kafka, Luca, and Jean-Luc Godard offer prime conditions for the occurrence of minor literature (*MP*, 123; *ATP*, 114). This is a product of the often-political nature of diglottic or polyglottic language situations, an idea which is illustrated by a discussion of the configuration of German, Czech, Hebrew, and Yiddish in Kafka's Prague. As Deleuze and Guattari suggest, situations of language contact involve a consciousness of the existence of a linguistic 'other', and a more immediate access to a position outside or exterior to the mother tongue, from which new possibilities for the stylistic properties of the major language might be gleaned (*MP*, 124; *ATP*, 114). However, as we have seen, Deleuze and Guattari stress that any given language is already constituted by a plurality of codes, varieties, and lects within it, which makes every writer a polyglot of sorts: 'C'est dans sa propre langue qu'on est bilingue ou multilingue' [It is in one's own language that one is bilingual or multilingual] (*MP*, 133; *ATP*, 122). Thus, within any one language there will be a similar situation of language contact between different codes, and a degree of exteriority and otherness permitted within a mother tongue. Although the sociolinguistic situations of the examples given have a heightened pertinence, the minor author might equally be a monolingual writer living in a monolingual community. Minor literature will appear wherever a writer resists the illusory monolingualism of the major language, developing a kind of multilingualism in his or her own language that accentuates variation rather than suppressing it:

> Être un étranger, mais dans sa propre langue, et pas simplement comme quelqu'un parle une autre langue que la sienne. Être bilingue, multilingue, mais dans une seule et même langue, sans même dialecte ou patois. Être un bâtard, un métis, mais par purification de la race. C'est là que le style fait langue. C'est là que le langage devient intensif, pur continuum de valeurs et d'intensités. (*MP*, 124–25)

> [To be a foreigner, but in one's own tongue, not only when speaking a language other than one's own. To be bilingual, multilingual, but in one and the same language, without even a dialect or patois. To be a bastard, a half-breed, but through a purification of race. That is when style becomes a language. That is when language becomes intensive, a pure continuum or values and intensities.] (*ATP*, 115)

In their analysis, Deleuze and Guattari configure the terms 'mother tongue'/'foreign language' onto 'langue majeure'/'usage mineur'. The 'major' quality of the mother tongue is felt primarily in the way that it requires a 'being within' or an 'être-chez-soi', to use Derrida's term; the 'minor' quality of a foreign language is that it involves a position of exteriority and an encounter with linguistic otherness.[78] In turn, minor literature is constituted by 'une agression contre la langue maternelle', as Prigent puts it, and is comparable, as Deleuze suggests, to a foreign language:[79]

> Ce que fait la littérature dans la langue apparaît mieux: comme dit Proust, elle y trace précisément une sorte de langue étrangère, qui n'est pas une autre langue, ni un patois retrouvé, mais un devenir-autre de la langue, une minoration de cette langue majeure, un délire qui l'emporte, une ligne de sorcière qui s'échappe du système dominant. (*CC*, 15)

> [We can see more clearly the effect of literature on language. As Proust says, it opens up a kind of foreign language within language, which is neither another language nor a rediscovered patois, but a becoming-other of language, a minorization of this major language, a delirium that carries it off, a witch's line that escapes the dominant system.] (*ECC*, 5)

As Deleuze points out, the evocation of literature as a form of foreign language is far from new: here he cites Proust, but one thinks also of Mallarmé ('le vers qui de plusieurs vocables refait un mot total, neuf, étranger à la langue' [verse which, from several expressions, reforms one total, new word, foreign to language]), Jean-Paul Sartre ('On parle dans sa propre langue, on écrit dans une langue étrangère' [One speaks in one's own language, one writes in a foreign language]), and, more recently, Pierre Alferi ('La littérature commence quand l'adhérence à la langue maternelle, son immanence, est conjurée' [Literature begins when the adhesion to the mother tongue, its immanence, is averted]).[80] In *A quoi bon encore des poètes?*, Prigent defines literary modernity precisely through its Rimbaldian desire to 'trouver' or 'créer une langue':

> J'appelle ici *modernité* l'objet de ce désir qui pousse quelques-uns à ne pas se contenter de l'expérience du monde telle que les langages communautaires la représentent, à vivre toute langue comme étrangère et donc à refonder un langage (à 'trouver une langue', disait Rimbaud) pour re-présenter autrement ces représentations.[81]

> [Here, I am calling *modernity* the object of this desire that compels some to not be satisfied with the experience of the world as communal languages represent it, to live all languages as if they were foreign, and so to re-create a language (to 'find a language' as Rimbaud said) to re-present these representations differently.]

Prigent contrasts foreign language with the 'langues communautaires' of the mother tongue, drawing attention to how the strangeness of alternative modes of representation engenders a novel experience of the world. This idea recalls the notion of defamiliarisation, now a commonplace in literary analysis, where the strange or foreign quality of literary language invites new modes of perception. In Victor Shklovsky's essay 'Art as Technique', which first formulated the concept of 'ostranenie' or 'estrangement', he sets up an opposition between automatic or habitual perception and 'the sensation of holding a pen or of speaking in a foreign language for the first time'.[82] This distinction between first language and foreign language is developed into a distinction between 'ordinary speech' and the 'deautomatized perception' involved in poetic language.[83] While both defamiliarisation and deterritorialisation capture the political potential of the new modes of perception provoked by dismantling conventional forms of representation, to conflate the two would be to oversimplify Deleuze and Guattari's analysis. The intersection of language and power plays a much more prominent role in their account, and as deterritorialisation reappears elsewhere in their writing as a phenomenon that occurs across various strata of experience, not just on the level of literary style, minor literature is subsequently linked to many other forms of political action.

The following chapters will illustrate how the mother tongue/foreign language paradigm is significant in the work of Fourcade, Cadiot, and Tarkos. Like Deleuze and Guattari who alternate between a literal understanding of maternal and foreign language, but go on to use the terms for their broader, conceptual value, we see a similar duality of reference in contemporary poetry, where the use of actual foreign language in the text configures with a theoretical consideration. The use of English in Fourcade's poetry, and minority regional languages in Cadiot's performance work, is representative of a broader tendency towards multilingual experimentation in the contemporary field, which takes its most radical form in the multilingual poetry of figures such as Ryoko Sekiguchi (writing in French and Japanese), Caroline Bergvall (English, French, and Norwegian), and Anne Tardos (French, German, English, and Hungarian).[84] The use of one or several foreign languages has various motivations in their work, indicating inter alia: a politically charged, transgressive gesture which refuses the superimposed limitations of national language boundaries; a desire to reflect the changing soundscapes of a globalised world; a quest for an extreme form of linguistic materiality, where the alterity of a foreign language forces signification to give way to the play of signifiers. Chapter 2 focuses on how Fourcade frequently uses English to create dialogic passages where the two languages act metonymically as different voices. The presence of English in his texts forms part of a broader exploration of 'langue maternelle' and 'langue étrangère', understood as two fundamentally different experiences of language. Fourcade's analysis accords in part with Deleuze and Guattari's (literature is understood as a form of foreign language), but he elaborates a more complex understanding of the mother tongue, closer to that of Derrida in *Le Monolinguisme de l'autre* [Monolingualism of the Other] (1996) and Abdelkebir Khatibi in 'La Langue de l'autre' [The Language of the Other] (2008). The chapter will examine how Fourcade harnesses the foreign/maternal paradigm to explore what literary language does, and how it relates to other types of language use.

Stuttering

Alongside references to 'la langue étrangère', a second significant motif in Deleuze and Guattari's analysis of minor literature is the stutter. In *Mille plateaux*, they write:

> Bégayer, c'est facile, mais être bègue du langage lui-même, c'est une autre affaire, qui met en variation tous les éléments linguistiques, et même les éléments non linguistiques, les variables d'expression et les variables de contenu. [...] Proust disait: 'les chefs-d'œuvre sont écrits dans une sorte de langue étrangère'. C'est la même chose que bégayer, mais en étant bègue du langage et pas simplement de la parole. (*MP*, 124)
>
> [It's easy to stammer, but making language itself stammer is a different affair; it involves placing all linguistic, and even nonlinguistic, elements in variation, both variables of expression and variables of content. [...] It was Proust who said that 'masterpieces are written in a kind of foreign language'. That is the same thing as stammering, making language stammer rather than stammering in speech.] (*ATP*, 114–15)

Understood in its most literal sense, the stutter deforms the structures of ordinary language: the course of speech is disrupted, its referential function is temporarily suspended, and the phonemic repetitions of the stutterer draw attention to the signifying elements. Both rhythmically and structurally, the linear, arborescent arrangement of the major language disintegrates and is cast instead into a minor, rhizomatic mode, as Deleuze suggests in his essay 'Bégaya-t-il' [He Stuttered] (*CC*, 140; *ECC*, 107). In such a way, the stutter operates as a metonym for the disordered language of minor literature more generally. Deleuze and Guattari's discussion of *bégaiement* has had a significant influence on contemporary French poetry, for example, on Game's multimedia experiments, or on Cadiot's schizophrenic protagonist Robinson in *Futur, ancien, fugitif*.[85] A brief glance at the lexical fields employed in contemporary criticism (*aphasique, autiste, balbutié* [aphasic, autistic, stammered]) flag up the way that literature is often conceptualised as a form of disordered language, with Deleuze and Guattari's stutter representing one recent and popular formulation of the idea.[86] As in the passage above, in 'Bégaya-t-il' Deleuze suggests that in minor literature the stutter appears on a systematic level, in 'la langue' of the author's style, not in 'la parole' of the text's characters. The distinction is an interesting one, and might well pose the question of whether, in fact, style is not simply the utterance or 'parole' of the writer. Deleuze addresses this question himself, asking 'Faire bégayer la langue: est-ce possible sans la confondre avec la parole?' [Is it possible to make language stutter without confusing it with speech?] (*CC*, 136; *ECC*, 108). The answer, he suggests, depends on how we conceive of language: if we see language as a homogenous system comprised of constants and universals, then the stutter represents malfunctional variants of these constants on the level of speech, but not on a structural level. If, as is the case for 'auteurs mineurs', the language system itself is conceived as characterised by continuous variation, then the stutter merely reflects the system as a whole, and the stuttered 'parole' is an expression of this internal, structural state. Deleuze gives Luca as an example ('Passionné nez passionnem je | je t'ai je t'aime je'), suggesting that through his 'parole [...] éminemment poétique [...] il fait du bégaiement un affect de la langue, non pas une affection de la parole' [If Gherasim Luca's speech is eminently poetic, it is because he makes stuttering an affect of language and not an affectation of speech] (*CC*, 139; *ECC*, 110). Given the emphasis in Deleuze's analysis on style as the locus of deterritorialisation (and therefore minor literature more generally), there is clearly a degree to which the writer can manipulate his or her 'parole' to be a greater or lesser expression of the continuous variation of the 'langue'. This will be explored further in the following chapters, where the stylistic use of foreign or disordered language in its most literal sense (asyntactic phrases, stuttered performance pieces, use of English in French texts) complements a broader engagement with these notions. For example, the decomposition of language into basic phonemic components in Fourcade's poetry operates a sort of performative stutter, acting as a 'tensor' or marker that in turn draws attention to the notion of poetry as disordered language more generally.

A Political Use of Language

In response to Deleuze's analysis of the stutter, Hocquard writes the following: 'Et si, précisément, le bégaiement était une manière de désobéissance, de résistance aux mots d'ordre de la grammaire imposée? Gilles Deleuze dit qu'écrire c'est bégayer dans la langue. En cela, bégayer serait aussi un comportement politique' [And if stuttering were a form of disobedience, of resistance to the order-words of imposed grammar? Gilles Deleuze says that writing is stuttering in language. Therein stuttering would also be a political behaviour].[87] In what sense might the stuttered quality of minor literature be seen as political? As Ronald Bogue suggests: 'Minor writers make language stammer; they deform and transform its regular patterns [...]. And in the process, minor writers contest and undo the power relations immanent within the dominant, major usage patterns of a language'.[88] As minor literature is, by definition, constructed in its opposition or resistance to various major discourses, and these major discourses are, following Deleuze and Guattari's analysis, intrinsically founded on relationships of power, then this makes the transformational linguistic capacity of minor literature a political phenomenon of sorts. In the following analysis of Deleuze, Prigent elaborates this idea, offering a particular example of how this might be the case:

> Ce que je nommais d'entrée 'contrat verbal socialisé' est un système articulé de représentations. C'est ce système que nous appelons 'réalité' [...]. Les 'lignes de fuite' que trace la littérature *mineure* sont des gestes de résistance à cette dictée idéologique. Elles creusent des trous dans ce décor et dérèglent son système. Inclure dans la langue des trouées de négativité venue de l'expérience réelle, c'est empêcher que ne coagule sans reste la représentation idéologique [...]. Un geste poétique digne de ce nom est une action contre les 'dispositifs de pouvoir qui travaillent nos corps' [...]. C'est en cela qu'il 'fait de' la politique. Voire, comme dit Deleuze, que 'tout y est politique'.[89]

> [What I was calling at the outset the 'socialised verbal contract' is an articulated system of representations. It's this system we call 'reality' [...]. The 'lines of

flight' that *minor* literature traces are acts of resistance to this ideological dictation. They dig holes in this set design and disrupt its system. The inclusion in language of gaps of negativity originating in real experience prevents ideological representation from coagulating entirely [...]. A poetic act worthy of its name is an act against the 'devices of power which work upon our bodies' [...]. This is how it 'does' politics. Or indeed, as Deleuze says, how 'everything about it is political'.]

Here, Prigent stresses the political dimension of the treatment of language in Deleuze and Guattari's theory of minor literature, which in turn flags up several parallels with a current of thought to which he himself belongs. In the 1970s, *Tel Quel* and *Change*, as well as several smaller revues such as Prigent's *TXT*, assembled writers and thinkers who theorised the relationship between political action and artistic activity. Both associated with *Tel Quel*, Julia Kristeva and Roland Barthes are two of the most well-known figures who are representative of this mode of thinking. Gleize, writing about the 'néo-avant-gardes' of the 1970s, evokes how they 'se donnaient pour mission de théoriser la coïncidence entre subversion formelle et désir de révolution politique: changer la langue, transformer la littérature, changer la vie, agir sur les représentations, changer le monde, la société' [set themselves the mission of theorising the coincidence of formal subversion and desire for a political revolution: change language, transform literature, change life, act on representations, change the world, society].[90] In the wake of Sartre's discussion of 'engagement' and his critique of poetry, these writers' work involved a form of 'langagement', which Gleize describes as:

> Subversion de l'ordre des représentations par la langue, par le travail sur la langue ou les langues (la contamination du haut par le bas, le familier, le vulgaire, le dialectal), subversion par la langue, subversion de la langue, transgression des codes, du code, dissidence par dissonance, discordance, néologisme, cacophonie, dérégulation morphologique et syntaxique, excentricité verbale, grandes irrégularités, en un mot 'mécriture'.[91]
>
> [The subversion of the order of representations through language, through working on language or languages (the contamination of the high by the low, the familiar, the common, the dialectal), subversion through language, subversion of language, transgression of codes, of code, dissidence through dissonance, discordance, neologism, cacophony, morphological and syntactic deregulation, verbal eccentricity, major irregularities, in a word, 'mécriture' [miswriting].]

We will recognise in this description certain parallels with Deleuze and Guattari's analysis of minor literature, in so far as both evoke not the engagement with overtly political themes, but the intrinsically political dimension of the use of language in certain literary texts.

The 'langagement' associated with the avant-gardes of the 1970s has seen a two-fold criticism in recent years. Firstly, the period that followed saw a disillusionment with the political potential of literary creation, a questioning of its capacity to have a real impact on the world, a wariness of literature that was too theoretically or politically motivated, leading, in part, to the return of lyricism in the 1980s.

Secondly, although the desire for a politically engaged form of poetry has returned in recent years, there has been a re-evaluation of the radical, stylistic 'irrégularités' of earlier avant-garde experiments, what Gleize describes as an opposition to the 'survalorisation avant-gardiste d'une certaine "monstruosité" idiolectale, ou sociolectale, de groupes constitués' [avant-gardist overrating of a certain idiolectal or sociolectal 'monstrosity' of the constituent groups].[92] Gleize argues that 'l'illisibilité' [illegibility] has itself become a marker of an avant-garde sociolect that has crystallised into what is paradoxically a major discourse wielding an equivalent power to the very discourses it originally aimed to dismantle. In response to the obscurity of earlier, radical experimentation, recently poets have sought to find more 'readable' — and, they would argue, more democratic — ways to experiment within a poetic language that is accessible to all, and not just to a literary elite. A number of poets would qualify for such an analysis: from Christophe Tarkos, Nathalie Quintane, and Charles Pennequin, whose poetry, with its emphasis on the paraphernalia of everyday life, expressed in straightforward, 'ordinary' language, formed an observable movement in the mid-1990s, to Valérie Rouzeau, whose work subtly transforms and agitates the linguistic tics of modern communication, from twenty-first-century slang to the 'langue de bois' of contemporary politics. For all of these poets, the referential, descriptive, and often narrative aspects that had been abandoned in previous decades return to the text, but are incorporated into an altogether different poetics, accompanied by a linguistically experimental inclination.

While the last two decades have seen the revival of a notion of 'langagement' inherited from this early period, it has also been revised in accordance with a more critical approach to how significant a political impact poetic language can have. In *Poésie action directe* [Direct Action Poetry] (2003), Christophe Hanna poses the question facing many contemporary poets: 'Quels sont les moyens d'action positive auxquels, non risiblement, la poésie actuelle peut prétendre?' [What are the modes of positive action that poetry today might plausibly aspire to?].[93] Surveying the contemporary field, a direct engagement with current affairs is widespread; the chapters that follow will make reference to a number of works by Fourcade, Cadiot, and Tarkos that consider overtly political subjects, from terrorist attacks to 'ouvriers sans papiers' [undocumented workers], from the extinction of minority languages to the treatment of Iraqi prisoners by American troops. Beyond this very immediate form of engagement, contemporary poetry demonstrates above all a preoccupation with the way that literary language challenges the dominant discourses of today, discourses that have changed over the course of the last half century.[94] Jean-Michel Espitallier, when asked by Nathalie Wourm about the political dimension of his poetry, responded: 'Les terrains de travail clairement politiques ont changé. On n'est plus du tout dans le politique du début du vingtième siècle. Aujourd'hui on s'intéresse beaucoup plus à l'action des médias, à la question de la représentation' [The fields clearly defined as political have changed. We are very far from early twentieth-century politics. Nowadays we are much more interested in the activity of the media and the question of representation].[95] He goes on to give some examples of the forms of discourse his own poetry tackles, such as the economic discourses of global tourism and the financial services industry. When Wourm puts the same question to Eric Sadin, he gives us a further example, identifying the 'technodiscours' of Silicon Valley, to which he wishes to 'opposer une contre-langue poétique en quelque sorte, à la fois capable de signaler la dimension grotesque de ces discours et d'exposer d'autres régimes de vérités possibles, qui nécessairement passent par d'autres régimes de langage' [oppose a poetic counter-language as it were, that is able to both flag up the grotesque dimension of these discourses and to present other possible regimes of truths, which necessarily appear through other regimes of language].[96]

Drawing inspiration from the novel metaphors offered by technological developments, Sadin, like other contemporary poets and critics, employs the metaphor of the virus to conceptualise the way poetic language infiltrates and disrupts major discourses. As Gleize suggests, certain contemporary poets 'travaillent dans la langue de l'ennemi pour mieux s'insinuer dans ses réseaux de communication, pervertir ou détourner ses messages, ses systèmes de figuration etc.' [work in the enemy's language to better infiltrate its communication networks, distort or hijack its messages, its systems of figuration etc.].[97] Wourm identifies a link between Deleuze and Guattari's philosophy and the viral metaphor, when discussing the contemporary poets Christophe Hanna, Vannina Maestri, and Christophe Fiat:

> Hanna uses the metaphor of a virus — seeing poetic activity as insidiously infiltrating and sabotaging the symbolic systems in place in a given society [...]. Such poets as Hanna, Maestri, and Fiat push the viral analogy further, playing on the obvious relation between biological and computer viruses. Deleuze had already brought this relation to the fore when he suggested that the use of computer viruses represented a new form of resistance against controlling regimes (Deleuze, *Pourparlers*, 237). Computer viruses insidiously infiltrate the communication networks of society, mutating within them in a rhizomatic and uncontrollable manner, bringing the dominant and dominating communication systems to a standstill.[98]

Where the image of the virus presents a useful way of conceptualising the experimental practices of contemporary poets, it has a clear parallel with Deleuze and Guattari's analysis of minor literature more broadly, both capturing the contingency of literature that disrupts and makes minor the major discourses within which it operates.

At the risk of oversimplifying the complexity of their analysis, Deleuze and Guattari's theory of 'littérature mineure' nonetheless reframes the idea that literature performs certain operations on language, making it foreign and strange. The idea that literary language is constituted by its difference or deviation from other discourses is, of course, far from new, and a notable example of such an approach would be Jean Cohen's *Structure du langage poétique* [Structure of Poetic Language] (1966), which defines poetry by its 'écart' from ordinary language, or by its difference from prose.[99] However, what sets Deleuze and Guattari's analysis apart from that of Cohen and others, and what renders it a more appropriate prism through which to consider the contemporary poets gathered here, is that the difference they identify in minor literature, namely the minor usage of major discourses, is a form of difference operating within a system of power, and therefore one that is inflected with a political dimension. Elsewhere, Kelly highlights the similarities between Deleuze and Guattari's analysis and Noël's in 'Où va la poésie?' [Where Is Poetry Going?], where he writes, 'la poésie est le foyer de résistance de la langue vivante contre la langue consommée, réduite, univoque' [poetry houses the resistance of living language against worn-out, paired-down, unequivocal language].[100] He argues that Noël's comment is 'representative of a widely held version of the difference of poetic practice' and goes on to observe that, for Noël and Deleuze and Guattari, poetic language is understood as an 'othered' discourse to 'both established discourses and discursive sclerosis', and, in both of their accounts, 'Poetry's minority becomes bound to rhetoric's majority'.[101] In this regard, Deleuze and Guattari's analysis of the deterritorialising processes of minor literature applies well to many experimental modern French poets. Given the centrality of the experiment in their work, which involves the revision of accepted conditions and unmarked norms (of syntax, style, form, meaning, voice, and so on), and the seeking of differential forms, we might hypothesise that it is precisely this difference-seeking, experimental dimension of modern poetry that then qualifies it as 'littérature mineure'. As the final section of this chapter will explore, this same experimental dimension, coupled with contemporary poetry's preoccupation with its own generic identity, means that the deterritorialisation taking place occurs not only in the disruption to major discourses, but also in the uprooting of a previously held conception of what poetry is, wherein we might find one possible interpretation for the term 'poésie mineure'.

The Place of Poetry

In the narrowest sense of the words, poetry and poetic language are not granted any prominent position in Deleuze and Guattari's analysis, where questions of literary genre are largely absent. In their discussion, examples of minor literature are drawn from poetry as well as prose, and the 'auteurs mineurs' that they evoke are poets, novelists, playwrights, and film directors alike. That said, a number of references pose interesting questions in this regard, for example in 'Bégaya-t-il', where the term 'poétique' is used synonymously with the notion of 'littérature mineure'. Here, the stuttering of the linguistic system (as opposed to the character's 'parole') is described as 'une opération poétique' (CC, 135 ECC, 107), and Luca's verse is analysed as 'éminemment poétique' precisely because it sees the stuttering of 'la langue' (CC, 139 ECC, 110). Deleuze writes, 'Si la langue se confond avec la parole, c'est seulement avec une parole très spéciale, parole poétique qui effectue toute la puissance de bifurcation et de variation, d'hétérogenèse et de modulation propre à la langue' [If language merges with speech, it is only with a very particular kind of speech, a poetic speech that actualizes these powers of bifurcation and variation, of heterogenesis and modulation, that are proper to language] (CC, 136–37; ECC, 108). In these instances, Deleuze appears to be equating 'parole poétique' with the distinctive language use of minor literature (i.e. with the becoming-other of language, with deterritorialisation, with the presence of tensors and lines of flight, and so on). Taken alongside Deleuze's analysis elsewhere, poetic language as it is understood here is not confined strictly to the poem, and reflects a broader use of the term that transcends straightforward generic boundaries. It is nonetheless significant that he uses *poétique* rather than *littéraire*, and it certainly invites, for example, Prigent's argument that deterritorialisation might offer a possible definition for poetic language more generally.

With this in mind, the discussion that follows outlines a contrastive approach to poetic language, one which addresses these generic questions more directly, and which, despite several similarities to Deleuze and Guattari's approach in its conception of language and literature *in toto*, arrives at a very different conclusion. Bakhtin's essays on literary discourse, especially 'Discourse in the Novel' and 'From the Prehistory of Novelistic Discourse', provide a set of interesting parallels with Deleuze and Guattari's work.[102] Like Deleuze and Guattari, Bakhtin describes the language system as characterised by inherent variation: variation of style, lexis, phonology, grammar, syntax, and so on. Within this system two forces are at work: one that attempts to suppress variation, imposing norms and constants, desiring 'centralization and unification'; and one that desires 'decentralization and disunification', allowing variation to multiply and proliferate (*DI*, 272). These 'centripetal' and 'centrifugal' forces are at work throughout language, and intersect in every utterance of a given language system. Clear parallels can be found here with Deleuze and Guattari's notions of 'territorialisation' and 'deterritorialisation'. Bakhtin refers to this inherent variation of language as 'heteroglossia', as opposed to 'monoglossia' which describes the highly codified, unitary language.[103]

Bakhtin suggests that, throughout the history of Western literature, 'major' genres have reinforced the 'centralizing (unifying) tendency' (*DI*, 67) of periods of comparative monoglossia. He argues, for example, that the 'major straightforward genres of the ancient Greeks' — epic, lyric, and tragedy — were born out of a period of 'confident and uncontested monoglossia' (66). In turn, he argues that for every major genre there has arisen a 'parodic-travestying' counterpart. These parodic-travestying forms serve as a critique or corrective to their major counterparts, highlighting how these major forms are artificially narrow in their scope, suppressing heteroglossia, and with this, the inherent richness of reality. Bakhtin goes on to argue that authors of major genres express a singular and direct relationship to their language, they are forever *within* language. In contrast, authors of parodic-travestying forms inhabit an indirect relationship with the language(s) of their writing, they find an outside of the direct word and thus 'liberate the object from the power of language' and '[destroy] the homogenizing power of myth over language' (60). He argues that this ability to perceive language from the outside comes from a situation of polyglossia. His analysis begins by identifying particular historical periods of national polyglossia, where the presence of a second national language allowed the writers of the time to see their own language from the outside. He writes:

> After all, it is possible to objectivize one's own particular language, its internal form, the peculiarities of its world view, its specific linguistic habitus, only in the light of another language belonging to someone else, which is almost as much 'one's own' as one's native language. (*DI*, 62)

The suggestion that parodic-travestying forms (that align roughly with Deleuze and Guattari's term 'littérature mineure') typically arise in situations of bilingualism or multilingualism has clear resonances with Deleuze and Guattari's analysis, and like Deleuze and Guattari, Bakhtin goes on to qualify his definition of polyglossia. He describes 'the internal stratification of any single national language' (262), writing: 'one's own language is never a single language: in it there are always survivals of the past and a potential for other-languagedness that is more or less sharply perceived by the working literary and language consciousness' (66). Thus, although these historical moments of national polyglossia have been significant, Bakhtin argues that any given language is internally polyglottic, and an encounter with a 'foreign' language need not involve exposure to another national language.

Bakhtin contends that the parodic-travestying forms that worked against the monoglossia of major genres paved the way for the emergence of the novel. It is here that he establishes a fundamental distinction between poetic and novelistic discourse. He argues that the novel, unlike poetry, is characterised by heteroglossia. He writes: 'the language of the novel is a *system* of languages that mutually and ideologically interanimate each other. It is impossible to describe and analyse it as a single unitary language' (*DI*, 47). These languages are dialogised, in relationship with each other within the space of the text, and the novel is thus a heterogeneous 'system of intersecting planes' (48), a 'dialogized system made up of the images of "languages," styles and consciousnesses that are concrete and inseparable from language. Language in the novel not only represents, but itself serves as the object of representation' (49). The author, Bakhtin argues, is outside language; he has very little direct language of his own within the novel, but instead presents this system of languages that interanimates itself. As a result, the novel exposes two crucial myths: 'the myth of a language that presumes to be the only language, and the myth of a language that presumes to be completely unified' (68). In contrast to the novel, Bakhtin argues that poetry involves only the direct language of the author:

> The language of the poet is *his* language, he is utterly immersed in it, inseparable from it, he makes use of each form, each word, each expression according to its unmediated power to assign meaning (as it were, 'without quotation marks'), that is, as a pure and direct expression of his own intention. (*DI*, 285)

As there is 'no distance between the poet and his word' (297), the poet cannot turn language into an object within the text: the language of poetry represents but, unlike the novel, is unable to be the object of representation. Although Bakhtin rejects the possibility that true monoglossia can exist, as all language is characterised by intrinsic variation, poetic style is nonetheless monologic, in so far as it perpetuates the myth of a unitary language, gesturing towards monoglossia in its suppression of 'alien languages' (285), other discourses and voices. In a later passage, Bakhtin writes:

> Poetry behaves as if it lived in the heartland of its own language territory, and does not approach too closely the borders of this language, where it would inevitably be brought into dialogic contact with heteroglossia, poetry chooses not to look beyond the boundaries of its own language. (*DI*, 399)

This comment is starkly contrastive to Prigent's analysis of deterritorialisation as a potential definition for poetic language, or Perloff's description of poetry as the '"bumping of one's head" against the limits of language'. For Bakhtin, poetic discourse must be qualified, according to his own terminology or that of Deleuze and Guattari, as 'major'.

A fundamental distinction between Bakhtin's analysis and that of Deleuze and Guattari, is that he sees the different operations on language (i.e. those found in monologic or dialogic discourses) as properties of generic conventions, as opposed to as properties of the individual author's style. Indeed, Bakhtin argues that poetry is, by definition, monologic, and at the point where this ceases to be the case, it ceases to be poetry. Bakhtin writes that the foreign, alien languages of heteroglottic reality 'could not find a place in the *poetic style* of [the poet's] work without destroying that style, without transposing it into a prosaic key and in the process turning the poet into a writer of prose' (*DI*, 285). In both Bakhtin's and Deleuze and Guattari's analyses, style plays a central role. However, the same stylistic features that Deleuze and Guattari identify as tensors for deterritorialisation (such as Cummings's use of syntax or Luca's disordered phrases), for Bakhtin are evidence of a stylistic unity in poetry that sustains the myth of monoglossia.

The tension between these two analyses will be considered in further detail in relation to Tarkos's poetry in Chapter 4. Tarkos's *œuvre* is characterised by a direct poetic voice and a unity of style that Bakhtin would see as exemplary of monologic poetic discourse. However, that same unity of style manifests itself in the disconcerting syntactic revisions and reformulations of ordinary language that could be read as an example of the deterritorialising force of 'littérature mineure'. Tarkos's poetry poses the question: if a poet's style is characterised by difference and variation from a set of stylistic or linguistic norms, is it not therefore an internally dialogic discourse, and one that is interested precisely in an outside or other to an implicit major language? Could we see, in Tarkos's example, a form of discourse that, albeit taking a different overt shape to novelistic discourse and involving a unity of style or voice in a very immediate sense, nonetheless performs a dismantling of the monologic mode that Bakhtin would otherwise assign it? Indeed, as Kelly suggests above, the conception of poetic language as an othering of major or normative discourses is now widespread, and ultimately casts poetic discourse as implicitly dialogic (in so far as the language of the poem evokes, by implication, another language that is not present). Similarly, we saw above the significant motif of poetry as the creating or imagining of another language (cf. Rimbaud, Noël, or Prigent, to cite just a few already mentioned), a notion which sits directly at odds with Bakhtin's analysis of poetry as the upholding of the myth of a singular, unitary language.

In his analysis, it is clear that Bakhtin has a very particular notion of poetry in mind. As Michael Eskin suggests, writing in the 1930s and early 1940s Bakhtin is addressing 'lyric poetry as private, emotionalized and highly personal — in short, as the more or less unmediated expression of its author's states of mind, which was prevalent in Russia at the beginning of the twentieth century'.[104] In this respect, Bakhtin's conception resonates with other ways poetry was construed in the same period in France; we saw above how the mid-twentieth century witnessed a crisis, precisely in response to criticism levelled at a notion of poetry that was akin to Bakhtin's conception. In any case, if Bakhtin's analysis holds for certain types of poetic discourse (nineteenth-century Romantic or twentieth-century Surrealist poetry for instance), there are numerous counter-examples that predate his analysis, and it sits ill-at-ease with modern French poetry as we understand it today.[105] Several critics have already taken issue with Bakhtin's account: Rabaté offers Rimbaud, Apollinaire, and Ezra Pound as examples of poets whose work cannot be characterised by a singular, centralised voice; Perloff highlights how modern American poetry also refutes this monologic analysis.[106] Alferi and Cadiot draw the following conclusion in the second *Revue de littérature générale*: 'L'opposition entre le langage unique, autarcique et linéaire de la poésie et le dialogisme relativisant et discontinu du roman n'a plus cours' [The opposition between the unique, autarkic and linear language of poetry and the relativizing and discontinuous dialogism of the novel no longer stands].[107] To describe, for example, Cadiot's *L'Art poétic'*, a text composed of cut-ups from grammar manuals, as monoglottic, or as a unified, singular language of the author's direct discourse, simply does not hold. Cadiot's text, like the long lineage of cut-up and ready-made poetry that it belongs to, aligns much more readily to Bakhtin's description of the heteroglottic novel, with its system of representations of language depicted *from the outside*. It demands a distance between the author and his language, represents language as *object* of representation, and in turn places emphasis on the heterogeneity and multiplicity of the languages represented.

If we do take Bakhtin's analysis as a valid account of an earlier form of poetry, then applying Bakhtin's own literary-historical approach, we might well argue that the last century and a half of literary production has changed the shape of poetry, so much so that his analysis no longer holds true. Having developed through a series of experiments that radically revised the key characteristics of poetic discourse, modern French poetry is often determined precisely by its break with traditional forms, and has often worked against a previous conception of poetry, akin to the one Bakhtin describes in *The Dialogic Imagination*.[108] Following Bakhtin's own account, we might therefore see modern poetry, with its self-reflexive dismantling of the inherited generic conventions of a pre-existing mode, as a parodic-travestying or minor counterpart to a major poetic genre. Indeed, one of the motivations for identifying a 'poésie mineure' as opposed to 'littérature mineure' more broadly, may well rest in contemporary practice's relationship to its past, its contingency on some former conception of what poetry is, as well as its marked preoccupation with its own generic status. In this sense, Deleuze and Guattari's discussion of deterritorialisation serves as a model not only for the functioning of poetic language within the text, but also for the shifting shape of the genre as a whole, an idea that Sadin alluded to above, when he described the 'minor poetics' of multimedia experiments that displace poetry outside of the book.

Following from this, the ensuing discussion will also consider how modern poetic discourse should be construed, if not as monologic. On the one hand, experiments with voice that draw on ready-made language, cut-ups, and distancing techniques offer heteroglottic, dialogic texts that resemble, in many respects, Bakhtin's account of novelistic discourse. This would then invite questions about the generic status of the subsequent poems — questions that are posed not only by Bakhtin's analysis, but by broader discussions around generic boundaries in the contemporary field. Chapter 3 will explore this issue by investigating the paradox in Cadiot's work: Cadiot simultaneously sustains Bakhtin's own analysis of poetry as intrinsically monologic (ultimately resulting in his self-proclaimed abandonment of poetry, and his movement into prose), yet produces, under the title of a 'livre de poésie', a polyphonous collage of cut-ups that experiment with indirect language in the poem. On the other hand, Chapter 4 explores Tarkos's poetry which sustains a direct, authorial poetic voice, but experiments with conventions of representation or meaning, presenting linguistic variants to normative discourses. His poetry disrupts the myth of monoglossia, yet not in the way that Bakhtin would suggest novelistic discourse does.

For the current discussion, the value of Bakhtin's account lies not in the veracity of his analysis of poetic discourse, but rather in the way that, like Deleuze and Guattari, he develops a conception of the language system as a whole, understood as a sociopolitical phenomenon, before situating different forms of literature within that wider system. Unlike Deleuze and Guattari, he also introduces the questions of voice, discourse, and genre that will be key to the consideration of the work of Fourcade, Cadiot, and Tarkos, to the consideration of poetry's specificity and value today, and to the possibility of a 'minor poetry'. Using their analyses as a framework, a number of different motifs that are pertinent to contemporary poetry are configured together: foreign language, disordered language, grammar, heteroglossia or polyphony, style, syntax, and so on; through close readings of their texts, the following chapters trace how these aspects play out in the poetry of Fourcade, Cadiot, and Tarkos.

Notes to Chapter 1

1. Gilles Deleuze and Félix Guattari, *Mille plateaux* (Paris: Minuit, 1980), pp. 125–26 (henceforth abbreviated to *MP*); *A Thousand Plateaus: Capitalism and Schizophrenia*, trans. by Brian Massumi (London: Bloomsbury, 2013), pp. 115–16 (henceforth abbreviated to *ATP*).
2. 'Deleuze ne fait guère plus qu'agiter ce nom comme une clochette à chaque fois qu'il parle de bégaiement stylistique' [Deleuze does little more than ring this name like a bell each time he speaks about stylistic stuttering]. Christian Prigent, 'Deleuze / "Poésie"', *Sitaudis* (2015) <http://www.sitaudis.fr/Incitations/deleuze-poesie.php> [accessed 26 June 2020].
3. *Sens et présence du sujet poétique: la poésie de la France et du monde francophone depuis 1980*, ed. by Michael Brophy and Mary Gallagher (Amsterdam: Rodopi, 2006).
4. *Deleuze et les écrivains: littérature et philosophie*, ed. by Bruno Gelas and Hervé Micolet (Nantes: Cécile Defaut, 2007).
5. Jérôme Game, *Poetic Becomings: Studies in Contemporary French Literature* (Oxford & New York: Peter Lang, 2011).

6. Ibid., p. 1. Given Game's theoretical framework and corpus, there will be several instances in the following chapters where I will draw on his analysis; in Chapter 2, I take up his discussion of Fourcade's 'poetics of the rhizome', and in Chapter 3, his account of the stutter in Cadiot's *Futur, ancien, fugitif.*
7. Michael G. Kelly, 'Poetry as a Foreign Language: Unhoused Writing Subjects in the *extrême contemporain*', *Forum for Modern Language Studies*, 47.4 (2011), 393–407.
8. Emmanuel Hocquard, 'La Bibliothèque de Trieste', in *Ma haie* (Paris: P.O.L., 2001), pp. 16–31 (p. 26).
9. Prigent, 'Deleuze / "Poésie"'.
10. Michael G. Kelly, *Strands of Utopia: Spaces of Poetic Work in Twentieth-century France* (London: Legenda, 2008), p. 6.
11. David Nowell Smith, *On Voice in Poetry: The Work of Animation* (Basingstoke: Palgrave Macmillan, 2015), p. 5.
12. Mikhail Bakhtin, *The Dialogic Imagination* (Austin: University of Texas Press, 1981), pp. 296–97 (henceforth abbreviated to *DI*).
13. Dominique Rabaté, 'Enonciation poétique, énonciation lyrique', in *Figures du sujet lyrique*, ed. by Dominique Rabaté (Paris: PuF, 1996), p. 77.
14. Jean-Michel Maulpoix, *La Poésie comme l'amour* (Paris: Mercure de France, 1998), p. 123.
15. Jean-Marie Gleize, *Sorties* (Paris: Questions théoriques, 2009), p. 58.
16. Jean-Marie Gleize, *A noir: poésie et littéralité, essai* (Paris: Seuil, 1992), p. 16.
17. Michel Collot, 'Lyrisme et littéralité', *Lendemains*, 34 (2009), 14–24 (p. 14). Gleize writes, 'le sens est toujours déjà figuré' [meaning is always already figurative], but notes that there is nonetheless a tangible difference between the excess of poetic imagery in Surrealist poetry, and the resistance to imagery in 'littéraliste' poets. Gleize, *A noir*, pp. 15–16.
18. Jean-Claude Pinson, *Habiter en poète: essai sur la poésie contemporaine* (Seyssel: Champ Vallon, 1995), p. 251.
19. Roland Barthes, *Le Degré zéro de l'écriture* (Paris: Seuil, 1953), pp. 59–60; *Writing Degree Zero*, trans. by Annette Lavers and Colin Smith (New York: Hill and Wang, 2012), p. 77.
20. Ibid., p. 60; p. 77.
21. Dominique Viart, 'Blancheurs et minimalismes littéraires', in *Écritures blanches*, ed. by Dominique Rabaté and Dominique Viart (Saint-Etienne: Publications de l'Université de Saint-Etienne, 2009), p. 7.
22. Hocquard, 'La Bibliothèque de Trieste', p. 25.
23. Denis Roche, *La Poésie est inadmissible: œuvres poétiques complètes* (Paris: Seuil, 1995), p. 511.
24. By '*la poésie*', Gleize means a traditional mode of predominantly lyric poetry. Like Roche, Gleize believes '*la poésie*' has had its day, and advocates a form of '*post*-poésie' that, as Christophe Wall-Romana writes, will '[approach] poetry as if from the outside, bringing to it other media and discourses, in a different ecology of meaning built upon *dispositifs de montage*'. Christophe Wall-Romana, 'Is "postpoetry" still Poetry? Jean-Marie Gleize's *dispositif*-writing', *Forum for Modern Language Studies*, 47.4 (2011), 442–53 (p. 443).
25. Gleize, *A noir*, p. 102.
26. Christophe Tarkos, *L'Enregistré* (Paris: P.O.L., 2014), p. 245 (henceforth abbreviated to *E*).
27. Christian Prigent, *A quoi bon encore des poètes?* (Valence: ERBA, 1994), p. 12.
28. Ibid., p. 12.
29. Ibid., p. 14.
30. Ibid.
31. Pinson, *Habiter en poète*, p. 20.
32. Jean-Claude Pinson, *Sentimentale et naïve: nouveaux essais sur la poésie contemporaine* (Seyssel: Champ Vallon, 2002), p. 186.
33. Xavier Person, 'Olivier Cadiot', *Le Matricule des Anges*, 41 (2002), 14–22 (p. 23).
34. Agnès Disson, 'Poésie années 90: les enfants de Gertrude Stein et de Jacques Roubaud', *French Studies Bulletin*, 22.79 (2001), 13–17. For two further useful accounts of Alferi and Cadiot's essays, see Gaëlle Théval, *Poésies ready-made, XXe-XXIe siècles* (Paris: L'Harmattan, 2015), pp. 199–223, and Alain Farah, *Le Gala des incomparables: invention et résistance chez Olivier Cadiot et Nathalie Quintane* (Paris: Garnier, 2013), pp. 83–86.

35. Guillaume Apollinaire, *Œuvres en prose*, 2 vols (Paris: Gallimard, 1991), II, 954. Brion Gysin, 'Minutes to Go', in *Back in No Time: The Brion Gysin Reader*, ed. by Jason Weiss (Middletown, CT: Wesleyan University Press, 2001), p. 74. Francis Ponge, *Entretiens de Francis Ponge avec Philippe Sollers* (Paris: Gallimard, 1970), p. 72. William Carlos Williams, *The Wedge* (Cummington, MA: Cummington Press, 1944), p. 8.
36. Pierre Alferi and Olivier Cadiot, 'La Mécanique lyrique', in *Revue de littérature générale 95/1*, ed. by Pierre Alferi and Oliver Cadiot (Paris: P.O.L., 1995), pp. 3–22 (p. 5).
37. Eric Lynch, 'Unidentified Verbal Objects: Contemporary French Poetry, Intermedia, and Narrative' (unpublished doctoral thesis, City University of New York, 2016), p. 18.
38. Pierre Alferi and Olivier Cadiot, 'Digest', in *Revue de littérature générale 96/2*, ed. by Pierre Alferi and Olivier Cadiot (Paris: P.O.L., 1996) (unpaginated).
39. Collot, 'Lyrisme et littéralité', p. 23. See also Michel Collot, *La Matière-émotion* (Paris: PuF, 1997).
40. Alferi and Cadiot, 'La Mécanique lyrique', p. 5.
41. Jean-Michel Espitallier, *Caisse à outils* (Paris: Pocket, 2006), p. 48.
42. See, for example, Kenneth Goldsmith, *Uncreative Writing: Managing Language in the Digital Age* (New York: Columbia University Press, 2011), and Marjorie Perloff, *Unoriginal Genius: Poetry by Other Means in the New Century* (Chicago: University of Chicago Press, 2010).
43. Pierre Alferi, *Cinépoèmes & films parlants* (Aubervilliers: Laboratoires d'Aubervilliers, 2003). Anne-James Chaton, *Autoportraits* (Paris: Al Dante, 2003). Eric Lynch provides a useful survey of recent intermedia experiments, from Alferi's 'Cinépoèmes' and 'Films parlants', to Roche's use of photography, and Gleize's work on the polaroid. Lynch, 'Unidentified Verbal Objects', p. 31. For a detailed exploration of this subject, see the essays in *Porous Boundaries: Texts and Images in Twentieth-century French Culture*, ed. by Jérôme Game (Oxford: Peter Lang, 2007), notably Nathalie Wourm's article, 'Poetry in Moving Image: The French Avant-Garde' (pp. 101–19), which explores Alferi's and Chaton's projects in particular.
44. Nathalie Wourm, 'Anticapitalism and the Poetic Function of Language', *L'Esprit Créateur*, 49.2 (2009), 119–31. Nina Parish, 'From Book to Page to Screen: Poetry and New Media', *French Studies: Writing and the Image Today*, 114 (2008), 51–66.
45. Sadin's review, *éc/artS*, established at the end of the 1990s and subtitled 'Pratiques artistiques et nouvelles technologies' [Artistic practices and new technologies], gathers contributions from many well-known experimental poets (Chaton, Espitallier, Maestri, Pennequin, Quintane, among others).
46. Eric Sadin, *Poésie_atomique* (Lentigny: éc/artS, 2004) (unpaginated).
47. Espitallier, *Caisse à outils*, p. 23.
48. All three of the poets considered here haven written extensively about poetry and literature more generally. See Cadiot's *Histoire de la littérature récente*, 2 vols (Paris: P.O.L., 2016–17), Fourcade's reflections in *Est-ce que je peux placer un mot?* (Paris: P.O.L., 2001) (henceforth abbreviated to *EJP*), and Tarkos's literary 'manifestos' in *Ma langue* (Paris: P.O.L., 2000) (henceforth abbreviated to *ML*).
49. Carrie Noland, 'Poetic Experimentation', in *The Cambridge Companion to French Literature*, ed. by John D. Lyons (Cambridge: Cambridge University Press, 2016), pp. 168–86 (p. 171).
50. Gleize, *A noir*, p. 11.
51. Ibid., p. 21.
52. Didier Alexandre, 'Le Blanc, le brut, le transparent: sur Dominique Fourcade, Emmanuel Hocquard, James Sacré', in *Écritures blanches*, ed. by Rabaté and Viart, pp. 255–67.
53. Game, 'Dominique Fourcade, or a Poetics of the Rhizome', in *Poetic Becomings*, pp. 107–50.
54. Christian Prigent's term in *Salut les anciens: lectures; Salut les modernes: sur ce qui apparaît* (Paris: P.O.L., 2000), p. 82.
55. Nathalie Wourm, *Poètes français du 21ème siècle: entretiens* (Leiden: Rodopi, 2017), p. 7.
56. Ibid., p. 34.
57. For an example of Cadiot's use of Deleuze and Guattari's terminology, see Olivier Cadiot, Philippe Mangeot and Pierre Zaoui, 'Cap au mieux: entretien avec Olivier Cadiot', *Vacarme*, 45 (2008), 4–12. Rodolphe Burger and Olivier Cadiot, *Hôtel Robinson* (Dernière bande, 2002) [CD].

58. Philippe Castellin points this out in his introductory essay, 'Christophe Tarkos: "Poète de la lecture"' (*E*, 22).
59. Gilles Deleuze and Felix Guattari, *Kafka: pour une littérature mineure* (Paris: Minuit, 1975), p. 29 (henceforth abbreviated to *K1*); *Kafka: Toward a Minor Literature*, trans. by Dana Polan (Minneapolis: University of Minnesota Press, 1986), p. 16 (henceforth abbreviated to *K2*).
60. Marjorie Perloff, *Wittgenstein's Ladder: Poetic Language and the Strangeness of the Ordinary* (Chicago & London: University of Chicago Press, 1996), p. 21.
61. Ibid., p. 85. Here, Perloff echoes Wittgenstein: 'Do not forget that a poem, although it is composed in the language of information, is not used in the language-game of giving information'. Ludwig Wittgenstein, *Zettel*, trans. by G. E. M. Anscombe (Oxford: Blackwell, 1967), p. 28.
62. Perloff, *Wittgenstein's Ladder*, p. 181.
63. Prigent, 'Deleuze / "Poésie"'. See the description of Prigent's *La Langue et ses monstres* on the P.O.L. website <http://www.pol-editeur.com/index.php?spec=livre&ISBN=978-2-8180-2147-7> [accessed 27 August 2020], and Prigent, *A quoi bon encore des poètes?*, p. 11.
64. Dominique Rabaté, *Gestes lyriques* (Paris: José Corti, 2013), p. 235.
65. Gilles Deleuze, *Critique et clinique* (Paris: Minuit, 1993), p. 9 (henceforth abbreviated to *CC*); *Essays Critical and Clinical*, trans. by Daniel W. Smith and Michael A. Greco (London: Verso, 1998), p. v (henceforth abbreviated to *ECC*).
66. Bernard Noël, 'Où va la poésie?', in *The New French Poetry*, ed. by David Kelley and Jean Khalfa (Newcastle upon Tyne: Bloodaxe, 1996), pp. 212–21 (p. 218).
67. Zornitsa Dimitrova, *Literary Worlds and Deleuze: Expression as Mimesis and Event* (Lanham, MD: Lexington Books, 2016), p. 173.
68. Christian Prigent, 'On ne fait pas de poésie sans casser d'œufs: note sur la poésie, en parcourant Deleuze', in *Deleuze et les écrivains*, ed. by Gelas and Micolet, p. 435.
69. Ibid., p. 436.
70. Barthes, *Le Degré zero de l'écriture*, p. 60; *Writing Degree Zero*, p. 77.
71. Hocquard, 'La Bibliothèque de Trieste', p. 26.
72. The reason being that it is the dimension of language that is potentially innate, universal, and the element of human language that sets it apart from animal communication.
73. Emmanuel Hocquard, *Tout le monde se ressemble* (Paris: P.O.L., 2001), p. 232.
74. Hocquard, *Ma haie*, p. 279.
75. Francis Ponge, *Le Grand Recueil: Lyres* (Paris: Gallimard, 1961), p. 149, and *Le Grand Recueil: Méthodes* (Paris: Gallimard, 1961), p. 19.
76. Disson, 'Poésie années 90', pp. 13–14. Elsewhere, Hocquard conceptualises contemporary poetry as a series of 'enquêtes de langage' [language investigations] (*Ma haie*, p. 451), and when Tarkos established, with Katalin Molnàr and Pascal Doury, the review *Poézi Prolétèr* in 1997, they subtitled it 'Revue semestrielle de poésie contemporaine et de recherche expérimentale sur la langue française' [Biannual review of contemporary poetry and experimental research into the French language]. The idea has a much longer history, of course, and the Surrealists were among the first to formalise overtly the notion of the poet as 'researcher'. André Breton, 'Les Mots sans rides', *Littérature*, 7 (1922), 12–14 (p. 13).
77. Hocquard, *Tout le monde se ressemble*, p. 15.
78. Jacques Derrida, *Le Monolinguisme de l'autre, ou, La Prothèse d'origine* (Paris: Galilée, 1996).
79. Prigent, 'On ne fait pas de poésie sans casser d'œufs', p. 429.
80. Stéphane Mallarmé, *Œuvres complètes* (Paris: Gallimard, 1945), p. 920. Jean-Paul Sartre, *Les Mots et autres écrits autobiographiques* (Paris: Gallimard, 2010), p. 89. Pierre Alferi, *Chercher une phrase* (Paris: Bourgois, 1991), p. 17.
81. Prigent, *A quoi bon encore des poètes?*, p. 10.
82. Victor Shklovsky, 'Art as Technique' in *Modern Criticism and Theory: A Reader*, ed. by David Lodge (London: Longman, 1988), pp. 15–30 (p. 19).
83. Ibid., p. 27.
84. For further analysis of these more radical multilingual poets, see Eric Robertson, 'Writing in Tongues: Multilingual Poetry and Self-translation in France from Dada to the Present',

Nottingham French Studies, 56.2 (2017), 119–38, and Marjorie Perloff, 'Language in Migration: Multilingualism and Exophonic Writing in the New Poetics', *Textual Practice*, 24.4 (2010), 725–48.

85. As will be explored in Chapter 3, Robinson recalls Louis Wolfson and his compulsive translation procedures, which Deleuze discussed in his preface to Wolfson's *Le Schizo et la langue*, and later in *Critique et clinique*. See Gilles Deleuze, 'Schizologie', in Louis Wolfson, *Le Schizo et les langues* (Paris: Minuit, 1970), pp. 5–23.
86. For example, Prigent describes 'la figure dominante' [dominant figure] of Tarkos's poetry as 'une sorte de polyptote sérialisé [...] tautologiquement radicalisé [...], parfois aphasiquement hoqueté' [a sort of serialised polyptoton [...] tautologically radicalised [...], sometimes aphasically hiccoughed]. Prigent, 'Sokrat à Patmo', in Christophe Tarkos, *Écrits poétiques* (Paris: P.O.L., 2008), pp. 9–23 (p. 17) (henceforth abbreviated to *EP*). Elsewhere, he depicts Tarkos's poetry as 'secoué de tremblements parkinsoniens' [shaken with Parkinson-like trembling], evoking his 'phrases hoquetées' [hiccoughed phrases], his 'rythmique obsessionnelle' [obsessive rythmics], and his 'mécanique déréglée' [disrupted mechanics]. Prigent, *Salut les anciens*, pp. 85–87.
87. Hocquard, *Tout le monde se ressemble*, pp. 15–16.
88. Ronald Bogue, 'The Minor', in *Gilles Deleuze: Key Concepts*, ed. by Charles J. Stivale (Abingdon & New York: Routledge, 2011), pp. 131–41 (p. 134).
89. Prigent, 'Deleuze / "Poésie"'.
90. Jean-Marie Gleize, 'La Post-poésie: un travail d'investigation-élucidation', *matraga*, 17.27 (2010), 121–33 (p. 124).
91. Ibid., p. 126.
92. Ibid., p. 129.
93. This question appears on the back cover of Christophe Hanna's *Poésie action directe* (Paris: Al Dante, 2003).
94. Of course, the two are not mutually exclusive and there are many contemporary poets who focus on current affairs as well as the various media and political discourses that surround them. One thinks, for example, of Espitallier's *En guerre* or Christophe Fiat's *New York 2001* which consider the hyperbolic media treatment of, respectively, Saddam Hussein's capture and the 9/11 attacks in New York. See Jean-Michel Espitallier, *En guerre* (Paris: Inventaire-invention, 2004), and Christophe Fiat, *New York 2001* (Romainville: Al Dante, 2002).
95. Wourm, *Poètes français du 21ème siècle*, p. 57.
96. Ibid., p. 50.
97. Gleize, 'La Post-poésie', p. 126.
98. Wourm, 'Anticapitalism and the Poetic Function of Language', p. 125.
99. Jean Cohen, *Structure du langage poétique* (Paris: Flammarion, 1966).
100. Noël, 'Où va la poésie?', p. 214. Kelly, *Strands of Utopia*, p. 6.
101. Kelly, *Strands of Utopia*, p. 6
102. 'From the Prehistory of Novelistic Discourse' and 'Discourse in the Novel', in *DI*, 41–83 and 259–422 respectively. In *Mille plateaux* Deleuze and Guattari make a series of references to Bakhtin, particularly in relation to Bakhtin's conception of the language system as a whole. At various points in 'Postulats de la linguistique', they reference his work on indirect discourse (*MP*, 97; *ATP*, 89), the social inflection of enunciations (101; 92), his observation of the emphasis placed in linguistics on constants (104; 96), and his definition of language as a form of ideology (113; 104).
103. Whether monoglossia is possible within a living language (as opposed to a dead language or a literary genre) is questionable. In any case, it is always a question of relative states rather than absolutes.
104. Michael Eskin, 'Bakhtin on Poetry', *Poetics Today*, 21.2 (2000), 379–91 (p. 379).
105. Bakhtin does himself address certain counter-examples to his analysis, although in keeping with his earlier comments about poetry ceasing to be poetry and becoming prose, he describes these examples as the 'drastic "prosification" of the lyric' in twentieth-century poetry. See Mikhail Bakhtin, *Problems of Dostoevsky's Poetics* (Minneapolis: University of Minnesota Press, 1984), p. 200.

106. Dominique Rabaté, 'Énonciation poétique, énonciation lyrique', in *Figures du sujet lyrique*, ed. by Rabaté, pp. 65–79 (p. 77). Perloff, *Wittgenstein's Ladder*, p. 280.
107. Alferi and Cadiot, 'Digest'.
108. Hocquard's description of the poetry of 'modernité négative' as 'cette poésie sans accent poétique' typifies this. Hocquard, 'La Bibliothèque de Trieste', p. 26.

CHAPTER 2

Dominique Fourcade, 'L'Expérience de la poésie'

In an article on 'littéralité' and 'lyrisme', Michel Collot presents Dominique Fourcade as a primary example of a poet whose work bridges the division of the contemporary field, integrating a focus on linguistic materiality with a form of lyricism.[1] As Jean-Claude Pinson suggests, even when Fourcade's work exemplifies a form of 'écriture blanche', with its intransitive, self-referential dimension and its 'effacement du sens' [erasure of meaning], a lyric impulse persists, albeit in the form of a singular 'lyrisme désubjectivé' [desubjectivised lyricism].[2] This duality lends Fourcade's poetry a breadth of scope; his work pursues literary questions of voice, meaning, and subjecthood, and attends equally to metaphysical concerns of being and death. The latter dimension of Fourcade's work leads Pinson to situate him in a lineage of 'poésie pensante'.[3] While this ontological focus is very immediately present, Fourcade's writing embraces what the poet himself describes as the 'bas voltage' [low voltage] of the American Objectivists: it is often grounded in the contemporary and the everyday, which is sometimes also the trivial and the prosaic.[4] As a result, his poetry is characterised by a certain plasticity, reinforced by the formal properties of the texts, that resists easy definition. It explores the deterritorialising possibilities of the polyphonous, multilingual text, elaborating a heterogeneous form of poetry, that is stuttered or stammered in a disordered mode of articulation. Through close reading of extracts from *Xbo*, *IL*, and *Rose-déclic*, the following discussion will identify some of the features of Fourcade's work that might qualify it as 'poésie mineure', which begins with the significance of foreign language in Fourcade's work, both as a conceptual category to describe the atypical experience of literary language, and as a textual technique, whereby actual foreign language is incorporated into the poem.

'Plusieurs langues étrangères'

In the opening pages of *Est-ce que j'peux placer un mot?* (2001), a generically hybrid collection comprised of poetry and essayistic prose, Fourcade makes the following remark:

> Je n'ai jamais eu de langue maternelle [...].
> Tout ce qui touche à *Mütterlich*, à *Muttersprache*, à mütternel en somme, j'ignore.
> Zone interdite.

> [...] je n'ai donc pas de première langue, je n'ai que des secondes langues. Et la question est: mes secondes langues où les loger
>
> sinon non loin de l'absence de la première
> rien que des
> mots labo.
>
> Ainsi parle JE plusieurs langues étrangères, je ne parle que ça [...], écrire (avec la permission du temps et de l'espace) est, dis-je, une affaire très absentuée. (*EJP*, 9–10)
>
> [I have never had a mother tongue [...]. | Everything touching on *Mütterlich*, *Muttersprache*, mütternel in sum, I am unfamiliar with. No-go zone. | [...] I have therefore no first language, I have only second languages. And the question is: where to house my second languages | other than not far from the absence of the first | nothing but | lab words. | So I speak several foreign languages, I speak only that [...], writing (with the permission of time and space) is, I say, a very absentuated affair.]

Aligning with Deleuze and Guattari, Proust, and the various other accounts outlined in the previous chapter, here Fourcade conceptualises his writing as a form of foreign language. Where the mother tongue is unavailable to him, it is a plural ('plusieurs') and experimental ('mots labo') form of foreign language that takes its place. As the capitalisation of the pronoun 'JE' suggests, the foreign nature of literary language is, at least in part, a product of the divorce between first-person pronoun and poet. The poet is estranged from his own language, which he does not possess or inhabit. Fourcade writes, 'Le moi que je travaille est le mot. Le mot n'est pas à moi' [The me that I am working on is the word. The word is not mine] (*EJP*, 88). We find here certain resonances with Derrida and Khatibi's discussion of monolingualism, despite the obvious difference of the latter writers' focus on Franco-Maghrebin linguistic identity.[5] Derrida's famous phrase, 'je n'ai qu'une langue, or ce n'est pas la mienne' [I have only one language, yet it is not mine], or Khatibi's assertion, 'Quand j'écris, je le fais dans la langue de l'autre. Cette langue n'est pas une propriété' [When I write, I do so in the language of the other. This language is not a property], both capture the uninhabitable, unassimilable nature of language, which cannot be appropriated or owned.[6] The feeling of being alienated from one's own language is what prompts Fourcade's reflections above; he goes on to elaborate a paradigm whereby the maternal and the foreign represent not descriptive terms for a first and second language, but two opposing experiences of one and the same language. In 'Pas sans l'amitié' [Not Without Friendship], a later essay in *Est-ce que j'peux placer un mot?*, Fourcade describes how his first experience of a mother tongue was initiated by the experience of friendship. It involved a tender, amicable sensation of proximity that contrasted with the intransitivity and distance provoked by writing and, paradoxically, by his relationship with his mother:

> L'expérience que je n'ai pu faire avec ma mère, et qui m'a été refusée plus tard par l'écriture (laquelle n'est vraiment pas faite pour ça), celle d'une langue orgiaque complice et tendre et qui vous comble, et par elle un contact avec le monde en tous points aussi stupéfiant qu'elle, cette expérience s'est ouverte à moi dès le premier ami et je n'en suis pas encore revenu. (*EJP*, 76)

[The experience that I wasn't able to have with my mother, and which was denied to me later on by writing (which is really not made for that), that of an orgiastic, companionable, and tender language that fills you and that brings you into contact with an equally astonishing world, this experience opened up to me from my first friend onwards and I still haven't got over it.]

He summarises these two distinct linguistic experiences a few pages later:

> Je me résume: j'ai donc eu à ce jour l'expérience de deux langues: celle (de l'amitié) qui touche tout point du monde et se laisse toucher, et la langue de l'écriture, qui ne vient pas et dans laquelle, de toutes façons, on ne peut toucher à rien. (*EJP*, 80)

> [To summarise: to date, I have therefore experienced two languages: one (of friendship) that touches the world entirely and lets itself be touched, and the language of writing, which doesn't come and with which, in any case, one can't touch anything.]

In contrast to the language of friendship, which is transitive and associated with tenderness and interiority, Fourcade depicts the language of writing as hostile and intransitive; it provokes 'une expérience particulièrement inamicale' [a particularly unfriendly experience] (79). He describes, not without a good dose of literary exaggeration, the fear that writing provokes: 'J'ai peur, j'ai eu peur toute ma vie, c'est la trame de mon existence, fondamentalement je suis né pour la peur. Parmi toutes les peurs que j'éprouve c'est l'écriture la très grande peur' [I am afraid, I have been afraid my whole life, it is the fabric of my existence, fundamentally I was born for fear. Among all the fears I feel, writing is the greatest fear] (79). Fourcade then draws a parallel between the experience of writing and his relationship with his mother: both fill the poet with an anxiety at the prospect of 'placer un mot'. The book's title captures this duality: on the one hand, it reflects on the literary challenge of writing with or against the intrinsic properties of the linguistic system (the 'écart énonciatif', as Dominique Rabaté puts it).[7] On the other, it evokes the poet's childhood struggle to get a word in edgeways, and forms part of a broader motif in the collection, where fragments of conversation between mother and child depict a domineering power relationship. While both embody a hostile linguistic experience, this is where the parallels end, as they represent two polar ends of the 'major'/'minor' distinction in Fourcade's work. Where the mother becomes a figure of an imposing major language, poetry is the minor linguistic mode that might resist it.

It is clear then that for Fourcade there is a misalignment between the mother, 'ce détestable masculin mother | qui empêche d'en placer une' [this detestable masculine mother | that won't let you get a word in] (*EJP*, 12), and the mother tongue. Adopting a psychoanalytic approach, Daniel Leuwers suggests that, for Fourcade, the mother is:

> Une mère normative et castratrice, celle qui le coupe abruptement avec cette phrase 'Est-ce que j'peux placer un mot?' — celle qui empêche donc l'enfant de placer son mot à lui et qui crée en lui un sentiment de panique quant à la vraie place d'un mot dans une phrase et bientôt dans un recueil.[8]

[A prescriptive, castrating mother, one that cuts him off abruptly with the phrase 'Can I get a word in?' — one that consequently prevents the child from getting his own word in and who leaves him with a feeling of panic about the rightful place of a word in a sentence, and shortly in a poetry collection.]

Implementing what Fourcade describes elsewhere as a childhood education that was 'stricte, faite de règles, de principes et de pensées cloisonnées' [strict, made up of rules, principles, and compartmentalised thoughts], the poet's mother is a figure of the constrictive, authoritative force of language.[9] Her voice enters the text as a menacing presence: 'vous m'emmerdez | avec votre langue bébé' [you're bothering me | with your baby language], 'on ne parle pas la bouche pleine' [one doesn't talk with one's mouth full] (*EJP*, 8). She becomes the embodied symbol of a Deleuzo-Guattarian major language: she interrupts her son, forbidding him to speak, insisting that his words follow the norms and standards of the language she imposes. In this sense, the mother depicted in Fourcade's work is similar to the mother evoked in Louis Wolfson's *Le Schizo et les langues* [The Schizo and Languages] (1970). As Deleuze suggests, Wolfson's schizophrenic linguistic processes, which involved the systematic translation of his native English into approximate foreign forms (French, German, Russian, and Hebrew), expressed his desire to kill the mother tongue (*CC*, 21; *ECC*, 12). Following Deleuze's analysis, Wolfson's use of foreign language represents a visceral response to his hatred and fear of his mother and thus the language that she spoke. As with Wolfson, the polyphony and multilingualism of Fourcade's writing (both literal and conceptual), with its emphasis on subverting linguistic rules and multiplying variation rather than suppressing it, might also be conceptualised as a reaction to the normative, regulating monolingualism of the major language, embodied by the mother. For both Wolfson and Fourcade, a singular language is supplanted by multiple languages, which accords with the distinction that Deleuze and Guattari make between the singular major language, and the multiple 'langues mineures' that minor literature will carve into it (*MP*, 133; *ATP*, 122).

While Fourcade complicates the mother tongue/foreign language distinction by introducing a conceptual 'langue maternelle' of friendship, and by equating a certain experience of language, related to the mother, with the experience of writing, the resonances between Fourcade's and Deleuze and Guattari's conceptions of literature are manifold. As the following readings will consider, these conceptions rest on a series of distinctions that, alongside that of the mother versus the foreign tongue, oppose monophony to polyphony, constant to variant, and the major to the minor.

The following passage is from *Xbo*:

> Le s passe dans bleu et le b rejoint sang
> [...]
> Bang sleu beaux
> Corps linguistique corps chromatique de l'extraveineux
> Corps bleu inoubliable de la poche anonyme
> Corps phonique de tout sang
> Corps sleu insanglant

> Bleu boue des reines
> Sang alezan brûlé
>
> On sait qu'en écrivant on fait défaut
> On travaille un champ d'émail blanc sans dimension
>
> Menstrues des reines d'Égypte
> White enamel
> Sensuel
> Usuel
> On défaille.[10]
>
> [The s moves into bleu (blue) and the b joins sang (blood) | [...] | Beautiful bang sleu | Linguistic body chromatic body of the extravenous | Unforgettable blue body of the anonymous pocket | Phonic body of all blood | Unbloody sleu body | Blue mud of queens | Burnt chestnut blood | We know that in writing we are lacking | We work a dimensionless field of white enamel | Menses of the queens of Egypt | White enamel | Sensual | Usual | We fail.]

Fourcade's focus on the materiality of language, 'la matière du mot', is immediately apparent.[11] The sounds of speech, its musicality and its phonology, are evoked by the anaphora that transforms 'corps linguistique' into 'corps chromatique' and then 'corps phonique'. The description of letters or phonemes moving about on the surface of the page ('le s passe dans bleu et le b rejoint sang') highlights the graphic and phonological units of language as their shapes change and the resulting meaning is transformed ('sang' becomes 'bang' for instance). Phonemes and graphemes are further highlighted through patterns of repetition, so that the neologism 'sleu', repeated twice in the first stanza, alternates with two instances of the adjective 'bleu'. The initial /b/ of 'bleu' forms its own pattern of alliteration: 'bleu inoubliable' in the first stanza transforms in the second stanza into 'bleu boue', and resonates with other /b/ alliterations in the passage, 'Bang sleu beaux'. Likewise, in the final stanza the suffix '-uel' might suggest that 'Sensuel' becomes 'Usuel' by dint of phonological generativity. Many of the words in the passage are repeated twice or more, sometimes translated between languages ('émail blanc' becomes 'White enamel'). Coupled with the use of polyptoton ('sang' and 'insanglant'), attention is drawn to the material quality of the repeated graphemes and morphemes. The metapoetic description in the third stanza, 'On travaille un champ d'émail blanc sans dimension', reinforced by its later translation in English, highlights the physicality of the white page, a dimensionless, indeed unpaginated text that the poet works upon. Fourcade talks in *Outrance utterance* about his desire to decompose language in poetry, to segment its various components so as to fully explore its functioning.[12] While we see this to a certain extent in the passage above, elsewhere the isolation of discrete linguistic units is all the more explicit. In *Xbo*, for instance, words are frequently broken down into their component parts: consonants: 'Tmcl | Fst hrt | Ymbol', phonemes 'S | W | A | Y', and syllables 'Mot et | Mo e | Mu | Et | Motet'. In such a way, there is a greater equivalence of meaning and form in Fourcade's work, whereby the signifier is of equal prominence as the signified. This insistence on the material physicality of words is significant;

in Fourcade's poetry words exist not as abstract concepts or transparent vehicles of meaning but as referents in themselves, 'mots-choses' [word-things] equivalent to bodies, blood, or enamel. Throughout Fourcade's writing, the materiality of language is seen as one form of materiality among others, and it joins a broader network of motifs that have a high coefficient of 'thingness': elements, metals, birds, or flowers.[13] These motifs, and the language that evokes them, constitute what Fourcade calls 'notre substance', the building blocks of existence.[14] As Game suggests, 'In [Fourcade's] poetics, language and things form a unique materiality [...] that constitutes the world as concrete body [...]. Maintaining the opposition between reality and language is nothing but an empty abstraction'.[15]

Discussing Fourcade's focus on linguistic materiality, Frédéric Valabrègue observes:

> C'est dans la syllabe ou le phonème qu'il retrouve quelque chose d'irréductible. Il n'y a pas d'inanité sonore. Le son n'est jamais vain, il est corps. Il y a là une matière qui ne peut pas être niée. [...] La poésie de Fourcade est largement post mallarméenne dans la mesure où elle ne porte plus le deuil du sens.[16]
>
> [It's in the syllable or the phoneme that he finds something irreducible. There is no sonorous inanity. Sound is never vain, it is body. There is a substance there which is undeniable. [...] Fourcade's poetry is largely post-Mallarméan insofar as it no longer mourns meaning.]

Elsewhere, Valabrègue discusses Fourcade's 'désir de redonner de la chair et de la salive' [desire to restore flesh and saliva], to create poetry that comes, not from the mind, but 'de la gorge' [from the throat].[17] He argues that Fourcade's poetry marks a transition in focus from the negative to the positive, whereby poetry is no longer defined by lack or absence, but instead reclaims its affirmative value via an emphasis on the irreducible materiality of the 'corps-mot' [body-word]. For Valabrègue, this qualifies Fourcade's poetry as 'post-Mallarméan', a qualification we might consider with some caution as it works with a potentially oversimplified conception of Mallarmé's poetry. For Fourcade (and, I would argue, for Mallarmé), the negative and positive exist in a state of tension, both being present in his work. This is immediately apparent in the passage above, which simultaneously accentuates the physical presence of language, while also evoking the inescapable absence provoked by 'l'écart du mot d'avec le réel' [the gap between the word and the real] (*Xbo*): 'On sait qu'en écrivant on fait défaut [...] | On défaille'.

Fourcade's emphasis on the physicality of language is reinforced by his insistence on language understood as a function of the human body. In the passage above, the 'corps' anaphora in the first stanza, the repetition of 'sang' accompanied by the evocation of 'menstrues', the neologism 'extraveineux', and the adjective 'sensuel' all serve to root language firmly in its corporeal confines. Rather than taking language as an isolated, abstract, or purely textual phenomenon, the materiality of the text itself is seen as intrinsic to and inseparable from the materiality of the body that produces it. This focus on the corporeal place of writing is seen elsewhere in Fourcade's poetry, for example in *IL* where he writes 'voici le poème il a été fait des deux mains' [here is the poem it was made with both hands] (85). In a sequence of poems in *IL,* 'XVI', 'XVII', and 'XVIII', the emphasis on articulation, singing at full volume, and speaking aloud, also returns language to its bodily location. The poem is now a 'lungoem' (*Xbo*), produced in the 'poumons' (*IL,* 38), passing 'la glotte' (*Xbo*) in its physical exhalation from the respiratory tract, 'le souffle' (*IL,* 90). It is, by extension, part of the flesh and blood of the body that produces it, a type of 'poème-sang' [blood-poem], a 'langue corps efficace' [effective body language], or 'langue musculature' [musculature language] (*Xbo*). This focus on the human body might suggest a link with Artaud and the Dadaists, but rather than experimenting with glossolalia or para- and non-linguistic sound to find a beyond or outside of ordinary communication, Fourcade is interested in precisely how the body is a constitutional, but often forgotten part of ordinary language.

In keeping with this focus on 'la chair du texte' [the flesh of the text] is the importance of what Peter Consenstein identifies as 'le présent immédiat' in Fourcade's writing.[18] The passage above displays the two principal modes of writing in Fourcade's poetry: the first uses nominal and adjectival phrases which are static and verb-less, 'bleu boue des reines'. The second, typified by the third stanza, 'On sait qu'en écrivant on fait défaut', employs verbs exclusively in the present tense or as present participles. This serves to situate language and the writing process in an immediate present: it is experienced in the here and now, 'Maintenant je suis dans un mot' [Now I am in a word] (*Xbo*); and its materiality takes effect on the body: 'J'observe le monde, la nasalisation de laper en lamper, l'autre sens de l'autre son, l'abîme' [I observe the world, the nasalisation of laper (lap) in lamper (quaff), the other meaning of the other sound, the abyss] (*Xbo*). Thus, returning to our starting passage, language's effect is immediate and 'Sensuel'; it involves a simultaneous and multi-sensory experience, that is both acoustic ('corps phonique', 'corps chromatique', 'Bang'), and visual ('corps bleu', 'Sang alezan brûlé', 'un champ d'émail blanc').

The material dimension of the text is also foregrounded by Fourcade's frequent use of neologisms, such as 'sleu', 'insanglant', and 'extraveineux', which, like the interjection of phrases in English, serve to disrupt the reading process, drawing attention to the foreign or strange shapes of these unfamiliar words. Fourcade's neologisms are often compounded 'blend' terms such as 'lungoem' (*Xbo*), and derivations where a prefix or suffix is added to an easily identifiable root word: 'usinable' (*RD,* 131) (*Rose-déclic*), 'véralité' (*Xbo*), 'moderneraie' (*IL,* 21), 'hirondinately' (*EJP,* 90).[19] Elsewhere, Fourcade uses suffixes in isolation to draw attention to this frequent process of affixation and word creation: 'itude' (*IL,* 14), 'ilité' (*IL,* 39). Other neologisms are more obscure, such as 'sleu' in the passage above, or 'xbéité' in *Xbo*, where the meaning, or at least the process of derivation, is clear from the context in which it is found. This feature of Fourcade's work, while no doubt part of his poetics of decomposition described above, expresses a delight in wordplay that is reminiscent of the poetry of Francis Ponge. For both poets, writing prompts a certain fear or 'angoisse', but in equal measure, it can be a place for 'l'amour des mots' [the love of words] and 'la jouissance des choses' [the pleasure of things].[20]

A further feature of Fourcade's poetry that subverts the normal reading process is his unusual use of syntax. In the passage above, meaning is not constructed across linear, complete sentences, but arises in the juxtaposition of grammatically incomplete phrases, and resonances between individual words. Discontinuous syntax, anacoluthon, truncated clauses, and paratactic adjectival or nominal phrases are pervasive; they create an overall sense of agrammaticality, and engender a 'staccato' pace to the text which is rhythmically awkward and stunted. The following extract, from the opening pages of *Xbo* which draws heavily on English, typifies this:

> A weight
> Inner
> This does not relate to an invisible wind
> This emanates from a being
> Life
> Sways away like a January rose
> But why
> Do they
>
> Sqd
>
> The the
>
> Voix sans sang.

The word 'inner' on the second line can be interpreted as either an ungrammatical, postponed adjective describing the noun 'a weight' in the first line, or as a dislocated phrase that does not qualify anything, but stands in isolation. The reference of 'this' in the third and fourth lines is not entirely clear; possibly it refers back to the 'weight' of the first line, but given the proximity of the sentences, the article is redundant and need not be expressed. The use of enjambment requires a double take for the reader, who might at first interpret 'Life' as an isolated nominal phrase (as is common in Fourcade's writing), but will consequently interpret it as the subject of the following line 'sways away like a January rose'. The following lines, 'But why | Do they' cannot exist as a stand-alone question (or questions) as 'they' cannot refer to anything in the previous lines (there are no plural nouns). As a result, they can only be analysed as one, or possibly two, truncated or interrupted questions. At this point in the passage, the text descends into isolated words: the indecipherable 'sqd', the ungrammatical repetition of the definite article 'the the' (which cannot be a metapoetic reference to a preceding 'the' in the passage as there isn't one), and finally 'Voix sans sang' [voice without blood] which typifies Fourcade's frequent use of isolated nominal phrases. The consequence of Fourcade's agrammaticality is that his readers must work harder, constantly revising their interpretation of the text, continuously doubling back on themselves to rescan the lines of the poem. This necessitates a more active engagement with the text, and a greater awareness of the syntactic properties of the words on the page. This in turn subverts the normal writing/reading process whereby the writer uses syntax to facilitate the transfer of meaning, and the reader as a result focuses predominantly on the meaning of the text, with the syntax passing largely unnoticed. Indeed, the passage above enacts a disordered mode of articulation, where communication disintegrates into indecipherable phrases and ungrammatical formulations. Faced with the magnitude of his subject matter ('Life', 'Voix sans sang'), the poet stumbles over his words, advancing one approach ('But why'), before faltering and beginning another ('Do they').

In *Son blanc du un*, Fourcade writes that: 'La grammaire on l'apprend la vivre comme espace oui l'apprendre et simultanément l'espace on se prend à l'éprouver comme grammaire' [We learn to live grammar like space yes learn it and simultaneously we start to feel space like grammar] (*SB*, 59). Where grammar is lived or experienced as a space, the consequence, as Fourcade would have it, is that the elaboration of a novel grammar activates novel modes of experience and perception. In an interview, he described how conventional syntax, embedded with ideology and an impulse to 'hiérarchiser', does not reflect truthfully the simultaneity and multiplicity of the real. He continued, 'petit à petit il a fallu que je casse la syntaxe dont j'avais héritée, pour en créer une nouvelle, pour arriver à la simultanéité des plans du réel et à mettre tout ça sur le même plan' [little by little I had to break the syntax I'd inherited, to create a new one, to reach the simultaneity of planes of reality and to place it all on the same plane].[21] This spatial conceptualisation of grammar, coupled with an insistence on its significance above and beyond mere linguistic structure, resonates with Deleuze and Guattari's analysis of agrammaticality, where the marked syntax of an author's style induces deterritorialisation, that is the movement from a major territory to a novel, minor space beyond. In *Est-ce que j'peux placer un mot?* we find this deterritorialisation enacted from the first pages: the text opens with two grammatically correct questions — 'est-ce que je peux placer un mot? et à qui poser la question?' [can I get a word in? and to whom should I ask the question?] (*EJP*, 7) — that are subsequently reworked into non-sensical, ungrammatical phrases. In such a way, Fourcade depicts the acquired grammaticality of the mother tongue (notably the language of the mother, who insists on her son's correct use of French, and not the 'langue maternelle' of friendship evoked later on), disintegrating in the resistant, agrammatical language of poetry.

The agrammaticality of Fourcade's poetry is underpinned by the general absence of punctuation. His texts tend to exclude the use of full stops and commas, question and exclamation marks, although as can be seen in the extracts above, they often observe the beginning of a new line with a capitalised letter. This lack of punctuation reinforces the effects of the discontinuous syntax, impeding rather than aiding readers in their navigation through the text. The reading process is slowed down, as readers must constantly revise their comprehension of a phrase, rescanning it in light of a new clause introduced without the familiar guidance of a comma to delineate it. The lack of punctuation creates an impression of interconnectedness: words and phrases are juxtaposed in comma-less lines, replacing linearity with a rhizomatic relationship between parts. Fourcade's rejection of conventional punctuation represents a similar gesture to his rejection of conventional grammar rules; both involve an 'usage mineur' of the major language. It is as if the poet wishes to strip language of its grammatical and orthographical rules, and return to an idealised, infantile state, before 'le babil enfantin' has been subjected to the norms and standards of parental and pedagogical correction. 'Si vous arrêtez le babil vous arrêtez tout' [If you stop the babble you stop everything] (*EJP*, 40) Fourcade proclaims in *Est-ce que j'peux placer un mot?*, and to make his point, in the opening pages of the collection he writes:

> je suis l'enfant arriéré et sa mère
> aggeu aggeu dis aggeu mon chéri
> arreu il a dit arreu aggaggaguigui
> je suis l'enfant
> et la mère arriérée. (*EJP*, 8)

[I am the underdeveloped child and his mother | aggeu aggeu say aggeu my darling | arreu he said arreu aggaggaguigui | I am the child | and the underdeveloped mother.]

The glossolalic babbling that appears here and elsewhere in Fourcade's poetry is clearly linked to both his broader poetics of decomposition, as well as to the motif of the stutter. Significantly, it is acknowledged to be both childlike ('je suis l'enfant'), as well as a disordered form of adult language ('et la mère arriérée'). In *Son blanc du un*, Fourcade writes 'I am the infant language' (*SB*, 17); the significance of this 'infant language' is that it represents a pre-verbal stage in a child's linguistic development, prior to word formation. Rather than focusing on meaning and communication, the child is instead focused on the production of sound, and on experimenting with their newly developed vocal tract. The emphasis is thus on the material quality of language — how it sounds and how it feels to produce. Babbling also represents an interim stage in language acquisition, where speech has not yet been subjected to the various regulating structures of the major language. As a result, Fourcade's recourse to 'babil enfantin' represents a heightened example of a minor language, freed from grammatical correction, from the codified rules of the written word, and from the meaning-orientated norms of ordinary communication.

It should be clear from the various features of Fourcade's poetry highlighted thus far why Fourcade describes his writing as foreign. As well as evoking the foreign experience of the writer, who feels alienated from the language he uses, it describes the strangeness of a form of poetic language that diverges from the normal, unmarked mother tongue. This strangeness renders the reader's experience of the text akin to that of a second language speaker. The stunted pace of reading produced, as described above, by the discontinuous syntax and absence of punctuation contributes to this effect. Fourcade's accentuation of the material quality of language is also significant here. In a first language, the emphasis is predominantly on meaning: semantics and pragmatics, content and connotation. Language is an uncomplicated, transparent vessel for communication and it is the message not the medium that is foregrounded. Conversely, in a second language this situation is often inverted: the speaker has a heightened awareness of the unfamiliar shape of the target language, its sounds, phonemes, intonation, and morphosyntax (Am I pronouncing this correctly? Are the words in the right order? Is that the right conjugation?). So too in Fourcade's poetry the medium is foregrounded, playing an equivalent and sometimes more prominent role than the message that is conveyed. The parallel is reinforced by Fourcade's insistence on resituating language in the body, and in the immediate present. As a foreign language speaker, one is often more aware of language as a product of the body: the sound of one's own voice, one's accent, the performing of unnatural, non-native sounds that require a renegotiation of the space of the mouth, tongue, and lips. The deficiency in the speaker's linguistic competence, to use Saussure's distinction, has an immediate impact on their linguistic performance, and delays the processing time for speech. The result is that the usual fluency of the mother tongue is no longer available, and the speaker is often more aware of the present moment, forever conscious of the other participants in a conversation waiting for them to 'get the words out'. Kelly describes an 'aesthetic principle of writing *as if* one were writing in a foreign language', a remark that also recalls Prigent's description of 'modernist' poets as those who 'viv[ent] toute langue comme étrangère'.[22] These observations apply well to Fourcade's poetry which involves an experience of language akin to that of a foreign language, for both writer and reader.

This simulated experience of foreign language is reinforced by Fourcade's practice of using actual foreign language, predominantly English, although occasionally German, in the body of the text. While Fourcade speaks English more or less fluently, he cannot assume that the same is true for his French readers. The frequent presence of English in his texts therefore involves a very literal experience of a foreign language for his readers, the degree of which will clearly vary from person to person. This in turn produces a deterritorialising effect of its own. English words and phrases operate as markers of linguistic otherness; they represent concrete instances of the conceptual notion of foreign language that is explored in Fourcade's work. For the French reader, these unfamiliar English words often carry no signifieds but exist as pure signifiers. As if to accentuate the way in which foreign language can exist as empty signifiers, Fourcade frequently uses a Wolfsonian translation procedure where French words and phrases are translated in the text not semantically but phonologically into similar sounding English equivalents. Just as Deleuze observes how Louis Wolfson translated similar sounding words, rather than similar meaning words ('Don't trip over the wire' becomes 'Tu'nicht tréb über èth hé Zwirn', *CC*, 19), so too we find in Fourcade's work examples of these phonologically motivated translations. The most obvious of these is the bilingual wordplay of the title of *Outrance utterance*, but it is equally found elsewhere, for example in *Rose-déclic*: 'Rose T rose thé rose the rose thou not you I-beam rose abîme' (*RD*, 67).[23]

The use of English serves several other purposes within the text. As Fourcade suggests in an interview with Emmanuel Laugier, the inclusion of both French and English allows for the possibility of two different language systems with their prosodic and rhythmic differences, thus expanding the musical possibilities of the text.[24] Valabrègue sees Fourcade's use of English in *Outrance utterance* as another form of constraint-breaking, a product of the poet's 'volonté de dépassement des limites imparties au poème' [desire to go beyond the limits bestowed on the poem], an exercise in 'outrepasser la frontière entre deux langues' [overstepping the boundary between two languages].[25] Furthermore, code switching, particularly mid-sentence, can lend salience to a particular word or phrase: for example, in an otherwise French passage in *Xbo*, the English phrase 'did you say a hemless poem' is all the more prominent because of the switch to English. It marks a transition in subject matter and interjects with a brief metapoetic reflection. A further significant effect of the bilingual text is that it lends itself readily to a plurality of poetic voices, and to a dialogic rather than monoglottic mode of discourse. Often the voices that are interjected in English appear to be citations from real conversations and exchanges. In *IL*, the address 'Susan, could you please tell me your last name' (61) evokes a fragment of conversation between Fourcade and his close friend, the American poet Susan Howe. In *Manque*, a compilation of eulogistic texts, the phrase 'my darling, now you're on oxygen' suggests the poet's address to a dying friend, whose subsequent absence provides the focus of the collection.[26] These instances of direct speech often generate an internal, bilingual dialogue within the poem. For example, in *Xbo* the phrase 'Louis m'écrit "I am pleased you are back to writing again and so under the sway and in the way of language"' is subsequently developed into a motif of 'the rose's sway', that appears in the passage given above ('Life | Sways away like a January rose'). In *Manque*, Fourcade extends this effect in an exploration of 'prosopopée' (*M*, 84), that is the figure of speech in which an absent or deceased person is represented as speaking. Alongside the poet's own voice, the voices of his addressees (who are often English-speaking) proliferate in the text, as if to deliberately overpopulate the literary space or 'manque' left by their departure. Here, Fourcade exploits the use of foreign language within his poetry in order to accentuate its polyphonous quality.

The prevalence of foreign language intersects with a further significant dimension of Fourcade's work, whereby the poet anthropomorphises language, transforming it into a human 'other' with which a relationship can be played out. Bilingual code switching animates this relationship, so that one language represents the voice of the poet, and the other the voice of language itself. For example, *Xbo* ends with the reflection that, between the fear of not writing and the fear of writing, 'les mots se pelotonnent dans l'étendue et disent oh cuddle me, cuddle me' [the words snuggle in the expanse and say oh cuddle me, cuddle me]. In *IL*, the titular pronoun, whose identity is in constant flux, but which frequently comes to stand for language itself, is interpellated: 'oh IL please wave back to me' (37). The use of the capitalised French pronoun within the English phrase contributes to its re-analysis as a proper name designating the anthropomorphised figure of language itself. This anthropomorphism of language ties into other aspects of Fourcade's work, such as the focus on words as *corps*. It reinforces the idea that language exists independently of the poet, as a foreign, estranged 'other', with its own agency. We saw above how Fourcade evokes words moving around autonomously on the page ('Le s passe dans bleu et le b rejoint sang'). Likewise, in a direct address to language in *Est-ce que j'peux placer un mot?*, Fourcade describes returning to a passage he'd written the previous day, only to find that the words had somehow changed:

> Je ne te trouve jamais à la place où je t'ai laissé la veille [...], si j'étais sûr que personne ne m'entende je dirais bien, en français dans le texte: 'est-ce toi, mot aux volets bleu nuit?' — souhaitant trouver la question qui nous situe, toi, moi, l'existence. (*EJP*, 87)
>
> [I never find you in the same place where I left you the night before [...], if I was sure nobody would hear me, I would say, in French in the text: 'is that you, midnight-blue shutter word?' — hoping to find the question that situates us, you, me, existence.]

In an observation that would apply equally well to Fourcade's work, Beckett famously described the agency of words that appears in James Joyce's *Finnegans Wake*: 'Here words are not the polite contortions of twentieth-century printer's ink. They are alive. They elbow their way on to the page, and glow and blaze and fade and disappear'.[27]

This device of anthropomorphising language is, of course, far from new. In 'Les Mots sans rides' [Words Without Wrinkles], André Breton describes words as having their own independent lives, and the short text ends with the phrase 'Les mots font l'amour' [Words make love].[28] In *La Fabrique du pré* [The Making of the Meadow], Ponge describes the 'copulation' of words and things, writing, 'c'est leur copulation que réalise l'écriture (véritable, ou parfaite): c'est l'orgasme qui en résulte, qui provoque notre jubilation' [it's their copulation that writing realises (true, or perfect): it's the ensuing orgasm that provokes our jubilation].[29] In *Est-ce que j'peux placer un mot?* Fourcade employs this anthropomorphic expression of the romantic life of words to comic effect; in a scene that evokes the affectionate bickering of an elderly married couple he writes: 'Il y a des mots que j'appelle de loin et qui ne viendront pas je les appelle de trop loin les mots que j'appelle de trop près me disent je ne suis pas sourd' [There are words that I call from afar and that will not come I call them from too far away the words that I call from too nearby tell me I am not deaf] (*EJP*, 17). Likewise, in *En laisse*, we read:

> 'Au revoir mon chéri' disons-nous, 'au revoir mon amour' répond le poème, des 'tu vas me manquer horriblement' s'échangent, 'tu me manques déjà', ainsi redoublons-nous sans fin dans l'effusion réciproque, et des deux c'est ma voix qui s'étrangle en descendant l'escalier.[30]
>
> ['Goodbye my darling' we say, 'goodbye my love' replies the poem, some 'I'll miss you terribly's are exchanged, 'I miss you already', and so it goes on in a never-ending reciprocal outpouring, and of the two it is my voice that chokes up as I head down the stairs.]

Fourcade uses this technique to animate his own complex relationship with language. Thus, in *Outrance utterance*, we read that 'toute phrase' is 'so loving and companionable' (*OU*, 86), thus evoking the possibility of finding within writing an experience of language that is both tender and proximate, something akin to the 'langue de l'amitié' described in *Est-ce que j'peux placer un mot?* as a 'langue orgiaque complice et tendre [...] qui vous comble'. A summary on the P.O.L. website describes how the same is true in *Xbo*: 'il s'agit de l'amour des mots, considérés chacun comme un nom propre désignant une personne, des mots à sauver dans un acte d'amour et dans l'urgence' [it's about the love of words, each considered as a proper name designating a person, words to be saved in an urgent act of love].[31] At the same time, the device also illustrates the hostile, estranged relationship between poet and his words: in *IL*, an extended polyptoton depicts language, embodied by the figure of the third person pronoun, as the 'corps de l'étranger', whose strangeness prompts the poet's fear and mistrust (11–14). Discussing the 'étrangeté' of *IL*, Valabrègue writes the following:

> *IL* est l'expérience de l'altérité — presque celle de 'la familiarité non familière' ou de 'l'inquiétante étrangeté'. Sa propre voix peut être vécue comme méconnaissable ('ce matin j'ai reconnu dans ma voix la voix de quelqu'un n'ayant jamais parlé' [...]). Etre poète, c'est être son propre étranger. Cette voix altérée, c'est-à-dire abîmée et désirante, est une outrance: elle est monstrueusement méconnaissable. Elle n'appartient plus à 'l'auteur' ni à la soi-disant première personne.[32]

> [*IL* is the experience of otherness — almost that of 'unfamiliar familiarity' or the 'uncanny'. One's own voice can be experienced as unrecognisable ('this morning I recognised in my voice the voice of someone who's never spoken' [...]). To be a poet is to be a foreigner/stranger to oneself. This altered voice, damaged and yearning, is an excess: it is monstrously unrecognisable. It no longer belongs to the 'author' nor to the so-called first person.]

As Valabrègue suggests, for Fourcade, language prompts a feeling of the uncanny, of something that is both familiar and unfamiliar. Estranged from the poet at their conception, the poet's words are at once his own but also foreign and other, a duality that is captured by Derrida's phrase, 'je n'ai qu'une langue, or ce n'est pas la mienne'. The complexity of the poet's relationship with language is highlighted precisely through this device of anthropomorphisation, which figures the alterity of language, the dialogic and plural mode of discourse that such a divorce engenders, as well as the consequent hostility or complicity between poet and his words.

'Je balbutie'

Fourcade forges what Jean-Jacques Thomas and Steven Winspur would describe as a 'personal poetic dialect', characterised, as we have seen, by discontinuous syntax and agrammaticality, by the decomposition of language and an emphasis on linguistic materiality, by the prevalent use of English, as well as by devices such as the anthropomorphism of words themselves.[33] Destabilising the norms and standards of ordinary language use, this poetic dialect constitutes a form of minor literature, which, following Deleuze and Guattari's analysis, would lend it a political dimension. Fourcade himself describes the intrinsically political nature of poetry, writing: 'il n'y a pas de grande poétique sans politique' [there is no great poetics without politics].[34] Some of his texts engage directly with current affairs: *En laisse* takes as its starting point the photograph of an Iraqi prisoner at Abu Ghraib, held on a leash by an American soldier, and the poem 'après les attentats' was written in response to the terrorist attacks in Paris in November 2015.[35] However, most of his work does not have an overtly political focus, and instead, as Fourcade himself suggests, it is a particular use of language that might render his poetry political.[36] Discussing the significance of Subcomandante Marcos in *Le Sujet monotype*, Fourcade draws a parallel between Marcos's non-dogmatic subversion of power, and the language of poetry.[37] He states: 'J'ai voulu [...] dire que *le* politique, dans sa façon d'être dans la langue, a extrêmement d'importance et qu'écrire c'est aussi habiter cette conscience politique' [I wanted [...] to say that the politician, in his way of being in language, is extremely important and that writing is also inhabiting this political consciousness].[38] In the previous chapter, we saw how Deleuze and Guattari's discussion of the politically subversive nature of language in minor literature is grounded in their analysis of the stutter. So too, in Fourcade's work, the stutter operates as a metonym for the systematic disordering of language, and thus the disruption of power-encrypted norms of representation.

In 1990, Fourcade published two poems under the title 'Stutter' with Editions Chandeigne, that were later included in *IL*. His writing makes frequent reference to its own disordered mode of articulation: 'je balbutie' [I stutter] he proclaims in *IL* (67), 'les intervalles sont surtout bégayés' [the intervals are above all stuttered] (70). In *Est-ce que j'peux placer un mot?*, he writes, 'Mes problèmes de zézaiement sont allés croissant. S'y sont ajoutées les difficultés du balbutiement' [My problems with lisping increased. Added to that were difficulties with stuttering] (*EJP*, 49). In *Xbo*, Fourcade describes the bi-partite nature of his disordered writing, which is affected on both a systematic level and on the level of production: 'b comme speech defect' captures the idea of a cognitive, semantic disorder; his metapoetic reference to 'un poème toussé | Par quintes' [a poem coughed | in fits] evokes the disrupted articulation of the text. Readers and critics are quick to pick up on this aspect of Fourcade's work: in a special edition of *Java* dedicated to Fourcade's work, Cadiot, whose poetry at times employs a similar stuttering effect, entitled his contribution 'Bé-bégayer'.[39] Jean Khalfa describes Fourcade as 'lui qui a fait du bégaiement dans la langue, pour reprendre l'expression de Deleuze, une méthode' [he who turned stuttering in language, to use Deleuze's expression, into a method].[40] This raises the questions: how does this method operate on a textual level, and what is its effect? The following passage is from 'XXXVII' in *IL*, one of the two poems previously printed under the title 'Stutter':

> Susan, could you please tell me your last name
> is it mimosa — I mean acid green mmsa
> tangoed mimosa
> or is stuttered mimosa your last name Susan
> electric
> o please tll me
> you plus minus msmo ai
> [...]
>
> the wowowoman man
> the wo
> manliness
> of the disphony of your breath

> holds me
> in explosive mimosaliness. (*IL*, 61)

Juxtaposing the ordinary and the disordered, the poem opens with a seemingly straightforward question addressed to the poet Susan Howe, in whose work the stutter is also a significant motif.[41] The normality of the opening line is soon disrupted, as the central 'mimosa' motif becomes 'stuttered mimosa', decomposed into its constituent letters and sounds: 'mmsa', 'o', 'msmo ai'. The omission of certain letters, 'tll', 'mmsa', and the scrambling of others, 'msmo ai', is a notably visual illustration of the disordered language that characterises Fourcade's poetry. In the passage, the normal function of meaning is disturbed: rather than progressing in a linear fashion, a loose network of associations between words is created. Mimosa, for instance, is qualified by the following, often opaque adjectives: 'acid green' (mimosa is yellow), 'tangoed', 'stuttered', 'electric', 'crisp', 'stencilled', and 'explosive'. Some of the adjectives ('stuttered', 'stencilled') make sense when mimosa is analysed metapoetically as referring not to the flower but to the word 'mimosa' itself, others remain more cryptic. The second stanza opens with a literal stuttering, 'wowowoman man | the wo | manliness', that is accentuated by the enjambment, which reinforces the impression of suspension and hesitation. When Fourcade alludes to the 'dysphony' of the addressee's (Howe's) breath, we might read this metapoetically as describing the disordered 'souffle' of the poem in hand.[42] The repetition of the key words of the poem ('mimosa', 'Susan', 'last name', 'woman') generate echolalic *ritournelles* that turn back on themselves, impeding the progression of the text. This is reinforced by the syntax of the passage which is disrupted, for example, in the dislocated adjective 'electric', and the verb-less phrase 'you plus minus msmo ai'. The poem is typographically narrow, making frequent use of enjambment; longer lines containing complete sentences (such as the first and fourth) are outnumbered by shorter, truncated clauses ('the wo', 'holds me') and isolated nominal and adjectival phrases ('tangoed mimosa', 'electric'). Again, this contributes to the disordered, impeded delivery of the poem, creating hesitations and pauses between different syntactic segments of the sentence. The poem, published for a French readership, is written in English, and as a result elicits the same deterritorialising effects described in the previous section. The disordered features of the poem (the word scrambling, the discontinuous syntax, the opaque network of semantic associations) are exaggerated for the foreign reader, without the immediate reference points of a native speaker to decipher what is normal and what is abnormal.

For Fourcade, the stutter is a product of the 'angoisse' of writing, evoked in *Est-ce que j'peux placer un mot?*. In a poem from *IL*, we read:

> je balbutie parce que je n'ose pas prononcer les mots tout est à
> jamais si confus je ne sais pas qui IL est
> tu balbuties tu es une balbutieuse je sais qui tuée
> IL bégaie parce que IL sait la part d'ombre qui gagne chaque
> mot et que l'ensemble ombre-lumière ne peut pas se dire en
> une fois et parce que IL connaît la tragédie de l'énonciation
> nous balbutions
> vous balbutiez. (*IL*, 67)

[I stutter because I don't dare pronounce the words everything is | always so confused I don't know who IT is | you stutter you are a stutterer I know who you are | IT stammers because IT knows the portion of shadow that spreads to each | word and that the shadow-light ensemble cannot be said in | one go and because IT knows the tragedy of the utterance | we stutter | you stutter.]

In this extract, the poet describes how he stutters, paralysed by the fear, described above, to 'placer un mot'. This hesitation is compounded by his confusion at the elusive status of the third person pronoun ('je ne sais pas qui IL est'), and 'IL' being 'la figure du poème [...], la figure de la parole' [the figure of the poem [...], the figure of speech] (*IL*, 9), by his uncertainty around language more broadly. The repetition of *balbutier* reinforces the centrality of the stutter, and the structuring of the poem according to the conjugation of the verb, beginning with 'je' and running through to 'nous' and 'vous', serves to populate the poem with a plurality of different voices — with the stuttering of all possible grammatical persons. The errant verb in the third person singular form (*bégayer* instead of *balbutier*) highlights the distinction between the poet's stammering and the poem's stuttering, thus foregrounding 'la tragédie de l'énonciation', the critical divorce between poet and his language. Structured around the pedagogical convention of organising language into conjugations, the poem foregrounds prescriptive grammar, that most tangible aspect of the major language. It then subverts the rules and conventions of this prescriptive, organisational framework: the deliberate misspelling of 'tu es' as 'tuée' misanalyses the grammatical category of the singular second person form of a present tense verb as a past participle of 'tuer' [to kill]. This slight but conspicuous act of grammatical disobedience gestures towards the disorderly nature of poetic language more generally.

In Fourcade's work, the stutter is both a stumbling against the material shapes and sounds of words, and a metaphorical encounter with the vertiginous and elusive functioning of meaning. To return to Perloff's formulation, it sees poetry bumping its head against the limits of language. Just as, in psycholinguistics, researchers study disordered speech to gain a greater understanding of the non-disordered brain, Fourcade's poetry experiments with disordered language in order to explore the features of ordinary communication that usually go unnoticed. His writing engages in a self-reflexive language game that examines its own linguistic functioning: the operation of meaning (for example in relation to *il*), word creation (in his frequent use of neologisms), syntax (in his flagrant disregard of grammatical rules), and phonology (in the unusual phonemic combinations that glossolalia and childlike babbling produces). For Deleuze and Guattari, the stutter destabilises the normal language system, and from this point: 'C'est là que le style fait langue. C'est là que le langage devient intensif, pur continuum de valeurs et d'intensités' [That is when style becomes a language. That is when language becomes intensive, a pure continuum of values and intensities] (*MP*, 125; *ATP*, 115). Intensities are what Deleuze and Guattari describe as elements at the limit of perception, imperceptible in themselves, yet still felt or sensed, something akin, perhaps, to Fourcade's evocation of 'explosive mimosaliness' in the final lines of the poem 'Stutter'. Furthermore, for Deleuze and Guattari, the stutter disrupts the hegemony of the major language by making variation — in both form and meaning — proliferate

(*MP*, 124; *ATP*, 114), an idea that Fourcade will arrive at independently through his elaboration of a rhizomatic, 'toutarrivesque' poetics (*EJP*, 61).

The Rhizome

In the chapter of *Poetic Becomings* entitled 'Dominique Fourcade, or a Poetics of the Rhizome', Jérôme Game investigates Deleuze and Guattari's concept of the rhizome by exploring notions of the surface, the fold, and the line in Fourcade's poetry.[43] In keeping with the overall focus of his book, Game centres his discussion on the poetic subject and on the Deleuzian notion of becoming. The following analysis takes up Game's idea of a 'poetics of the rhizome' to explore various properties of Fourcade's writing, before mapping it onto what Fourcade himself describes as his 'tout arrive' poetics.

In the introduction to *Mille plateaux*, Deleuze and Guattari develop the concept of the rhizome, derived originally from the botanical term for an 'elongated, usually horizontal, subterranean stem which sends out roots and leafy shoots along its length' (*OED*). Typical examples of these botanical rhizomes are grass, ginger, and weeds; when separated or cut into pieces, each piece of the plant continues to expand and grow laterally. Deleuze and Guattari adopt the term to refer to systems defined by multiplicity, a lack of linear unity, and principles of interconnection and heterogeneity (*MP*, 13; *ATP*, 5). They describe how each point of a rhizome must be connected to any other, and how upon rupture the rhizome will start up again and proliferate. A rhizomatic system therefore has no beginning or end, no pivot or centre, and instead involves a horizontal, flat, or non-hierarchical structure. They establish an opposition between the rhizome and arborescent (tree-root) structure, the latter being organised vertically or hierarchically. Game summarises Deleuze and Guattari's adoption of the term as follows:

> Gilles Deleuze and Félix Guattari extract the notion of rhizome from its original context and use it to determine Being as becoming, non-individual and formless, locating the concept at the centre of their ontology and their aesthetics. The originally botanical concept now designates an open system of multiplicities that are not rooted in common history or teleology but related in non-arborescent ways on a plane without presupposing any centre or transcendence. A poetics of the rhizome can in turn be schematically explained as one in which the poem is the experience of a plane of composition [...] on which subjectivity and corporeity are disseminated into a flux — writing itself.[44]

Game's analysis elucidates how the rhizome provides a model for the operation of subjectivity in Fourcade's poetry, but it might equally apply to other dimensions of Fourcade's work. The metapoetic descriptions of Fourcade's texts themselves offer a starting point in this regard. Throughout the unpaginated, unpunctuated, book-length poem *Xbo*, the poet describes the text as 'seamless' and 'hemless', writing:

> Ne cherchez pas la fin dans ce poème
> Il ne peut y en avoir parce qu'il n'a pas commencé
> Dès la première ligne il a été cloué

> Le temps en a été éjecté
> Circulez dans ce poème. (*Xbo*)

[Don't look for the end in this poem | There cannot be one because it didn't start | From its first line it was nailed down | Time has been ejected from it | Circulate in this poem.]

Fourcade elaborates the idea of the poem as a single page or plane, without a beginning or an end. The lack of punctuation reinforces this notion; the absence of full stops, question and exclamation marks means that sentences quite literally have no end but instead make up an open and interconnected system. As Fourcade writes, the poem is a space where time is ejected, and where the reader is invited to circulate, rather than to progress in a linear fashion from beginning to end. In keeping with this, his poetry has little narrative progression, and, as discussed above, often uses present participles and static, verb-less clauses. His texts are not structured according to more conventional systems: they are not organised into structurally significant parts or sections, and do not employ established metric or verse forms (as Valabrègue puts it, Fourcade 'ne met pas en forme').[45] Instead, they are structured horizontally, with collections reading as entire poems that develop interlacing networks of key words and motifs. These motifs are not centres that subordinate other components of the text, but rather are identifiable threads in a network of equivalences.[46] They generate loose associations with further motifs that add to the rich, interconnected texture of Fourcade's writing. Game captures this 'principe de connexion' well when he describes how Fourcade produces 'non-hierarchical links between beings, moments, signifieds and signifiers on the immanent surface that is the poem'.[47]

Elsewhere in *Xbo*, Fourcade suggests that the text proceeds through a continuous series of uprootings and self-rupturings: 'Vous vous rappelez la première ligne elle n'inaugure pas une durée | Elle se déracine comme elle s'énonce' [Remember the first line doesn't usher in a duration | It uproots itself as it expresses itself]. Just as the rhizome continues to grow when it is severed, we might expect the same to be true for the rupture Fourcade describes in his own work. In this sense, Fourcade's use of the stutter presents itself as an archetypal form of rupture — it segments the text, breaking the fluidity and onward momentum of reading. Where the stutter appears, linguistic variation proliferates: phonological, semantic, and so on. Likewise, agrammaticality performs a similar form of rupture, by impeding the normal linear progression of ordinary syntactic structure. As we saw in the previous section, isolated nominal clauses, truncated phrases, and anacoluthon require meaning to be constructed rhizomatically (as opposed to arborescently), through juxtaposition and parataxis. The self-rupturing characteristic of the rhizome can also be traced onto the generic plasticity of Fourcade's writing. In an interview, Fourcade describes how, as he sees it, the fundamental difference between poetry and prose is that 'le vers scande différemment les choses' [verse scans things differently].[48] His comment reflects the posture of many contemporary poets and critics, such as Agnès Disson who suggests that, for the writers collected in the *Revue de littérature générale*, poetry's difference from prose continues to be predicated on 'le découpage, la mise en rythme' [the cutting up, the putting into rhythm].[49] We might then attempt to situate Fourcade's texts on a continuum, based on this rhythmic distinction. At the more conventionally 'poetic' end, texts such as *Xbo* and *IL* involve shorter verse lines, arranged into stanzas. On the prose end, texts such as *Est-ce que j'peux placer un mot?* and *Le Sujet monotype* resemble essays, written for the most part in complete sentences, arranged into paragraphs, with punctuation to denote the end of lines. However, such a taxonomy quickly disintegrates as Fourcade's most poetic texts frequently include passages of prose, and his more prosaic text are so poetic that they have very little bearing on a more prototypical notion of a prose text or essay. Instead of maintaining traditional generic distinctions, Fourcade's texts oscillate between prose and poetry, with one form continuously uprooting the other. This happens on the level of the prose/poetic line itself, as Game suggests: 'Dominique Fourcade has developed a line/fold that is a mutual deterritorialisation between verse and sentence whereby the verse *folds the sentence* and the sentence *continues (or stretches) the verse*'.[50] We saw in the passages from *Est-ce que j'peux placer un mot?*, cited above, how the text moves between essayistic prose (for example, the metapoetic reflections on the foreign language of literature) and poetic stanzas (the glossolalic babbling of the poet-child). In this folding and stretching of the line, the same themes, subject matters, and words alternate continuously between two rhythmic patternings, with punctuation, line length, and the use or non-use of enjambment reinforcing the distinction. Discussing this dimension of his work, Fourcade states:

> En somme j'établis ou s'établit un réseau mobile vers-proses, un filet en apparence très lâche mais extrêmement dynamique, dont le maillage se recalibre sans cesse, système espace-temps qui m'autorise des combinaisons infinies — ce qui veut dire dont le nombre est infini et dont les possibilités opératoires sont infinies. Une organisation, une tensilité (élasticité?), une multiplicité de détentes internes dont l'énergie déborde le texte, au moins je crois, et en tout cas ne se cale nulle part.[51]

> [In short a mobile poetry-prose network is established, a net that appears very loose but which is extremely dynamic, whose meshing is constantly recalibrated, a space-time system that allows me infinite combinations — meaning the number of combinations is infinite and the operational possibilities are infinite. An organisation, a tensility (elasticity?), a multiplicity of internal springs whose energy overflows the text, at least I think so, and in any case doesn't settle anywhere.]

The 'réseau mobile vers-proses' of Fourcade's writing thus involves a certain elasticity, where form is not superimposed upon a work, but rather is found organically in the writing process. It lends his texts a rhythmic and formal multiplicity, which involves the continuous deterritorialisation between one form and the next; as Fourcade says of *Le Sujet monotype*, the text 'procède par déplacements incessants' [advances through constant displacements], and he goes on to state:

> Élaborant, à un degré que je n'avais jamais osé auparavant mais qui ne m'aurait pas été possible auparavant, des textures de proses et de vers mêlés, j'abolissais dans le même geste la distinction, dont j'ai par ailleurs la nausée, entre prose et poésie.[52]

[By elaborating, to an extent that I had never previously dared but which wouldn't have been possible beforehand, textures of prose and verse combined, in the same gesture I did away with the distinction that I am otherwise sick of, between prose and poetry.]

While Fourcade insists on this being a distinct feature of *Le Sujet monotype*, the mixing of prose and verse that he describes is clearly apparent in his earlier work too. What he conveys here is a rhizomatic approach to genre, where prose and poetry successively deterritorialise one another within the text, existing in a relationship of continuity. In turn, as Fourcade suggests, such a practice destabilises the distinction between poetry and prose altogether, resisting their discrete classification as genres. 'Une prose c'est un poème-bloc,' he writes, 'Vers et prose? Dans les deux cas c'est pour moi un travail de poésie.' [A prose text is a poem-unit [...]. Verse and prose? For me they are both a work of poetry].[53] His writing is thus 'un travail de poésie': not poetry understood in that first, narrower sense as a distinct rhythmic form, but something which transcends the formal properties of traditional generic classifications.

Linked to this collapsing of the distinction between prose and poetry is Fourcade's exploration of the boundaries between different art forms, specifically, poetry, art, music, film, and dance. Rather than simply exploring how these different artistic domains can offer poetry conceptual models, or how, to use Valabrègue's term, a 'système de vision' can be passed from one domain into another, Fourcade demonstrates how they are all part of one and the same thing.[54] The poet is a choreographer, an artist, a film director, and a musician, as once again the discrete system of classifications is collapsed: 'Je veux rendre le réel, et c'est une idée tout à fait infantile, et pour le rendre, il me faut être moi-même un chorégraphe, un ingénieur du son, un cadreur, un monteur, un peintre, etc.' [I want to render the real, and it's a totally infantile idea, and to render it, I have to be a choreographer, a sound engineer, a cameraman, a film editor, a painter, etc.].[55]

Thus, Fourcade alternates between these various roles, drawing on different artistic domains in his poetry. As an art critic as well as a writer, it is unsurprising that the visual arts play a significant role in Fourcade's poetry.[56] He describes the poem as a surface, a canvas rather than a page, where words relate to each other spatially, as objects within a composition. As Pinson suggests, 'la poésie, pour Dominique Fourcade, est devenu aussi un art de l'espace'.[57] *Xbo* extends this idea to its extreme by eliminating page numbers, describing instead the 'champ d'émail blanc sans dimension' (which might evoke Duchamp's 'Fountain' — that foundational work of twentieth-century art which had, in its turn, posed its own questions about the boundaries of artistic practice). *Le Ciel pas d'angle* is particularly concerned with the relationship between art and poetry. It was the first book Fourcade published after his ten-year break from writing poetry, during which time he studied at length the artists that have continued to influence his work to this day: Manet, Cézanne, Matisse, Degas, and Hantaï. The collection explores a number of dimensions of visual art: line, shape, composition, light, and colour. It depicts a series of geometric shapes, from the more basic 'lignes' (*CPA*, 33) and 'angles'

(63), to the more obscure 'hélice' (33) and 'trapèze' (34), and evokes traditional aspects of artistic composition, such as 'cadre' (33), and 'toile' (67). These evocations frequently appear in metapoetic descriptions of the text itself, and references such as the following are pervasive:

> Mots
> Leur sculpture
> Aplat
> O formidable bas-relief des mots. (*CPA*, 81)
>
> [Words | Their sculpture | Flat tint | O tremendous bas-relief of words.]

Colour and light are equally prominent, with references throughout: 'un rouge magnifique' (67), 'lumière violette' (68). The poet explores not only the very composition of pigment, 'le bleu est fait du cuivre' [blue is made from copper] (47), but also colour understood more metaphorically: 'La couleur accidentelle de Buffon; la couleur sollicitée de Goethe; la couleur non exprimée de Matisse' [Buffon's accidental colour; Goethe's solicited colour; Matisse's non-expressed colour] (68). The most prominent colours of the collection are blue and white, evoking in turn Cézanne's skies, Matisse's cut outs, and Simon Hantaï's 'pliage' compositions. These pivotal colours acquire a further metapoetic significance when Fourcade qualifies the blue as 'bleu d'encre' (83), and the white as the whiteness of 'la page' (23).

Paul Cézanne, whom Fourcade describes as a poet as well as a painter (*CPA*, 65), is omnipresent in *Le Ciel pas d'angle*; the oranges and blues of his provençal landscapes form the basis of a key visual motif. Taking a quotation from Cézanne as his starting place, 'Quand la couleur est à sa richesse la forme est à sa plénitude' [When the colour is at its richest, the form reaches plenitude] (65), Fourcade goes on to discuss the relationship between form and content:

> Cézanne voulait dire que le contenu est à lui-même sa forme et simultanément que l'être du contenu, la substance du contenu (le contenu du contenu?) réside dans sa forme. N'est pas un contenant; la forme est un contenu — elle est le contenu — le seul visage et la seule âme et la seule vérité possible du contenu qu'elle a en propre de dire et d'intégralement produire. (*CPA*, 65)
>
> [Cézanne meant that content is its own form and, at the same time, that the being of content, the substance of content (the content of content?) resides in its form. It is not a container; form is a content — it is the content — the only face and the only soul and the only possible truth of content that it truly possesses to say and fully produce.]

Fourcade deduces from Cézanne's reflection that form *is* content, which, in an immediate sense, resonates with a number of aspects of Fourcade's writing already discussed: notably its metapoetic dimension, where language is both medium and subject matter, and its emphasis on language as referent, indistinguishable from other forms of materiality. In *Citizen Do*, Fourcade suggests that the focus on the materiality of language in his work expresses a continuistic, monistic conception of the relationship between language and world: 'Syllabe-être. A ce point, réel de la langue et réel du monde ne font qu'un' [Syllable-being. At this point, the real of language and the real of the world are one].[58] The significance of colour in *Le Ciel pas d'angle* is an expression of this same idea: the motif of blue and white binds the material reality of the poet's ink and paper to Cézanne's brush strokes, to a provençal summer sky, creating a continuum between language, art, and world, where all are constituted from the same basic matter. The distinction between form and content is collapsed, a single substance remains: 'Cuivre, bleu étale, notre substance sans origine ni départ | Notre substance notre limite nos cendres' [Copper, blue spreads, our substance without origin or beginning | Our substance our limit our ashes] (*CPA*, 47). Without the semiotic structure of language to complicate the matter, it is in the visual arts that Fourcade finds a very immediate example of this continuity between form and content. In this sense, we understand why Fourcade is keen to stress the significance of Cézanne, Matisse, and Cubism, over and above literary figures such as Stéphane Mallarmé.[59]

In the citation above, Fourcade also describes himself as an 'ingénieur du son', and by extension the poem is as much a sound composition as a textual one. In an interview with Mathias Lavin, he reiterates this: 'je dirais aussi que je travaille à partir des sons, je fais de la façon la plus modeste possible de la musique, et sur ma page je fais des agencements de sons' [I would also say that I work from sounds, I make music in the most modest way possible, and on my page I arrange sounds].[60] These arrangements or compositions of sounds are heterogeneous and multiple. First and foremost, Fourcade draws attention to the phonemes and syllables of human language, 'un *pu* doux | un *tlu* clair et liquide [...] un *tuh* un *puh* un *huih* un *pluih*' (*IL*, 79), to the various modes of articulation that modulate it (words are murmured, sung, coughed, stuttered, and hummed). Alongside human language, various forms of animal communication appear: bird song, the calls of nightingales and larks, and the sonar 'cris' of porpoises in *Son blanc du un* (*SB*, 28). References to music proliferate: we find allusions to traditional musical notation (*M*, 33), to classical composers such as Bach and Shostakovich, as well as to jazz: 'saxophone' (*SB*, 90), 'riffs' (*RD*, 25) and 'effusion parkerienne' (*CPA*, 40). Pinson points out the significance of the *berceuse* or 'système lullaby' in *Citizen Do*, and the prominence of the motif of the *chant* is well-documented in criticism of Fourcade's work.[61] Fourcade's poetry depicts the variegated soundscapes of modern life, right down to the most banal aspects of everyday existence: in *Le Ciel pas d'angle* the poet describes 'la rythmique d'une machine à écrire' [the rhythm of a typewriter] joined by 'cinquante sonneries de téléphone' [fifty ringtones] and 'du riz sur le zinc on a craqué une allumette quelque part | O diesel de musiques rue de n'importe quelle ville' [rice on the zinc counter a match being lit somewhere | O diesel of music road of whatever city] (*CPA*, 35). Like a sound engineer or score composer, the poet constructs 'des agencements de sons' that are simultaneous and multiple, not simply in the eclectic range of sounds that are assembled, but also in the nature of those sounds themselves. The motif of jazz riffs, classical music chords, and a cappella vocal ensembles all involve multiple voices or sounds that are synchronised in polyphonous compositions. In this way, the heterogeneity and polyphony of the lyric *je*, discussed in the first section, is matched by the heterogeneity and polyphony of the auditory collages that Fourcade's poetry presents.

As Fourcade suggests when he describes himself above as 'un chorégraphe', dance forms a prominent motif in his work, from classic ballet (*IL*, 60), to the contemporary dance of choreographers such as Merce Cunningham and Pina Bausch (*M*, 72). 'A partir de Balancine,' the poet states, 'j'ai appris notamment comment chorégraphier différents éléments sur un plan donné' [From Balancine, I learnt how to choreograph different elements on a given plane].[62] In an extension of the anthropomorphism device discussed earlier in the chapter, words are conceived as bodies that are choreographed in grammatical patternings across the space of the page: 'Le mot est le corps chorégraphié du poème' [The word is the poem's choreographed body] (*OU*, 24). Evoking the influence of dance on his work, Fourcade remarks: 'On pourrait voir comment le placement d'un geste puis sa répétition simultanée, mais à peine décalée dans l'ampleur, dans les chorégraphies de Pina Bausch, m'a conduit à penser des déplacements similaires dans l'intensité et le rythme de la langue' [We might see how the placing of a gesture, then its repetition, at the same time but slightly different in scale, in Pina Bausch's choreography, led me to think about similar movements in the intensity and rhythm of language].[63]

Fourcade draws a parallel between choreography and poetic composition, describing how poetry involves the manipulation of language's rhythms into patterns of repetition and movement. Extending this parallel further, he presents language and dance as constituted by the same basic elements — material presence, movement, rhythm — and the frequent choreographic metaphors he employs emphasise this continuity by fusing signifier and signified. For example, in a passage from *IL* discussed earlier, we read 'acid green mmsa | tangoed mimosa | or is stuttered mimosa'. The repetition of the word 'mimosa' in a poem characterised by abrupt pauses and discontinuous syntax means that 'tangoed mimosa' has a dual reference, evoking not only the dancing flower, but also the movements of the word 'mimosa' itself. Likewise, when we read in *Rose-déclic*, 'cheek to cheek dans la roseraie elles dansent un slow mortel' (*RD*, 165), the slow dance of flowers in a rose garden is also that of the words on the page. In *Manque* Fourcade evokes *Shards*, a piece of contemporary dance choreographed by Cunningham, in which the choreographer plays on the contrast between stillness and movement. The piece involves short phrases where one dancer moves and the rest of the dance corps are immobile. The significance of this evocation is apparent in *Manque*, a collection of eulogistic texts, where Fourcade describes a sensation of being the 'last one standing', having watched many of his friends pass away before him. This idea is reworked later in the text when Fourcade likens the text to a tango ('ce livre n'est qu'un tango', *M*, 100), but a tango where despite there being two people involved (the poet and the eulogised friend), the dance is now a solitary one.

In *Est-ce que j'peux placer un mot?*, following a passage that evokes the spatiotemporal dimensions of writing, Fourcade intertwines the composition of the poem with the movements of a dance:

> je place un mot [...]
> je place, je fais un pas rien de plus (deux je n'ai pas deman-
> dé on verra bien)

> mon premier souci est de ne pas saboter la gestuelle mon
> deuxième souci est de saboter la gestuelle
> je mets un pas (un pas se lance un mot se met dans tous ses
> états)
> un pas, nice toe-work, lovely, dans le temps (à la renverse)
> je
> mets mot mets pas mets pas
> j'espace (à la renverse, une seconde fois)
> mot pas mot (son instep, ses assoiements)
> pas un. (*EJP*, 14)

[I put down a word [...] | I put down, I take one step nothing more (two I didn't ask | we'll see) | my first concern is not to botch the body language my | second concern is to botch the body language | I place a step (a step is taken a word is placed in all its | forms) | a step, nice toe-work, lovely, over time (backwards) | I | place word place step place step | I space out (backwards, a second time) | word step word (its instep, its sittings) | step one.]

The dance/poem progresses across the space of the page ('j'espace'), taking place 'dans le temps', configured in movements or 'pas'. The initial reference to the tentative words of the writer 'je place un mot' is subsequently abstracted to more generalised verbs of movement 'je place', 'je fais un pas', 'je mets un pas'. When the English voice interjects ('nice toe-work, lovely'), the comparison to dance is made explicit, and is then sustained in the references to 'instep' and 'assoiement', as well as in the parathentical instructions '(à la renverse)', '(à la renverse, une seconde fois)', that might then be read as choreographic directions. Following the English interjection, the syntactic uncertainty of the phrases 'je | mets mot mets pas mets pas', 'mot pas mot', and 'pas un' activates the two lexical fields that have been developed thus far in the poem (that of writing and of dance). By playing on the polysemy of the word *pas* which means not only a step in the chorographical sense, but also a step forward, and the particle of negation, the poem elaborates various planes of meaning, suspending them simultaneously throughout the passage. The parallel between dance and language highlights their similarities, as scripted patterns of movement and rhythm, and as two different forms of semiotic systems. The gestures of dance have a dual status, whereby they can exist as both pure signifier or sheer movement, but also enclose the possibility of meaningful interpretation and signification. Language also maintains this duality: it is both material sound and printed ink, but also a system of signs with the capacity to signify and be meaningful.

The fourth and final art that Fourcade evokes in the citation above is film. Cinematic terminology is prevalent in his work, from 'dubbing', 'lip-sync', and 'play-back' (65) in *Citizen Do* (the title of which is a play on Orson Welles's *Citizen Kane*), to 'la bande des sous-titres' in *Rose-déclic* (141). The significance of cinema for Fourcade is found not so much in the centrality of the image, poetic or cinematographic, but rather in the way it offers a parallel to the spatial composition of poetry. As we have just seen with regard to choreography, the poet, like the film director, is involved in the staging of words as bodies. In this sense,

Christophe Wall-Romana's observation in *Cinepoetry* applies well to Fourcade: 'the cinematic (and precinematic) imaginary [...] brought a new focus to the scene and materiality of writing, and to the spatial and visual dimension of the page'.[64] For Fourcade, as for many other contemporary poets, cinema offers new modes of perception, and invites a return to the question of the real in artistic representation. It presents poetry with novel ways of seeing: in *Rose-déclic*, for example, the poet uses cinematographic language to describe how the text focuses in on the motif of the rose: 'Rose en zoom sur la chose zeroing in on', referencing in turn 'le gros plan' (*RD*, 27), whereby the camera isolates a single object to focus on in detail. In *Outrance utterance*, the Barthesian 'death of the author' or Mallarméan 'disparition élocutoire du poète' is figured in cinematographic terms: the poet describes 'le champ de la caméra' where 'Le principal personnage joue hors du champ. Off off' [The main character acts off screen. Off off] (*OU*, 29). The poem itself becomes a type of screen, 'un poème l'écran' (*SB*, 78), or a word-film, 'Le poème mon film à syllabes' (*Xbo*). Writing becomes synonymous with filming, a notion that Fourcade explores at length in *Est-ce que j'peux placer un mot?*: 'Je ne vois maintenant qu'à travers cet écran portable dont je ne peux plus me défaire; [...] j'expérimente le grain de l'image, et des rapports d'ombres (en cassettes immédiates). Je filme tout ce qui m'arrive' [Now I see only through this portable screen that I can no longer get rid of; [...] I experiment with the grain of the image, and the shade ratios (on instant cassettes). I film everything that happens to me] (*EJP*, 78). The image of the poem as a camera, set up in the midst of day-to-day life, filming everything that comes into shot ('Jour ordinaire | Je filme', *Xbo*), is closely linked, as we shall shortly see, to Fourcade's 'tout arrive' poetics. He describes how, as a writer, he has taught himself to resist the desire to sift, sort, and categorise, so that the simultaneity of real experience can be better represented in the poem.[65] When Fourcade writes 'Le poème un vide le seul réel mon film' [The poem a vacuum the only real my film] (*Xbo*), we see how he is equating cinema with a particular mode of representing the real. Indeed, in the initial citation where he suggests that the poet must become a cameraman or a film editor, it is precisely because it facilitates his desire to 'rendre le réel'.[66] This mode of representation is, for Fourcade, necessarily intransitive or 'surfaciste'; the task for the poet is to 'filmer des corps ininterprétables' (*Xbo*).[67] Here, we are reminded of Hocquard's description of the poet's role, inspired by American Objectivism, which is to:

> Se contenter de donner à voir, à la manière d'un témoin devant un tribunal, sans chercher à influencer le jugement ou l'émotion du lecteur. Pour cela il met en place un espace neutre, il ménage une distance sans laquelle aucune tentative d'élucidation ne saurait être possible. Cette distance, cet écart, est le (théâtre du) travail poétique, un théâtre de mots.[68]
>
> [Make do with simply showing, like a witness in court, without trying to influence the judgement or emotion of the reader. To do so, [the poet] establishes a neutral space and maintains a distance without which any attempt at elucidation would be impossible. This distance, this gap, is the (theatre of) poetic work, a theatre of words.]

In this instance Hocquard evokes theatre, but the parallel to cinema, to the poem as film, is clear. Whether a 'théâtre de mots' or a 'film à syllables', in both instances the poet sets about the staging of language, which, as direct embodiment of the real, involves a point of contact, an 'être au contact du réel' (*CD*, 15), not mediated by literary conventions of representation.

Fourcade incorporates cinema, art, music, and dance in his poetry, tracing the transferable dimensions of each domain: from art, his poetry derives an exploration of colour and line, and the collapsing distinction between form and content; from cinema, a return to the notion of representation and the real; from dance, the importance of movement and gesture, configured across a given space; and from music, the irreducible presence of sound, and a principle of simultaneity and multiplicity. In Fourcade's poetry, these different artistic domains form a rhizome: they are not isolated, individual practices, separated off from each other, but rather are interconnected, part of the same overall structure, with shared concerns of form, representation, signification, and so on. Just as Deleuze and Guattari discuss the 'principe de connexion' which connects each point of a rhizome to any other, the various artistic domains in Fourcade's poetry create a similar interconnected network. They exist in a horizontal, flat relationship of equivalence and reciprocity, with each domain relating to every other. In turn, this constitutes an expression of Fourcade's 'tout arrive' poetics, which, as we shall see, foregrounds the principles of multiplicity, simultaneity, and heterogeneity.

'Tout arrive'

In a text entitled 'Tout arrive' in *Est-ce que j'peux placer un mot?*, Fourcade recounts meeting Olivier Cadiot at an exhibition on Stéphane Mallarmé. Among the various exhibits the two poets find a letter addressed to Mallarmé from Édouard Manet, and both are struck by the letterhead with its simple yet arresting maxim, 'tout arrive'. For Fourcade, the phrase encapsulates the principles of multiplicity, simultaneity, and heterogeneity central to his own work. His reflections in an interview with Emmanuel Laugier provide further insight into the significance of Manet's expression:

> Pour moi, utiliser tous les degrés de perception d'une langue, toutes les façons qu'elle a d'agir, jusqu'à ses propres inconnues, me conduit à prendre les choses comme un tout, et dans le temps où elles arrivent. Il a fallu que je me rééduque pour ne plus trier, puisque trier c'était remplacer la venue simultanée des événements et des choses par des méthodes de perception rigides et sclérosées. Il faut un effort suprême pour sortir d'une pensée de l'épure qui est un seul et grand mensonge sur le monde.[69]

> [For me, using all of the degrees of perception of a language, all the means it has to act, even its own unknowns, leads me to take things as a whole, and in the time in which they happen. I had to retrain myself to stop filtering, because filtering replaces the simultaneous appearance of events and things with rigid and sclerotic methods of perception. A supreme effort is required to leave behind a way of thinking based on refinement, which represents one great lie about the world.]

A key constituent of Fourcade's 'tout arrive' poetics is a resistance to 'trier'. In an interview in *Action Restreinte*, he discusses how his education reinforced the idea that 'il faut faire une seule chose à la fois' [you should do one thing at a time], and that in his poetry he has attempted to free himself from this mode of thought: 'je me suis concentré sur le multiple et non pas sur le un' [I focused on the multiple and not on the singular].[70] Rejecting the implicitly selective and hierarchical value judgements that underpin the acts of categorising and sorting, Fourcade insists that his poetry must draw on various modes of perception, must be receptive to all possibilities, and heterogeneous in its subject matter, lexis, register, form, and rhythm. The poetics that Fourcade elaborates finds a clear resonance with Deleuze and Guattari's analysis of minor literature, in so far as both envisage a resistance to variation-suppressing modes of discourse through an emphasis on multiplicity.

For Consenstein, Fourcade's adoption of Manet's phrase involves the implementation of a 'système de vision des peintres modernes':

> Tout arrive en même temps. Tous les cinq sens, dont le cerveau se compose, capturent le monde entourant l'interprétation de ces sensations et enlisent l'individu, le sujet pensant, dans une synesthésie totale. Fourcade ne cherche pas l'ordre de cette synesthésie, il préfère en déduire une poésie ou ce que j'appelle un forme-rythme langagier.[71]
>
> [Everything happens at the same time. All five senses that make up the brain capture the world around the interpretation of these sensations and immerse the individual, the thinking subject, in a complete synaesthesia. Fourcade is not looking for the order of this synaesthesia, instead he extracts poetry from it, or what I call a linguistic rhythm-form.]

Using all modes of perception at the same time, without attempting to separate off one from another or to 'mettre en ordre', Fourcade's poetry has a synaesthesic, 'kaleidoscopic' quality.[72] Crediting early twentieth-century painting and twentieth-century sculpture, Fourcade suggests that this system of vision, which captures, on the single surface of the poem, 'la simultanéité des plans du réel', requires a break with the implicit hierarchy and ideology of traditional syntax, and the elaboration of a new form of syntax in its place.[73] Fourcade's novel syntax, with its agrammatical phrases and its emphasis on juxtaposition and parataxis, complements the collapsing of the implicitly hierarchical structure of traditional representations of perception. Significantly, Disson identifies experimentation with perspective as a defining feature of the 'mécanique lyrique' generation. In her discussion of Alferi and Cadiot's *Revue de littérature générale*, she identifies the accumulation of perspectives and viewpoints as a unifying characteristic of the poets gathered in the review (Fourcade included).[74] She writes, 'tout est question de regard, de focalisation, de jeux d'angle et de perspectives' [it's all a question of gaze, of focus, of playing with angles and perspectives], and offering the poet Yannick Liron as an example, she describes how 'le regard bouge, change, tourne autour de l'objet, le saisit au ralenti, sous toutes ses facettes, tous ses angles, toutes ses couleurs' [the gaze shifts, changes, turns around the object, grasps it in slow-motion, in all its aspects, all its angles, all its colours].[75] This description might equally well apply to Fourcade, whose poetry rotates through multiple perspectives, hinging, as we shall soon see, on a 'mot-pivot' such as the rose of *Rose-déclic* or the titular pronoun of *IL*.

Fourcade's 'tout arrive' poetics engenders what he calls a 'multipiste' quality to his work: 'Ma page d'écriture est un débat permanent entre le successif et le simultané. Il n'y a pas qu'une piste sur la machine à enregistrer, mais des enregistrements multipistes' [My writing page is a permanent struggle between the successive and the simultaneous. There is not just one track on the recording machine, but multitrack recordings].[76] This image sustains the metaphor of the poet as a sound-engineer, producing recordings that are characterised by multiplicity and simultaneity. On this subject, Valabrègue writes:

> L'écriture de Fourcade se met au service d'une multiplicité de voix qui en constitue une seule, résultante parfois atone d'une polyphonie. L'enjeu est d'accueillir cette multiplicité et faire en sorte que les éléments qui la constituent jouent le plus librement possible. C'est une affaire de vitesse et de mobilité.[77]
>
> [Fourcade's writing serves a multiplicity of voices which make up one single voice, whose polyphony sometimes renders it atonic. The challenge is to embrace this multiplicity and make sure that its constituent elements play as freely as possible. It's a matter of speed and mobility.]

The same multiplicity that pervades every other aspect of Fourcade's work necessarily applies to poetic voice. His poetry is characterised by polyphony, by a 'voix d'une plasticité remarquable' (*IL*, 79), which is doubtless a corollary of a post-Mallarméan 'disparition élocutoire du poète'. Fourcade describes how the poet is 'asleep at the wheel' (*CD*, 14), leaving in his place a lyric *je* that operates as an open space of possibility, in which a multitude of voices proliferate. Among the various studies that exist on the lyric subject in Fourcade's poetry, Kelly's analysis is of particular interest as it emphasises Fourcade's focus on the 'experience of a disappearing linguistic security', and the consequent 'unhousedness' of the subject.[78] Kelly reads Fourcade's mother tongue/foreign language paradigm, discussed above, as an expression of the poet's desire to get closer to the perceived subjective ease of a mother tongue.[79] As we saw, the absence of a singular mother tongue provokes a plural, foreign language in its place; monologic voice is replaced by heteroglossia. Kelly's evocation of the 'unhoused writing subject' accords with Pinson's description of Fourcade's 'lyrisme désubjectivé'.[80] Employing a similar metaphor to the poet-sound-engineer, Pinson describes Fourcade as a composer, constructing poems out of 'unités de son-sens' [units of sound-meaning].[81] In this conception, which closely resembles Alferi and Cadiot's 'mécanique lyrique', lyric voice is a product of the linguistic assemblages of the poem. Language is already endowed with a certain lyricism, and the poet is effectively spoken *through*. His compositions and assemblages will, to return to Hocquard's formulation, 'donner à voir', 'mettre en place [...] un théâtre de mots'. The singularity of the poet's voice is thus displaced by the multiplicity of voices that this theatre of words will bestow. A single writing subject becomes, as Game suggests, a 'proliferation of subjective positions', or, as Leuwers would have it, 'une affirmation de toutes les virtualités du "je"' [an affirmation of all the virtualities of the 'I'].[82]

The principles of multiplicity and heterogeneity that render Fourcade's writing a form of 'poésie mineure' are found not only in relation to voice and subjecthood, but also in the systematic variation of registers and tonalities, influences and inspirations, and subject matter and lexis. On this last point, Fourcade employs multiple lexical fields simultaneously so that, in their juxtaposition, one emphasises the difference of the other. References to the natural world, to the provençal landscapes of Char or Cézanne, are intertwined with evocations of a developed, post-industrial society, where referential markers, such as 'le Chrysler Building' (*RD*, 35), join broader evocations of the spaces of modern life, like the neon-lit concrete of a multi-storey car park (*RD*, 21). The markers of material existence that have permeated poetry since its very origins — constellations, skies, and meteorological phenomena — appear alongside descriptions of the physical world, derived from modern science: 'antiquarks et quarks' (*IL*, 111), 'neutrons' (*RD*, 9), 'uranium' (*CD*, 81), 'berylium' (*Xbo*). Lexis associated with more traditional poetic vocabularies, the Ronsardian 'rose' of *Rose-déclic*, the Mallarméan 'blancheur' and 'voix interstellaire' of *Le Ciel pas d'angle*, juxtapose vocabulary not typically associated with a poetic lexicon: 'SLAM DUNK' (*IL*, 115), 'tailgaiting' (*IL*, 159), 'frisbee' (*SB*, 65), 'boite de Q-tips' (*SB*, 11). Indeed, we can trace the technological developments and trends of modern life across Fourcade's œuvre. In *Le Ciel pas d'angle* (1983), we find pagers (*CA*, 85) and 'telex' (30); in *Xbo* (1988), 'Pan Am 747' and 'steadycam'; in the more recent *Citizen Do* (2008), 'faux cils' (*CD*, 64) and 'monokini' (76), as well as ludic reworkings of email address formatting: 'aube.récidive@talc', 'claquedecalme@gomina.socquettes', 'merleoblong@wanadooprune' (79).

This lexical variation reflects a heterogeneity of subject matter, both of which are a product of Fourcade's desire to mobilise all aspects of reality within the poem. He states:

> Le poème se fait en objectivant toute réalité, sans exclusion, qu'elle soit d'ordre psychologique, sexuel, métaphysique, matériel, et en étalant tout cela sur la page, à plat, en travaillant la langue qui est la seule façon dont toutes ces notions peuvent exister.[83]
>
> [The poem is created by objectifying all reality, without exception, whether it's from the psychological, sexual, metaphysical, or material realm, and by laying that all out flat on the page, by working with language which is the only means through which all of these notions can exist.]

Fourcade's comment recalls a passage on the rhizome from the introduction to *Mille plateaux*: 'L'idéal d'un livre serait d'étaler toute chose sur un tel plan d'extériorité, sur une seule page, sur une même page: événements vécus, déterminations historiques, concepts pensés, individus, groupes et formations sociales' [The ideal for a book would be to lay everything out on one plane of exteriority of this kind, on a single page, the same sheet: lived events, historical determinations, concepts, individuals, groups, social formations] (*MP*, 16; *ATP*, 8). Like Deleuze and Guattari, Fourcade envisages a rhizomatic representation of reality, where all dimensions unfold horizontally upon the page. Thus, while *Manque* tackles vast metaphysical subjects of death and grief, often apostrophising the deceased, *Le Ciel pas d'angle* engages in a more prosaic address: 'Merci Ville de Paris d'avoir doté ma rue d'une benne à ordures' [Thank you Paris City Hall for equipping my street with a wheelie bin] (*CPA*, 34). *IL* circumnavigates the abyssal experience of language and referentiality, interwoven with references to the most fleeting, commercial aspects of modern life, like brand names. In *Rose-déclic*, Fourcade juxtaposes an exploration of poetic inspiration with pervasive sexual imagery. These references oscillate between what might have traditionally been divided into 'high' and 'low' culture, producing a destabilising, often comic, effect. Discussing this amalgamation of forms and flattening of hierarchies, Fourcade says:

> Je me suis entraîné pendant quarante ans à transcrire simultanément la totalité des perceptions: regarder une peinture de Cézanne dans une exposition est *inséparé* et inséparable du fait qu'une personne mâche du chewing-gum en regardant le même tableau à côté de moi, qu'il émane d'elle un certain parfum, ou que le téléphone sonne [*à ce moment-là, le téléphone sonne dans la pièce*], et si le téléphone sonne et bien il sonnera également dans mon poème. Je ne lis pas Heidegger séparément du bruit du téléphone. J'ai essayé de mettre au point une écriture qui permette de transcrire le fait que 'tout arrive' simultanément — ce que j'ai essayé de faire précisément dans le texte *Tout arrive*, qui était le cœur de mon précédent livre. Et je me suis beaucoup entraîné pour tendre vers un mode d'écriture qui rende possible cette transcription de différents plans en même temps.[84]

> [For forty years, I taught myself to transcribe simultaneously the totality of perceptions: looking at a Cézanne painting in an exhibition is *inseparate* and *inseparable* from someone chewing gum while looking at the same painting beside me, from that person smelling of a certain perfume, from the telephone ringing [*at that moment, the telephone rings in the room*], and if the telephone rings, well, it will also ring in my poem. I don't read Heidegger separately to the sound of the telephone. I tried to develop a form of writing that allows the fact that 'everything happens' simultaneously to be transcribed — which is precisely what I tried to do in the text *Everything Happens*, which was the core of my previous book. And I really trained myself to move towards a mode of writing that makes this transcription of different aspects at the same time possible.]

Here, Fourcade observes how the more prosaic aspects of everyday life shape his poetry as much as literary, philosophical, and artistic influences such as Heidegger and Cézanne. His eclectic references eschew traditional French writers in favour of American poets (Dickinson, Stein, Howe, Palmer) and visual artists (Degas, Hantaï, Matisse). Fourcade reiterates that Mallarmé and La Fontaine, Proust and Baudelaire, have equal sway to a song by Bashung or Gainsbourg, or 'la trivialité du bruit d'une voiture qui passe dans la rue' [the triviality of the noise of a car passing by in the street].[85]

This variation in influence, subject matter, and lexis is matched by a variation in tone and register. Fourcade's writing oscillates between different tonalities — the grandiloquent and the trivial, the serious and the comic — that in turn often present themselves as different voices in the text. In the following passage, Pinson analyses the contrastive registers of *Citizen Do*:

Les superlatifs ne manquent pas dans la langue de Fourcade ('Dans la vie, l'ordre de l'art est une charge immense'). Mais toujours l'audace du plus trivial ('je m'excuse c'est l'heure de ma Suze') vient déjouer la menace de l'enflure; toujours le 'reportage' du réel le plus immédiat (le beau nom par exemple de 'Michelle LaVaughn Robinson Obama') vient rappeler dans quel monde effectif nous sommes.[86]

[There is no shortage of superlatives in Fourcade's language ('In life, the duty towards art is an immense responsibility'). But the daringly trivial ("Please excuse me, it's time for my Suze" [trans. note: this is an advertising jingle for a popular alcoholic drink]) continuously thwarts the threat of pomposity; the 'reporting' of the most immediate reality (the beautiful name of 'Michelle LaVaughn Robinson Obama' for example) is a constant reminder of the world we're actually living in.]

As Valabrègue puts it elsewhere, Fourcade juxtaposes major and minor modes, so that one complements the other: 'Il sait doser et mêler le majeur et le mineur, éclairer l'un par l'autre' [He knows how to combine the major and the minor in just the right doses, how to elucidate one with the other].[87] This oscillation between contrastive registers and tones is often accentuated by the intrusion of an otherwise 'out of place' phrase, written in English, which creates the impression of a plurality of voice. In a passage cited above, the English phrase 'nice toe-work' disrupts the altogether more reflective tone of the surrounding passage, with its metapoetic reflections on writing and dance. Likewise, in a poem in *IL* that explores 'l'expérience de l'oubli' [the experience of oblivion] and the possibility of a world without words, the single line 'what's the rumpus' interjects with a bathetic effect (*IL*, 93). In *Xbo*, a self-reflexive passage that describes the decomposition of words ('Des terminaisons en d en eb en id en b', 'Des combinaisons azotées') is interrupted by the English phrase 'Type you stupid deb'. In each instance, the alternation of voice serves, as Pinson writes, to 'déjouer la menace de l'enflure', operating as a corrective to the introspective impulse of modern poetry.

Alongside identifying the sheer variation that characterises Fourcade's work, one way to explore how the poet attempts to 'transcrire simultanément la totalité des perceptions', is to consider how he treats just one given subject. Many of his books take a primary motif, for example the titular pronoun in *IL* or the 'murmure' in *Son blanc du un*, and then elaborate a multiplicity of perspectives around this pivotal word or phrase. The following analysis will explore how this operates on a textual level, taking the rose of *Rose-déclic* as an example. As the hyphenated title suggests, the rose is first and foremost a catalyst or trigger for the text: an 'appareil propulseur' (*OU*, 10), an 'engin' or 'moteur' (15). In the text itself, the rose is described as a powerful and transformative 'catapulte' (*RD*, 35): 'rose cyclonique œil de la source puissance de l'o de cyclone' [cyclonic rose of the source power of the o in cyclone] (37). It is the source of the poem's imagery, a point of origin from which the poem is generated: 'rose des comme et des comme et des ainsi que rose-déclic des comparaisons' [rose of the 'like's and 'as if's and 'just as's rose-trigger of comparisons] (9). It brings with it a network of associations — auditory (the buzzing of the rose garden, 11), visual ('rose blanche', 143), and haptic ('rose velvet', 43) — that are often interwoven into synaesthesic images: 'Rose | Blancheur au chant de rossignol' [Rose | Whiteness of the nightingale's song] (11). The long history of the poetic symbolism of the flower, and the rose in particular, is evoked in the numerous references in *Rose-délic* to writers such as Ronsard, Stein, Rilke, and indeed Mallarmé ('[rose], tu es maintenant loin du bouquet' [rose, you are now far from the bouquet], 91). Fourcade depicts the rose as a traditional trope in love poetry, in his use of sensual and sexual imagery, 'rose nuque' [rose nape of the neck] (81), 'rose [...] nue sous ta jupe' [rose [...] naked under your skirt] (37), and by frequently apostrophising the rose as a female addressee. Elements of courtly love are evoked, from the rose garden setting (11), to the suggestion of unconsummated desire: 'rose tes lèvres ne doivent jamais venir sur les miennes' [rose your lips must never meet mine] (37). Wordplay transforms 'rose' into the anagram 'éros' (163), which again maintains its traditional romantic symbolism, as well as evoking Desnos and Duchamp and the wordplay of 'Rrose Selavy' / 'Éros, c'est la vie'. No sooner are the more conventional aspects of the rose evoked, than they are quickly supplanted by more unusual images, 'rose blanche' becomes 'rose ligne noire' [black line rose] (143), and 'rose velvet' transforms into 'rose béton' [concrete rose] (23). The motif of the rose mutates from one clashing, violent image to the next: 'Rose éclabousse d'urine' [rose splattered with urine] (9), 'Rose bombe à neutrons' [neutron bomb rose] (9), 'off-shore rose' (153), 'Rose o yellow cab and whalesque' (177). The rose becomes a 'rose poumon' [rose lung] (49), breathing air and life into the poem: 'Rose ô colonne d'air structure du poème' [Rose o column of air structure of the poem] (63). The sheer 'thingness' of the rose, as both a referent-object and a word-object, provides the poet with the delight in the irreducible materiality of the poem that Valabrègue describes above. Its quiddity is drawn out in the text through bilingual wordplay, 'Rosities rose it is rosités | Rose de la chosité' (17), which seems to illustrate its point as it describes it, evoking the 'thingness' of the rose while it highlights, through their decomposition in the poem, the material constitution of the words themselves.

As is true for all of Fourcade's texts with their various motifs and pivot-words, Fourcade describes how the different permutations of the rose in *Rose-délic* operate as 'des courants intérieurs au poème', producing a kind of 'flux' (*RD*, 71). The polysemy of the word *courant* amalgamates four significant dimensions of Fourcade's work: firstly, taken in its broadest sense, it describes the varying speeds and rhythms of the movement of language within the poem, recalling again the parallel Fourcade draws between poetry and dance. Secondly, it evokes currents of water and resonates with Fourcade's description elsewhere of his own 'écriture alluvionnaire' [alluvionary writing], whereby the poem, comprised of multiple textual currents, leaves behind a verbal sediment.[88] Thirdly, it evokes 'électricité (73), where words are charged particles circulating in the flux of electrical currents in the 'moteur'-poem. And finally, it describes the currents of air generated not only by the rose-cyclone text alluded to above, but also by the humble 'souffle' (61) of language — the inhalation and exhalation of breath that punctuates the text, both in the writing and the reading.

The rose therefore operates, as Game suggests, as 'a poetic rhizome'.[89] It is multidimensional: a material object, a word, an imagined addressee and a literary trope. A 'brutale rose de toutes les simultanéités' [brutal rose of all simultaneities] (RD, 9), it appeals to the different senses, provoking various visual, auditory, olfactory, and haptic responses. In these rotations or gyrations around the pivot of the rose, we see how Fourcade's poetry involves, to return to Consenstein's phrase, a 'système de vision des peintres modernes'. The desire to capture simultaneous and multiple perspectives, as well as different responses and reactions to an object, clearly resonates with the Cubist practices that Fourcade describes as having an important influence on his work.[90] In this respect, there are unsurprising parallels between Fourcade's poetry and that of Francis Ponge, the latter also being an art critic, who transposed into a written medium the visual practices of artists such as Georges Braque.[91] Like Ponge's 'textes ouverts', with their rhizomatic, draft-like reworkings of a subject, Fourcade's poetry takes a pivotal word or object, exploring a series of possible ways to approach it, generating endless possible unfoldings and expansions in the text. Even where the poem must necessarily reach its end, within the practical constraints of the published book, the generativity of the text means that the poem's end is but an artificial closure. Like the rhizome when it is severed, the text will continue to proliferate, if not in the poet's ongoing poetic project, then in the reading process that follows. As if to illustrate this ongoing generativity, the motif of the rose from *Rose-déclic* continues to permeate the texts that follow; references to 'drumming' roses in *Son blanc du un*, to a 'rose of great sway' or a 'rose never idle' in *Xbo*, create a network that transcends the individual text.

By accentuating multiplicity, simultaneity, interconnectivity, and heterogeneity, Fourcade's 'tout arrive' poetics align in several ways with Deleuze and Guattari's analysis of the rhizomatic nature of minor literature. Returning to the initial starting point of this chapter, we recall how Fourcade conceptualises his writing in terms of the different experiences, foreign and maternal, involved in literary and non-literary uses of language. The minor quality of Fourcade's poetry rests, it appears to me, in the dual interpretation of this term 'expérience', which captures two principal and interrelated dimensions of his project. On the one hand, his poetry presents a series of *experiments*: foregrounding the essentially heterogeneous nature of language, favouring multiplicity and difference over the suppression of variation. A number of tensors serve to simultaneously highlight the norms of the major language that usually pass unnoticed, and to signal the divergence of his own poetic language from such norms. Polyphony, dialogic multilingual play, and the anthropomorphic voicing of language disrupt a monologic mode of poetic discourse. The decomposition of language within the text, alongside the use of foreign words and neologisms, accentuates the materiality and musicality of words as bodies, subverting in turn the unmarked referential mode of normal communication. Agrammaticality and stuttered syntax rupture the underlying structuring principles of normative grammar. In each instance, Fourcade's use of language is deterritorialising, creating lines of flight by outlining the possibility of different linguistic modes, and with that, a different *experience* of language within the text. Throughout his writing, Fourcade foregrounds the various ways we experience language as a sensorial, psychological, or affective phenomenon:

he describes the oppressive sensation of the rule-governed language of his education and upbringing, the anguish of writing, the comforting physicality of language reinstated within the human body. Set against this emphasis on linguistic experience, the reader is all the more aware of his or her own experience of the text. The experimental, minor quality of Fourcade's language means that this experience, however it manifests itself, is a marked one. Where writing may be intransitive in other ways, may face the eternal problem of the gap between word and world, the fact that the text will prompt a novel experience of language for the reader enables a form of transitivity, a contact with the real, that Fourcade describes as so compelling:

> Une obsession majeure commande ce travail: être au contact du réel — une obsession, et toute l'angoisse d'un grand amour. Le réel, l'époque, le monde. Un désir fou un besoin fou de le toucher. [...] Seule l'écriture. Le contact donc, la vérité de ce contact, et l'expérience de la connaissance qui est indissociable de l'écriture-contact — aspiration d'une vie d'écrivain. (CD, 15–16)
>
> [This work is driven by a major obsession: to be in contact with the real — an obsession, and all the anguish of a love affair. The real, the current moment, the world. A crazy desire a crazy need to touch it. [...] Writing alone. So contact, the truth of this contact, and the experience of consciousness which is indistinguishable from writing-contact — the aspiration of a writer's life.]

Notes to Chapter 2

1. Collot, 'Lyrisme et littéralité', p. 15.
2. Pinson, *Habiter en poète*, p. 49, and *Sentimentale et naïve*, p. 255.
3. Pinson, *Habiter en poète*, p. 24.
4. Dominique Fourcade, 'Entretien avec Hervé Bauer', *Java*, 17 (1998), 57–70 (p. 63).
5. For an account of Derrida and Khatibi's dialogue on the subject, see Dominique Combe, 'Derrida et Khatibi — autour du *Monolinguisme de l'autre*', *Carnets*, 7 (2016), 1–6 <https://carnets.revues.org/897> [accessed 26 June 2020].
6. Derrida, *Le Monolinguisme de l'autre*, p. 15. Abdelkebir Khatibi, *Essais* (Paris: La Différence, 2008), p. 119. Unlike Fourcade, Derrida does not structure his discussion around a mother tongue/foreign language paradigm. In *Le Monolinguisme de l'autre* he writes: 'En disant que la seule langue que je parle n'est pas *la mienne*, je n'ai pas dit qu'elle me fût étrangère' [In saying that the only language I speak is not *mine*, I didn't say that it was foreign to me] (p. 18).
7. Rabaté, in *Figures du sujet lyrique*, ed. by Rabaté, p. 77.
8. Daniel Leuwers, 'Dominique Fourcade: une question de cordes vocales', in *Sens et présence du sujet poétique*, ed. by Brophy and Gallagher, pp. 203–08 (p. 204).
9. Dominique Fourcade, '"La Langue en crue": entretien avec Emmanuel Laugier', *Le Matricule des Anges*, 22 (1998), 46.
10. Dominique Fourcade, *Xbo* (Paris: P.O.L., 1988) (unpaginated).
11. Dominique Fourcade, *IL* (Paris: P.O.L., 1994), p. 21.
12. Dominique Fourcade, *Outrance utterance* (Paris: P.O.L., 1990), p. 35 (henceforth abbreviated to *OU*).
13. So extensive are these motifs that one researcher has created an inventory of the vast network of references to birds in Fourcade's work. Abigail Lang, 'What's in a Bird?', in *Dossier Dominique Fourcade, Cahier Critique de Poésie*, 11 (2006), 31–48.
14. Dominique Fourcade, *Le Ciel pas d'angle* (Paris: P.O.L., 1983), p. 47 (henceforth abbreviated to *CPA*).

15. Game, *Poetic Becomings*, pp. 143–44.
16. Frédéric Valabrègue, 'Une chose fuitive', *Java*, 17 (1998), 21–25 (p. 24).
17. Frédéric Valabrègue, 'Dominique Fourcade: "La page langue monde"', *Critique*, 8 (2008), 710–18 (p. 715).
18. Dominique Fourcade, *Son blanc du un* (Paris: P.O.L., 1986), p. 91 (henceforth abbreviated to *SB*). Peter Consenstein, 'Le Présent immédiat dans la poésie de Dominique Fourcade', *Contemporary French and Francophone Studies*, 10 (2006), 447–62.
19. Dominique Fourcade, *Rose-déclic* (Paris: P.O.L., 1984), p. 131 (henceforth abbreviated to *RD*).
20. Francis Ponge, *Œuvres complètes*, 2 vols (Paris: Gallimard, 1999–2002), II, 432. The parallels between Fourcade's and Ponge's projects are manifold, particularly with regard to how they describe their relationship with language, the anguish of writing, and the compulsion to persist despite the inevitable failure of the task. Both animate this troublesome relationship by anthropomorphising language within the poem.
21. Fourcade, 'Entretien avec Hervé Bauer', p. 57.
22. Kelly, 'Poetry as a Foreign Language', p. 397. Prigent, *A quoi bon encore des poètes?*, p. 10.
23. Fourcade is not the only one to employ a Wolfsonian procedure of phonological translation. Cadiot uses a similar technique in *Futur, ancien, fugitif*, as does Pierre Alferi in *Sentimentale journée* (Paris: P.O.L., 1997), where the title itself is a deliberate mistranslation of Laurence Sterne's *Sentimental Journey*.
24. Fourcade, '"La Langue en crue"', p. 46.
25. Valabrègue, 'Dominique Fourcade', p. 714.
26. Dominique Fourcade, *Manque* (Paris: P.O.L., 2012), p. 15 (henceforth abbreviated to *M*).
27. Samuel Beckett, 'Dante... Bruno. Vico... Joyce', in *I Can't Go On, I'll Go On: A Selection from Samuel Beckett's Work*, ed. by Richard W. Seaver (New York: Grove Press, 1976), p. 117.
28. Breton, 'Les Mots sans rides', p. 14.
29. Ponge, *Œuvres complètes*, II, 431.
30. Dominique Fourcade, *En laisse* (Paris: P.O.L., 2005), p. 56.
31. Dominique Fourcade, 'Xbo', *P.O.L. Website Catalogue* (2013) <http://www.pol-editeur.com/index.php?spec=livre&ISBN=2-86744-136-6> [accessed 26 June 2020].
32. Valabrègue, 'Une chose fuitive', p. 24. The citation is from Fourcade, *IL*, p. 24.
33. Jean-Jacques Thomas and Steven Winspur, *Poeticized Language: The Foundations of Contemporary French Poetry* (University Park: Pennsylvania State University Press, 1999), p. 5.
34. Fourcade, '"La Langue en crue"', p. 46.
35. The poem 'après les attentats' (2015) is one of several 'feuillets' published by Editions Chandeigne.
36. In this respect, Fourcade aligns with Gleize's account of the 'langagement' of certain contemporary poets. See Chapter 1 for further discussion, as well as Gleize, 'La Post-poésie', p. 126.
37. Dominique Fourcade, *Le Sujet monotype* (Paris: P.O.L., 1997).
38. Fourcade, '"La Langue en crue"', p. 46.
39. Olivier Cadiot, 'Bé-bégayer', *Java*, 17 (1998), 39–40.
40. Jean Khalfa, 'Ontologie et subjectivité chez Césaire', in *Sens et présence du sujet poétique*, ed. by Brophy and Gallagher, pp. 191–201 (p. 191).
41. For more on Howe and the stutter, see Elisabeth W. Joyce, *'The Small Space of a Pause': Susan Howe's Poetry and the Spaces Between* (Lewisburg, PA: Bucknell University Press, 2010).
42. Fourcade frequently uses 'souffle' as a metonym for the voice of the poem.
43. Game, *Poetic Becomings*, pp. 107–50.
44. Ibid., p. 116.
45. Valabrègue, 'Dominique Fourcade', p. 717.
46. Valabrègue writes: 'Si Fourcade sort de Mallarmé, c'est parce qu'il remet en question la notion du centre. Il n'y a plus de centre. C'est en cela que sa poésie est devenir-chose, devenir-corps et devenir-monde' [If Fourcade leaves Mallarmé behind, it's because he calls into question the notion of the centre. There is no centre any more. It is through this that his poetry is becoming-thing, becoming-body and becoming-world]. Valabrègue, 'Une chose fuitive', p. 25.
47. Game, *Poetic Becomings*, p. 115.

48. Dominique Fourcade, 'Entretien avec Frédéric Valabrègue', in *Dossier Dominique Fourcade*, 5–18 (p. 15).
49. Evoking the widespread 'brouillage des genres' in contemporary practice, Disson asks, 'Mais comment distinguer la poésie de la prose, si son matériau privilégié est désormais de "la prose découpée"? Simplement: par le découpage, la mise en rythme. Le vers devient mouvement, élan, flux, symétries de séquences, "puissance rythmique, velléité de fuite et de suspens, de répétition et de retournement"' [But how do we distinguish poetry from prose, if its form of choice is now 'cut-up prose'? Put simply: through the cutting up, the setting into rhythm. Verse becomes movement, momentum, flux, symmetries between sequences, 'rhythmic power, the vague desire of evasion, suspense, repetition and reversal']. Disson, 'Poésie années 90', pp. 14–15.
50. Game, *Poetic Becomings*, p. 123.
51. Fourcade, 'Entretien avec Frédéric Valabrègue', pp. 15–16.
52. Fourcade, 'Entretien avec Hervé Bauer', p. 58.
53. Fourcade, 'Entretien avec Frédéric Valabrègue', p. 15.
54. Valabrègue, 'Une chose fuitive', p. 21.
55. Fourcade, '"La Langue en crue"', p. 46.
56. For a detailed study on this subject, see Irina Anelok, 'Les Écrits sur l'art de Dominique Fourcade: la naissance d'une poétique' (unpublished doctoral thesis, Université Paris Ouest Nanterre, 2013).
57. Pinson, *Sentimentale et naïve*, p. 253.
58. Dominique Fourcade, *Citizen Do* (Paris: P.O.L., 2008), p. 15 (henceforth abbreviated to *CD*).
59. Claude Royet-Journoud, 'Entretien avec Dominique Fourcade', *Banana Split*, 11 (1983), 18–29.
60. Dominique Fourcade, 'Entretien avec Mathias Lavin', *Action Restreinte*, 7 (2006), 90–91.
61. Jean-Claude Pinson, 'Citizen Do de Dominique Fourcade' (2008) <http://www.sitaudis.fr/Parutions/citizen-do-de-dominique-fourcade.php> [accessed 26 June 2020].
62. Fourcade, 'Entretien avec Mathias Lavin', p. 90.
63. Fourcade, '"La Langue en crue"', p. 46.
64. Christophe Wall-Romana, *Cinepoetry: Imaginary Cinemas in French Poetry* (New York: Fordham University Press, 2013), p. 30. *Cinepoetry* includes a brief consideration of Fourcade's *Citizen Do* (p. 373).
65. Fourcade, '"La Langue en crue"', p. 46.
66. Ibid.
67. Gleize, using Fourcade's description of Degas as a 'surfaciste', writes that this term applies equally well to the poet himself. Jean-Marie Gleize, 'Le Poème est l'afflux de cela', *Java*, 17 (1998), 47–51.
68. Hocquard, *Ma haie*, p. 28.
69. Fourcade, '"La Langue en crue"', p. 46.
70. Fourcade, 'Entretien avec Mathias Lavin', p. 87.
71. Consenstein, 'Le Présent immédiat', p. 448.
72. In the essay 'Tout arrive', Fourcade links the 'toutarrivesque' with 'le kaleidoscope lampe à pétrole de l'enfance Marcel Proust' [the kaleidoscope lantern of Marcel Proust's childhood] (*EJP*, 61).
73. Fourcade, 'Entretien avec Hervé Bauer', p. 57.
74. Disson, 'Poésie années 90', p. 15.
75. Ibid.
76. Fourcade, '"La Langue en crue"', p. 46. Immediately after this remark, Fourcade comments on the multilingual dimension of his work, thus insisting on the link between multilingualism and polyphony in his poetry.
77. Valabrègue, 'Une chose fuitive', p. 25.
78. Kelly, 'Poetry as a Foreign Language', p. 395.
79. Ibid., p. 398.
80. Pinson, *Sentimentale et naïve*, p. 255.
81. Ibid., p. 254.
82. Game, *Poetic Becomings*, p. 139. Leuwers, 'Dominique Fourcade', p. 205.

83. Marguerite Haladjian and Jean-Baptiste Para, 'Une partie qu'on ne gagne jamais: entretien avec Dominique Fourcade', *Europe*, 744 (1991), 136–46 (p. 136).
84. Fourcade, 'Entretien avec Mathias Lavin', pp. 86–87.
85. Ibid., p. 86.
86. Pinson, 'Citizen Do de Dominique Fourcade'.
87. Valabrègue, 'Dominique Fourcade', p. 717.
88. Fourcade, '"La Langue en crue"', p. 46.
89. Game, *Poetic Becomings*, p. 130.
90. Royet-Journoud, 'Entretien avec Dominique Fourcade', pp. 18–29.
91. See Shirley Ann Jordan, *The Art Criticism of Francis Ponge* (London: W. S. Maney, 1994), for a detailed study on this subject.

CHAPTER 3

Olivier Cadiot, 'La Poésie par d'autres moyens'

Olivier Cadiot is often heralded as an important figure in contemporary poetry, which is perhaps surprising given that he has only published one book under the straightforward designation of a 'livre de poésie'. This book, his first, is entitled *L'Art poétic'* (1988) and is composed of cut-ups from grammar manuals. Its experimental redefinition of poetic genre has attracted much attention from critics and other poets. His second book, *Futur, ancien, fugitif* (1993), Cadiot calls a 'roman par poèmes' [novel comprised of poems].[1] It marks the transition from his early poetry towards his later prose work: *Le Colonel des Zouaves* (1997), *Retour définitif et durable de l'être aimé* (2002), *Fairy Queen* (2002), *Un nid pour quoi faire* (2007), *Un mage en été* (2010), and *Providence* (2014). Alongside his prose writing, characterised by its idiosyncratic, fast-paced, and humorous style, Cadiot has written an opera, translated Gertrude Stein, and adapted his own texts for the stage. He has also collaborated with the French musician Rodolphe Burger, producing three albums with Dernière bande: *Welche; On n'est pas indiens c'est dommage* [Welche; We're not Indians, that's too bad] (2000), *Hôtel Robinson* (2002), and *Psychopharmaka* (2013). With Pierre Alferi, he co-founded and edited the *Revue de littérature générale* (1995–96), and more recently, he published the two volumes of his *Histoire de la littérature récente* (2016–17). Given that Cadiot's prose writing forms the majority of his recent literary output, it is understandable that this is what has attracted the most critical attention. However, the chapter that follows will leave this aspect of Cadiot's work to one side in order to focus on his poetry. It will trace the development of his poetic project across three key moments: *L'Art poétic'*, *Futur, ancien, fugitif*, and then his recent musical collaborations with Burger, which I argue see the extension of his earlier written poetry into a performed, auditory medium.

Of all three poets considered here, Cadiot's work is the most explicitly engaged with Deleuze's philosophy. As a young writer he attended Deleuze's lectures at Vincennes, and he frequently alludes to the influence of the philosopher on his own writing. This has led to a number of Deleuzian readings of Cadiot's work: in 'Le Monologue extérieur d'Olivier Cadiot' [Olivier Cadiot's External Monologue], Jean Renaud traces the rhizome in Cadiot's prose writing; Jérôme Game's chapter in *Poetic Becomings*, 'Olivier Cadiot, or the Stuttering Self', and his article on 'La Répétition différenciante dans la poétique deleuzienne' [Differentiating Repetition in Deleuzian Poetics], explore the stutter and the *ritournelle* in *Futur, ancien, fugitif*.[2] The protagonist introduced in this latter text, who reappears throughout Cadiot's subsequent novels, is the polymorphous, schizophrenic writing subject Robinson. Robinson in particular has attracted a number of Deleuzian readings, from Game, but also Alain Farah and Eric Lynch, who see him as an illustration of Deleuze's notion of the 'conceptual persona'.[3] Nathalie Wourm traces how Cadiot's Robinson owes more to Deleuze's reading of Robinson in *Logique du sens* [The Logic of Sense] (1969), than to Michel Tournier's or Daniel Defoe's original texts.[4] Drawing on various aspects of Deleuze and Guattari's account of minor literature, the discussion that follows will explore four key elements of Cadiot's poetic project: i) his use of cut-ups, sampling, and the ready-made; ii) the polyphonous, heteroglottic quality of his work; iii) the significance of dictionaries, grammar books, and other reference works; and iv) the parodic dimension of his poetry. Having used these four prominent features to outline some of the key issues at play, the fifth and final section will consider the broader questions that arise with regard to genre and the intersection of poetry, prose, theatre, and music in Cadiot's work.

Cut-up, Sampling, and the Ready-made

The ready-made plays a key role in Cadiot's poetic practice. *L'Art poétic'* presents a collage of cut-ups from grammar books, dictionaries, and other reference works, interspersed with citations from canonical writers. In *Futur, ancien, fugitif*, the protagonist Robinson is shipwrecked on an island, compelled to reconstruct himself out of the linguistic fragments of his previous existence that have washed up ashore with him: letters, etiquette manuals, and dinner party invitations. In Cadiot's later musical compositions, cut-ups are transposed into a phonic medium as pre-recorded samples. His albums present heteroglottic collages of music, the spoken word, ambient noise, sound effects, and samples from a whole range of sources: Deleuze's lectures on Spinoza, Kurt Schwitters at the Cabaret Voltaire, interviews with minority-language speakers in Alsace.

Despite the long history of the ready-made in modern literature, Cadiot describes how his initial use of cut-up in *L'Art poétic'* was more an accidental discovery than a considered literary choice:

> Un jour, je tombe sur la *Grammaire générative* de Dubois. 'Pierre est fatigué', 'Pierre est malade', 'Pierre a mal à la tête'. Je pleure, c'est cela que je veux faire, je veux avoir cette frappe-là. Tout à coup, je passe de l'autre côté du miroir. Je me retrouve tout petit face à la langue française. Et je me mets à faire des cut up sans le savoir. Je ne fais pas un geste néo-Burroughs, néo-Stein, néo-surréaliste. Je suis devenu moderne par erreur, par accident industriel. Et voilà que je passe quatre ou cinq ans à découper des milliers de livres au cutter. J'ai lacéré des Pléiade, j'ai saccagé des bibliothèques entières.[5]

> [One day, I stumbled upon Dubois's *Generative grammar*. 'Pierre is tired', 'Pierre is ill', 'Pierre has a headache'. I cried. That is what I wanted to do, I wanted to have that same impact. All of a sudden, I passed through the looking glass. I found myself tiny confronted with the French language. And I started doing

cut-ups without knowing it. It wasn't a neo-Burroughsian, neo-Steinian, neo-Surrealist gesture. I became modern by error, by industrial accident. And then I spent four or five years cutting up thousands of books with a Stanley knife. I lacerated Pléiade collections, I pillaged entire libraries.]

In a recent interview with Wourm, Cadiot repeats these reflections, emphasising how he felt *L'Art poétic'* was misread by his critics:

> Je fais [*L'Art poétic'*] par des moyens lyrico-mécaniques, sans avoir l'impression d'être moderniste, comme un artisan. Le but n'était pas de faire du William Burroughs. C'est la grande différence avec les générations qui suivent: je n'étais pas préparé au moderne. Quand j'ai fait cela, je n'ai pas fait du cut up. J'ai accompli cela comme un enfant fait du collage. C'est pourquoi ce travail est très émotionnel. J'ai cherché des ritournelles, j'ai cherché le poétique collectif dans des phrases, et je l'ai fait plutôt avec les larmes aux yeux qu'avec un sourire vengeur.[6]

> [I created *L'Art poétic'* through lyrico-mecanical means, without having the impression of being a modernist, but rather as an artisan or craftsman. The aim wasn't to do a William Burroughs. That's the great difference with the generations that followed: I wasn't prepared for the modern. When I created it, I wasn't doing cut-ups. I created it like a child making a collage. That's why this work is very emotional. I looked for *ritournelles*, I looked for the collective poetics in sentences, and I did it with tears in my eyes rather than with a vengeful smile.]

Rather than a defiant or ludic gesture inscribed in a lineage of modernist literature experimenting with aleatory writing techniques, Cadiot's interest in the ready-made stemmed from the discovery of a surprising and intrinsic lyricism embedded within existing language, and, subsequently, in the potential effects of displacing these fragments into poetry. In this respect, Cadiot's practices in *L'Art poétic'* are more akin to Charles Reznikoff's in works such as *Testimony* and *Holocaust*, than to Dadaist collages or Burroughs's and Gysin's cut-ups.[7] Indeed, Reznikoff's three-volume poem *Testimony* (1934–79), translated into French by Jacques Roubaud, has been a particularly influential text for the 'mécanique lyrique' generation, with extracts from it appearing in the second *Revue de littérature générale*.[8] A lawyer by training, Reznikoff spent a large part of his literary career working from legal documents, rearranging testimonies from criminal trials into poetic 'compilations' of lines, stanzas, and cantos.[9] The testimonies, which through legal obligation must avoid conveying emotion or rhetoric, offer an exemplary instance of the neutrality and flatness that the Objectivists sought in poetic language, yet despite the descriptive neutrality of the original testimonies, the poem produces moments of extraordinary affect, delivering a powerful political commentary on American society and its justice system. Significantly, the political or affective dimensions of the text do not come from any traditionally recognisable lyric voice, but instead, are the product of the poem's compositional techniques, thus representing a prototypical illustration of Alferi and Cadiot's 'mécanique lyrique'. Acting as a linguistic archive, presenting, without comment, the sociohistorical realities encoded within the language that is documented, *Testimony* exemplifies how, without exploring overtly political subject matters in the first-person voice of the poet, poetry can nonetheless contain a 'dimension politique très singulière' that rests on the use of certain literary techniques.[10] It therefore presents a model for a mode of post-lyrical poetry that, far from being affect-less and apolitical, can offer a novel form of 'engagement'.

In this vein, Cadiot describes the conception of *L'Art poétic'*, recounting how, having found emotion where he might least expect it, he then acted as an archaeologist, extracting it from its unlikely location:

> Il ne s'agissait pas de coller ou réunir de force ou par le hasard des bouts de choses, je me comportais plus comme un archéologue qui enlève le sable autour des ossements avec un petit pinceau, le plus délicatement possible.[11]
>
> [It wasn't about sticking together or assembling bits and pieces by force or at random, I acted more as an archaeologist who removes the sand around the bones with a little brush, as delicately as possible.]

As an 'archéologue' or an 'artisan', the poet sets about the construction of the poem 'par des moyens lyrico-mécaniques'. The cut-up lends itself particularly well to the pursuit of a 'mécanique lyrique', in so far as it captures the same duality of the latter term, generating texts that oscillate continuously between the personal and the impersonal, depth and surface, meaninglessness and signification.[12] On the one hand, the cut-up permits an exaggerated distance between poet and the language of the poem, creating an impersonality or objectivity that traditional lyric poetry does not. It emphasises the surface, producing what Prigent calls 'poésie "faciale", sans rêve de profondeur ni bouclage sur du "secret"' ['facial' poetry, without the aspiration of depth nor the concealment of something 'secret'].[13] This 'poésie faciale' is primarily concerned with its own linguistic materiality, and is typically resistant to deeper meaning or signification. On the other hand, it offers the possibility of a renewed proximity; Cadiot writes that the cut-up is 'd'abord une opération de "neutralisation" de la langue, de remise à plat. [...] Une distance devient possible, et une nouvelle proximité' [firstly an operation of neutralising language, of starting from scratch [...] A distance becomes possible, and a new proximity].[14] Elsewhere he states that in *L'Art poétic'* 'L'enjeu était finalement de **produire du lyrisme par d'autres moyens,** de dépasser les oppositions traditionnelles entre forme et fond, émotion et concept... J'avais besoin de me recréer un territoire de poésie neuf' [The challenge was ultimately to **produce lyricism by other means,** to go beyond the traditional oppositions between form and content, emotion and concept... I needed to create a new poetic territory for myself].[15] Echoing his earlier essay with Alferi in the *Revue*, Cadiot describes here the quest to replace a traditional conception of lyricism with a novel one, constructed as an artisanal object comprised from 'des boules de sensations-pensées-formes' inherent in language.[16] This 'mécanique lyrique' constructs a platform in the poem whereupon the nascent energy in words can produce resonant, affective responses in the encounter between reader and text.

The following extract from the beginning of *L'Art poétic'* demonstrates how such an idea might work in practice:

> Je vois Pierre — Je vois qu'il est là
> Ta robe bleue. C'est ta robe bleue. Ta robe est bleue

> Leur amour grandit face à: Il grandit les difficultés
> admirablement belle
> bien trop peu, bien peu, trop peu, bien trop
> ah! oh!
> brrr!
> Viens là à côté de moi
> Songe, / songe, / Céphi // se à cette nuit / cruelle
> (dire, raconter, penser, croire...)
> Viens que je te parle
> Aussi est-il venu
> Je l'ai vu depuis le balcon (du balcon)
> en hiver, en été, en automne.
>
> [I see Pierre — I see that he's there
> Your blue dress. It's your blue dress. Your dress is blue
> Their love grew in the face of: it grew the difficulties
> admirably beautiful
> much too little, very little, too little, much too
> ah! oh!
> brrr!
> Come sit here by my side
> Dream, /dream, / Céphi // se of this cruel / night
> (to say, to tell, to think, to believe...)
> Come and I'll tell you
> And he arrived as well
> I saw him from the balcony (on the balcony)
> In winter, in summer, in autumn.][17]

The reader is made aware that the passage is composed of a number of cut-ups; some from grammar books, others presumably from textbooks on poetic versification ('Songe, / songe, / Céphi // se').[18] Certain phrases recall the most conventional textbook examples ('Ta robe bleue. C'est ta robe bleue'), and the appearance of 'Pierre', the archetypical grammar book protagonist, reinforces the reader's awareness of the origins of these linguistic fragments. As a result, we read the passage with a heightened consciousness of the formal properties of the words in front of us — their grammatical categories, their syllabic structure, and so on. We subsequently engage in an unconventional mode of reading: we are prompted to focus on the signifiers not the signifieds, and so resist the desire to make sense of the passage. The extract begins with a number of declarative, descriptive sentences which reinforce the apparent objectivity and neutrality of the language it presents. However, if there is an initial attempt to depict a form of language that is neutral or flat, something akin to what we might expect to find in dictionaries and grammar books, this attempt soon performs its own failure. Declaratives are intercut with exclamations, 'ah! oh!', which resist this neutralisation, by alluding to some form of affective response. Furthermore, the possibility of a neutral linguistic mode is quickly dismantled by the encounter between the reader and the text; language is embedded with traces of residual meaning, and any given reader approaches the poem carrying the baggage of all their previous linguistic and literary experiences, so the passage cannot help but prompt the possibility of further, deeper signification. We find ourselves constructing a rudimentary narrative, trying to piece together an ensemble of characters (a *je*, a *toi*, a 'Pierre'), tracing the motif of a developing romance, growing difficulties and a 'nuit cruelle', set against the passing seasons. The 'balcon' of the penultimate line, which conjures, perhaps, a distant allusion to Baudelaire and his mistress, might offer a number of possible metaphorical readings — the balcony as a liminal place, suspended between the domestic interior and the outside world, the balcony as a place of observation, and so on. Likewise, the line '(dire, raconter, penser, croire...)', while very likely a cut-up from a grammar exercise book, might now be read as a metapoetic comment on the processes at work in the writing or reading of the text. The very fact that the cut-ups are relocated to the space of the poem amplifies the possible resonances of the words in the passage; readers bring to the text their expectations about the operation of poetic language, with its propensity for metaphor, self-reflexivity, or semantic density. A whole range of possible literary and non-literary resonances arise, with different, idiosyncratic configurations for each reader, but, significantly, where possible resonances arise, they never evolve into anything more than a hint or glimmer of possible signification. No authoritative, comprehensive meaning is sustained over more than a handful of phrases. The text continuously resists interpretation just as quickly as it invites it, no sooner is one meaning conjured up than another takes its place. This constant oscillation produces in turn a distinctive, vacillating movement or rhythm in the reading process. Given the cut-ups in the poem are short, single-clause sentences or phrases, semantically unrelated to one another, and not combining to form one complete, comprehensive narrative, meaning is constructed in isolated sentential or phrasal units, rather than across larger chunks of text. Heightened by the juxtaposition of different tones, styles, and registers, Cadiot creates a fast-paced reading experience, where the reader moves quickly from one fragment to the next, resisting the attempt to read meaningful connections between lines.[19]

One of the dominant motifs in *L'Art poétic'*, apparent in the passage above, is the tension between the individual and collective, and the personal and impersonal dimensions of language. This is particularly apparent in the way Cadiot makes use of the most semantically empty lexical fields. Discussing the poet's use of grammar book examples, Lia Kurts writes:

> Le fort degré de banalité sémantique des phrases les rend 'transparentes' d'un point de vue dénotatif et référentiel: dans les énoncés d'origine, le lexique est peu polysémique, non connoté, le niveau de langue est non marqué et peu subjectif. [...] Ce qui est 'neutre' dans ce cas, c'est donc le niveau locutoire de l'énoncé premier, qui permet de mettre spécifiquement l'accent sur le niveau illocutoire, c'est-à-dire sur l'acte d'enseignement, l'acte de transmission de compétences grammaticales, de focalisation et d'insistance sur une difficulté grammaticale dont la visibilité est justement garantie par l'absence de toute originalité sémantique. Le champ lexical de la météorologie, largement présent, constitue à cet égard un signal de la banalité, une forme d'emblème du lieu commun, au sens courant du terme: 'Il pleut. Il fait beau.'[20]

> [The sentences' high degree of semantic banality makes them 'transparent' from

a denotative and referential point of view: in the original utterances, the lexis is seldom polysemic, non-connotated, the language level is unmarked and rarely subjective. [...] What is 'neutral' in this instance is therefore the locutionary level of the initial utterance, which allows for emphasis to be placed specifically on the illocutionary level, namely, on the act of teaching, the act of transmitting grammatical competence, of focus and stress on the grammatical difficulty whose visibility is guaranteed precisely through the absence of any semantic originality. The lexical field of weather, which is very present, constitutes in this regard a marker of banality, a kind of emblem of a commonplace, in the usual sense of the word: 'It is raining. The weather is nice.']

Kurts develops a convincing argument that the theme of transparency reappears throughout *L'Art poétic'* — from the diagram of an X-ray on the back cover, to the motif of water, and the purposefully mundane quotations from canonical authors. Through the frequent use of clichés and banalities, Cadiot stresses the impersonal, communal origins of the cut-ups, which come from linguistic reference works that explicitly resist subjectivity and attempt to occupy an objective space in language. However, this impersonality constitutes just one half of Cadiot's enterprise, as even the most impersonal language can be inflected with a highly personal, lyrical intonation. To use Prigent's formulation, 'la grammaire de Cadiot fait du personnel avec de l'impersonnel' [Cadiot's grammar creates something personal out of the impersonal], an idea that Cadiot himself describes when he outlines how his interest in the cut-up lay in the possibility of 'trouver des choses personnelles au fond de la langue morte' [finding something personal at the heart of a dead language].[21] He states:

> Dans *L'art poétic'*, j'expérimentais d'une certaine manière le 'je'. Paradoxe: j'y étais dans un 'on' complètement usé, celui des exemples de grammaire, des vieux proverbes, de ces bouts du bout de la langue, saisie au moment où elle est tellement collective qu'elle en est morte. Or cette langue devenue morte est à tout le monde. C'est *l'autobiographie de tout le monde*. Quand on est dans ce 'on'-là, à un moment donné, on est très proche du 'je'. *L'art poétic'* a donc l'air aussi impersonnel que possible, mais au fond, j'y fais une autobiographie déguisée.[22]
>
> [In *L'Art poétic'*, I was experimenting to a certain extent with the 'I'. The paradox was that I was immersed in this completely worn-out 'one', the pronoun of grammatical examples, of old proverbs, of these scraps of language, captured at the point where it has become so collective that it has died. Yet this now-deceased language is everybody's. It is *everybody's autobiography*. When one is immersed in this 'one', at a certain point, one is very close to the 'I'. So *L'Art poétic'* seems as impersonal as possible, but fundamentally, I created an autobiography in disguise.]

Here Cadiot evokes the significance of pronouns, their dual status as both an impersonal or universal space, and the locus onto which the personal is projected, where, in ordinary language, our affective lives are anchored. He nuances the idea of a monodirectional process whereby the impersonal is reanimated and made personal, and instead describes the sustained duality of *L'Art poétic'*, where every instance of language use, every *je* or *on*, oscillates continuously between the personal and the impersonal. The paradox of describing *L'Art poétic'* as 'l'autobiographie de tout le monde' captures this dualistic quality, not simply of the text itself, but of the language system as a whole, which is simultaneously collective and individual, impersonal and personal.[23]

On a textual level, in any given phrase both poles of a neutral 'écriture plate' and a dynamic lyric mode are activated. For instance, the characters that appear in *L'Art poétic'* — 'Pierre', 'Peter', 'Bill', 'Paul' — are all common male names that might be used as default examples in a grammar book, and thus represent a certain impersonality. In the phrase 'Pierre se tue' [Pierre kills himself] (*AP1*, 58; *AP2*, 58), 'Pierre' is both the empty, prototypical name from a grammar example, a monodimensional signifier or 'nobody' with no referent, but also the book's protagonist who gains depth over the course of the text, and an 'everyman', a blank space that the reader might project themselves into. Significantly, many of these names appear in the aptly-named section 'Invented Lives', which evokes the possibility of re-motivating the space of these otherwise empty signifiers, breathing new life into them. As with the entirety of *L'Art poétic'*, 'Pierre se tue' can be read on two levels: firstly, it can be read with a focus on the signifier, on the grammatical functioning of the sentence itself, as an exercise book cut-up, an example of a reflexive verb where Pierre is both the subject and object of the action. Secondly, it can be read with a focus on the signified, as a dramatic turn of events for our protagonist, who, it would seem, leads a rather tragic life: 'Paul est malade et Pierre l'est aussi' [Paul is sick and Pierre is too] (57; 58), 'des ennuis accablent Pierre' [Pierre is overwhelmed by worries] (61; 62), 'Pierre se tue dans un accident' [Pierre kills himself in an accident] (58; 59).

Lyricism in *L'Art poétic'* is therefore not the poet's subjective expression anchored in a 'je lyrique', but rather the possibility of lyricism constructed through the encounter between reader and textual object. This distinction is captured in the epigraph to the section 'The Tempest', which is composed of the grammar cut-up 'sujet –> objet' (177). As Anna Boschetti writes, this new lyric mode requires the complicity of the reader, *L'Art poétic'* 'ne peut prendre un sens que pour un lecteur complice, disposé à réactiver les connotations que sa compétence linguistique et son expérience lui permettent d'associer à ces matériaux' [can only take on a meaning for a complicit reader who's willing to reactivate the connotations that their linguistic competence and experience allow them to bring to these texts].[24] Consequently, as Prigent suggests:

> Une sorte de lyrisme en creux renaît alors sur l'impersonnalisation affectée de l'auteur, un lyrisme à la fois désabusé et allègre qui, comme l'a bien noté Alain Bideau, nous renvoie sans cesse, à force de faire dans l'archétype, 'à nous-mêmes, à nos troubles et à nos manques, à nos amours'.[25]

> [A sort of inverse lyricism arises from the affected impersonalisation of the author, a lyrism that is both disillusioned and light-hearted which, as Alain Bideau rightly noted, continuously returns us, through the use of archetypes, 'to ourselves, our problems, and our failings, our love affairs'.]

There is, of course, an editorial process behind the construction of an 'objet lyrico-mécanique'. The poet does not disappear entirely and, as Cadiot suggests in the interviews cited above, the cut-ups he chooses are often selected precisely so as to prompt an affective response from the reader. In the section 'futur, ancien, fugitif' of *L'Art poétic'*, for example, where passages of cosmic proportions evoke the sun, moon, and skies, his choice of source materials is clearly motivated by their readiness to suggest greater signification or symbolism. The evocation of the most primal, universal symbols, 'astres' and 'ciel', 'jour' and 'nuit' (*AP1*, 119), gestures towards the long history of imagery of the natural world, celestial bodies and diurnal rhythms in poetry (particularly lyric poetry). In one passage, 'venir au monde, c'est   perdre la vie, c'est   devenir *grand*, c'est   devenir *vieux*, c'est   ' [to enter the world is   to lose your life is   to become *grown-up* is   to become *old* is   ] (119; 105), while we can read it as a further textbook example and fill in the blanks accordingly, these pregnant spaces also evoke the vast swathes of literary, philosophical and theological thought that have attempted to make sense of birth, death, and the passage of time, and to provide answers to these existential questions. There is a playful mocking of the overly simplistic way that textbooks might assume right or wrong answers to such boundless questions, which in turn ties back in to Deleuze's assertion that major structures, such as tyrannical regimes of thought or language, superimpose a lack of nuance that doesn't adequately reflect the inherent variation and complexity of reality.

In Cadiot's use of cut-ups, we find a significant reworking of poetic voice that challenges in turn Bakhtin's analysis of the monoglossia of poetry. Although there is an editorial process of selection and assemblage, the cut-ups in *L'Art poétic'* nonetheless allow for the juxtaposition of multiple voices that are clearly distinct from that of the poet. When the compositional techniques of *L'Art poétic'* are translated into sampling procedures in *Welche*, *Hôtel Robinson*, and *Psychopharmaka*, which collage recordings of other people speaking — Deleuze, Henry Miller, native Welche speakers, and so on — this idea is made all the more apparent. Instead of being the direct expression of the poet, in *L'Art poétic'* we find the disembodied voice of language itself. In *Un privé à Tanger* [A Sleuth in Tangier], Hocquard points out that in Cadiot's work, we witness a kind of 'prosopopée' of language: '[la] vacance d'un sujet qui écrit produit, à partir de choses pourtant familières, l'impression très étrange que c'est quelque chose comme la langue qui parle' [the fact that the writing subject is vacant produces, from things that are otherwise familiar, the very strange impression that it's something like language itself that is speaking].[26] Cut-ups enable the poet to make objects out of the language(s) of the other, and consequently to create what Bakhtin describes as 'dialogized system[s] made up of the images of "languages", styles and consciousnesses that are concrete and inseparable from language' (*DI*, 49). In Cadiot's work, this heteroglottic, dialogic system of languages is embodied in the image of the poem as a composite form, a sort of linguistic Frankenstein's monster. This motif is a significant one in criticism on contemporary poetry, appearing, for example, in Prigent's recent book of critical essays, *La Langue et ses monstres*, and in Alferi and Cadiot's essay 'La Mécanique lyrique'.[27] In the following passage, Xavier Person considers the surgical procedure at work in Cadiot's writing:

> Le geste est précis, chirurgical. Un morceau de chair morte se verrait amoureusement découpée, puis recousue sur un organisme vivant, rajeuni dès lors (l'image est d'Olivier Cadiot). Redisposés sur la page, les énoncés prennent une nouvelle dimension, se font écho d'une manière inattendue, dégageant des nouvelles zones de significations, de sensations.[28]
>
> [The gesture is precise, surgical. A piece of dead flesh sees itself lovingly cut up, then sown back onto a living organism, from then on rejuvenated (the image is Olivier Cadiot's). Reconfigured on the page, the utterances take on a new dimension, echo in an unexpected way, release new areas of meanings and sensations.]

The image of a clinical operation, of the transplanting or grafting of flesh, ties into a number of issues outlined in 'La Mécanique lyrique', such as the poem as a constructed artefact, and the emphasis on the poem's materiality, on its skin or surface. The Frankenstein image aptly captures how inanimate linguistic parts are assembled to create a living, breathing poetic organism, thus tying in with Hocquard's notion of the prosopopoeia of language in Cadiot's work, and with the notion at the heart of 'La Mécanique lyrique', where the lyric force of the poem lies not in the poet who speaks, but in language itself. Tantamount to Frankenstein's famous exclamation 'It's alive!', Cadiot describes how the grammar book cut-ups in *L'Art poétic'* assemble a surprisingly animate text: 'Loin de la littérature, ces petits bouts de langue morte étaient de l'énergie pure' [Far from literature, these little scraps of dead language were pure energy].[29]

L'Art poétic' emphasises the monstrous, composite nature of its own creation; various linguistic scraps are sewn together — different styles, registers, and forms — resulting in a discordant whole where the different parts are animated by their dialogue with each other. Stylistically, this is reinforced by its non-systematic use of typography. Take, for example, the use of literary citation: quotations in English retain their quotation marks, and quotations in French their *guillemets*. Some are capitalised, others italicised, and font sizes vary, presumably according to their original typography. There is no cohesive formatting process, no removal of the stitches of these linguistic *greffes*, so the marked typography draws attention to the disparate parts. In *Futur, ancien, fugitif*, Cadiot extends many of the same features of *L'Art poétic'* — linguistic heterogeneity, collage, and *greffes* — but the conception of the poem-monster is incarnated in the protagonist himself, Robinson. In the first two sections of *Futur, ancien, fugitif*, 'Le Naufrage' [The Shipwreck] and 'L'Île' [The Island], Robinson finds himself shipwrecked on an island, reconstructing himself from the linguistic fragments of his life before the wreckage. He composes himself out of these scraps of his prior existence like a self-assembling Frankenstein's monster, a self-constructing machine or 'auto-usine' as Cadiot puts it.[30] Despite the obvious link to Defoe's Robinson, Cadiot stresses that his interest lies in Robinson's 'méthode' and not his 'solitude ni son île'.[31] For Cadiot, what makes the Robinson figure so appealing, and one of the reasons why he reappears in so many of his subsequent novels, is that, as the poet writes, 'A chaque livre, je pars avec lui de zéro' [With every book, I start from scratch with him].[32] To use the title to the fourth and final section of *Futur, ancien, fugitif*, Robinson represents a 'zero-sum', a blank space latent with possibility, and equipped with a toolbox to self-construct. In this sense, Robinson is also a highly Deleuzian figure of potential becoming, as the repeated phrase 'QU'EST-CE QUE TU VAS DEVENIR' [WHAT WILL YOU BECOME] reminds us when it reappears throughout *Futur, ancien, fugitif*, often capitalised to highlight its significance.[33] Indeed, we might read Robinson as a figure of the poet himself: a craftsman, working from the ground up, rebuilding in language. After the shipwreck of poetry prompted by the likes of Stéphane Mallarmé or Denis Roche, the young poet is left assessing what remains after the wreckage, what can be salvaged, and what can be rebuilt.

Polyphony/Heteroglossia

One of the characteristics that unites all three stages of Cadiot's poetic project is how the proliferation of linguistic forms and styles engenders dialogic systems of different 'images of languages'. Composed of literary citations, dictionary entries, grammar book examples, and extracts from encyclopaedias, *L'Art poétic'* draws on several national languages: French, English, Italian, and Latin. This multilingualism extends into *Futur, ancien, fugitif*, with its frequent use of English and occasional Latin and German, and is particularly salient in *Welche*, *Hôtel Robinson*, and *Psychopharmaka* which use French, English, and German, alongside the regional dialect Welche and a Breton dialect from L'Île de Batz. As we saw with Fourcade, multilingualism in contemporary poetry often forms part of a broader exploration of the conceptual notion of a foreign mode of poetic language, with actual foreign language operating as a marker of radical linguistic otherness. In Cadiot's work, the foreign and the minor are connected in his exploration of minority languages on the brink of extinction. This will be considered in greater depth in relation to *Welche*, but in *L'Art poétic'* we find the seeds of this later theme, namely in the section 'the West of England'. The epigraph contains a poem, written in English, composed of cut-ups from the *Life of Kate Crozier*, a text originally written in Hualapai, an endangered Native American language, as an act of language conservation. The original text, dictated by a Hualapai elder Kate Crozier, recounts the arrival of white colonialists and the often-violent imposition of their language on the indigenous Hualapai people. The symbolism of the text, now presented in 'the white man's language' (*AP*, 129) is hard to miss. Just as Bakhtin and Deleuze develop their respective analyses of heteroglossia and minor literature via specific historical examples from distinct sociolinguistic situations, so too Cadiot announces a broader exploration of literature and language and their major and minor axes through these markedly political instances of major national languages being imposed upon minority-language speakers.

In *Futur, ancien, fugitif*, Cadiot experiments with voice through his elaboration of the polyphonous figure of a solitary, shipwrecked Robinson, which gives Dominique Rabaté the title of his essay 'Polyphonie de solitaire: le Robinson d'Olivier Cadiot'.[34] As Cadiot writes, 'rempli du langage des autres' [filled with the language of others], Robinson is the 'porte-voix de plein de langues' [mouthpiece of many languages]; he functions as 'an empty site for the performance of the heterogeneous language of the contemporary world', as Lynch suggests.[35] Compared to *L'Art poétic'*, in *Futur, ancien, fugitif* there is a greater focus on intra-linguistic heteroglossia: the internal variation of one particular national language. The text contains a multitude of different forms, what Game summarises as 'pluralités de styles: lettres, journal, calendrier, listes, catalogues, rêves, traductions, résumés, exercices de lecture, élocutions poétiques, devinettes, cut-ups de livres d'écoles, imitations de romans réalistes' [pluralities of styles: letters, diary, calendar, lists, catalogues, dreams, translations, summaries, reading exercises, poetic speech, riddles, cut-ups from school books, imitations of realist novels].[36] Written communication, in the form of letters and party invitations, is juxtaposed with spoken language, alluded to in both the play on phonetic transcription, '[inaudible]' (*FAF*, 9), '<ouf>' (11), and in the pervasive interjection of exclamations: 'ah!', 'oh!', 'Aïe!', and 'Ouf!'. These gasps of delight and cries of disbelief are prime examples of how the attempt to encode spoken language in written texts can lose much of the original, expressive effect, in turn appearing highly codified and contrived.[37] They serve as reminders of the moments in everyday speech when language is insufficient and the non-linguistic, or para-linguistic, takes over. Appearing throughout Cadiot's *œuvre*, these exclamations form part of a broader exploration of a Deleuzian 'au-delà de la langue' or an Artaudian passage towards the 'cri'. Several features of Cadiot's work draw attention to non-linguistic modes of expression: in *Futur, ancien, fugitif*, for example, pervasive stage directions such as '[piano]' (106), '[chanté]' (206) anticipate the passage in Cadiot's later work from the written to the performed. In the section 'La Dame du lac' [The Lady of the Lake] in *L'Art poétic'*, hand-drawn staves and musical notation accompany choreographic directions. In the section 'the West of England', each page contains a large grey square composed of black dots, as if evoking a once present, now absent image. The anatomical diagram on the back cover announces the distorted, disfigured language of the text itself.

In *Futur, ancien, fugitif*, and later in *Hôtel Robinson* and *Psychopharmaka*, the theme of animal language and bird song represents a further exploration of an 'au-delà de la langue'. For Cadiot, animal communication presents a counterpart to human language, a further form of minor language that an anthropocentric perspective relegates to an inferior form of expression. Game explores this same idea in his discussion of the 'becoming-bird' at work in *Futur, ancien, fugitif*, writing, 'Le devenir-oiseau est ici une déterritoralisation réciproque entre l'homme et l'oiseau' [The becoming-bird is here a reciprocal deterritorialisation between human and bird].[38] At various points in *Futur, ancien, fugitif*, bird song is transcribed into roman alphabet; the notably poor approximations of bird song — 'ff-fff-fff', 'piii', 'liri-liii', 'takatss-takatss' (32) — appear to exaggerate their own failure to transliterate animal noises, as if to highlight their resolute resistance to being translated into human language. Bird song is thus represented as impenetrable, incomprehensible to the human ear, an assemblage of sounds that elude linguistic representation, and exist only as music without meaning, or pure signifier.

In his experiments with the limits of linguistic expression, Cadiot also explores child language and babbling. Recalling Fourcade's use of 'babil enfantin', in *Futur, ancien, fugitif* Robinson recalls his earliest memories:

> Oh le bébé à sa maman
> Oh le bébé qu'il est gentil oh le bébé
> ça c'est un bébé ça c'est un bébé ça c'est un bébé
>
> [...]
> c'est mon bébé
> c'est mon bébé
>
> [ad lib.] (FAF, 40–41)

[Oh mummy's baby | Oh such a kind baby oh the baby | that's a baby that's a baby that's a baby | [...] | that's my baby | that's my baby | [ad lib.]]

This child-oriented speech, with its grammatical reworkings and repetitions, appears in *Futur, ancien, fugitif* but is also found in *Hôtel Robinson*, for example in 'Cheval-mouvement' [Horse-Movement]: 'What's in the box? Can you open it? Can you open it? The box? Well Mummy's gonna see what's in it'.[39] In recent linguistic research, a key theory of why adults talk to children in this way is that it facilitates the child's acquisition of grammatical constructions and word order.[40] This mode of communication parallels both experimental modernist literature, such as the grammatical *ritournelles* of Gertrude Stein, and the generation of 'poètes-grammairiens' to which Cadiot belongs, in that emphasis is placed on the structural functioning of language, the signifier and its grammatical category, rather than on the transfer of semantic information. In the section of *Futur, ancien, fugitif* entitled 'LES PREMIÈRES PAROLES DE ROBINSON' (FAF, 20), the focus is on an earlier stage of language acquisition — babbling. Strings of letters, 'Vo ro jo botopolodo' (20), enact Robinson's reconstruction from his linguistic past, with these 'premières paroles' referring to both his first words as a child and his first words uttered on the island. Babbling reappears on the album *Psychopharmaka*, in the song 'Dadasophe' which samples Kurt Schwitters's glossolalic performances at the Cabaret Voltaire, and in 'Da da da', a cover of a song by the German synthpop band Trio, which revolves around the consonant-vowel clusters that children typically start to produce in early infancy. Linguists suggest that child babbling represents a pre-verbal, pre-semantic developmental stage in speech production where children begin to exercise their vocal tracts and start to produce the physical shapes and sounds of speech. The emphasis is again on the material signifier, rather than on the meaning. One of the reasons why *le babil* is so significant in Cadiot's work (as it is, in different ways, for Fourcade and Tarkos) is because it occupies a double position. It is the point at which language stops being language and becomes something non-linguistic or non-verbal. And, just as in childhood it represents the point at which language begins to emerge and develop, so too in literature it offers a departure from the 'regime of meaning' in the elaboration of a new, experimental mode of expression.[41] Babble understood as a pre-verbal developmental stage that consolidates the building blocks of a language to come, provides an apt metaphor for the development of Cadiot's own poetry. Like the infant, so too the poet tentatively explores the possibilities of the tools in his poetic 'caisse à outils'. He experiments with linguistic decomposition, the cut-up, heteroglossia, polyphony, assembling a number of procedures and techniques that constitute the foundation of an 'art poétic'' to come.[42]

Moving from the most elementary, innate forms of language to the most ritualised, *Futur, ancien, fugitif* also explores the highly codified practices of phatic language and social convention. In the first section of the book, 'Le Naufrage', phatic speech is pervasive, often pushed to its extreme in parodic passages such as the following:

> Ah mon cher
> Cher Monsieur
> C'est avec plaisir que
> Eh bien recevez acceptez croyez cher Monsieur,
> à mon meilleur souvenir [...]
> Votre si dévoué fidèle entièrement à vous
> votre ami — .   (*FAF*, 10–11)

[Ah my dear | Dear Sir | It's with great pleasure that | Well, receive accept have faith dear Sir, | in my fondest recollections [...] | Your devoted faithful entirely yours | your friend — .]

This passage, which recalls Heidsieck's 'Biopsie 6: Stratimelo' (with its repetitions of the 'formules de politesse' used at the beginnings and ends of letters), pokes fun at phatic language.[43] The excessive accumulation of pleasantries undermines the sincerity of what is being expressed, rendering the expressions themselves semantically null. This semantic emptying takes place throughout *Futur, ancien, fugitif*, and is perhaps best exemplified in the following passage from the opening lines of the book:

> *Mr. et Mrs.* ★★★
> *auraient la joie de recevoir*
> ———————————
> *pour le dîner*
> *du* .... (*FAF*, 9)
>
> [*Mr. and Mrs.* ★★★
> *would be delighted to receive*
> ———————————
> *for dinner*
> *on*........................]

This extract constitutes one of the many linguistic fragments that Robinson has salvaged from the shipwreck. By leaving the blanks incomplete, Cadiot accentuates the phatic quality of ritualised language use; the overt sentimentality of the fixed expression *avoir la joie de recevoir* is undermined by its depersonalisation — it has no expressed subject and no expressed object. In these passages, we might read a broader comment on the iterative nature of the linguistic system, and on the tension between the communal, impersonal nature of language and the highly individual nature of each given instance of speech. In the context of *Futur, ancien, fugitif*, where Robinson has washed up ashore on an island on his own, the emphasis on phatic language is all the more poignant. In the absence of society, language is stripped of its social function, and phatic speech, which is already semantically null, loses its pragmatic force too. Like the bird call and glossolalia above, Robinson's 'formules de politesse' are also reduced to the status of pure signifier.

The frequent use of phatic language makes Robinson's absent interlocutor all the more salient, and reinforces the themes of madness and schizophrenia which are pervasive in the text. Following the shipwreck in the first half of the book, in the second half the action is transplanted to the doctor's office. Here Robinson is being treated for schizophrenia, and his previous island existence is declared to be a figment of his imagination. Robinson's illness is introduced from the off; in the first section he enumerates a list of symptoms:

>   1. Impossibilité de marcher et de se tenir debout.
>   2. Perte de la voix haute.
>   3. Paralysie locale et rêveries diurnes.
>   4. Amnésie lacunaire.
>   5. Mutisme de type lucide. (*FAF*, 20–21)

[1. Incapable of walking or standing up. | 2. Unable to speak out loud. | 3. Local paralysis and daydreaming. | 4. Selective amnesia. | 5. Lucid-type mutism.]

The various communicational and cognitive symptoms on the list invite a metalinguistic reading, encouraging the reader to assess the language of the text itself as disordered. Symptoms such as 'le style télégraphique' (22), a common feature of aphasia, and 'le dédoublement vocal' (22), with its psychiatric connotations, offer self-reflexive comments on the stylistic properties of *Futur, ancien, fugitif*. A brief glance at some of the characteristics of schizophrenic speech reveals clear parallels with the text: i) non-sequiturs, fragmentation, and difficulty maintaining a train of thought; ii) repetition of words and phrases; iii) use of neologisms and nonsensical words; and iv) 'clanging', where sentences are composed according to similarity of sound rather than according to a target meaning. In *Futur, ancien, fugitif*, manic *ritournelles* and clanging ('grune greil grace grob gran grette gri gro', 20) reappear throughout the text, which jumps from one subject to another, switching from one voice to the next. This polyphonous quality creates an impression of a schizophrenic monologue, a multitude of voices rooted in the single figure of Robinson. In the second half of the book, particular emphasis is given to this schizophrenic monologue, with Robinson observing, 'Depuis longtemps déjà je me surprenais à parler tout seul' [For a long time now, I have been catching myself talking to myself] (82), an observation reinforced by the paranthetical stage directions: '[à part]' (10), '[seul]' (205).

One particularly salient aspect of Robinson's schizophrenic speech is the frequent oscillation between French and English, often intrasententially. In the passage 'LETTRES RETROUVÉES ET TRADUITES DE MA LANGUE MATERNELLE' [LETTERS FOUND AND TRANSLATED FROM MY MOTHER TONGUE] (*FAF*, 23), the reading process is disrupted by the constant intrusion of the French translated into English:

> Cher Jack,
> Pourquoi ne viendriez-vous pas chez nous pour le thé
> sur le pré (lawn) vendredi le quinze? Les fraises
> (strawberries & roses) et les roses
> sont mûres tout de suite

> les fraises et les roses sont prêtes
> in their prime now. (*FAF*, 24–25)

[Dear Jack, | Why don't you come to ours for tea | on the meadow (pelouse) Friday the fifteenth? The strawberries | (fraises & roses) and the roses | are ripe right now | the strawberries and roses are ready | maintenant au mieux de leur forme.]

This continuous translation process creates a dialogic effect, and the two voices, one French and one English, reinforce the impression of a schizophrenic writing subject. As Game points out, Cadiot's Robinson demonstrates striking similarities with Louis Wolfson.[44] Like Wolfson or Fourcade revolting against the mother figure, Robinson's disordered speech resists the phatic formulations of 'Mr and Mrs ★★★', the enigmatic characters evoked in the extract above, as well as the normative, medicalising discourse of Dr Lawrence, the psychotherapist who treats Robinson in the latter half of the book. As Game writes, 'the stutter [in *FAF*] is the de-territorialization called for by the tyrannical attempts at re-territorialization perpetrated on Robinson'.[45] As we saw in the last chapter, Wolfson's schizophrenic translation procedure exemplifies, for Deleuze, a form of 'becoming-minor', whereby the major language of the mother tongue is rendered foreign and minor in a broken, often agrammatical, French. In the passage above Cadiot's translation procedure has a similar effect. It makes the text stutter, for example in the mistranslation of 'pré' as 'lawn', or in the disruption of the original French clause 'les fraises et les roses' with the translated phrase '(strawberries & roses)'. As the passage continues, the translation process is abandoned, and the text decomposes into strings of sounds, where English and French morph into one another: '*dipli dipli dipli hi | oui wou no ha chairin yourloss*' (26). As was the case for Fourcade, in these multilingual passages, we see how Cadiot initially takes the notion of the 'langue étrangère' in the shape of actual foreign language, before transforming it into a conceptual form of foreignness, characterised, in this instance, by agrammaticality, discontinuity, and nonsense. Game concludes his account of *Futur, ancien, fugitif* with the following suggestion: 'structured around the cyclical uttering of a delirium, the book becomes the story of a border-line language. The true locutor of *FAF* is generic and subjectless, purely processual yet not schizophrenic: it is poetic language itself'.[46] That Robinson becomes a figure for poetic language is a convincing argument in that his unstable and shifting identity clearly aligns with the properties of a minor poetry that have been outlined thus far: the destabilisation of voice in polyphonous and heteroglottic discourse, a literal and conceptual foreignness, an uprooting agrammaticality, and so on.

As *Futur, ancien, fugitif* progresses, Robinson's schizophrenic monologue often builds into manic, hysterical speech, with excessive exclamations, 'ricanements hystériques soupirs' (*FAF*, 30) and 'hurlements de joie et rires sauvages' (30). The pervasive effect of speed in Cadiot's work is amplified by extreme repetition, for example in a passage depicting someone fussing over their dog (revolving around the phrase '*oh le chien le petit oh le petit chien il est à qui le petit chien?*' [oh the doggie the little the little doggie whose little doggie is it?], 35) where the parallels between clinical disorder and social silliness are clearly drawn.[47] This manic excess in his speech creates the impression that Robinson is attempting to fend off silence by filling the void with noise. After all, silence looms in *Futur, ancien, fugitif* as an omnipresent threat: 'D'un coup: rien. Silence' [Suddenly: nothing. Silence] (33), 'silence. Noir' [silence. Dark] (89), 'Silence. Rien. Et après silence silence' [Silence. Nothing. And after silence silence] (202). The word itself appears with increasing frequency as the book progresses, culminating in the final passage of the third section, 'Le Retour' [The Return]. This might be read as a metapoetic comment on the impending threat of silence in modern poetry, summarised in Roche's previously cited formulation that Cadiot will later re-use: 'La poésie est inadmissible, d'ailleurs elle n'existe pas'. Silence becomes a metonym for the non-existence or non-continuation of poetry, for its irrelevance, its contentious ethical status, and its potential death as a genre. The presence of this theme in *Futur, ancien, fugitif* is significant as the text marks a threshold between Cadiot's first book, a book of poetry, and his later written work, which has been exclusively prose. This question will be considered in detail later in this chapter, but for the time being we note how, inscribed in the text itself, is a comment on the endangered status and uncertain future of poetry.

Where poetry is presented as constructing itself against the threat of silence, this is then mirrored in the instability of Robinson as poetic subject. This represents a further way in which *Futur, ancien, fugitif* interweaves, and at times conflates, the character Robinson and the metapoetic abstraction of Robinson as figure for poetry itself. As Game writes, '*Futur, ancien, fugitif* [...] operates a powerful destructuring of the narrative, the locator and his language, from which the subject emerges as incessant self-production rather than representation of an ideal and stable formation'.[48] The polyphonous collage of voices in the text produces a constant construction and deconstruction of the subject, which oscillates continuously between its own becoming and its undoing, as Jean Renaud suggests, citing Deleuze:

> *Je* se constitue et se déconstitue sans cesse, se déterritorialise et reterritorialise, sans que jamais prenne forme une totalité (aussi secrète, enfouie, qu'on voudra). 'On parlera donc d'un *plan de consistance* des multiplicités.' Ce plan ne connaît pas de 'sujets', mais seulement 'des rapports de mouvement et de repos, de vitesse et de lenteur, entre éléments non formés, molécules ou particules emportées par des flux'.[49]

> [*I* constructs and deconstructs itself continuously, deterritorialises and reterriorialises, without a totality (however secret or buried) ever taking shape. 'We will therefore speak of a *plane of consistency* of multiplicities.' This plane doesn't recognise 'subjects', but only 'relations of movement and rest, speed and slowness, between unformed elements, molecules and particles carried by the flux'.]

This oscillation between self-construction and self-deconstruction is exemplified first and foremost in the overarching narrative framework: Robinson has, prior to the start of the novel, been decomposed by the shipwreck. He subsequently rebuilds himself out of linguistic fragments washed ashore and is then undone again by the revelation in the second half of the book that his island escapades were schizophrenic delusions. We are left wondering what of the previous episodes was true and what was delusion, which is undermined again by the recognition that Robinson is a fictional character, and therefore, in any case, a subject constructed exclusively through language. The polyphonous fragments of the first section result in a 'RECONSTITUTION' (*FAF*, 41), but by the end of the book Robinson is 'Décomposé' (202), and it has all been 'Beaucoup de bruit pour rien' [Much ado about nothing] (202). These constructions and deconstructions, expansions and contractions, structure the entire text. For example, the 'Zero-sum' of the final section title appears at intervals throughout the book: 'Résultat nul: Zero-sum' [Null result: Zero-sum] (86), '*Zero-Sum*. Somme zéro. Résultat final de toute opération. Somme de toutes choses' [*Zero-Sum* Sum zero. Final result of all operations. Sum of all things] (149). Robinson, as a post-modern experiment in poetic subjecthood, is presented as an unstable locus of continual self-construction and effacement, on the level of the narrative, his functioning as a fictional character, and as a poetic voice, constructed necessarily within language.

Cadiot and Burger's album *Welche* returns to many of the same themes of *L'Art poétic'* and *Futur, ancien, fugitif*, translating the same formal features of these earlier texts into an acoustic medium. Its lyrics, sound effects, and stuttered samples constitute a similar heteroglottic collage and demonstrate the same incongruous juxtaposition of linguistic fragments, images, and voices. Bob Dylan lyrics appear alongside a passage from *Billy the Kid*, read by the American poet Jack Spicer; the sound of running water is juxtaposed with the voices of native Welche speakers. The context in which the album was recorded is significant in so far as it engages directly with language, power, and their intersection, evoking relationships between different language variants in a socio-political setting. As we have seen, these considerations are at the centre of Deleuze and Guattari's discussion of minor literature, and, consequently, fundamental to the form of 'poésie mineure' that I believe Cadiot's work constitutes. The album was recorded in the 'Val de Lièpvre' in Alsace, where Burger and Cadiot interviewed members of the local community who spoke Welche, an endangered minority dialect with only 1,000 or so speakers left. Given its geographical situation, Alsace of all places witnessed the struggle between different national languages, principally German and French, as well as the resistance of local dialects and regional languages to superimposed national ones.[50] Instances of minority dialects such as Welche being ousted by major national languages, represent clear examples of how a 'langue de pouvoir' suppresses regional variation in a political campaign of standardisation, typically linked to nationalism. Cadiot and Burger's album formed part of a broader linguistic conservation project that attempted to record and promote awareness of a language on the brink of extinction. In the promotional material for the album, Welche is described as being, historically, a language of resistance:

> La langue welche, qui est en réalité un patois, est une survivance unique. Enclave romane en territoire germanique (le mot welche signifie 'non allemand' en langue allemande...), elle n'est plus parlée que par un millier de personnes réparties sur un petit nombre de vallées des Vosges alsaciennes. Elle aura probablement disparu dans quelques années. La survivance du parler

welche jusqu'en l'an 2000 s'explique en partie par la succession des occupations allemandes. Durant la dernière guerre, le welche a survécu comme une résistance à la dictature linguistique allemande.⁵¹

[The Welche language, which is actually a patois, is a unique survival. A Romance enclave in a Germanic territory (the word Welche means 'non-German' in the German language...), it is now only spoken by a thousand people spread across just a few valleys in the Alsatian Vosges. It will probably die out in a few years. The fact that Welche has survived until the year 2000 can be explained in part by the succession of German occupations. During the last war, Welche survived as a form of resistance to the linguistic dictatorship of German.]

In this account of the historical status of Welche, there are clear resonances with Deleuze's notion of a 'langue majeure' and a 'langue mineure', taken in their most literal senses. While, as we saw in Chapter 1, Deleuze and Guattari's analysis extends beyond this literal understanding, we also saw how such heightened sociolinguistic settings were significant for the majority of the authors they considered. Similarly, I would argue, the particular context of Cadiot and Burger's project frames the centrality of the broader issues around language, variation, and power at play in their work.

The interviews Burger and Cadiot conducted with the Welche speakers Monsieur Humbert, Madame Rosa, Madame Bauman, and Monsieur Baradal are reworked into the five tracks of the album. The phonological variants of their regional accents represent a very tangible component of the variation that Deleuze and Guattari suggest a minor use of language will carve into the major language. The motif of the accent, and the wider theme of foreign language, were already present in *Futur, ancien, fugitif*, where Cadiot transcribed English spoken with a foreign accent in French orthography, for example: 'Maï dieur frennd, aï challe nevveur forguette youre kaïnnd-ness and djènérosité' (*FAF*, 119). Here, it appears not only in the Welche accents, but also in the track 'Try to Understand', which overlays Jack Spicer reading in his native English accent, and Burger, repeating the same text with a French accent, in such a way as to draw attention to their differences in pronunciation and intonation. Translation, in and out of different languages and dialects, is central to the project Cadiot and Burger pursued in *Welche*. In the track 'Tante Elisabeth' [Aunt Elizabeth], Welche is translated into standard French; in 'Zo Love', standard French is translated into Welche. The phrase that forms the second part of the album's title, *Welche; On n'est pas indiens c'est dommage*, and which reappears in the tracks themselves, comes from a Welche speaker at a translation workshop held at Orbey in July 1999, that formed part of the project, and which focused on the translation of Navajo songs into French and Welche. In an interview for France Culture, Cadiot and Burger evoke the importance of the workshops and interviews they conducted, stressing the centrality of the *rencontre* in the production of *Welche*.⁵² The significance of the encounter can be traced in the album's themes: translation sees the interaction of two different languages, and the foreign accent sees the expression, in voice, of the intersection between a native language and the target foreign one. In this respect, the heteroglossia or polyphony of *Welche* is not merely the juxtaposition of different linguistic forms, but precisely the interaction and the meeting point between them.

The recordings of Welche speakers, while sometimes presenting entire phrases, are often cut short, spliced into phonemes and syllables, beginnings of words and ends of phrases. These segmented samples are then superimposed on one another and transformed into auditory collages with a musical accompaniment (guitar, drumming, voice, and so on). This feature culminates in the final track of the album, 'On n'est pas indiens c'est dommage', which presents a number of samples from the Welche speakers, radically reworked so that what were once recordings of their complete, meaningful phrases are now decomposed into an auditory assemblage of verbal segments and para- or non-linguistic sound (laughter, exclamations, the inhalation of breath). This final track provides a prototypical example of the same Deleuzian stutter found in Cadiot's earlier writing, but is rendered all the more salient in an acoustic medium. In *Mille plateaux*, Deleuze and Guattari write that the 'auteur mineur' will 'faire bégayer la langue, [...] tendre des tenseurs dans toute la langue, même écrite, et en tirer des cris, des clamés, des hauteurs, durées, timbres, accents, intensités' [make language stammer, [...] stretch tensors through all of language, even written language, and draw from it cries, shouts, pitches, durations, timbres, accents, intensities.] (*MP*, 131; *ATP*, 121). The stuttering, cacophonous collage of 'On n'est pas indiens c'est dommage' extracts from language its constitutional rhythms, tones, and timbres, so that, as the linguistic becomes non-linguistic, language extends to its limits, is deterritorialised and transformed into pure music. In the transition from the preserved, full-length recordings of Welche that appear in the initial tracks 'C'est dans la vallée' [It's in the Valley] and 'Tante Elisabeth', to the barely recognisable samples of the final track, we might read a gesture towards the fate of Welche itself, as it gradually disappears, and the remaining speakers of the dialect pass away. In this respect, there is an ambiguity in the cutting up and splicing of the Welche recordings: on the one hand, it is clearly an experimental, poetic gesture, aesthetically and formally motivated; on the other hand, there is a certain violence behind the act of deforming the recordings, rendering them incomprehensible. In a project concerned with a language in danger of extinction, we might expect the focus to be conversely on the preservation of such recordings.

Alongside recordings of interviews with Welche speakers, a number of features of traditional Welche culture are woven into the musical fabric of the album. The sampling of running water found throughout *Welche* is a recording of 'La Lièpvrette', the river that outlines the boundary of the Welche territory, and that has provided a life source for generations of Welche inhabitants. In the track 'Tante Elisabeth', Madame Rosa, a local of Labroche, sings a traditional Welche song, a *ritournelle* with an accumulative refrain that acquires additional clauses with each repetition. The 'cinépoème' of this track, produced by Alferi in conjunction with Burger and Cadiot, features a montage of video clips: Madame Rosa singing, footage from old films, the running waters of the Lièpvrette.[53] The *ritournelle* of the Welche song, with its repeated grammatical refrain, is reinforced by the visual images:

the rotating steps of a waltz, a model bed spinning on a trapeze, a mechanism being wound up, and a dancer twirling fabrics into circles. In *Mille plateaux*, the *ritournelle* forms a key part of Deleuze and Guattari's analysis of territorialisation and deterritorialisation.[54] Taking bird song as their point of departure, they demonstrate how the refrain is used to stake out the perimeters of a territory. The refrain can have a reassuring, stabilising effect; it creates order out of chaos. To use Deleuze and Guattari's examples, it is the tune hummed under one's breath as one potters around one's home, or the nursery rhyme a child sings to herself in the dark. However, as Deleuze and Guattari argue, the *ritournelle* contains within it the potential for deterritorialisation; it has no beginning or end but is rather involved in a constant production of variations, and with that, the possibility of coding those variations differently. It offers, therefore, new lines of flight that move outside the familiar, repeating, but repeating differently with each variation.

The oscillation between the territorialising and deterritorialising dimensions of the *ritournelle* is apparent in 'Tante Elisabeth'. In the central refrain, the repetition of the phrase 'Tante Elisabeth' returns us continuously to a familiar starting point, but the repetitions are not exact repetitions; they are thrown off-centre, acquiring additional clauses with each rotation. The clip wavers continuously between the familiar and the unfamiliar, the recognisable and the strange. The montage of images has a disorientating effect: we are left trying to configure sense from their juxtaposition, and to establish their relationship with the words of the song. For the non-Welche speaker, the foreign, unfamiliar sounds of Madame Rosa's voice are alienating and opaque, but the standard French subtitles, running along the bottom of the screen, serve to ground us. There is, nonetheless, a temporal lapse between the Welche recording and the appearance of the subtitles on screen, which is matched by the syncopated rhythm of the musical accompaniment. A similar slippage appears between the apparent slightness of the song's lyrics, and its broader significance in a language conservation project, where it represents the vestiges of a language and a culture under threat. One of the prominent images of the 'cinépoème', the clip of a model bed spinning on a miniature film set, represents a visual expression of these opposing centrifugal and centripetal forces. The image is territorialising in its presentation of a familiar, household object, and in the hypnotic gyrations of the bed spinning on an invisible string. However, this familiarity is quickly subverted by the fact that the bed is a model, a miniature variation, markedly different from the original. A number of questions are left unanswered: 'What are we watching?', 'Why is the bed spinning?' The entire scene produces an unsettling and strange effect. In a very visual representation of Deleuze and Guattari's conception of the *ritournelle* and its subsequent lines of flight, the bed's rotations grow ever faster until it breaks out of its established path and flies off the set and out of shot entirely. This is just one example of the Deleuzo-Guattarian refrain in Cadiot's work, where bird song, child and child-oriented language, and nursery rhymes are all significant motifs.[55] The most pervasive form of refrain is undoubtedly the grammatical refrain; we read above how, in the construction of *L'Art poétic'*, the poet set about finding 'ritournelles' in grammar books:[56]

> Pierre se tue (1)
> Pierre se tue lui-même (2)
> Pierre se tue dans un accident. (*AP*, 58)

These grammatical repetitions reappear throughout Cadiot's *œuvre*, and as we shall see shortly, oscillate between a major and minor axis in their vacillation between grammaticality and agrammaticality. Significantly, the focus on refrains and repetition in Deleuze's and subsequently Cadiot's work returns us again to questions of poetry and its constitutive generic properties. For as long as it has existed, repetition has been a primary feature of poetic form: in its verse forms, its prosodic effects (assonance, alliteration, end rhyme, etc.), and in its stylistic devices (anaphora, epistrophe etc.). As Gaëlle Théval points out in her discussion of repetition in *L'Art poétic'*, Cadiot's grammatical refrains have the opposite effect to the usual function of stylistic figures of repetition in poetry: instead of 'adding value', they have 'un effet appauvrissant' and a 'fonction "littéralisante"'.[57] In this respect, we see a further instance of deterritorialisation, where the same features of a major poetic genre are repeated, but used to a different effect.

Like *Welche*, *Hôtel Robinson* involves an eclectic assemblage of voices and sounds: Gilles Deleuze talking about Spinoza, Henry Miller speaking in broken French, Burger's grammatical *ritournelles* in 'B à Batz'. These voices are offset by techno music, guitar, drumming, and samples of horses braying, bells ringing, and machines rattling. Like *Welche*, the album involved a similar sociolinguistic excursion: Cadiot and Burger recorded residents of the Île de Batz in the Finistère in Brittany in 2002. As in *Welche*, the recordings are reworked on the album, so that, for example in 'Totem & Tabou', Mamie Dirou's voice, with its strong Breton accent, is made to stutter. One of the central motifs of the album is the island identity of the Île de Batz: the title, *Hôtel Robinson*, evokes the shipwrecked Robinson of *Futur, ancien, fugitif* (reinforcing the idea that Cadiot's albums present an extension of his written project). The theme of water generates the inclusion of Deleuze's voice in the track 'Je nage' [I swim], which opens with the following words of the philosopher: 'Je plonge au bon moment, je ressors au bon moment, j'évite la vague qui approche ou au contraire je m'en sers' [I dive at the right moment, I emerge at the right moment, I avoid the approaching wave or, quite the opposite, I make use of it].[58] The track assembles fragments of recordings of Deleuze's lecture on Spinoza, given in Vincennes in 1981 (which Cadiot attended), where he illustrated Spinoza's theory of knowledge through the example of swimming. Talking about the encounter of the human body with the approaching waves, Deleuze argues that, instead of 'une connaissance mathématique ou physique, scientifique du mouvement de la vague' [a mathematic or physical, scientific knowledge of the movement of the wave], the swimmer possesses a 'savoir faire':

> Un savoir faire étonnant, c'est-à-dire que j'ai une espèce de sens du rythme. La rythmicité. Qu'est-ce que ça veut dire, le rythme ? Ça veut dire que mes rapports caractéristiques je sais les composer directement avec les rapports de la vague. Ça ne se passe plus entre la vague et moi, c'est-à-dire que ça ne se passe plus entre les parties extensives, les parties mouillées de la vague, et les parties de mon corps, ça se passe entre les rapports.[59]

[An astonishing know-how, which is to say that I have a kind of sense of rhythm. Rhythmicity. What does that mean, rhythm? It means that I know how to compose my characteristic relations directly with the relations of the wave. It's no longer happening between the wave and me, which means that it is no longer happening between the extensive parts, the wet parts of the wave, the parts of my body, it's happening between the relations.]

Deleuze's theory of rhythm, his questions 'qu'est-ce que ça veut dire le rythme?', 'qu'est-ce que ça veut dire tout ça?', form the pivot of 'Je nage' in *Hôtel Robinson*, which returns to the same themes of rhythm and movement introduced in *L'Art poétic'* and *Futur, ancien, fugitif*. The track's samples, with their unanswered questions, suspend the notion of rhythm in the mind of the listener, both highlighting it as a thematic concern of the album, and drawing attention to the album's formal composition, the rhythmic quality of the music in hand. The rhythm of the track itself is markedly syncopated or arrhythmic, which paradoxically draws the listener's attention to precisely the regular, steady rhythm that is absent. The samples of Deleuze's lecture run throughout the track, but the musical accompaniment (guitar, samples of swilling water) builds in momentum, and then quickly dissolves. The track's gradual crescendo and subsequent diminuendo takes the form of the rising and falling wave that Deleuze describes in the recordings ('Ah, maman, la vague m'a battu' [Ah, mum, the wave hit me]). The samples centre on a number of verbs of motion — *plonger, nager, barboter, voler, se lancer* — evoking the movements of the wave and the philosopher swimming. Elsewhere in *Hôtel Robinson* this focus on movement takes the form of the gallop, for example in 'Cheval-mouvement', where phrases found originally in *Futur, ancien, fugitif* describe the movements of the horse. The motif reappears in *Psychopharmaka*, notably in the track 'Dada-Bewegung', *Bewegung* being the German word for motion/movement. The track features a variation on the guitar chords from 'Cheval-mouvement', like the previous track it also samples horses neighing, and now includes recordings of Deleuze talking about 'le galop' ('le galop c'est la cavalcade du présent qui passe' [the gallop is the stampede of the passing present], 'la musique aurait pour éléments principaux le cheval et l'oiseau' [music has as its principal elements the horse and the bird).[60] Deleuze's phrase then generates a motif of 'le cheval et l'oiseau', which is found throughout the album in the frequent sampling of birds singing and horses whinnying.

Psychopharmaka, recorded in Germany and German-speaking Switzerland, is Cadiot and Burger's third musical excursion. The first track's title announces the artistic endeavour in hand: 'Sing mir ein neues Lied' [Sing Me a New Song], a request that is then reiterated as the sample is repeated at intervals throughout the album. The parallels here with Cadiot's earlier aspiration to find a new form of poetry, to 'produire du lyrisme par d'autres moyens', are clear, and are reinforced by Cadiot and Burger's own reflections in interviews.[61] Evoking the transfer of the 'cut-up' and *découpage* from a literary medium to an auditory one, they describe how, behind their use of sampling, of assembling other people's voices in their recordings, lay a desire to 'fabriquer des chansons par d'autres moyens' [create songs by other means].[62] More broadly, this practice also responds to the desire to house poetry within music, as Cadiot suggests: 'Comment une chanson peut-elle devenir accueillante pour la poésie? L'idée est alors venue, pour aller très vite, de sampler' [How can a song start to accommodate poetry? Then, to cut a long story short, we thought of using samples].[63] Cadiot and Burger set about their quest for a 'neues Lied' by elaborating a rich and hybrid network of interconnected linguistic and musical images, dialogising the old and new, the classical and the modern, 'high culture' and pop culture. Renowned figures of German and Austrian Romanticism — Brahms, Schubert, and Goethe — are interwoven with philosophers, Deleuze and Nietzsche, literary figures, such as Paul Celan, and chart-topping cult bands, like Trio and Grauzone. A primary reference point in *Psychopharmaka* is Dada: three of the album's track titles contain explicit references, 'Dadasophe', 'Dada-Bewegung', and 'Da da da'; Kurt Schwitters's Cabaret Voltaire performances are sampled extensively in 'Dadasophe', with all the characteristic glossolalia, vocal tics and trills that we might expect of a Schwitters poem. *Psychopharmaka* itself experiments with para- and non-linguistic sound: laughter, babbling, animal noises, as well as frequent samples of ambient noise (a busy restaurant, the sound of a car door, and so on). In featuring Dada so heavily, there is a clear acknowledgment of its influence, and a confirmation of *Psychopharmaka*'s situation in a lineage of experimental, performance poetry. The significance of Dada experiments, which radically redefined the parameters of poetic form and language, is apparent in the uncertain generic status of Cadiot and Burger's albums. A second key reference in *Psychopharmaka* is the German electronic band, Kraftwerk. In the third track 'Eisbär' [Polar Bear], a sample from a 1975 BBC documentary announces: 'Kraftwerk have a name for this, it's machine music. Sounds are created at their laboratory in Düsseldorf, programmed, and then recreated on stage'.[64] Kraftwerk were instrumental in the development of electronic music, and, as their album titles would suggest, *Die Mensch-Maschine* [The Man-Machine], *Computerwelt* [Computer World], at the centre of their enterprise was the importance of the machine. Working in a 'sound laboratory', the band pioneered new uses of technology in their songs, experimenting with computer-programmed speech generators and custom-built instruments. In this respect, Kraftwerk sought to produce music by other means; their relevance for Cadiot and Burger, who supplant the traditional French *chanson* with a heteroglottic, hybrid form, composed through machinic processes of sampling and arrangement, is apparent. The centrality of the machine in *Psychopharmaka*, which appears in the allusions to Kraftwerk, and in the very techniques of the album's composition, sees a continuation, in an acoustic medium, of the 'mécanique lyrique' of Cadiot's earlier poetry.

How does the heteroglossia of Cadiot's work sit in terms of the relationship between language, discourse, and genre introduced in the first chapter? We will remember that, when Bakhtin sets up the opposition between poetic and novelistic discourse, the type of poetry he is evoking is implicitly lyric poetry; other forms of poetry are largely absent from his discussion, and when they do appear, they are considered to be 'novelistic', and therefore no longer poetry. Bakhtin's analysis of poetic monoglossia, and his underlying assumption that poetry = lyric poetry, are still widely preserved in popular opinion and among certain critics and poets. Frustratingly, given the argument I want to make, Cadiot himself discusses poetry in a way that perpetuates Bakhtin's distinction. He states: 'C'est pour ça que j'ai abandonné la poésie, parce que je n'y ai pas trouvé, comme dans le roman, le moyen de **faire entendre des voix multiples**, de plonger dans des logiques sociales, de m'y "engager" techniquement' [That's why I abandoned poetry, because I didn't find in it, as I did in the novel, the means to **make multiple voices heard**, to dive into social logics, to 'commit' myself technically].[65] In a turn of phrase that echoes Bakhtin's, Cadiot writes, 'La poésie est parole du poète, et même s'il n'y a pas un mot de lui dans le poème, reste l'acte conceptuel toujours en surplomb: la poésie ne permet pas une parole vraiment démultipliée; c'est sa beauté et sa spécificité' [Poetry is the poet's speech, and even if there isn't a single word of his in the poem, the conceptual act still hangs over it: poetry does not allow a truly multiplied speech; that is its beauty and its specificity].[66] Elsewhere, he states:

> Au fond, moi je préfère la poésie. Simplement, la part concrète de poésie que je peux m'autoriser diminue à chaque livre. J'ai de moins en moins le droit de faire de la poésie parce que la poésie comme chacun le sait est inadmissible. Je le pense vraiment.[67]
>
> [Fundamentally, I prefer poetry. Only the actual portion of poetry that I can allow myself decreases with every book. I have less and less right to create poetry because poetry, as everyone knows, is inadmissible. I truly believe that.]

If nothing else, these assertions are confusing: it is not clear how *L'Art poétic'* is more Cadiot's own 'parole' than *Futur, ancien, fugitif*, as a generically hybrid text, or *Un mage en été*, as a novel. As the preceding discussion of *L'Art poétic'*, *Futur, ancien, fugitif*, and Cadiot's musical compositions has suggested, the same forms, devices, and themes reappear in various ways throughout these different genres and mediums. While certain distinctions might be made between *L'Art poétic'* and *Futur, ancien, fugitif*, with regard to character, narrative, or mode of composition for example, it is hard to identify what separates them in terms of voice or discourse, despite Cadiot's insistence that they are generically distinct, and that poetic and novelistic discourse are markedly different. Cadiot's claim prompts a number of further questions: given the poet's description of *Futur, ancien, fugitif* as 'un roman par poèmes', what are the implications for poetic voice in this liminal text? Would Cadiot envisage an interim form of discourse, poised between poetic and novelistic, some kind of hybrid of the two? Is monologic discourse something that can even exist in degrees? Or, following Bakhtin's analysis, is monologic/dialogic discourse a binary that separates texts into two distinct camps?

I choose ultimately to disregard Cadiot's own analysis of a prose-poetry distinction, as I do not believe the difference is borne out in his work itself. It appears that Cadiot, despite his nuanced exploration of poetry elsewhere, is using a narrow definition of poetry as, essentially, lyric poetry, which is staking out the boundaries in a more conservative way than I intend to here. Instead, I would argue that all of his poetic endeavours (*L'Art poétic'*, *Futur, ancien, fugitif*, and the three albums discussed above) are examples of a Deleuzian 'littérature mineure', subverting an ideological mother tongue in their heteroglottic linguistic assemblages. The use of cut-up and sampling, which facilitates a polyphonous quality to his work, is engaged in a subversive act of undoing and destabilising the domination of the major language, in all its various forms. Cadiot himself touches on this idea, describing the potential tyranny of certain types of language:

> J'ai envie de confronter plusieurs régimes de parole: style direct oppressé contre indirect oppresseur, style actif contre parlé inactif, protocole intérieur contre monologue extérieur agressif, etc. [...] Le tyran, c'est la parole en excès, la parole ininterrompue, atrocement autonome (ça représente, si on veut que tout fasse sens, le mauvais côté de la littérature, le caractère monomaniaque, grenouille devenue bœuf, aussi tyrannique que son contraire poétique: l'aphorisme à prétention philosophique). En anglais, on dit un *close talker*: celui qui vous perfuse sa parole pendant un dîner, qui vous serre le bras en vous psalmodiant à l'oreille. [...] J'écris pour traiter ce flux. Pas pour l'interrompre, mais pour l'inverser, pour le dé-tyranniser. Écrire des livres, c'est dé-tyranniser sa propre parole.[68]

> [I want to compare several regimes of speech: oppressed direct style against oppressor indirect, active style against inactive speech, interior protocol against aggressive exterior monologue, etc. [...] The tyrant is excessive speech, atrociously autonomous, uninterrupted speech (which represents, if we want everything to make sense, the negative side of literature, the monomaniac character, the frog that's turned into an ox, as tyrannical as its poetic counterpart: the aphorism that purports to be philosophical). In English, they say a *close talker*: someone who drip-feeds you their speech over dinner, who grips your arm while droning on in your ear. [...] I write to process this influx. Not to stem it, but to counteract it, to de-tyrannise it. Writing books is de-tyrannising your own speech.]

Any type of language that dominates or oppresses, that claims to be the only legitimate form, suppressing other variants in turn, is dangerous, particularly when it passes unchallenged and starts to look like a 'natural', singular language. This tyrannical monologism of the 'langue majeure' will take various forms. The most immediate example is that of major national languages in periods of political change, for example in the imposition of standard French in the period after the French Revolution, where regional languages were largely eradicated, either directly or indirectly, through various power structures: national education, military conscription, etc. As we have seen, there are echoes of this very concrete example of major-minor language power struggles in Cadiot's work, particularly in his references to Welche, Breton, and Hualapai. However, the various possible forms of a major language are multiple, constantly proliferating and forever in flux. The monoglottic voice of lyrical poetry becomes a form of 'langue majeure' to be dismantled into polyphonous, heteroglottic collages. The regime of meaning, of the signified, is destabilised by an emphasis on the signifier, on the materiality of language — its shapes and sounds and rhythms. Human language is undercut with animal communication, adult speech with child babbling, grammar with agrammaticality, and 'healthy' forms of linguistic communication are subverted by Robinson's disordered, schizophrenic speech. The major language of poetry, as a traditionally written, printed, and published form, is challenged by the relocation of poetry from the written page to the recording studio.

Dictionaries and Grammars

One of the most pervasive types of major language found in Cadiot's work appears in the form of linguistic reference works, dictionaries, phrase books, and grammar manuals. As described above, Cadiot first began *L'Art poétic'* after he stumbled across Dubois's *Grammaire générative* and witnessed the nascent energy of the semantically hollow examples. The cut-ups in *L'Art poétic'* are not just French grammars, but also Latin primers and English textbooks, dictionary entries, and phrase books. Written under the influence of Georges Perec, *Futur, ancien, fugitif* is also concerned with glossaries, indexes, encyclopaedias, and manuals.[69] On the back cover, *Futur, ancien, fugitif* is described as a survival manual: 'Ce livre contient: la liste complète de ce qu'il faut faire en cas d'exil. Des conseils précis pour la fabrication d'objets simples à réaliser soi-même. [...] Un manuel raisonné d'exercices poétiques. [...] Une méthode de dialogue à une voix' [This book contains: the complete list of what should be done in case of exile. Precise advice for manufacturing objects that are easy to make yourself. [...] A comprehensive manual of poetic exercises. [...] A manual for dialogue using just one voice]. Cadiot is, of course, not the first to use linguistic reference works in his writing. In *Eau sur eau* (1997), Christophe Lamiot explores the use of dictionaries in the works of Mallarmé, Flaubert, Bataille, Michaux, Leiris, and Ponge.[70] More recent examples that we might add to this list are Georges Perec, Bernard Heidsieck, and a number of Oulipian texts that experiment with dictionary-based constraints. I want to briefly consider just two of these examples, to highlight some of the similarities to Cadiot's project.

Bernard Heidsieck's *Derviche/Le Robert* (2004) uses a dictionary-based compositional constraint: it is a 'poème sonore', a sound poem made up of twenty-six sections, one for each letter of the alphabet.[71] Each section uses the first ten unfamiliar or obscure words found in the given letter's corresponding section of *Le Robert*: for example, section 'K' begins with the words *kacha, kadsura, kaempferie*. These rare and abstruse words are then incorporated into refrains of phatic language and empty exclamations, similar to those found in Cadiot's own work: 'OH! ... Oh! là! là! [...] OH NON! .... NON! ... non! ... Ce n'est pas possible! ... Ça n'aurait pas pu être cela... ! ... C'est évident!'. Through the juxtaposition of dictionary words and phatic formulae, two different but equivalent forms, Heidsieck's intention was to construct an *abécédaire* made out of 'matériau vide de sens' [meaningless material], and in so doing, to explore the materiality and musicality of these linguistic signifiers freed from their usual referential function.[72] Heidsieck foregrounds the dictionary with its own implicit set of linguistic ideologies (e.g. words as principally referential, fixed, and definable) and simultaneously undermines those ideologies with a set of opposing conceptions of language (e.g. language as a more fluid system of sound, sign, and gesture, resistant to any attempt to pin it down). A second example that resonates with Cadiot's work is Leiris's *Glossaire, j'y serre mes gloses* [Glossary: My Glosses' Ossuary] (1939) which subverts the usual function of the glossary, which is to provide definitions for rare and specialised terms. Leiris's 'glossaire' dismisses etymology and institutionalised meaning, and emphasises the idiolectal and personal, rather than the objective and universal. We note, for example, the first-person pronoun in the French title — the *je* would not usually be present in a dictionary or glossary, except for in illustrative examples. Rather than attempting to pin it down, Leiris's glossary plays with language; this wordplay is frequently multilingual, thus not respecting the usual institutionalised boundaries between different national languages. Likewise, his glossary refuses the traditional boundary between the literary and the pictoral, including calligrams in amongst its definitions.

In *Futur, ancien, fugitif*, Cadiot also experiments with the glossary, elaborating a three-page alphabetical list of abbreviations used in the book, alongside expanded definitions of these terms. The very status of this list, which is part way between a glossary and a list of abbreviated terms, represents one initial way in which it serves to undermine the form. The position of the list in the middle of the book rather than at the end or the beginning is a further subversion of the formatting conventions of the glossary, and its function as an easily locatable reference tool. Like that of Leiris, Cadiot's glossary is distinctly personal and full of idiosyncrasies: 'D.R.' stands for '*Dossier Robinson*', 'D.T.' for '*Disparition Totale*' [total disappearance] (*FAF*, 147). Cadiot extends this to its extreme with protracted abbreviations such as 'L.B.V.D.M.E.': '*Le But Ultime De Mes Efforts*' [the ultimate goal of my efforts] or the quasi-acronymic 'M.S.R.': '*Members are Requested to keep Silence in this Room*' (148). The inclusion on the list of 'H.' for '*Hapax*' might be read as a metapoetic comment on the singular, idiosyncratic words and phrases included in his glossary. The singularity of the hapax legomenon represents the opposite pole to the shared, universality of language embodied in a conventional glossary. Like Leiris's, this glossary of terms is also multilingual, fusing Latin, French, and English. The list is wholly unsystematic: certain conventional abbreviations appear, '*Ante Meridiem*', '*Ante Christum*', alongside conventional abbreviations with unexpected interpretations: 'B.D.' is not *bande dessinée* as we might expect, but '*Bachelor of divinity. Exilé*' (147). Many of the items on the list are pivotal terms in *Futur, ancien, fugitif* ('disparition totale', 'zero-sum'), which might lead us to interpret the glossary as a unique 'key to reading', a tool kit for unpacking the various motifs at work in the book. The inclusion of the term 'X' could be read as a playful gesture towards an 'X marks the spot' on a treasure map that guides the reader in their navigation of Robinson's island. However, these key terms are interspersed with the most mundane and irrelevant ones too: 'P.S.' ('*Post-scriptum*'), 'D. Incert.' ('*Date Incertaine*'), which quickly undermines the possibility that this glossary is a comprehensive guide to decoding the text. One by one, the various conventions of the glossary are subverted; Cadiot's text is unsystematic, illogical, incomplete, idiosyncratic, and the glossary entries are often more confusing than they are enlightening. Like Leiris's *Glossaire*, Cadiot's list of abbreviations is a very clear example of a major mode dismantled from the inside, picked apart, and put back together in a strange lopsided assemblage that at once resembles the original model, and yet is constituted precisely by its difference.

In *L'Art poétic'*, Cadiot's use of linguistic reference works serves a number of purposes. Firstly, as previously discussed, the grammar book cut-ups place emphasis on the surface of language, on the materiality of its signs, which are decomposed, broken down into phonemes, syllables, parts of speech, grammatical constructions, and so on. This systematic decomposition of language is announced in the epigraph to *L'Art poétic'* where, in an allusion to Gutenberg and printing, a short passage describes how the letters of the alphabet would be engraved one by one onto a separate piece of metal or wood. From the outset, the normally invisible process of printing and publication is rendered visible; the reader is compelled to engage with the materiality of the book and of language itself. There is also in this image of language deconstructed into the twenty-six letters of the alphabet, a further significance for a text comprised of cut-ups. Just as all language is composed from a small number of basic orthographic or phonological building blocks, so too all literature is composed of a finite set of possible words and phrases, all of which will have been found before, in different combinations, in previous literary and non-literary texts. We are reminded of Barthes's evocation in 'La Mort de l'auteur' [The Death of the Author] of an 'immense dictionnaire', with each individual literary text being 'un tissu de citations, issues des mille foyers de la culture' [a fabric of quotations, resulting from a thousand sources of culture].[73] The cut-up text represents an extreme extension of this idea, a very literal interpretation of the text as a 'tissu de citations', but it is also a reminder that all literature operates on the same basic principle of iteration, as Burroughs suggests when he observes, 'What is any writing but a cut-up?'[74] The cut-up, with its focus on assembling an original whole from a set of unoriginal composite parts, presents broader reflections on the iterative and finite nature of the language system as a whole. The significance of dictionaries in Cadiot's poetry might also be read as a gesture towards this Barthesian notion of the vast 'dictionnaire' of literature, or indeed of the linguistic system *in toto*. Elsewhere, in *Le Degré zéro de l'écriture*, Barthes offers a further reflection on the relationship between literature and linguistic reference works. In an essay entitled 'Y a-t-il une écriture poétique?' [Is There Any Poetic Writing?], he draws a parallel between the operation of language in modern poetry and the operation of language in dictionaries:

> Ainsi sous chaque Mot de la poésie moderne gît une sorte de géologie existentielle, où se rassemble le contenu total du Nom, et non plus son contenu électif comme dans la prose et dans la poésie classique. Le Mot n'est plus dirigé *à l'avance* par l'intention générale d'un discours socialisé; le consommateur de poésie, privé du guide des rapports sélectifs, débouche sur le Mot, frontalement, et le reçoit comme une quantité absolue, accompagnée de tous ses possibles. Le Mot est ici encyclopédique, il contient simultanément toutes les acceptions parmi lesquelles un discours relationnel lui aurait imposé de choisir. Il accomplit donc un état qui n'est possible que dans le dictionnaire ou dans la poésie, là où le nom peut vivre privé de son article, amené à une sorte d'état zéro, gros à la fois de toutes les spécifications passées et futures.
>
> [Thus under each Word in modern poetry there lies a sort of existential geology, in which is gathered the total content of the Name, instead of a chosen content as in classical prose and poetry. The Word is no longer guided *in advance* by the general intention of a socialized discourse; the consumer of poetry, deprived of

the guide of selective connections, encounters the Word frontally, and receives it as an absolute quantity, accompanied by all its possible associations. The Word, here, is encyclopaedic, it contains simultaneously all the acceptations from which a relational discourse might have required it to choose. It therefore achieves a state which is possible only in the dictionary or in poetry — places where the noun can live without its article — and is reduced to a sort of zero degree, pregnant with all past and future specifications.][75]

Despite the differences between the 'major' and 'minor' dimensions of poetic language and language in dictionaries and encyclopaedias, here Barthes offers us a surprising parallel. In both instances, language is stripped of its usual pragmatic force; meaning is not selected or narrowed down by the context of the utterance, and thus, is freed from its habitual social function. To use Barthes's terms, this form of discourse is: 'un discours [...] sans prévision ni permanence d'intention et par là si opposé à la fonction sociale du langage' [a discourse [...] without foresight or stability of intention, and thereby so opposed to the social function of language].[76] In poetry, as in the dictionary, language is, to a certain degree, in a paradoxically 'context-less' context, with each word thus activating and suspending the plurality of possible meanings and interpretations it contains. This same property of multiplicity, the suspension of multiple variants as opposed to the selection of just one, is what would render poetry particularly hospitable to the proliferation of variation that is constitutive of Deleuze and Guattari's minor literature. Yet reference works are the institutional tools of a Deleuzo-Guattarian major language in their strict demarcation of prescribed linguistic norms. In any case, the parallel is an interesting one, and particularly apparent in Cadiot's *L'Art poétic*. Coupling the lack of sustained narrative, character development, or a singular lyric *je* with the poetic *mise en page* and the isolation of words and phrases into disjointed fragments, the effect of this suspension and plurality is exaggerated. The parallels between the two forms are nowhere more apparent than in the section 'Delenda est Carthargo' [Carthage Must Be Destroyed], where cut-ups from Latin dictionary entries, retaining the conventional formatting of the original, resemble the typographical experiments of a post-Mallarméan lineage of modern poetry. While attention is drawn to certain typographical similarities, and to certain parallels in the semantic function of words, the comparison also invites us to explore their differences.

Indeed, throughout *L'Art poétic*, Cadiot draws attention to the rule-governed properties of linguistic reference works, not only in their own conventions (of formatting etc.), but also in the projection of those rules onto the classification and organisation of language itself. As Lia Kurts points out, Cadiot's selection of the most semantically hollow grammar book examples emphasises, first and foremost, the 'acte de transmission de compétences grammaticales', foregrounding the conventions of grammatical instruction. The elaborate metalanguage of linguistic reference works takes a prominent position, often disrupting the text that it describes: 'Les feuilles [no, dér. et verbe comp.] Les feuilles deviennent jaunes jaunes [adj. et verbe dér.] et rouges [nom, adj. et verbe dér.] rouges et tombent et tombent une à une' [The leaves [noun and verb complement] The leaves become yellow yellow [adj. and linking verb and red [noun, adj. complement and linking verb] red and falling and falling and falling one by one] (*AP1*, 220; *AP2*, 208). By retaining the typography and formatting of their original sources, the cut-ups highlight the highly contrived formal conventions of reference works, such as the use of bold and italic fonts, square brackets, and line arrangements in the dictionary entries in the section 'Delenda est Carthargo'. Throughout the text a number of different conventions of linguistic reference works are used: symbols marking metrical feet such as dactyls and spondees (*AP1*, 85), syllabic counts marked by superscript numbers (*AP1*, 138), phonetic transcription in square brackets, written in the International Phonetic Alphabet (IPA) (*AP1*, 59), arrows marking grammatical transformations or relationships between clausal constituents (*AP1*, 98). Cadiot presents the language of dictionaries and grammars as the ultimate exemplars of what Deleuze and Guattari would analyse as the territorialising, norming axis of the major language. Indeed, Cadiot's foregrounding of the elaborate metalinguistic systems of grammatical description resonates with Deleuze and Guattari's discussion of linguistics as a discipline in *Mille plateaux*. For Deleuze and Guattari, the desire in linguistics to systematise and to find standards and universals (grammatical, phonological, semantic, etc.) makes it, ultimately, an 'institution majeure'. They write: 'La linguistique en général n'a pas encore quitté une espèce de mode majeur, une sorte d'échelle diatonique, un étrange goût pour les dominantes, les constantes et les universaux' [Linguistics in general is still in a kind of major mode, still has a sort of diatonic scale and a strange taste for dominants, constants, and universals] (*MP*, 123; *ATP*, 113). To illustrate this notion with one particular example, the development of the IPA, which is found in *L'Art poétic'* and *Futur, ancien, fugitif*, and used in most dictionaries, was an attempt to create a universal system that encapsulates all possible phonologies of all world languages. At first glance this might seem like a useful, productive exercise; however, Deleuze and Guattari might argue that this is a necessarily reductive, 'territorialising' task which suppresses variation in order to impose a set of standards. Such an analysis gains credibility when one considers two key aspects of the IPA: i) the symbols it uses are predominantly Western, based on the Roman and Greek alphabets, which in itself represents a form of dominance whereby the institutions that created the IPA (French and English linguists) superimposed their own system on others (e.g. the vast number of world languages that have no written script, or languages that use syllabic or logographic writing systems); ii) the reality of sub-national, regional, and inter-personal variation on a phonetic level — where pronunciation can vary according to geographic location, socioeconomic group, and as many variables as there are speakers of a given language — is necessarily too complex to fit neatly into a small number of discrete phonological units. An international phonetic alphabet will, by definition, be unable to account for the variation and complexity of communication in a system that is both concise and usable, without being overly reductive. Following Deleuze and Guattari's analysis in 'Postulats de la linguistique', the metalanguage of linguistic reference works found in Cadiot's writing might be read as both a tool and a symbol of the broader 'institutions majeures' (of prescriptive grammar, of linguistics, etc.) that they were conceived by. In Cadiot's texts they operate as constant, concrete reminders of the major language in action.

Closely linked to this, a further pervasive marker of the major language in *L'Art poétic'* is prescriptive grammar, remaining in its residual form in the reworked cut-ups from grammar books and manuals. By using cut-ups from grammar books, by rendering them agrammatical in their novel arrangement in the text, Cadiot initiates a process of deterritorialisation. His reworkings of the cut-ups destabilise one of the most territorialising forms of language, thus highlighting both the centripetal force of grammar and centrifugal force of agrammaticality precisely through their polarisation. The following passage from *L'Art poétic'* demonstrates these oscillating processes:

>A *white-sailed* ship
>faire beau, venter un peu
>   — Elles (maigrir) — Il (tomber)
>nuit... belle
>   [And ¹every²one did ³swink [⁴silence]
>   And ⁵every⁶one did ⁷sweat [⁸silence]
>   (Dans la plaine), (les détonations)
>[...]
>   He passed his hand ... his eyes
>L'œil ... protégé par les paupières ... par les cils
>many years (*to go*) by, since those days; and he (*to forget*) how
>he (*to feel*) then [...]
>   ... sirènes; ... cabines; ... canots.
>   (*AP1*, 135–36)
>
>[A *white-sailed* ship
>to make beautiful, a little breezy
>   — They (to get thinner) — It (to fall)
>night... beautiful
>   And ¹every²one did ³swink [⁴silence]
>   And ⁵every⁶one did ⁷sweat [⁸silence]
>   (On the plain), (explosions)
>[...]
>   He passed his hand ... his eyes
>The eye ... protected by the eyelids ... by the lashes
>many years (*to go*) by, since those days; and he (*to forget*) how
>he (*to feel*) then [...]
>   ... sirens; ... cabins; ... rowboats.] (*AP2*, 121–22)

The unconjugated, parenthetical verbs ('Elles (maigrir)') and 'fill in the blank' ellipses ('les paupières ... par les cils') alert the reader to the grammar book origins of the cut-up phrases. In the transplanted fragments, language is broken down into its component parts; grammatical structure and syntactic categories are isolated in bracketed verbs '(maigrir)', '(tomber)', italicised adjectives '*white-sailed* ship', absent articles '... sirènes; ...cabines; ... canots', and missing prepositions 'He passed his hand ... his eyes'. The reader's attention is drawn to the aspects of speech and writing that usually pass unnoticed: its orthography (the 'correct' spelling for the homophones *est* and *et*), its syllabic structure and rhythmic properties ('And ¹every²one did ³swink [⁴silence]'), and its morphosyntax ('maigrir' giving *maigrissent*, 'to go' giving 'went').

The grammar book cut-ups evoke a particularly prescriptive approach to language, one that takes language as a fundamentally rule-governed system, and one that assumes that behind the given grammar exercise ('fill in the blanks', 'conjugate the verb') is a right or wrong answer.

In the passage, and throughout *L'Art poétic'*, Cadiot exploits a tension between the major, territorialising dimension of the original grammatical cut-ups, and their deterritorialisation within the poem. We find both the residual *grammaticalité* of the exercise book cut-ups, and the subsequent *agrammaticalité* — the discontinuous syntax, anacoluthons, and grammatically 'incorrect' forms — produced by their assemblage. For example, when re-analysed in the poem, the phrase 'many years (*to go*) by, since those days' is simply 'wrong', the verb is left unconjugated and the normal reading process is disrupted. The overall effect of this passage (and of *L'Art poétic'* as a whole) is one of dysfluency and rhythmic disruption. The reader is impeded by the discontinuous syntax of the transplanted cut-ups and the overriding sense of the text's 'expression atypique' (*MP*, 125): its lack of coherent narrative, the unclear relationship between one constituent of the passage and the next, its suspension of reference, and its subversion of traditional lyric voice.

The cut-up lends itself particularly well to Deleuze and Guattari's conception of deterritorialisation, as it involves a very literal displacement or relocation of language from its original context into the novel space of the poem. This displacement prompts a re-examination of the source information, for example the ideologies and assumptions about language that lie behind the linguistic reference works (that grammar has absolute rules that are embodied in the standard variant, that words have fixed meanings or essences that are identical for all speakers of a given language, and so on). Alongside dictionaries and grammars, a significant number of the cut-ups in Cadiot's work come from non-linguistic reference works: encyclopaedias, science manuals, and educational textbooks. In these instances, there is a similar questioning of the implicit assumptions that lie behind discourses of knowledge and pedagogical systems based on absolute truths, as well as an examination of the conventions of representation within sciences and other such disciplines. Thus, in *L'Art poétic'* we find fragments of taxonomies and classification systems that might come from an encyclopaedia or an introductory zoological textbook: 'BIRDS | SNAKES | FISH | INSECTS' (*AP1*, 133). In *Futur, ancien, fugitif*, many of the fragments washed ashore with Robinson are from manuals and almanacs: one passage enumerates the three types of heraldic figures (*FAF*, 31), another appears to be a description from an old science textbook about vegetation and water consumption (57). One prevalent form of instruction manual in *Futur, ancien, fugitif* is the etiquette handbook:

> 1. Ne touchez pas vos couverts inutilement.
> 2. Laissez une main au moins posée sur vos genoux.
> 3. Ne vous balancez pas en avant en arrière.
> 4. Ne mangez pas tout ce que vous avez dans l'assiette.
> 5. Ne vous réservez jamais même si on vous le propose.
> 6. Ne parlez d'aucun sujet qui puisse provoquer des désaccords.
> 7. Ne pelez pas les poires sans fourchette. (*FAF*, 29)

[1. Do not touch your cutlery needlessly. | 2. Leave at least one hand resting on your lap. | 3. Do not rock back and forth. | 4. Do not eat everything on your plate. | 5. Never have second helpings even if you are invited to. | 6. Do not talk about any subject that might provoke disagreement. | 7. Do not peel pears without a fork.]

The fact that Robinson is stranded on an island, estranged from society, permits a distance that highlights the arbitrary and highly codified nature of social rituals. In this example, table manners appear as an illustration of a major institution at its most ridiculous. Throughout Cadiot's œuvre, a wide range of established systems of codes are undermined, the most obvious being literary authority. As Farah suggests, Cadiot's writing involves 'un pillage désinvolte de la tradition littéraire' [a nonchalant pillaging of literary tradition], where the conventions that support and reinforce the idea of a 'canon' are subtly subverted.[77] *L'Art poétic'* makes reference to many canonical literary figures: Ovid, Shakespeare, Hugo, and Proust, to name a few. However, following in the lineage of Lautréamont in *Poésies*, Cadiot undermines these literary authorities, as well as the conventional use of citations and epigraphs, by choosing the most clichéd or banal quotations from their works. Thus Blake's '*Tiger! Tiger! burning bright*' (*AP1*, 134) and Ovid's 'O lente, lente currite noctis equi' (142) appear in the text as isolated passages, without commentary or apparent function, gesturing towards the use of citation for the sake of citation, or the recourse to a higher authority in order to lend weight to a given text. In the context of the pedagogical cut-ups in *L'Art poétic'*, these citations recall the schoolchild trotting out the famous lines of canonical poets in a monotonous rhythm, not in an act of engagement with the words themselves, but as a form of memory exercise. Likewise, prosaic quotations, such as 'Serait-il trop tard pour que je revienne chez vous? (PROUST)' [Is it too late for me to come back to you?] (*AP1*, 95; *AP2*, 81), are wrenched from their original contexts and incorporated into the text with no further expansion, left as seemingly banal and insignificant citations. Elsewhere in *L'Art poétic'*, as the title of the collection would suggest, the literary greats offer nothing more than poetic clichés: 'La rivière était toute couverte de plis d'argent (V. HUGO)' [The surface of the river was completely folded silver] (143; 129), 'Grande pour tous les êtres est la tristesse du soir (MICHELET)' [The sadness of evening is equally grand for all] (211; 199). This forms part of a systemic practice throughout Cadiot's work, whereby authority — be it linguistic, scientific, social, or literary — is called into question. This is, of course, a characteristic feature of a work of 'littérature mineure', as well as a constitutive aspect of what makes Cadiot's writing parodic.

Parody

Cadiot is often heralded as a funny writer. Hocquard, like many others, celebrates the comic aspect of Cadiot's œuvre, describing how it constitutes a break from a dominant strain of contemporary French literature that is 'of a more serious kind, of a graver nature'.[78] The centrality of parody in Cadiot's work no doubt contributes to this. As touched on above, the poet frequently ridicules social rituals and linguistic conventions: his texts repeat 'formules de politesse' in frenzied *ritournelles*, so much so that their excess morphs them into grotesque, absurd exaggerations. As Prigent points out, the title itself of *L'Art poétic'* is 'parodique', reworking the conventional literary formula of an *ars poetica*, evoking Horace, Boileau's *L'Art poétique*, and Queneau's *Pour un art poétique*, among others.[79] The title critiques some of the literary pretensions that lie behind the quest to outline a definitive art of poetry, while also foregrounding the notion of the literary or stylistic 'tic' — a compulsive and subconscious type of behaviour or language use, explored earlier by Lautréamont. As Prigent suggests, the title of the collection announces 'tout un programme' [an entire programme], whereby literary tics and conventions are one by one subverted and parodied.[80] In the previous section, we saw how Cadiot exploits the redundant use of citation and epigraphs from certain literary greats; elsewhere a whole range of features of 'high literature' are gently mocked. The conventions of plot development, literary themes, and poem titles are undermined in *L'Art poétic'*: the headings 'Le Départ' [Departure] (*AP1*, 33), 'La Poursuite' [Pursuit] (31), 'L'Amour' [Love] (30), 'Le Regret' [Regret] (28) do not follow any conventional order, and do not correspond whatsoever with the content of the passages that they precede. The section 'Voyages anciens' [Past Travels] introduces a pastiche of travel literature that *Futur, ancien, fugitif* later extends. In both texts, certain aspects of Romantic lyricism are subverted. For example, in *Futur, ancien, fugitif*, the slight variation on Lamartine's canonical line from 'Le Lac', 'O *tempssuspendtonvoletvousheurespropices* | [piano]' [O *timesuspendyourflightandyouhappyhours* | [piano]] (*FAF*, 106), transforms the original: the elision of the words, so that the whole phrase is no longer parsed into units of individual meaning, but rather comes to symbolise one single thing — a clichéd marker of Romantic poetry, is reinforced by the tongue-in-cheek stage instructions, the evocation of a muted musical accompaniment.

In an essay on *Futur, ancien, fugitif*, Prigent evokes the pervasively parodic tone of Cadiot's writing, with its 'pastiches divers, rumination d'idiolectes insignifiants, gnomisme drolatiquement nul (un peu comme chez Beckett), refrains idiots, mime de la bêtise du parler convivial' [diverse pastiches, rumination in trivial idiolects, comically bad pithy sayings (a bit like in Beckett's work), idiotic refrains, mimicry of the silliness of congenial speech].[81] Following this line of thought, he goes on to describe *Futur, ancien, fugitif* as:

> Moins un roman que la doublure d'un roman [...]; moins un récit pour de vrai qu'un récit 'pour rire'; [...] moins un texte qu'un évitement du texte, un retrait au texte, un pas de texte, un texte zéro, un texte marqué, à la clausule, d'un 'Zéro-sum'.[82]
>
> [Less a novel than the understudy of a novel [...]; less a 'for real' story than a 'for laughs' story; [...] less a text than the evasion of a text, a no-text, a zero-text, a text marked, by way of a coda, with a 'zero-sum'.]

The idea of the text as a negative or negating counterpart, defined by its deviation from a generically-exemplary hypotext, appears to me a useful way to conceptualise Cadiot's work as a whole. Extending Prigent's analysis further, I would argue that the parodic dimension of Cadiot's writing exists not only in the narrower sense (intermittent pastiches of particular literary forms, mocking of specific codes, etc.) but also in the broader sense that it engages with and revises the wider conventions of pre-existing genres. In *L'Art poétic'*, *Futur, ancien, fugitif*, and in his albums with Burger, Cadiot stages an internal and often implicit dialogue between the work itself — the song, the poem, or the text — and the whole host of generic forms that it derives from: variously, lyric poetry, the 'Robinsonnade', the adventure novel, sound poetry, the traditional French *chanson*, and so on. These genres or forms are multiple, but of particular interest for this chapter is how his work revises an established 'major' mode of poetry. This takes us back to a line of argument outlined in Chapter 1, where I asked whether, following Bakhtin's analysis of genre, we might see certain forms of contemporary poetry as a parodic-travestying counterpart to a major genre. In each of Cadiot's poetic projects, I think we find precisely this — an internally dialogistic form that parodies the conventions of the major genre.

Again, following Bakhtin's account, any parodic-travestying form will involve heteroglossia, which breaks the illusion of the direct word. As already discussed, heteroglossia is a defining feature of Cadiot's work. Various linguistic forms are not only juxtaposed, but parodied, as Anna Boschetti suggests in her analysis of *Futur, ancien, fugitif*:

> Le récit de Robinson est une traversée de formes et de codes, évoqués par des échantillons parodiques [...]. Ce jeu avec les genres s'inscrit dans la même logique, fondée sur le choc des contraires. Ainsi, loin de confondre les codes, en brouillant les différences, le texte tend à accentuer les écarts, pour entretenir la tension, qui est une caractéristique fondamentale de la poésie. La modernité remplace la tension traditionnelle entre le mètre et la syntaxe par la tension entre les matériaux, entre les codes.[83]

> [Robinson's story is a crossing of forms and codes, conjured by parodic samples [...]. This generic play abides by the same logic, based on the clash of opposites. So, far from conflating the codes by blurring the differences, the text tends to accentuate the gaps, to sustain the tension that is a fundamental characteristic of poetry. Modernity replaces the traditional tension between metre and syntax with a tension between materials, between codes.]

Prigent also analyses this feature of *Futur, ancien, fugitif*, evoking how it situates Cadiot's work in a particular literary tradition:

> En bref, rien n'est assignable (à un genre, à un style): c'est un patchwork disparate, un dialogue de formes décousues qui décline, ravageur et moqueur, dans l'opacité narrative et se soustrait à toute prise cimentée des intentions (fables et morale). Si cela relève d'une tradition, c'est celle de la *satire* (le pot-pourri critique et burlesque de la littérature 'carnivalesque': Rabelais, Sterne, Gadda — mais blanchis — allégés par l'ironie et le ressassement rêveusement radoté façon Gertrude Stein).[84]

> [In short, nothing is attributable (to a genre or a style): it's a disparate patchwork, a dialogue of disjointed forms that unfolds, scathing and mocking, in the narrative opacity and avoids being tethered to any (moral or allegorical) agenda. If it belongs to any tradition then it would be *satire* (the burlesque,

critical medley of 'carnivalesque' literature: Rabelais, Sterne, Gadda — but whitewashed — lightened by irony and dreamily rambling repetitions à la Gertrude Stein.]

Prigent's image of 'un patchwork disparate' resonates with the key image in 'La Mécanique lyrique' of the poem as a monster composed from various linguistic *greffes* and different literary forms and styles. It also evokes Barthes's analysis of the text as a 'tissu de citations', 'un espace à dimensions multiples, où se marient et se contestent des écritures variées' [a multidimensional space in which various forms of writing blend and clash].[85] Cadiot's poetry might be read as a grotesque or carnivalesque exaggeration of literature's pre-existing status as an immense fabric composed of heterogeneous threads. Prigent describes here how the patchwork of disparate forms inscribes Cadiot's work in a lineage that draws on satire and the 'carnivalesque'. The terms *pastiche* and *parodique*, and more specifically *burlesque* and *carnivalesque*, are often used by critics discussing Cadiot's work.[86] As outlined in Chapter 1, Bakhtin uses the term 'parodic-travestying forms' to capture the wide variety of parodic forms that co-exist with major genres, but elsewhere he develops more specific analyses, for example of the carnivalesque.[87] As in his exploration of novelistic discourse, Bakhtin traces the development of the carnivalesque via its origins in particular historical events: street carnivals and public feast days in Medieval Europe. During these carnivals, laughter and subversion of the major institutions of the day (the Church, the state, etc.) were permitted, and even ritualised. This transgressive mode of the carnival soon found its way into literature, and although the events themselves petered out, the carnivalesque quality of certain forms of literature remained. Where carnivalesque literature uses humour, satire, and the excess and exaggeration of the grotesque to destabilise and undermine power structures, we see a parallel with certain forms of minor literature, notably in their deterritorialising of major modes from within the major mode itself. Central to both is the idea of repetition and difference: the repeating of the major refrain, but repeated or performed differently.

Significantly, in Bakhtin's analysis of both the carnivalesque and the parodic-travestying genres that precede and pave the way for the development of novelistic discourse, is the idea that the laughter they provoke is also a moment of revelation — an unveiling of the illusions behind monoglottic, single genres. Bakhtin writes:

> Parodic-travestying literature introduces the permanent corrective of laughter, of a critique on the one-sided seriousness of the lofty direct word, the corrective of reality that is always richer, more fundamental and most importantly *too contradictory and heteroglot* to be fit into a high and straightforward genre. (*DI*, 55)

He suggests that 'all these diverse parodic-travestying forms constituted, as it were, a special extra-generic or inter-generic world' (*DI*, 59) and goes on to describe 'an immense novel, multi-generic, multi-styled, mercilessly critical, soberly mocking, reflecting in all its fullness, the heteroglossia and multiple voices of a given culture, people and epoch' (*DI*, 60). Although Bakhtin's own analysis is concerned ultimately with mapping the prehistory and defining the constitutive features of the novel, what is significant for the present discussion is that he envisages a form of inter- or extra-generic writing project, a heteroglottic, hybrid text that is more apt to represent the intrinsic variation of language and life. These notions of 'parodic-travestying genres', the 'carnivalesque', and the 'multi-generic, multi-styled' text map onto Deleuze and Guattari's reflections on minor and major forms of literature, and their relationships to variation and norms in language and reality. Indeed, there are certain parallels to be drawn between the 'permanent corrective of laughter' in Bakhtin's analysis, and the stutter in Deleuze and Guattari's account: both repetitious, compulsive, paralinguistic gestures that disrupt the flow of language. Both are deterritorialising, breaking the illusions, and destabilising the operation of a major mode or genre.

'L'Incertitude générique'

This final section will draw together some of the threads of the preceding analysis by exploring what Rabaté calls the 'incertitude générique' [generic uncertainty] of Cadiot's writing and considering how this links into the discussion of minor literature set out hitherto.[88] The heteroglottic, hybrid, and often parodic nature of Cadiot's work makes it unsurprisingly resistant to sitting within a single, major genre. The aspects of his *œuvre* considered in this chapter all reside, in various ways, at the convergence of different mediums and traditional genres — poetry, the novel, text, performance, music, and so on. As already noted, *L'Art poétic'* is the only text that Cadiot himself designates as a straightforward work of poetry, yet from the off, the task was precisely to destabilise the conventions of the genre within which Cadiot so firmly locates the text. We read above how, in using cut-ups to disrupt the monoglossia of a traditional lyric mode, Cadiot set about finding a 'territoire de poésie neuf'. As Wourm suggests, Cadiot sought to 'déhiérarchiser les genres, [...] déloger la poésie de ses quartiers traditionnels pour en réinterroger la definition, pour la décharger de cette définition' [dehierarchise the genres, [...] dislodge poetry from its traditional locations so as to re-interrogate its definition, release it from this definition].[89] If he was ultimately successful in this task, which I think he was, Cadiot nonetheless evokes the impasse that *L'Art poétic'* led him to. He describes how the cut-up renders the poet an 'artisan', and edges literature towards the visual arts, towards a 'travail plastique', 'presque un travail de plasticien'.[90] He remarks:

> À l'époque de *L'art poétic'* ce qui m'intéressait, c'était de faire de l'ultra-simple: du marbre, du conceptuel. La page de *L'art poétic'* est une cimaise. Si j'avais continué, je serais devenu peut-être plasticien — imitateur de Laurence Weiner ou de Joseph Kossuth [sic]: j'aurais fait des installations de mots. Ou je serais devenu poète sonore, ce qui n'est pas très différent: la musique et les arts plastiques sont dans la même zone, la zone matériologique. C'est merveilleux, mais je ne peux pas le faire; ou bien je ne voudrais faire que ça. Il fallait abandonner le bateau. Pour arriver au roman, disons au livre, il a fallu faire à nouveau naufrage.[91]
>
> [What interested me with *L'Art poétic'* was to do something extremely simple: marble, the conceptual. In *L'Art* poétic', the page is a picture rail. If I had continued, I would have perhaps become an artist — a Lawrence Weiner or

Joseph Kosuth impersonator: I would have made word installations. Or I would have become a sound poet, which isn't that different: music and the visual arts are in the same domain, the materiological domain. It's marvellous, but I can't do it; or at least I didn't want to do it. I had to abandon ship. To get to the novel, or let's say the book, required another shipwreck.]

Here Cadiot elaborates the dilemma he faced after writing his first book of poetry. He writes that 'au moment de *L'art poétic'* [...] je sors du littéraire', and thus could either pursue an artistic or musical trajectory, or abandon the project and return afresh to the 'littéraire' in the shape of the novel.[92] Ultimately, it appears that he did both, pursuing the 'littéraire' in his novels, and extending the 'plastique', 'matériologique' dimension of *L'Art poétic* in his subsequent work on *Welche*, *Hôtel Robinson*, and *Psychopharmaka*. Unsurprisingly, by importing many of the same features of *L'Art poétic'* into the later albums, the result is a similar hybrid and generically unclassifiable form. The compositional techniques — sampling and rearrangement — express clearly the 'plasticien' dimension; that the material he is working with is primarily linguistic means we find an 'installation de mots', set within a musical framework. The importance of music in Cadiot's *œuvre* begins well before his collaborations with Burger. From the start of his literary career, Cadiot wrote lyrics and worked with musicians and composers such as Pascal Dusapin and Kat Onoma. Musical allusions are pervasive in his earlier writing, from the musical staves of 'La Dame du lac' in *L'Art poétic'*, to the annotations of *Futur, ancien, fugitif*: '[chanté] ... [parlé]' [[sung] ... [spoken]] (*FAF*, 210), '*Allélulia* 1. (voix suraiguë)' [*Hallelujah* 1. (high-pitched voice)] (180). Tellingly, criticism of Cadiot's earlier work often conceptualises it with musical vocabulary: Mark Alizart, for example, describes *L'Art poétic'* as 'un livre fait de *samples*' [a book composed of samples], and Prigent evokes its 'musicalité ironique et légère, un peu rêveuse, un peu cassée, un peu répétitive, alanguie et parfois discordante' [musicality that is ironic and light, a little dreamy, a little broken, a little repetitive, languid and sometimes discordant].[93] In the background is, of course, the longstanding connection between music and poetry, with the latter often being distinguished from prose in the emphasis it places on language as a rhythmic, phonic material, rather than a naming, signifying entity. From the focus on linguistic materiality in *L'Art poétic'*, via the manic repetitions and glossolalia of Robinson in *Futur, ancien, fugitif*, to the reworked samples of Welche speakers in *Welche*, we see how Cadiot is interested in the point where language overlaps or transforms into music, where the rhythmic patterning of poetry 'déporte la langue littéraire vers une sorte de contiguïté avec la *musique*' [veers literary language towards a kind of contiguity with *music*].[94]

Also significant for these later albums is their status as performance. All three albums were performed live at various art festivals and concerts: *Welche* at the 'Babel' festival in Strasbourg, *Hôtel Robinson* at the 'Festival des Vieilles Charrues' in Brittany, and *Psychopharmaka* at the 'Festival d'Avignon' and the Centre Pompidou. Looking at the trajectory of Cadiot's work as a whole, we see an organic movement from *L'Art poétic'*, via *Futur, ancien, fugitif*, with its dramatic monologues and stage directions, towards actual performance, both in his musical collaborations, but also in his prose writing adapted for the stage (*Roméo & Juliette*, for example, was made into an opera, and *Fairy Queen* was performed as a play). Even Cadiot's public readings of his written poetry have the dramatic dynamism and comic interpretation of a one-man show. In the passage from text to performance, we find an interim stage in *L'Art poétic'* and *Futur, ancien, fugitif* that explores linguistic performativity. The focus on language as doing rather than saying manifests itself both in the emphasis on the '*acte* de transmission de compétences grammaticales' in *L'Art poétic'*, and in the emphasis on phatic speech in *Futur, ancien, fugitif*, where language operates primarily as a form of social gesture. As discussed above, in the latter text Robinson is built, performatively, in language, and then subsequently dismantled in the same gesture. Between Robinson's dramatic monologue in the first half of *Futur, ancien, fugitif* and the stage directions throughout, Dominique Rabaté's assertion that the book represents a 'passage au théâtre, au *one man show*' rings true.[95]

Writing about *Futur, ancien, fugitif*, Rabaté describes Cadiot's 'manière d'écrire très singulière, entre roman et poésie et théâtre' [very singular way of writing, between the novel, poetry, and theatre].[96] Cadiot himself evokes how, in *Futur, ancien, fugitif*, 'L'idée était de faire un "roman par poèmes", comme on fait un "roman par lettres"' [the idea was to produce a 'novel comprised of poems', just as one can produce a 'novel comprised of letters'].[97] He expresses his desire to 'greffer' poetry onto prose, to house poetry within prose, using prose as a 'famille d'accueil' for poetry.[98] It might be tempting to pursue Cadiot's reflections here, and to explore how his texts fuse features of both genres in a hybrid form of contemporary prose poetry.[99] However, we might equally want to move away from this polarisation altogether, and to envisage instead the dismantling of the distinction, as Cadiot himself gestured towards in 'La Mécanique lyrique', where he and Alferi elaborated the term 'OVNI'. In this essay, Alferi and Cadiot write:

> Ce dont la fiction a besoin, c'est d'un matériau de construction spécifique: des boules de sensations-pensées-formes. Des calculs, des nids d'hirondelles. On peut les appeler Objets, parce qu'ils sont manufacturés [...]. Plus que des contours lisses et familiers, ces petites agglutinations, sensibles-affectives-langagières, sont des sortes de monstres. Monstres de fidélité, des Objets verbaux non identifiés.[100]

> [What fiction needs is a specific construction material: balls of sensations-thoughts-forms. Sums, swallows' nests. We can call them Objects, because they are manufactured [...]. Rather than smooth, familiar contours, these little sensory-affective-linguistic agglutinations are sorts of monsters. Monsters of fidelity, unidentified verbal objects.]

The term 'OVNI' thus resists the temptation to polarise, and acts either to suspend or evade the impasse of the prose-poetry debate. With its evocation of UFOs, it encapsulates the alien quality of a monstrous, generically hybrid or generically unidentifiable form. In his thesis on OVNIs, Lynch writes:

> The Ovni implies experimental works that may be far from resembling traditional literary forms. Appearing instead as 'monstres,' these creations may combine multiple genres and several registers of language within a single

work. As the title *Revue de littérature générale* implies, contemporary poetry may incorporate numerous sorts of prose as a sort of 'general,' post-genre literature. These hybridized forms also take verse and prose alongside works involving drawings, photographs, video, and other media. This theory of textual mechanics orients post-genre poetry by characterizing methods of intermedial composition proper to a specific work.[101]

Like Gleize and his theory of 'post-poésie' discussed in Chapter 1, Alferi and Cadiot identify the presence of a form of post-genre literature in contemporary practice. In their essay 'Digest' that concludes the second *Revue*, they express overtly the resistance to classifying along generic lines:

> Il ne s'agit pas d'inclure artificiellement des poèmes dans un roman ou de la prose découpée dans un poème. Plutôt de travailler à une forme où l'on verrait les genres et les registres se justifier en cours de route. Cette forme, faut-il encore l'appeler 'roman'? Ou 'texte'? Ne pas l'appeler du tout?[102]
>
> [It's not about artificially including poems in a novel or cut-up prose in a poem. It's more about working on a form where the genres and registers justify themselves along the way. Should we still call this form a 'novel? Or a 'text'? Or not call it anything at all?]

In the conclusion to this book, I will return to the issues raised by Alferi and Cadiot's post-generic analysis, particularly with regard to the place for poetry within it. For the time being, and by way of an interim conclusion, we might maintain that their account also applies to the various aspects of Cadiot's *œuvre* considered in this chapter. Indeed, we might conceptualise Cadiot's work as a vast literary or artistic rhizome, a Barthesian multidimensional space or a Bakhtinian intra- or extra-generic practice, where poetry and prose, music, and theatre all exist on one single interconnected plane. Rather than superimposing particular generic distinctions onto a given work, and then attempting to identify how certain features relate back to some established notion of a 'novel', 'poem', or 'song', it can be more useful to explore the properties that transcend generic distinctions and forge links between one literary enterprise and the next. The cut-up, the heteroglottic assemblage of variegated images of languages, the destabilising 'usage mineur' of the major language, all of these practices transcend literary classification and translate throughout Cadiot's work from his early texts to his most recent performances. Having distilled from poetry, prose, and music the fundamental, supra-generic or supra-media building blocks that Deleuze analyses — rhythm, refrain, repetition, and movement — Cadiot then assembles these building blocks to produce a number of effects, literary and formal, but also affective and political. Like Bakhtin's carnivalesque or parodic-travestying forms that undermine the conventions of major genres, the generic rhizome of Cadiot's *œuvre* presents one further way in which his work operates as a 'littérature mineure', challenging and destabilising the clear delineation of genre in 'littérature majeure'.

Notes to Chapter 3

1. Cadiot, Mangeot and Zaoui, 'Cap au mieux', p. 3.
2. Jean Renaud, 'Le Monologue extérieur d'Olivier Cadiot', *Critique*, 677 (2003), 763–75. Game, 'Olivier Cadiot, or the Stuttering Self', in *Poetic Becomings*, pp. 151–88, and 'La Répétition différenciante dans la poétique deleuzienne: bégaiement et ritournelle', in *Deleuze et les écrivains*, ed. by Gelas and Micolet, pp. 401–20.
3. Game, 'Olivier Cadiot, or the Stuttering Self', p. 187. Lynch, *Unidentified Verbal Objects*, pp. 149–58. Alain Farah, 'La Possibilité du choc: invention littéraire et résistance politique dans les œuvres d'Olivier Cadiot et de Nathalie Quintane' (doctoral thesis, Ecole Normale Supérieure; Université du Québec à Montréal, 2009), pp. 207–08.
4. Gilles Deleuze, 'Michel Tournier et le monde sans autrui', in *Logique du sens* (Paris: Minuit, 1969), Appendix 4. Nathalie Wourm, 'Non-readings, Misreadings, Unreadings: Deleuze and Cadiot on Robinson Crusoe and Capitalism', in *Stealing the Fire: Adaptation, Appropriation, Plagiarism, Hoax in French and Francophone Literature and Film*, ed. by James T. Day (Amsterdam: Rodopi, 2010), pp. 177–90.
5. Cadiot, Mangeot and Zaoui, 'Cap au mieux', p. 10.
6. Wourm, *Poètes français du 21ème siècle*, p. 28.
7. For a detailed study of the history of the ready-made, and the difference between different practices within this broader appellation, see Théval, *Poésies ready-made*.
8. Emmanuel Hocquard writes extensively about *Testimony* in *Ma haie* (2001) and elsewhere; as does Jean-Marie Gleize, who entitled the third section of *Néon: actes et légendes* (2004) 'Témoignage', in homage to the American poet.
9. Emmanuel Hocquard uses the term 'compilations' to describe Reznikoff's practice. See Hocquard, *Ma haie*, p. 289.
10. Hocquard, *Ma haie*, p. 449.
11. Olivier Cadiot, Ludovic Lagarde and Laurent Poitrenaux, *Un mage en été: dossier pédagogique* (Paris: Centre Pompidou, 2010) (unpaginated). Hocquard, a friend and mutual influence of Cadiot, and to whom a section of *L'Art poétic'* is dedicated, makes a similar remark in his introduction to *Tout le monde se ressemble*. He describes how the poets collected in the anthology (Cadiot included) handle words like fragments of a vase or a fresco uncovered on an archaeological dig (p. 12).
12. Théval considers the relationship between the ready-made and the 'mécanique lyrique' in depth in Part III of *Poésies ready-made*, pp. 199–223.
13. Prigent, *Salut les anciens*, p. 53.
14. Person, 'Olivier Cadiot', p. 14.
15. Cadiot, Lagarde and Poitrenaux, *Un mage en été*.
16. Alferi and Cadiot, 'La Mécanique lyrique', p. 4.
17. Olivier Cadiot, *L'Art poétic'* (Paris: P.O.L., 1988), pp. 16–17 (henceforth abbreviated to *AP1*); *Art Poétic'*, trans. by Cole Swensen (København: Green Integer, 1999), pp. 16–17 (translation amended here and elsewhere; henceforth abbreviated to *AP2*).
18. This line is from Racine's *Andromaque*, although the notation suggests it is an example given in a versification textbook.
19. The speed of Cadiot's texts has been discussed at length by various scholars, particularly in relation to his prose writing. Michel Gauthier, *Olivier Cadiot, le facteur vitesse* (Dijon: Presses du réel, 2004), section 2.1. Anne Woelfel, 'Mouvement', in 'Le Système Cadiot: l'hétérogène dans le champ de l'expérience' (unpublished doctoral thesis, Université de Pau et des Pays de l'Adour, 2014). Game, *Poetic Becomings*, pp. 168–70. In their analyses, the speed of Cadiot's prose is often seen as the importing of something 'poetic' into a novelistic genre. See, for example, Farah, *Le Gala des incomparables*, p. 97.
20. Lia Kurts, 'Olivier Cadiot, ou La Poétique des objets trouvés', in *Formes et normes en poésie moderne et contemporaine*, ed. by Laurence Bougault and Judith Wulf (2011), pp. 35–36 <https://www.academia.edu/4461615/FORMES_ET_NORMES_EN_POÉSIE_MODERNE_ET_CONTEMPORAINEPréface> [accessed 22 June 2020]. I would add to this that meteorological expressions often involve impersonal verbs ('il fait beau', 'il pleut', 'il y a du vent'), which represent heightened examples of a form of subjectless, impersonal language.

21. Christian Prigent, *Ceux qui merdRent* (Paris: P.O.L., 1991), p. 252. Person, 'Olivier Cadiot', p. 21.
22. Cadiot, Mangeot and Zaoui, 'Cap au mieux', p. 13.
23. Cadiot's phrase echoes both Roubaud ('La poésie est autobiographie de tout le monde. La poésie est autobiographie de personne' [Poetry is everybody's autobiography. Poetry is nobody's autobiography]), and the French translation of Stein's *Everybody's Autobiography*. Jacques Roubaud, *Poésie, etcetera: ménage* (Paris: Stock, 1995), pp. 106–07. Gertrude Stein, *Autobiographie de tout le monde*, trans. by Marie-France de Paloméra (Paris: Seuil, 1989).
24. Anna Boschetti, 'Le Formalisme réaliste d'Olivier Cadiot: une réponse à la question des possibles et du rôle de la recherche littéraire aujourd'hui', in *L'Écrivain, le savant et le philosophe*, ed. by Eveline Pinto (Paris: Sorbonne, 2003), p. 241.
25. Prigent, *Ceux qui merdRent*, p. 252.
26. Emmanuel Hocquard, *Un privé à Tanger* (Paris: P.O.L., 1987), p. 213.
27. The image is hardly a new one, and was significant for a number of writers who were instrumental in shaping Cadiot's generation of poets, such as Blaise Cendrars in *Kodak: (documentaire)* (Paris: Stock, 1924), or more recently, Bernard Heidsieck in *Biopsies: 1965–1969* (Al Dante, 2009) [CD].
28. Person, 'Olivier Cadiot', p. 14.
29. *Olivier Cadiot*, ed. by Jean-Michel Espitallier and Jacques Sivan, special issue of *Java*, 13 (1995), 61.
30. Cadiot, Mangeot and Zaoui, 'Cap au mieux', p. 3. For a detailed consideration of this subject see Eric Lynch, 'Olivier Cadiot's Robinson, or, A Portrait of the Artist as "Auto-usine"', *L'Esprit Créateur*, 54.1 (2014), 86–99, as well as the chapter on Cadiot in his thesis, 'Unidentified Verbal Objects'.
31. Cadiot, Mangeot and Zaoui, 'Cap au mieux', p. 3.
32. Ibid., p. 4.
33. Olivier Cadiot, *Futur, ancien, fugitif* (Paris: P.O.L., 1993), p. 201 (henceforth abbreviated to *FAF*).
34. Dominique Rabaté, 'Polyphonie du solitaire: le Robinson d'Olivier Cadiot', in *Nuove solitudini: mutamenti delle relazioni nell'ultima narrativa francese*, ed. by Matteo Majorano (Macerata: Quodlibet, 2012), pp. 83–97.
35. Cadiot, Lagarde and Poitrenaux, *Un mage en été*. Lynch, 'Unidentified Verbal Objects', p. 35.
36. Game, 'La Répétition différenciante', p. 409.
37. For an expanded discussion of the codification of non-linguistic or non-verbal sound, see Steven Connor, *Beyond Words: Sobs, Hums, Stutters and Other Vocalizations* (London: Reaktion Books, 2014).
38. Game, 'La Répétition différenciante', p. 416.
39. Like many of the lyrics in the later albums, this passage reprises phrases found earlier in *Futur, ancien, fugitif*. In the text it appears under the title 'souvenir très ancien II' [very early memory II], as part of a longer passage that seems to be a cut-up from a linguistic transcript depicting a conversation between 'Mommy' and a young child 'S.' (*FAF*, 135–37). The transcript resembles those used by syntacticians and child development specialists in the study of language acquisition.
40. See, for example, Matthew Saxton, *Child Language: Acquisition and Development* (Los Angeles & London: SAGE, 2010).
41. In his work on glossolalia, Michel de Certeau also evokes this dual status, describing how glossolalia combines something of both the pre- and post-linguistic. Michel de Certeau, 'Utopies vocales: glossolalies', *Traverses*, 20 (1980), 26–37.
42. An interesting figure in this regard is Giorgio Agamben, who connects the transition from the non-linguistic state of infancy (etymologically 'in-fans', 'unable to speak') to the acquisition of language in childhood, with the development of subjectivity and coming into being, that can only happen within language. Giorgio Agamben, *Infancy and History: The Destruction of Experience*, trans. by Liz Heron (London: Verso, 1993). The relationship between child language or babble and poetry has been explored by a number of writers, among whom Agamben, Kristeva, Herder, and more recently Steven Connor. See Nowell Smith, *On Voice in Poetry*, pp. 23–34, for a good account of these approaches.

43. Heidsieck, *Biopsies*.
44. Game, 'Olivier Cadiot, or the Stuttering Self', p. 181.
45. Ibid., p. 171.
46. Ibid., p. 187.
47. We might detect here an implicit commentary on the political dimension of mental illness and power structures which decide that, say, Louis Wolfson's behaviour is 'disordered', but abiding by the arbitrary codes of social behavior is 'normal'.
48. Game, 'Olivier Cadiot, or the Stuttering Self', p. 153.
49. Renaud, 'Le Monologue extérieur d'Olivier Cadiot', p. 770.
50. For further detail on the sociolinguistic history of Alsace, see Dennis Ernest Ager, *Sociolinguistics and Contemporary French* (Cambridge: Cambridge University Press, 1990), p. 50.
51. 'Biographie', in *Ici d'ailleurs* <http://www.icidailleurs.com/index.php?route=product/category&path=68> [accessed 26 June 2020].
52. 'Olivier Cadiot et Rodolphe Burger: nouvelle géographie sonore', *L'Atelier du son*, France Culture (2012), 26:00 <https://www.franceculture.fr/emissions/latelier-du-son/olivier-cadiot-et-rodolphe-burger-nouvelle-geographie-sonore> [accessed 26 June 2020].
53. Alferi, *Cinépoèmes & films parlants*.
54. Deleuze and Guattari, 'De la ritournelle' (*MP*, 381–433).
55. On the subject, see Game, 'La Répétition différenciante'.
56. Wourm, *Poètes français du 21ème siècle*, p. 28.
57. Gaëlle Théval, 'Poésies ready-made, XXe-XXIe siècles' (doctoral thesis, Université Paris-Diderot-Paris VII, 2011), p. 206.
58. 'Cours 12 du 17/03/1981', *La Voix de Gilles Deleuze en ligne* <http://www2.univ-paris8.fr/deleuze/article.php3?id_article=151> [accessed 26 June 2020].
59. Ibid. For a simple outline of Deleuze and Guattari's theory of rhythm, see Eugene B. Young, with Gary Genosko and Janell Watson, *The Deleuze and Guattari Dictionary* (London & New York: Bloomsbury Academic, 2013), p. 266. The subject will be explored in greater detail in the following chapter.
60. These samples are taken from Deleuze's lecture on the *ritournelle* and the gallop, 'Cours 58 du 20/03/1984', *La Voix de Gilles Deleuze en ligne* <http://www2.univ-paris8.fr/deleuze/article.php3?id_article=337> [accessed 26 June 2020].
61. Cadiot, Lagarde and Poitrenaux, *Un mage en été*.
62. 'Olivier Cadiot et Rodolphe Burger: nouvelle géographie sonore', 24:00.
63. Rodolphe Burger and Olivier Cadiot, 'Une petite guérilla intérieure', *Vacarme*, 52 (2010), 54–58 (p. 55).
64. *Tomorrow's World* (BBC, 25 September 1975).
65. Cadiot, Lagarde and Poitrenaux, *Un mage en été*.
66. Cadiot, Mangeot and Zaoui, 'Cap au mieux', p. 5.
67. Person, 'Olivier Cadiot', p. 21.
68. Ibid., p. 4. I'm not sure we do say this in English, but Cadiot's meaning is clear.
69. Cadiot describes the influence of Perec's *La Vie mode d'emploi* on his first draft of *Futur, ancien, fugitif*. Person, 'Olivier Cadiot', p. 19.
70. Christophe Lamiot, *Eau sur eau: les dictionnaires de Mallarmé, Flaubert, Bataille, Michaux, Leiris et Ponge* (Amsterdam: Rodopi, 1997).
71. Bernard Heidsieck, *Derviche/Le Robert* (Roumainville: Al Dante, 2004).
72. Heidsieck, 'Notes a posteriori', in *Derviche/Le Robert*, p. 10.
73. Roland Barthes, 'La Mort de l'auteur', in *Le Bruissement de la langue: essais critiques IV* (Paris: Seuil, 1984), p. 65.
74. William Burroughs and Brion Gysin, *The Third Mind* (New York: Viking Press, 1978), p. 8.
75. Barthes, *Le Degré zero*, p. 39; *Writing Degree Zero*, p. 48.
76. Ibid., pp. 39–40; p. 48.
77. Farah, *Le Gala des incomparables*, p. 79. Farah gives a good account of the role of these literary references in the section 'Ce que *L'art poétic*' fait à la notion d'intertextualité' [What *L'Art poétic*' does to the notion of intertextuality] (pp. 69–75).

78. Serge Gavronsky, *Toward a New Poetics: Contemporary Writing in France* (Berkeley: University of California Press, 1994), p. 237.
79. Prigent, *Ceux qui merdRent*, p. 241.
80. Ibid., p. 242.
81. Christian Prigent, 'Le Fugitif présent', in *Olivier Cadiot*, ed. by Espitallier and Sivan, p. 38.
82. Ibid., p. 39.
83. Boschetti, 'Le Formalisme réaliste d'Olivier Cadiot', p. 242.
84. Prigent, 'Le Fugitif présent', pp. 38–39.
85. Barthes, *Le Bruissement de la langue*, p. 65.
86. For example, Cusset uses the term *burlesque* to describe Cadiot's prose writing, and Kurts uses the same term in her analysis of *L'Art poétic'*. François Cusset, 'politique de Cadiot', *Vacarme*, 40 (2007) <http://www.vacarme.org/article1341.html> [accessed 26 June 2020]. Kurts, 'Olivier Cadiot, ou La Poétique des objets trouvés', p. 43.
87. For a detailed consideration of these various terms, see the chapter 'Approaches to Parody' in Simon Dentith, *Parody* (London & New York: Routledge, 2000), pp. 1–38. Bakhtin elaborates the notion of the 'carnivalesque' in *Rabelais and His World*, trans. by Hélène Iswolsky (Bloomington: Indiana University Press, 1984).
88. Rabaté, 'Polyphonie du solitaire', p. 86.
89. Wourm, *Poètes français du 21ème siècle*, p. 4.
90. Cadiot described this 'travail plastique' at the *Colloque Olivier Cadiot: expérience morte, expérimentez* at the Bibliothèque nationale de France (BnF) in September 2015. Cadiot, Lagarde and Poitrenaux, *Un mage en été*.
91. Cadiot, Mangeot and Zaoui, 'Cap au mieux', p. 12.
92. Ibid., p. 13.
93. Mark Alizart, 'Les Trois Ages du sample', *Critique*, 677 (2003), 776–84 (p. 776). Prigent, *Ceux qui merdRent*, pp. 250–51.
94. Prigent, 'On ne fait pas de poésie sans casser d'œufs', p. 435. Here Prigent is describing the four principal characteristics of poetry according to Deleuze.
95. Rabaté, 'Polyphonie du solitaire', p. 86.
96. Ibid., p. 86.
97. Cadiot, Lagarde and Poitrenaux, *Un mage en été*.
98. Cadiot elaborated these ideas at the *Colloque Olivier Cadiot*.
99. Game does so in his chapter on Cadiot in *Poetic Becomings*. He writes: 'Neither novel nor poem *FAF* is a generic de-territorialization taking place between the all-encompassing continuity of a *récit* and the conspicuous self-consciousness specific to the poetic function of language in the Jakobsonian sense. In a word it is *the becoming-poem of prose as much as the becoming-prose of poetry*' (pp. 162–63). This analysis resonates with what we saw in Fourcade's work in Chapter 2.
100. Alferi and Cadiot, 'La Mécanique lyrique', pp. 5–6.
101. Lynch, 'Unidentified Verbal Objects', pp. 17–18.
102. Alferi and Cadiot, 'Digest'.

CHAPTER 4

Christophe Tarkos, 'Pour la poésie'

Several aspects of the preceding discussion — on minor literature, style, monoglossia, and genre — configure differently in Christophe Tarkos's work, due in no small part to his conception of language, which sets him apart from many of his contemporaries. The result is a form of experimentation that is markedly different from that found in Cadiot's and Fourcade's poetry, and which lends a new prism through which to consider Bakhtin's and Deleuze and Guattari's analyses. Although perhaps less well-known than the other two poets, since his premature death 'un mythe Tarkos' has begun to take shape.[1] This myth depicts Tarkos as a strange, somewhat subversive figure, a talented poet and thinker, troubled by illness throughout his brief but prolific career. In many respects, Tarkos invited a degree of mythologising upon himself, producing, throughout the course of his lifetime, a number of slippery 'auto-présentations': playful, semi-autobiographical descriptions that deliberately wrong-foot the reader in their combination of fact and fiction.[2] These passages include reflections on his poetic practice: 'Poète: bouleur, prononciateur, crieur, improvisateur [...]. Produit autant de textes que de sons. Travail poétique traditionnel' [Poet: baller, pronunciator, shouter, improviser [...]. Produces as many texts as sounds. Traditional poetic work] (*E*, 7), and seemingly straightforward assertions about himself:

> Je suis intelligent
> Et
> sérieux.
> [...]
> Je suis
> un homme
> d'une trentaine d'années.
> [...]
> Je suis de gauche.
> Je suis athée. (*E*, 415–16)

[I am intelligent | And | serious. | [...] | I am | a man | of around 30. | [...] | I am left-wing. | I am atheist].

Things that we know to be true, 'Vit à Marseille et Paris' [Lives in Marseille and Paris] (*E*, 7), and things that we know to be false, 'Je n'ai pas de femme et pas d'enfants' [I have no wife and no kids] (*E*, 35), are interspersed with provocative statements, the truth of which is uncertain: 'Profession alimentaire: vol, gardiennage' [Day job: stealing, working as a security guard] (*E*, 7), 'je suis anormal, sexuellement' [I am abnormal, sexually] (*E*, 35). This makes constructing a clear sense of Tarkos's life somewhat difficult, but there are a number of facts that we know for certain. He was born near Marseille in 1963, where he spent a large part of his life. He studied politics, and later literature, before beginning a teaching career which he soon abandoned. In the 1990s, he moved back and forth between Paris and Marseille, while holding down a number of jobs to put bread on the table: motorway tollbooth operator, toy salesman, temp at the BnF. In the early 1990s, poetry became Tarkos's primary focus; he gave numerous performances of his work, for example at the Centre International de Poésie in Marseille and the Centre Pompidou in Paris, and published his texts, initially with various small publishers, and later with P.O.L. and Al Dante. As well as contributing frequently to poetry reviews, *Nioques*, *Doc(k)s*, *TXT*, *Java*, and the *Revue de littérature générale 96/2*, for example, Tarkos co-founded *R.R.* with Nathalie Quintane and Stéphane Bérard, *Poézi Prolétèr* with Katalin Molnàr and Pascal Doury, *Quaderno* with Philippe Beck, and *Facial* with Charles Pennequin and Vincent Tholomé. In the last ten years of his life, Tarkos wrote prolifically, publishing, among others: *Morceaux choisis* (1995), *Oui* (1996), *Le Train* (1996), *Processe* (1997), *Le Bâton* (1998), *Caisses* (1998), *Le Signe =* (1999), *PAN* (1999), *Ma langue* (2000), and *Anachronisme* (2001). In November 1999, after suffering from severe headaches, Tarkos was told that he had a brain tumour. In the years that preceded his death on 4 November 2004, his illness consumed his day-to-day life, inflecting his poetry in numerous ways, and ultimately bringing his writing to a premature end. Since his death, critical attention to Tarkos's work has grown steadily, increasing in recent years after P.O.L.'s posthumous publication of *Écrits poétiques* (2008) and *L'Enregistré* (2014). The first of these volumes presents Tarkos's written poetry, collecting together his earlier texts, often hard to get hold of due to their small print runs; the second, accompanied by a CD and a DVD, assembles his performance work.

Whether written or performed, there is a stylistic and thematic unity to Tarkos's poetry. In her thesis on Tarkos, Anne-Renée Caillé describes this unity as a 'projet totalisant'.[3] Tarkos's *œuvre* presents itself as a distinct, cohesive whole, which means that, as Thomas Clerc suggests, it constitutes an immediately recognisable art.[4] His poems, with their obsessive repetitions and revisions that circulate around a central, pivotal word or idea, have what Christian Prigent describes as an arrogant simplicity to their mode of expression.[5] Marking a noticeable contrast to many experimental poets of the preceding generation, Cadiot and Fourcade included, Tarkos's poetry reinstates the much-maligned lyric *je*, and often has a personal, if not autobiographical, inflection. His poetry is firmly grounded in 'la matière vécue' of the everyday, and, as Jocelyn Bonnerave points out, it often demonstrates a narrative inclination, particularly in the later texts.[6] These features of Tarkos's work are typically associated with 'les poètes du signifié', yet his poetry presents itself in an entirely different way to other poets assembled under this paradigm. His concern with the everyday suggests certain resonances with Jacques Réda, Henri Thomas, and Paul de Roux, for example, and his emphasis on presence offers parallels with Yves Bonnefoy, but his preoccupation with language and linguistic experimentation gives his poetry a different orientation. It is precisely this idiosyncratic configuration that distinguishes Tarkos from many of his contemporaries, and that serves to cement his position as a unique voice in his generation.

Despite its manifest singularity, the 'filiations' in Tarkos's poetry are apparent and manifold. In his written texts, we see the influence of, among others, Francis Ponge, Samuel Beckett, Gertrude Stein, Georges Perec, and Valère Novarina; in his performance work, Antonin Artaud, Kurt Schwitters, and Bernard Heidsieck. Likewise, links are often drawn between Tarkos and certain other contemporary poets — Nathalie Quintane, Charles Pennequin, and Philippe Beck — who formed a new generation of poets publishing in the 1990s. Their work, while different in many respects, constituted an observable movement, 'un phénomène *nouveau*' that Prigent argues began to crystallise in the mid-1990s.[7] Their poetry was characterised by a new *lisibilité*, a readability that arose from a twofold rejection of the state of poetry as they had inherited it. On the one hand, with figures like Bonnefoy and Du Bouchet in the background, they were wary of poetry that, driven by the philosophy underpinning the texts, resulted in poems that were highly conceptual, often difficult, and paradoxically removed from the world that they purported to accentuate. On the other, responding to formalist or textualist poetry, typified by poets associated with *Tel Quel* or the Oulipo, they sought to move away from self-negating linguistic play, and the perceived stagnation of impossible meaning, absent reference, and the problematising of poetic voice. However, like others of this generation, if Tarkos's work appeared as more immediately readable, it was no less experimental, and many of the same preoccupations of twentieth-century poetry were sustained, albeit in a different guise. Despite features that often appear as markers of a traditional or lyric mode of poetry — the reprise of first-person voice, the narrative or descriptive dimension — Tarkos's work does not represent a return to a previous state of poetry.[8] It is not a form of 're-poésie', to use Jean-Marie Gleize's term, nor was it associated with the new lyricism or 'néo-lyrique' movements discussed in Chapter 1.[9] Instead, these features arise from the idiosyncratic theoretical underpinnings of Tarkos's project — his notion of the 'pâte-mot' [word-dough], which envisages the relationship between language and the world it describes differently. This chapter examines these theoretical underpinnings and their consequences for poetic form and voice, before considering how Tarkos's *œuvre* highlights an important divergence in Bakhtin's and Deleuze and Guattari's analyses, as well as an alternative form of discourse to those accounted for in Bakhtin's monologic/dialogic distinction.

A Poetic Project

In the final stanza of 'Je m'agite' [I am Restless] (1999), a poem in which Tarkos expresses a sense of anxiety prompted by uncertainty, he writes the following:

> je ne sais pas sur quoi je vais m'appuyer pour savoir.
> pour dire.
> pour appuyer ce que je suis.
> [...]
> je ne sais pas ce sur quoi je vais bientôt m'appuyer pour dire.
> pour dire que je suis.
> pour savoir. (EP, 315)

[I don't know what I can depend on to know. | to say. | to stress what I am. | [...] | I don't know this thing that I will soon depend on to say. | to say that I am. | to know.]

The concluding lines of the poem evoke the enterprise at the heart of Tarkos's poetic project. For Tarkos, poetry responds to the demand for a means 'pour savoir'; it is, to use Gleize's expression, a work of investigation-elucidation.[10] It presents itself as a mode to pursue a further understanding of existence, to make sense of the self and the world, and to elaborate, as Tarkos writes in *Le Baroque*, a 'théorie de ce qui est' [theory of what is], a 'théorie de ce qui existe' [theory of what exists].[11] In *Processe*, he describes this project outright: 'je m'engage à chercher la vérité et à rester dans la vérité les yeux tournés vers le sens du monde' [I commit to seeking out the truth and to remaining within this truth, my eyes turned towards the meaning of the world] (EP, 88). In an interview with Bertrand Verdier, Tarkos highlights certain similarities between poetry, as he conceives of it, and philosophy, suggesting that there is an equivalence in their quest for truth.[12] In this sense, poetry is seen as one practice among many engaged in a pursuit of truth, in its various forms, and Tarkos was, perhaps unsurprisingly, a wide reader in a number of disciplines: philosophy, theology, history, science, economics, sociology, and so on.[13] Throughout his work we find references to the various ways in which people have attempted to glean insight into the world: in *Le Baroque*, for example, Tarkos refers to anthropology (B, 20), linguistics (14), Whitehead's and Russell's class logic (14), genealogy (14), and a range of other disciplines besides.

The scope of Tarkos's subject matter is broad: in his writing we find meditations on, inter alia, substance, things, reality, consciousness, thought, feeling, bodily experience, language, literature, poetry, and meaning. His poetry touches on various ethical concerns; a recurring motif is the desire to ascertain not only what is true, but also what is of value and what is good, and in each instance, he is equally interested by the power structures that lie behind value systems and discourses of knowledge. Throughout his work we find recurring declarations such as the following: 'l'amour est bon' [love is good] (ML, 33), 'la drogue est bonne' [drugs are good] (EP, 220), 'les textes sont vrais, sont sincères' [texts are real, are sincere] (EP, 135), 'l'argent est la valeur sublime' [money is the sublime value] (EP, 263). In this respect, Tarkos's œuvre might be seen to belong to a form of 'poésie pensante', concerned, in turn, with a 'poéthique' more commonly associated with figures such as Yves Bonnefoy, Philippe Jaccottet, Michel Deguy, or René Char.[14] However, unlike many (although not all) of the twentieth-century poets that fall under this appellation, Tarkos's work resists abstraction and its ontological dimension is consistently grounded in the slightness of the everyday. In this sense, Tarkos's project sees an often surprising and occasionally disjunctive combination of the major and minor. It is major in so far as his work is ambitious in scope, tasked with nothing less than pursuing a further understanding of the world; minor in so far as these broader questions are always rooted in the resolutely small, and are expressed in simple, straightforward terms. A theory of monistic materialism is elaborated via the consideration of a fruit compote (*EP*, 243); the sight of crowds moving outside the metro station at Barbès forms the pivot for a wider reflection on a theory of the 'ensemble'.[15] This derives, in part, from the way in which Tarkos presents what might in grander terms be called a 'philosophical investigation', as 'un modeste petit effort de mettre au clair certaines petites choses' [a modest little effort to make a few things clear] (*EP*, 96). Philosophy is understood as event, and an entirely ordinary, quotidian event at that.

Tarkos's poetry often reads as a series of straightforward observations, postulates, and assertions. In *Ma langue*, he writes:

> Une chose est sûre. Une chose est sûre.
> Il y a une chose de sûr. [...] Une chose est claire. Une chose
> est sûre. Une chose est certaine à 100%. (*ML*, 29).

> [One thing is sure. One thing is sure. | There's one thing that's for sure. [...]
> One thing is clear. One thing | is sure. One thing is 100% certain.]

This metapoetic refrain evokes his own modus operandi: begin with stating clearly what is certain and proceed from there. Tarkos was interested in modal logic and truth conditional semantics; we saw above his reference to Russell and Whitehead, and logical propositions such as the following occur throughout his work: 'Ma mère est un homme est faux. Ma mère n'est pas un homme. Ma mère est une femme. [...] Une femme n'est pas un homme. Un fils n'est pas une femme' [My mother is a man is false. My mother is not a man. My mother is a woman. [...] A woman is not a man. A son is not a woman] (*EP*, 238). Starting with tautological statements such as these, Tarkos constructs a philosophy from scratch, commencing with basic assertions of things that are certain and true. Complementing this desire to begin at the beginning, Tarkos's attempt to make sense of the world as a material entity starts with a consideration of the constitutive elements of its substance. 'La grande substance' (*EP*, 163) is a pivotal motif in Tarkos's poetry: as we shall shortly see it is intimately linked to his theory of the 'pâte-mot', but it is also there in its most literal form, as a term that incorporates the sheer variety of different forms of matter from which the world, and everything in it, is constituted. As a result, we find prevalent references to the most basic, material particles: in *Anachronisme*, Tarkos lists the elements from the periodic table (*A*, 185); in *Processe*, we find references to quarks, ions, and other primordial elements (*EP*, 126). Certain types of substance are granted a prominent position, most notably elemental forms (earth, water, stone) and viscous substances (dough, purée, jam, faeces). Beyond this emphasis on substance itself, Tarkos elaborates a network of motifs — usually physical objects or geometric shapes — that reappear throughout his poetry. 'Carrés' [squares], 'ronds' [circles], 'bâtons' [batons], 'boules' [balls]: these shapes operate not only as typographic models for the poem, but constitute primary forms, the patterns of which are then traced across multiple levels of existence and lived experience. To give just one example, in *Morceaux choisis* Tarkos focuses on the ball as an abstract, geometrical form, describing its spatial arrangement, the relationship between part and whole, centre and sides, as well as the forces that act upon it and the movements it makes (*MC*, 32). The 'boule' then returns in various different manifestations: in *Ronds*, for example, it constitutes the shape of the poems themselves (*EP*, 207). Alongside its cognates *boulette* and *globule*, it reappears in 'Quelle belle terre' [What a beautiful earth] in reference to the spherical shape of the Earth itself (*E*, 472–73), and in *Le Signe* = it describes units of meaning: 'Les expressions, les tirades sont des boulettes, des poches d'eau, des bombes d'eau' [Expressions and speech are little balls, water pockets, water bombs].[16] In a letter to Christophe Hanna, Tarkos acknowledges the way in which he traces the patterns of the 'boule' across multiple fields, from the human head to 'des corps sphériques topologiques que l'on retrouve dans le voyage autour du Monde' [the topological spherical bodies that one finds on the journey around the World] (*E*, 49).[17] In this respect, there is something Deleuzo-Guattarian about Tarkos's project; like Deleuze and Guattari with the plateau or rhizome, Tarkos identifies a number of basic forms, the 'boule', the 'bâton', or the 'beignet' for example, which manifest themselves on various strata of experience, and which then serve as conceptual models for his philosophical project. Just as Deleuze and Guattari might use the rhizome to think about different forms of literature, Tarkos uses the 'boule' to think about the operation of meaning within language. There is an arbitrariness to the selection of these models, which reflects the fact that neither Deleuze and Guattari's nor Tarkos's project attempts to create an exhaustive or systematic philosophy. Instead, both projects involve the elaboration of an idiosyncratic vocabulary, a small, generative set of basic concepts that form a conceptual toolbox from which to construct a broader philosophical programme.

Linguistic Experiments/Experiences of Language

In the quest 'pour savoir', Tarkos's poetry advances through a series of experiments. The experiment is the operational principle for Tarkos's project, and references are found throughout his work to experimentation of various kinds. In *Anachronisme*, for example, he details a medical trial that monitors the effects of zuclopenthixol, an antipsychotic drug (*A*, 188), and evokes the battery circuit tests conducted by the physicist Édouard Branly (205). In a comment that might equally well apply to his own poetics, he describes Branly using his radio wave detector, 'à noter les résultats, à enregistrer les phénomènes, à expérimenter tous les phénomènes avec toutes les matières' [to jot down the results, to record the phenomena, to experiment with all phenomena using all materials] (205). Elsewhere his reflections on the experiment are more directly self-reflexive:

> Une expérience, un truc expérimental, une expérimentation, il est possible d'expérimenter, expérimenter sur soi, nous allons faire une expérience, faire l'expérience de certains produits cérébraux, de certains états d'âme, de certaines ambiances, de certaines substances qui suintent, qui coulent de la pensée, [...] un certain attentisme, un flottement et c'est parti, l'expérience peut commencer. (*A*, 21–22)
>
> [An experiment, an experimental thing, an experimentation, it is possible to experiment, to experiment on oneself, we're going to do an experiment, experiment with certain cerebral products, certain states of mind, certain atmospheres, certain substances that ooze, that flow from thought, [...] a certain waiting and seeing, a hesitation and we're off, the experiment can begin.]

Here Tarkos evokes the thought experiments that form the inaugural point of departure for his poems, which begin with an attentiveness to the states and modulations of the mind. As we saw with Fourcade, Tarkos also plays with the dual meaning of *expérience*, this time evoking an experiment grounded in the experience of different cognitive states. In *Processe* he describes how:

> Les textes ne sont que le fruit d'un modeste petit effort de mettre au clair certaines petites choses, ne peuvent pas répondre intégralement d'un coup aux énormes demandes qui surestiment les possibilités d'un simple petit texte qui ne peut être que le résultat d'un petit effort de penser à quelque chose. (*EP*, 96)
>
> [Texts are just the fruit of a modest little effort to make a few things clear, can't respond fully in one go to the huge demands that overestimate the possibilities of a simple little text that can only be the result of a little effort to think about something.]

Describing the text as the result of such an effort might suggest the poem is the end-product — a set of conclusions or outcomes of a prior process. This conjecture would be misguided though, as in Tarkos's work the poem itself *is* the experiment. The process of experimentation is represented as if it is taking place in real-time, within the language of the poem itself, rather than in the mind prior to the production of the text. As we shall see, the formal properties of Tarkos's poetry reinforce this idea; they often demonstrate the advancing of a proposition, its repetition, and subsequent revision, in a form of 'mastication verbale' which in turn replicates or indeed performs the movements of thought itself.[18]

The experiment, although described thus far as a form of thought experiment, might therefore be seen as both an experiment in thought and simultaneously an experiment in language. Given that it is represented as taking place in the writing, the experiment involves language and thought synchronously, and their inextricability is reinforced by a focus in Tarkos's work on their locus within the body. The adjectives Tarkos uses to describe thought and language, such as hormonal or corporeal, form part of a broader conception of the two phenomena as temporal, bodily events that involve a change of physical or neurological states.[19] One of the principal, recurring forms of experiment in Tarkos's poetry is the transcription of the sensorial experience of the body: the lungs inflating and deflating, the heart beating, the movement of the arms and the elbows. Deriving from this attentiveness to the body is an attentiveness to the experience of thought and language as embodied phenomena. We saw this in Fourcade's work too, but for Tarkos, a performance poet as well as a written poet, references to the experience of speech are particularly pervasive. His performances often comment on their own delivery, describing the movement of the tongue in the mouth, the sensation of air exhaled from the lungs, punctuated by the contraction of the vocal tract.[20] In written texts such as *Processe*, the feeling of pronouncing different vowel sounds is transcribed on the page:

> A est différent de O. Il faut prononcer A et O. Montre l'incroyable différence. Aaaaaaaaaaaa / Ooooooooooo. S'imprégner de la prononciation, en prononçant longuement dans la bouche. En vocalisant un a continu. Puis un o continu. Sentir l'évolution, les métamorphoses complexes dans la bouche. (*EP*, 117–18)

> [A is different to O. Pronounce A and O. Show the incredible difference. Aaaaaaaaaaaa / Ooooooooooo. Immerse oneself in the pronunciation, by pronouncing slowly in the mouth. By vocalising a continuous a. Then a continuous o. Feel the evolution, the complex metamorphoses in the mouth.]

Here Tarkos appeals to the physical experience of language, which is felt in the body, or in the mouth. The verbs that Tarkos uses to describe this experiment, 's'imprégner' and 'sentir', reinforce this emphasis on sensation or feeling, which is found elsewhere, in *Signe =*, in a series of fourteen poems all given the same title: 'Le Sentiment'. In the following passage, which comes from this series, Tarkos begins with a description of the sensation of breathing, before drawing attention to consciousness situated within that same breathing body:

> Le sentiment du battement balancement régulier de la poitrine du ventre du devant, de l'oscillation lente, plus lente que le battement, le balancement lent du devant, du poitrail, de ce n'est pas la poitrine, c'est la personne, le centre de la personne qui se balance, trouve l'air en entier, trouve dehors, trouve de quoi, trouve son inspiration, trouve son balancement, [...] le sentiment de la conscience, de la conscience qu'elle est en présence d'une personne, qu'elle a vu une personne, qu'elle est en face d'une personne, plus qu'en face, en phase d'une personne, qu'elle est avec une personne, que c'est une personne qui est trouvée dans le un balancement. (*S*, 112–13)

> [The feeling of the beat regular swaying of the chest of the stomach of the front, of the slow oscillation, slower than the beat, the slow swaying of the front, of the breast, of this isn't the chest, it's the person, the centre of the person that sways, finds the air in its entirety, finds outside, finds something, finds its inspiration, finds its swaying, [...] the feeling of consciousness, of the consciousness of being in the presence of a person, of having seen a person, of being in front of a person, more than in front, in sync with a person, of being with a person, that it's a person that is found in the swaying.]

This passage moves from the observation of the beating of the heart in the chest to the awareness of the presence of consciousness. The regular beat of the heart is reflected in the marked rhythmic effects of the text: alliteration ('poitrail', 'poitrine', 'personne') and internal rhyme and assonance ('lente', 'ventre', 'devant') create a steady pulsation. At times, this is reinforced by the syntactic divisions of the text which, in the penultimate lines of the passage for example, present clauses of regular durations. The repetition of certain words ('lente', 'trouve', 'personne') forms pivots for the transition from one phase of the passage to the next, subsequently driving the language of the text forward with a sustained rhythm. These rhythmic effects replicate 'le battement' described and serve to hold the passage together as an 'ensemble', creating a formal unity. As the focus of the passage shifts, this formal unity creates an equivalence or parallelism between the description of the regularity of the heart and the constant presence of consciousness, something which Tarkos alludes to in a previous poem from this same series on 'Le Sentiment', where he describes 'Le sentiment constant de la conscience' (S, 109). Consciousness is therefore presented in the poem, both in the words themselves and in the prosodic effects, as a constant presence which is 'en phase' with a person, synchronised with the beating heart, with the movement of thought, and with the production of language itself.[21]

In *Processe*, Tarkos applies a similar attentiveness to the movements of thought: 'La pensée flotte, elle existe. Circulent. M'amusaient. S'ouvrent. Se désaltèrent. Virent. La pensée flotte, elle existe' [Thought drifts, it exists. Circulates. Amuses me. Opens. Quenches its thirst. Turns. Thought drifts, it exists] (*EP*, 69). His observations attempt to catch thought in the act, as it were, to trace its repetitions, revisions, and derivations. As suggested above, the displacement of the locus of experimentation from a time prior to the poem to taking place in the poem itself, accounts for many of the formal and stylistic characteristics of Tarkos's work. His poetry represents the flux of thought in language; as Kate Campbell observes, the 'pulsation' of the poet's thought provides the rhythm of the text, shaping the direction it takes.[22] The following passage, from the poem 'F', illustrates this idea in practice, exemplifying many of the formal properties that are prevalent in Tarkos's poetry:

> Ce qui est se forme. Ce qui est est sans forme. Ce qui est n'est pas les choses. Ce qui est est sans choses. Ce qui est forme ses petites formes. Ce qui est est la formation des petites formes. Ce qui est voit apparaître une forme. Les formes se réalisent. Ce qui est forme. Ce qui est n'est pas rien. Ce qui est est quelque chose. Ce qui est est dangereux. Ce qui est fait un effet. Ce qui est a une présence effective. Ce qui est prend forme pour s'être. Ce qui est prend forme. Ce qui est ne prend pas toutes formes. Ce qui est prend certaines formes. Les formes sont formées. (*EP*, 177)

> [What is forms. What is is formless. What is isn't things. What is is thingless. What is forms its little forms. What is is the formation of little forms. What is sees a form appear. Forms come into being. What is forms. What is isn't nothing. What is is something. What is is dangerous. What is has an effect. What is has an effective presence. What is takes a form to be itself. What is takes a form. What is doesn't take all forms. What is takes a certain form. Forms are formed.]

Here, as throughout his poetry, the basic pattern of Tarkos's style is the *ritournelle*, where repetition, and variations on that repetition, enact continuous processes of de- and re-territorialisation between phrases. Tarkos begins with a pivotal phrase, the anaphora 'ce qui est', which is then repeated and qualified as the passage develops. Polyptotons, in this instance 'former', 'formes', 'formation', are prevalent, reinforcing the effect of derivation and reformulation that exists between one sentence and the next. At times the passage appears to develop in logical sequence, 'Ce qui est n'est pas rien. Ce qui est est quelque chose', with one phrase following as a logical corollary of the previous. Elsewhere, an initial assertion is subsequently qualified, revised, or negated: 'Ce qui est est sans forme' becomes 'Ce qui est est la formation des petites formes', and 'Ce qui est n'est pas les choses' becomes 'Ce qui est est quelque chose'. These revisions or reworkings appear throughout Tarkos's *œuvre*, sometimes in close proximity (i.e. within the same passage), sometimes from one poem or text to the next. They often appear to negate each other, or to create paradoxes that are not easily overcome. For example, in *Le Signe=* Tarkos makes the following proclamation, 'Les mots n'existent pas' [Words do not exist] (S, 28), but in *Ma langue est poétique* writes 'Ma langue vit, est vivante, est poétique, est pleine de mots' [My language lives, is alive, is poetic, is full of words] (EP, 48). In this sense Tarkos's thought experiments involve the advancing of an idea or the extending and elaborating of an assertion, in order to test whether it holds up, before revising it or modifying it. Often the poet says one thing, and then says precisely the opposite, which can lead to a number of conflicting or contradictory statements on the same subject.[23] As we shall see, Tarkos's argumentation is thus in a state of continuous flux, which lends his work a slippery quality, inviting contrasting analysis from critics, depending on which part of Tarkos's argument they choose to focus on. Furthermore, Tarkos frequently ventures deliberately problematic statements, such as the suspiciously rapturous exaltations of drugs and money in 'Drogue' and *L'Argent*, where the cracks in the argument are made overtly visible, yet sit in contrast with the apparent certainty of the rhetoric. In an interview, Tarkos resolutely denies that these texts are ironic.[24] This claim makes sense when we consider that Tarkos is instead testing an argumentative stance, trying it out for size in the space of the text, rather than offering, via the poem, a pre-established conclusion on a topic, delivered directly, or indirectly through ironic voice.

Alongside these revisions and contrasting assertions, Tarkos often uses tautological phrases, such as 'Les formes sont formées'.[25] However, rather than being Barthesian tautologies, of the sort 'Racine, c'est Racine', Tarkos's phrases draw attention to the subtle distinctions in meaning that appear when polyptotons displace sense across different grammatical categories. Here we see how Tarkos earns his place among Hocquard's poet-grammarians: his phrases highlight how, in the transition from noun to adjective to verbal form, the semantic force of a word is modulated, with emphasis being placed, for example, on fixed essence, transient attribute, or process and movement itself.[26] Furthermore, in Tarkos's poetry tautologies often constitute a form of linguistic *mise en abyme* which link into a broader dimension of his work, clearly visible in this passage. His writing is often highly self-referential; here, the description of forms could easily be read as a metalinguistic comment on the verbal forms of the text itself. In this way, we could read 'Ce qui est forme ses petites formes. Ce qui est est la formation des petites formes' as describing the words of the text as they take shape. The final line, 'Les formes sont formées', might then be read as not only a logically tautological proposition, but also a metapoetic reflection on the composition of the text. Read in this way, the text is therefore both tracing the patterns of thought, while also continuously describing the language that shapes it, which in turn serves to sustain the impression of their inextricability.

In the passage above, the sequences and drifts of thought are presented in tangential series, where each sentence generates the next through some form of conjunctive relationship. In *Anachronisme*, Tarkos writes, 'La philosophie fait la chenille, une idée amène à une autre idée, un sentiment à un autre sentiment, un ami à un autre ami, une couleur à une autre couleur, un chemin à un autre chemin' [Philosophy does the conga, one idea leads to another idea, one feeling to another feeling, one friend to another friend, one colour to another colour, one path to another path] (*A*, 175–76). Thus, in *Oui* (1996), in the poem 'F' where the passage above appears, Tarkos circulates through a series of interconnected subjects: forms, ensembles, combinations, mixtures, organisations. In the final paragraphs of the poem, the speed at which Tarkos passes from one subject to the next accelerates, and references accumulate in a series of tautologies that conclude with an epistrophe: 'La vérité est vraie. La pensée pense. La parole dit. Le destin destine. Ce qui est est clair. Les définitions sont par définition. Les mots sont par définition. Les choses sont par définition' [The truth is true. Thought thinks. Speech speaks. Destiny destines. What is is clear. Definitions are by definition. Words are by definition. Things are by definition] (*EP*, 179). Talking about Tarkos's work, Philippe Castellin describes a drift, a series of deviations whereby 'tout mot peut conduire à tout mot et par des chemins multiples: la langue est cet enchevêtrement qui sans arrêt prend la tangente' [every word might lead to every other word and via multiple paths: language is this jumble which continuously goes off on a tangent].[27] This tangential quality, where language and thought diverge endlessly, tending towards an infinite number of possible derivations, is performed in Tarkos's poetry to excess. This is something that Tarkos himself describes in the performance poem 'Improvisation-lieder', where, after a long list of words, generated by semantic or phonological similarities, he writes:

> petite série
> série
> série
> série
> [...] où vas-tu?
> où m'emmènes-tu?
> jusqu'où continues-tu?
> vas-tu jusqu'à l'infini? (*E*, 122).[28]

[little series | series | series | series | [...] where are you going? | where are you taking me? | where are you heading? | are you heading to infinity?]

Describing this serial quality of Tarkos's poetry, which for him is grounded in the rhetorical figure of the polyptoton, Prigent writes, 'cette rhétorique est d'une part délibérément *abusive* (elle en fait trop)' [on the one hand, this rhetorical device is deliberately excessive (it's overdone)].[29] As Prigent suggests, there is a desire on Tarkos's part to represent this tangential or sequential generativity in its excess, consequently provoking a vertiginous sense of accumulation.

The mode of thought that is represented (or, indeed, performed) in Tarkos's work is at odds with the usual way in which thought is presented in writing as structured according to a pre-determined argument that is then delivered as an organised whole. Consequently, the accumulative tangents and repetitions of Tarkos's poetry prompt a form of disorienting reading experience akin to 'le vertige' that he describes as being an intrinsic characteristic of thought itself (*EP*, 378–79). The proliferating deviations of the subject matter are reinforced by certain formal characteristics — sentence length and long, unformatted paragraphs — that create an impression of an excess of language. The usual signposts and breathing spaces that guide the reader through the text (typically punctuation or typographical arrangement) are often minimal or absent in Tarkos's work. The consequent sense of disorientation is one of the many means by which Tarkos's poetry subverts the ordinary experience of language, and thus one of the ways in which his poetry might be read as minor, in Deleuze and Guattari's sense of the word. There are several instances in Tarkos's *œuvre* where this form of disoriented language is more readily apparent, for example in the agrammatical poems in *Donne* ('tu le tu donné ma de nouveau avec moi il par il même', *EP*, 322), or the *babil* in *Le Train* ('Ta na ta na ta — ne te ne te ne te ne ---- to no to no to no to no', *T*). However, in keeping with Deleuze and Guattari's analysis, the minor quality of Tarkos's work appears not just in these more extreme examples, but in the comprehensive stylistic and syntactic variation on unmarked linguistic norms that, even in passages that are sensical and grammatically correct, render language strange and disorienting. His use of *ritournelles*, where 'normal' language is repeated excessively, continuously revised and reformulated until it becomes abnormal, presents an exemplary illustration of the deterritorialising process of minor literature. Where in Fourcade's and Cadiot's poetry we have encountered a more radically foreign type of literary language — in Fourcade's use of neologisms or Cadiot's multilingual cut-ups, for example — in Tarkos's poetry there is an *unheimlich* effect, whereby the immediately recognisable mother tongue appears at once familiar and unfamiliar. In an article that discusses the coincidence of familiarity and strangeness in literary style, Laurent Jenny writes the following: 'Dans la "langue étrangère" de l'art se creuse et se différencie l'étrangeté familière de la langue commune. On y est d'emblée chez soi, quoique dans une forme d'habitation inédite' [In the 'foreign language' of art, the familiar strangeness of the common language digs and differentiates itself. One is at home within it straightaway, even if it's a new form of dwelling].[30] In Tarkos's poetry, we find this same 'étrangeté familière de la langue commune'. It might seem paradoxical that the strangeness of Tarkos's language arises precisely in the attempt to represent the experience of thought, an experience which is familiar to every reader. However, the atypicality of Tarkos's language flags up its difference to conventional modes of representation, and thus points to the illusory quality of linguistic norms that appear to represent reality unproblematically (in this instance, the way we think or experience consciousness). In this respect, returning to Prigent's formulation, we see a desire on Tarkos's part to 'ne pas se contenter de l'expérience du monde telle que les langages communautaires la représentent, à vivre toute langue comme étrangère et donc à refonder un langage (à "trouver une langue", disait Rimbaud) pour re-présenter autrement ces représentations'.[31]

'Pâte-mot'

The distinct formal and stylistic features of Tarkos's poetry discussed hitherto are equally motivated by the particular way in which he conceives of language. Throughout his work, Tarkos elaborates the concept of the 'pâte-mot', which begins as a way of conceptualising the operation of meaning within language. Rather than seeing words as the foundational units of meaning, Tarkos, via the image of a vast and viscous mass or 'pâte', sees language as an 'ensemble' in which meaning is located in a more complex configuration. In *Le Signe =*, he writes: 'le sens n'est pas donné avant toutes les paroles dites, c'est la masse des paroles dans leur masse qui va donner leur sens aux blocs de paroles qui sont proférés, qui sont sortis, qui sortent de la bouche' [meaning is not given before all spoken words, it's the mass of words in their mass which give meaning to the groups of words that are spoken, that have come out, that come out of the mouth] (S, 40). Meaning is therefore not a discrete property of the individual word, but forms instead 'des nuées, [...] des nappes, [...] des durées [...], des boulettes' [clouds, [...] layers, [...] durations [...], little balls] (28). This enumeration of several ways of conceptualising the units of meaning is deliberate, as Tarkos wishes to avoid the recourse to a singular or fixed location of sense. However, one particular term that he frequently returns to is that of the 'poussée de sens' — the thrust or upsurge of meaning — which attaches itself onto clusters of words: 'on ne peut plus prendre les mots pour des éléments de sens, pour les éléments de tirades sensées, il n'a pas de mots, il y a le sens qui pousse, qui s'attache à la poussée' [we can no longer take words as components of meaning, as components of meaningful speech, there are no words, there is meaning that thrusts, that is attached to the thrust] (28). The choice of term is significant: it marks a transition from envisaging meaning as grounded in a discrete entity (i.e. a word, taken as a graphic or phonological unit), to envisaging it as force or momentum in a speech (or text) event, where it attaches itself as an attribute.[32] For Tarkos, meaning is thus not a fixed or stable locus, but melts between words and phrases:

> [Les mots] se fondent, ils sont fondus, ils sont regroupés en une masse indistincte pour pousser une petite poussée de sens, ils ne voudraient pas rester seuls, ils ne sauraient que faire en restant seuls, ils se mettent à plusieurs et le sens des mots est donné par le sens qu'ils voudraient donner en s'y mettant à plusieurs. (S, 29–30)
>
> [[Words] merge, they are merged, they are regrouped into an indistinct mass to thrust a little thrust of meaning, they wouldn't like to stay on their own, they wouldn't know what to do on their own, they group together and the meaning of the words is given by the meaning that they'd like to give by grouping together.]

The repetition of the verb *fondre* is significant here for two reasons: firstly, because it reinforces the emphasis on meaning as movement and event; secondly, because it forms part of the extended metaphor Tarkos employs to envisage language as a viscous 'pâte'. Indeed, while meaning is understood as movement, language itself is a substance: 'pâte-mot est une substance' (S, 32). It is a substance where meaning circulates and where words are stuck together in an amorphous, elastic mass. The viscosity of the linguistic substance is significant because, as opposed to a solid substance, it is an object that contains the potential for movement. A viscous substance occupies an interim state between solid and liquid. It forms a resistance to forces acting upon it, but ultimately, as Jeff Barda points out in his discussion of Tarkos's 'pâte-mot', can be moulded at will: 'This amorphous material is also characterized by its plasticity and malleability [...], one that rejects fixed identities or solidification in favour of a texture that can be infinitely kneaded'.[33]

Significantly, this conception of language places emphasis on the whole as opposed to the fragment, which in turn marks a rupture with the modernist emphasis on fragmentation, disjunction, and detachment.[34] It also sets Tarkos apart from several of his contemporaries; his metaphor of language as a totalising 'pâte' marks a stark contrast to, for example, the image used by Cadiot and Hocquard of the poet as archaeologist, constructing the poem from fragments unearthed on a dig.[35] On a formal level, this manifests itself in an immediately striking visual distinction between Tarkos's agglutinative 'carrés' or 'blocs', and the cut-ups of Cadiot's work, where isolated clauses are dispersed across the page.[36]

As Castellin remarks, Tarkos's interest in the relationship between parts and whole, and his focus on structural relations in the production of meaning, offers an immediate resemblance to Saussure.[37] I want to briefly outline the similarities and differences in their approach to language, precisely because Saussure's conception forms the foundation for many (if not most) of the poets thinking about language across the twentieth century. It is where Tarkos diverges from Saussure's thought that we find some of his most interesting and innovative ideas, and where we see certain resemblances with Deleuze and Guattari's own critique of Saussure's theory of the sign.[38] Like Saussure, Tarkos describes the relational construction of meaning, where things are defined by their situation within a broader system: '[les choses se définissent] par la place qu'elles occupent aux côtés des autres à l'intérieur d'une constellation de places' [[things are defined] by the position they occupy alongside others within a constellation of positions] (E, 53). However, Tarkos soon highlights the problem with this image of the constellation, borrowed from Saussure.[39] He writes, 'L'image de la constellation est ici trop discrète pour donner l'idée de la continuité des places' [The image of the constellation is too discrete to convey the notion of the continuity of positions] (53). The distinction Tarkos draws here between the discrete and the continuous is an interesting one, and highlights where his analysis differs from that of Saussure. If Saussure's analysis still maintains the word as a discrete unit of sense, albeit constructed by its relationship within a system, then Tarkos, while still employing the same framework of relational construction of meaning, sees sense as configured in a continuous series of relationships that transcend the individual unit of the word. In *Le Signe =*, which is prefaced by the phrase 'le signifiant = le signifié' (*S*, 7), Tarkos writes: 'Le mot n'est pas le référenceur, n'est pas le signifiant, le mot est sans référence, n'a pas deux côtés, n'est pas un signe' [The word is not the referencer, is not the signifier, the word is without reference, doesn't have two sides, is not a sign] (37).[40] In such a way, Tarkos sets about the dismantling of the very notion of the linguistic sign, a gesture which is reflected in the ambiguous title *Le Signe =*, one possible reading of which is that the sign equates to nothing. This rejection is no doubt in part because Saussure's theory of the sign is grounded on the word as the ultimate unit of meaning. Indeed, in a later passage in *Le Signe =*, Tarkos describes words as little more than empty sacks or shells (28), because meaning is to be found elsewhere. Conversely, for Tarkos, meaning arises at the intersection of various systems of 'relations'. In an interview with Pascale Casanova, he says the following:

> Le problème c'est que ces groupes de mots sont souvent attachés à des relations, c'est-à-dire les relations que l'on a entre nous [...], elles sont déjà toutes fourrées d'intérêts et de structures, donc ce qu'on va dire ça va être des groupes de mots qui sont toujours attachés à ces structures. (*E*, 55)
>
> [The problem is that these groups of words are often attached to relationships, namely the relationships that exist between us [...], these relationships are already full of interests and structures, so what we'll say will be groups of words that are already attached to these structures.]

In this emphasis on 'relations', we see the pragmatic dimension of Tarkos's work, which Castellin describes as being close to the theoretical approaches developed by Grice, Austin, Searle, and Labov.[41] Meaning cannot be isolated from the social context in which it is found, and from whose systems it derives; the 'pâte-mot' is part of a broader 'pâte-monde' (*E*, 216), and sense is therefore not anchored in word-units but encoded throughout the relational structures that contain them.

A further divergence between Tarkos's and Saussure's conceptions of language appears in *Le Signe =*, where Tarkos rejects the dualism between world and word that is a corollary of Saussure's analysis of the linguistic sign. When asked in an interview to expand on Saussure's analysis, Tarkos responded:

> Ce que je trouve bizarre dans cette idée-là, c'est le fait que la langue et le monde soient séparés. Pour moi la langue n'est pas en dehors du monde, c'est aussi concret qu'un sac de sable qui te tombe sur la tête, c'est complètement réel, complètement efficace, efficient, utile.[42]
>
> [What I find bizarre in that idea is the notion that language and the world might be separated. For me, language is not outside the world, it's as concrete as a bag of sand falling on your head, it's completely real, completely effective, efficient, useful.]

Here, as elsewhere, Tarkos argues that language does not reflect or represent the world from the outside, but is interior to it, a constitutive part of a broader 'ensemble'. In 1997, during an interview given at the Poetry International Festival in Rotterdam, Tarkos addresses this point directly. He gave the following explanation of 'pâte-mot', emphasising the inextricability of language and world as two constituents of the same substance:

> Toute la langue, elle est collée entre elle, et on peut pas lui prendre des petits morceaux pour s'inventer une histoire ou pour construire quelque chose. Alors on est obligé de tout prendre à la fois. Tout prendre le réel et tout prendre la langue qui est toute collée ensemble. Alors pour pouvoir avancer un tant soit peu là-dedans, pour faire même un geste, pour faire n'importe quoi dans une telle réalité cohérente, et collée, on est obligé, au départ, d'avoir un 'oui'. (*E*, 244)

> [All language is stuck together, and we can't take little bits of it to make up a story or to construct something. So we have to take it all at the same time. Take all of reality and take all of language which is all stuck together. So to be able to progress even a little bit within it, to do something, to do anything in such a cohesive, stuck-together reality, we have to start with a 'yes'.]

The final section of this chapter will address in detail the significance of the 'oui', a recurring motif in Tarkos's poetry, but in the interim I want to focus on this monistic conception of language and world, which sets Tarkos apart from many of his contemporaries. It is important to emphasise that Tarkos is not merely observing that language exists as a material phenomenon among others, a fact which, as we have seen in the previous chapters on Cadiot and Fourcade, is hardly remarkable or unique. Nor is it merely a reiteration of the fact that language is a social phenomenon, a series of linguistic events grounded in human interaction, as opposed to an abstract semiotic system. What makes Tarkos's analysis distinct is that it emphasises a levelling down, a flattening of distinctions, where language, no longer conceived as being outside or exterior to the world that it purports to describe, is therefore stripped of its privileged status. This levelling is in part a response to the linguistic turn of the twentieth century, manifested in formalism, structuralism, or in the emphasis on linguistic materiality and surface in contemporary poetry. In all of these instances, language is granted a special status and conceived as a phenomenon set apart from others. In Tarkos's analysis however, it is understood as a cluster of phenomena — actions, movements, impulses, events, gestures, material substances, sensations, perceptions, etc. — that form the basis of all that is, and which configure in various arrangements in all things, language included. Tarkos frequently focuses on language as a series of 'actes', where speaking or writing are actions among other types of actions, such as smoking, sleeping, or walking in a park. This parallelism is particularly apparent in *Anachronisme*, where reflections on language and poetry are interwoven with a focus on a whole host of daily activities; each action presents itself as a sensorial experience, involving motor-neurological responses within the body, each taking place in a particular time period, involving a change of physical state, and so on. In such a way, Tarkos seeks to diminish the distinction between word and world, in a gesture which aims to avoid setting language apart as a singular phenomenon. Language is conceived as existing on a broader plane of consistency, to use Deleuze and Guattari's term, in a relationship of continuity and interiority with 'la Grande substance'. Here we see, as Castellin describes it, Tarkos's 'ontologie radicalement *immanentiste, moniste, continuiste*' in practice.[43] Likewise, in arguing that language is part of a continuous, monistic reality, Tarkos then translates the same formal properties of 'pâte-mot' into a broader 'pâte-monde', emphasising structural parallels between the two levels. Patterns of the linguistic 'pâte' are traced across a number of different strata of experience; in *Anachronisme*, for example, Tarkos observes the movement of crowds outside the metro station at Barbès (*A*, 39), and in an interview he compares 'pâte-mot' to demonstrators at a protest.[44] In both instances, he describes how the crowd forms an amorphous, elastic whole, in which the constituent parts, the individuals in the group, move together as a 'flux' (*A*, 39).

In the light of Tarkos's theory of the 'patmo', and the analysis he offers of the linguistic sign, the following remark by Prigent appears problematic:

> Peu de poètes, du coup, savent nous faire éprouver avec autant d'aisance ironique la sensation violente qui se dégage de ça: l'étrangeté de la langue, son tournis ahuri, sa distance implacable aux corps, aux choses, au réel. Peu savent nous introduire avec un aussi imparable mélange de tendresse subtile et de cruauté pince-sans-rire au malaise de la langue qui passe comme une lame entre le monde et nous.[45]

> [Few poets know how to make us feel, with such ironic ease, the violent sensation that this engenders: the strangeness of language, its stupefying dizziness, its relentless distance to bodies, to things, to the real. Few know how to introduce us, with such an unstoppable combination of subtle tenderness and deadpan cruelty, to the uneasy sensation of language sliding like a blade between us and the world.]

This reading, which reflects that of a number of critics who adopt a similar theoretical stance to Prigent's, conveys less about Tarkos's own position than about Prigent's. Prigent appears to be appropriating Tarkos into his own critical framework, where the division between word and world is taken as given, and where all writing begins from the negative, from the absence of the real in the text. While, as previously suggested, the 'étrangeté de la langue' that Prigent identifies here is certainly present, this strangeness of language, which is integral to minor literature, does not necessarily entail a divorce or a distanciation from the world as Prigent goes on to suggest. There are many instances where this might be the corollary, or indeed the desired effect, of the defamiliarisation of language within poetry (Francis Ponge being one such example).[46] However, if anything, the opposite is true for Tarkos, and the following section will argue that the 'ontologie radicalement *immanentiste, moniste, continuiste*' of his work aims to bring the world into closer proximity, and language, as a constituent part of the world, likewise.[47]

One of the ways in which Tarkos sets about the desired immersion in language and world in his poetry is through the exaggerated performance of 'pâte-mot' in the poem. As Castellin writes: '[Le poème] ne "dit" rien, ne "sert" à rien, ne "démontre" rien. *Il montre dans sa forme patmot en acte*. Il colle à patmot. La déploie. L'étale. Exagère ce qui est patent' [The poem 'says' nothing, 'serves' no purpose, 'reveals' nothing. *It shows, through its form, patmot in action*. It sticks to patmot. Deploys it. Spreads it. Exaggerates what is patently obvious].[48] To illustrate this idea in practice, the following extract is taken from 'Je fume' in *Caisses*:

> Je fume, la fumée s'échappe, la fumée sort, la fumée me sort
> de la tête, ma tête laisse échapper de la fumée, je laisse
> échapper de la fumée au-dessus de ma tête, ma chaleur
> part en fumée, une fumée monte du dessus de ma tête dans
> le ciel, je fume.[49]

[I smoke, the smoke drifts away, the smoke leaves, the smoke leaves | my head, my head lets the smoke drift away, I let | the smoke drift away above my head, my heat | goes up in smoke, smoke rises from above my head in | the sky, I smoke.]

In this passage, the formal features replicate and exaggerate the properties of the 'patmo'. To give just two very basic examples, here, as elsewhere, words do not appear in isolation (on separate lines in the text) as they do, for example, in Fourcade's work, but are always in large blocks of texts, often in lengthy sentences (here, the nineteen-line poem is composed of one long sentence). The revision and reworking of phrases, alongside the use of polyptoton and anaphora ('la fumée', 'je fume'), gives the impression that the poet is bogged down, caught in the sticky mass of words. The effects of accumulation produced by these features contribute to an impression of excess in Tarkos's work: an excess of language, and with that, an excess of the world that is evoked. This excess no doubt contributes to the strangeness of Tarkos's poetic language that Prigent describes above, and is further reinforced by the prevalence of lists in Tarkos's work.

Lists

Lists are pervasive in Tarkos's poetry and take a number of different forms. Often they are based on a straightforward semantic category: animals (*MC*, 33), parts of the body (*A*, 33), musical instruments (*A*, 9). Often they revolve around linguistic similarities: words beginning with 'k' (*A*, 57) or verbs commencing in 'a' (60). Elsewhere, they are assembled according to more eclectic resemblances; in *Anachronisme*, for example, Tarkos presents a list of things that he stole one winter (*A*, 53), objects that make a loud noise (95), and, in an exercise reminiscent of Perec, items on his table (143). In *Le Baroque*, Tarkos enumerates a list of lists, creating a sort of metapoetic *mise-en-abyme* of this property of his work:

> Liste des étoiles connues
> Liste des couleurs disponibles
> Liste des objets vendus en France
> Liste des insectes nommés
> Liste des classification. (*B*, 11)

[List of known stars | List of available colours | List of objects sold in France | List of named insects | List of classifications.]

The final line evokes one of the many functions of the list in Tarkos's work, drawing attention to classification, taxonomy, and the many ways in which language divides and structures reality. In Tarkos's poetry, there is an exploration of the normative modes of thought which seek to find patterns in otherwise formless substances. The eclecticism of the 'family resemblance' for each series demonstrates the variety of ways in which we look for relationships between one entity and the next. Many of the lists are reminiscent of games of word association, depicting in turn the rhizomatic nature of language, characterised by endless points of juncture, and infinite relations between the words within it:

> orange
> ogre
> horrible
> autorisation
> obligation. (E, 117)

The arbitrariness of certain sequences serves to emphasise the plurality of possible paths that might be navigated through 'la pâte faite de mots' (E, 231).

Certain lists prompt a distinct type of reading process which reinforces the idea, outlined above, of the performance of 'patmo' in the poem. The more prosaic lists, such as long enumerations of cheeses (A, 164–65) or fruits (A, 50), might well see the reader skimming through the poem, gathering an impressionistic sense of the ensemble ('a list of cheeses'), as opposed to reading each individual name, word by word ('sainte-maure, chèvre, chaource, vache, le vieux lille', and so on). In *Morceaux choisis*, in a text entitled 'La Liste', Tarkos quotes the German mathematician Rudolph Lipschitz: 'Si on veut avoir une vue d'ensemble de plusieurs choses, on en choisira d'abord une, et on ajoutera une nouvelle chose à la première choisie jusqu'à épuisement' [If we want to have an overview of several things, first we choose one of them, then we add another new thing to the first, until the point of exhaustion] (MC, 22). The poem composed of lists will often place emphasis on the ensemble, as opposed to the individual unit, an idea that is reinforced by the formal properties of certain texts, such as *Anachronisme*, *Processe*, or *Ma langue est poétique*. Tarkos does not divide these texts into individual poems, distinguishing them by titles or separate layout on a new page. A degree of distinction is made between one block of text and the next, either through paragraphs or alternating justifications on the page, but the division of the text as a whole is minimal. Coupled with the thematic unity that sees the same subjects returning from one passage to the next, this means that these books function as broader textual 'ensembles'. In this sense, there are then two layers of symmetry in the formal constitution of Tarkos's work: each list is constituted from several words or phrases, forming a complete paragraph, and each paragraph forms a series with the previous and the next, in turn constituting the text as a whole. When Jean-Michel Espitallier talks about lists in *Caisse à outils*, he writes that 'Toute liste est un objet fractal'.[50] We could conceptualise certain texts by Tarkos as 'objets fractals' — where the list provides a set of formal properties, the patterns of which are then mirrored on a broader structural level within the book. Given Tarkos's theory of the 'patmo', and his consideration of the relationship between part and whole in language and substance more generally, it is unsurprising that the list, which prompts these same questions, is such a prevalent feature in his work.

As Lipschitz suggests in the quotation above, the accumulative nature of the list, which involves a continuous process of supplementation or addition, tends towards a state of exhaustion. This practice of attempting to exhaust a subject, or to exhaust language itself in the process, recalls various pivotal figures for Tarkos: Perec, Ponge, and Beckett, for instance.[51] In *Morceaux choisis*, Tarkos professes the following intention:

> Je vais écrire la liste des choses. Il y a beaucoup de choses. [...] Je m'appliquerai. Je vais écrire la liste de toutes les choses, c'est possible en faisant attention, elles ne sont pas infinies. [...] Les choses essayent toujours de s'échapper. Avec leur nom chacune, ni plus, ni moins, elles ne s'échapperont pas. (*MC*, 22)
>
> [I'm going to write the list of things. There are lots of things. [...] I'll apply myself. I'm going to write the list of all things, it's possible by paying attention, they're not infinite. [...] Things always try to escape. Each with their own name, not a single one of them will escape.]

The obvious impossibility of writing a comprehensive, exhaustive list of 'toutes les choses', coupled with the poet's apparent certainty, or indeed faux naivety, lend this passage a clearly ironic tone. In a similar gesture in *Anachronisme*, after enumerating an (admittedly long) list of animals, he writes, 'voilà il n'y a pas d'autres animaux, ce sont là tous les animaux, [...] tous les animaux qui existent sont ceux-là' [there you have it, there are no other animals, all the animals are here, [...] those are all the animals that exist] (*A*, 15). This claim, which again can only be read as ironic as it clearly sits at odds with the non-exhaustive list that precedes it, identifies the way in which any attempt to enumerate exhaustively is ultimately destined to fail. The types of lists that Tarkos details in his work, rather than being closed-set classifications such as days of the week, are predominantly based on subjects that are, by definition, inexhaustible. In such a way, Tarkos's poetry sets up an apparent attempt to exhaust language, and subsequently performs the failure of such a task. This in turn serves to highlight the sheer vastness of language (and consequently the world it evokes), by juxtaposing its enormity with the comparative slightness of any one text's attempt to exhaust it.

The structural or syntactic properties of the list as a form contribute to the accumulative effect that characterises Tarkos's poetry. Typified by proliferation and interconnection, the list forms a rhizomatic structure.[52] If the list represents an '(n + 1)' equation, with the possibility of supplementation being an intrinsic property, then its inclusion in the poem complements the notion of an endless, ongoing project. This sense of continuity or interminability is alluded to in the final pages of *Anachronisme*, which ends with a three-page enumeration of the infinite number pi. There is a clear symbolism in the fact that pi can only be represented in the book to a certain number of decimal places. It offers a metapoetic reading, highlighting the way in which the poem, faced with the sheer expanse of reality, can only ever offer up some slight endeavour, necessarily carving out a meagre portion to present, and drawing itself to an artificial close.

The motif of the list, coupled with the way Tarkos's poetry advances through a series of revisions and rectifications, mirror his broader conception of poetry as no longer a completed, verbal artefact, the final product of a poetic process, but rather the process itself, suspended in a continual state of rewriting and reworking. This conception owes much to Ponge, who, as Noland puts it, 'introduced the genre of the poem-as-work-in-progress', which goes hand-in-hand with the focus on the poem as an 'enquête' or 'expérience'.[53] When Ponge's œuvre transitioned from the earlier, page-length, completed 'textes clos' in *Le Parti pris des choses* [The Nature of Things] (1942), to the later, open-ended, draft-like 'textes ouverts' in, for example, *Pièces* [Pieces] (1961), *Le Savon* [Soap] (1967), and *La Fabrique du Pré* [The Making of The Meadow] (1971), he initiated a draft-like, process-orientated writing that resists petrifaction and maintains momentum: repeating, redefining, and rearranging. In a description that applies equally well to Tarkos's own practice, Ponge writes: 'Que mon travail soit celui d'une rectification continuelle de mon expression (sans souci *a priori* de la forme de cette expression) en faveur de l'objet brut' [Let my work be that of a continual rectification of my expression (without an *a priori* concern for the form of this expression) in favour of the raw object].[54] Crucially, the conception of poem as work-in-progress often implies both its own inexhaustibility, and its ultimate, inevitable failure, leading Philippe Sollers to describe Ponge's 'volonté d'inachèvement perpétuel' [desire for perpetual incompletion].[55] In this sense, both Ponge and Tarkos exemplify the following reflection by Deleuze:

> Ecrire n'est certainement pas imposer une forme (d'expression) à une matière vécue. La littérature est plutôt du côté de l'informe, ou de l'inachèvement, comme Gombrowicz l'a dit et fait. Ecrire est une affaire de devenir, toujours inachevé, toujours en train de se faire, et qui déborde toute matière vivable ou vécue. C'est un processus, c'est-à-dire un passage de Vie qui traverse le vivable et le vécu. L'écriture est inséparable du devenir: en écrivant, on devient-femme, on devient-animal ou végétal, on devient-molécule jusqu'à devenir-imperceptible. (*CC*, 11)

> [To write is certainly not to impose a form (of expression) on the matter of lived experience. Literature rather moves in the direction of the ill-formed or the incomplete, as Gombrowicz said as well as practiced. Writing is a question of becoming, always incomplete, always in the midst of being formed, and goes beyond the matter of any liveable or lived experience. It is a process, that is, a passage of Life that traverses both the liveable and the lived. Writing is inseparable from becoming: in writing, one becomes-woman, becomes-animal or vegetable, becomes-molecule to the point of becoming-imperceptible.] (*ECC*, 1)

Deleuze's conception of the text as 'une affaire de devenir, toujours inachevé, toujours en train de se faire' certainly resonates with what we find in Tarkos's experimental poetic practice. As his use of the list demonstrates rather aptly, his attempts to give form to the formless matter of existence continuously perform their own failure. Tarkos, like Cadiot, was well-known for his animated public readings; this emphasis on performance also leaves the poem in a state of impermanence, no longer a published text but a series of events, anchored spatially and temporally, and subject to constant revision, with endless variations generated by the circumstances of each reading. The poem as a 'work-in-progress' is therefore mobilised in a continuous state of becoming. And, with the current 'crise de poésie' looming in the background, these formal expressions of a 'rectification continuelle' might also reflect the way poetry is engaged in a sustained process of becoming-poetry, constantly re-inventing and redefining its very identity as a genre.

For Tarkos, the list also plays a role in his broader project which seeks to affirm the presence of the world within the text. As Campbell writes, 'For Tarkos, the poetic act is primarily an affirmation of presence'.[56] This affirmation of presence is clearly opposed to the tradition, discussed in Chapter 1, of 'poésie négative'. Following from Mallarmé, 'poésie négative' derives from a certain conception of language, outlined above, whereby the nature of the linguistic sign produces an inescapable separation between language and world, leaving the text characterised by negation and absence. On the question of presence and absence, we find a significant divergence in critical responses to Tarkos's work. While Campbell describes Tarkos's poetics of presence, Prigent, like others, suggests that certain linguistic effects (such as fast pacing or the semantic interchangeability of one clause with the next) serve to empty Tarkos's texts of meaning, resulting in an 'effacement' [erasure].[57] Prigent extends his analysis of this supposedly self-cancelling mode of writing by looking at the significance of whiteness in Tarkos's work, again aligning the younger poet to the 'poésie blanche' associated with 'poésie négative'.[58] However, Tarkos himself rejected this reading of his work strongly. In response to a letter from Yves di Manno, who said he found Tarkos's poetry 'assez vide de sens' [quite empty of meaning], he wrote:

> Je ne veux pas jouer avec le manque de sens. [...] Je ne supporte pas, pour vous dire la vérité, qu'un texte n'ait aucun sens, comme il s'en voit trop dans la poésie, des textes qui ne font que glisser, ruisseler, sur des ambiances de miroitement de sens de mots comme mutité par exemple. (E, 492–93)
>
> [I don't want to play with the absence of meaning. [...] I can't stand, to tell you the truth, that a text should have no meaning, as is seen too often in poetry, texts that just slip around, overflow with ambient glimmers of meanings of words like muteness for example.]

Here Tarkos is quick to refuse the analysis that his poetry is emptied of meaning; elsewhere, he extends these comments, refuting the possibility of meaningless texts altogether: 'tout ce qui est imprimé, est un texte, a un sens' [everything that is printed, is a text, has a meaning] (EP, 119). Although grounded ultimately in his conception of the 'pâte-mot' or 'pâte-monde', throughout his poetry Tarkos makes frequent use of a number of declarative, anaphoric refrains that reinforce this affirmation of presence: 'il y a' or 'il existe' [there is], 'je suis' [I am], and 'j'ai' [I have]. These phrases, marked in their simplicity, are often followed by lists or accumulative phrases: 'J'ai des pieds, des mains, [...] des paupières, des cheveux, des ongles' [I have feet, hands, [...] eyelids, hair, nails] (A, 33). We see here Tarkos's desire to render reality immanent in the poem and to immerse the reader in the material presence of the world. The focus on presence offers an immediate parallel with the work of Yves Bonnefoy. However, if, as John T. Naughton suggests, Bonnefoy's 'highly abstract, even "conceptual" diction' and the absence of 'personal experience' means that 'the *specifically* human face is effaced or even obliterated in the highly "essentialized" landscape of [Bonnefoy's] poetic world', then quite the opposite is true for Tarkos.[59] Castellin describes Tarkos's emphasis on material presence as 'une poétique de l'immersion: une *endopoétique*. Un réalisme si sauvage qu'il emboutit toute altitude. Le réel est infiniment plus vaste et contourné que nous ne le croyons, mais sans abîme, ni ciel' [a poetics of immersion: an *endopoetics*. A realism that is so wild that it crashes into any altitude. Reality is infinitely vaster and more convoluted than we believe it to be, but without depths or sky].[60]

The poem 'Quelle belle terre', originally a performance piece, illustrates Castellin's comment rather aptly:

> Quelle belle terre,
>
> Un vaste, et très grand paysage,
>
> C'est une belle terre,
>
> Une bonne bouille
>
> La simple richesse de sa richesse
>
> Elle est très vaste et très grande.
> [...]
> Un souffle
> Un immense retentissement
> Un poumon grand comme
>
> Un camion
>
> Comme une inspiration,
>
> Sa beauté, une grande et vaste réalité nue, riante, chantante, qui danse.
>
> Oui.
> Elle est une grande, et belle, et vaste, et très nue.
>
> D'une rare violence, imprègne
>
> Ma pigeonneuse éponge. (*E*, 471–72)

[What a beautiful earth, | A vast, and very large landscape, | It's a beautiful earth, | A nice mug | The sheer richness of its richness | It is very vast and very large. | [...] | A breath | An immense impact | A lung large like | A lorry | Like an inspiration [trans. note: or inhalation] | Its beauty, a large and vast reality, bare, laughing, singing, that dances. | Yes. | It is a large, and beautiful, and vast, and very bare. | With a rare violence, permeates | My pigeonly sponge.]

The power of the passage lies in the simplicity of its phrasing; the adjectives 'nue' and 'simple', used in the passage to describe reality, might therefore also be read as metapoetic, describing the language of the poem itself. The text rotates around a relatively small set of words that are repeated ('belle', 'vaste', 'richesse', etc.), an effect which is reinforced by the use of polyptotons ('beauté', 'belle', 'riante', and the nominal form found later in the poem 'rire'). Reality is described as stark or bare, and the formal properties echo this minimalism, with the lines being relatively short in length, and dispersed across the page so as to emphasise the empty space between them. On the one hand, we might read the slightness of the phrasing as a gesture towards the insufficiency of language to capture the vastness or richness of the world it evokes. The opening lines of 'Quelle belle terre' present a cliché, the paired-down language of the passage is constantly at risk of appearing naff or trite, and the lacklustre simile 'comme | Un camion' has a bathetic effect which is reinforced by the subsequent need for revision or modification in the following line 'Comme une inspiration'. However, the apparent slightness or simplicity of the language might also lend the text the same properties that it attributes to the world: a richness or pregnancy, where the words are charged with latent possibility. The image of the sponge might also be read as metapoetic; the words of the passage are absorptive, they contain more than the slightness of their exterior form might initially suggest. This metapoetic analysis gains some credibility when we consider the way in which Tarkos conflates reality, subject, and language in the poem. Proceeding through a series of metaphors, Tarkos conceptualises the world as a human body — describing its 'bonne bouille', its 'souffle', its 'poumons', and its 'inspiration'. Basing the imagery on the vocal tract thus evokes language itself. Set amongst this series of anthropomorphising images, Tarkos describes the Earth's 'retentissement', which evokes in turn the effect or impact of the world on the human subject. The world lives, breathes, and inhales, and in turn is lived, breathed, and inhaled. This anthropomorphism is sustained in the qualification of reality as 'riante, chantante, qui danse' (and indeed the word 'danse' reappears later in the passage in the first-person form, 'je danse', E, 473). In the final lines of the three-page poem, the isolated nominal phrase 'Un globule' (E, 473) also serves to conflate world, subject, and language into a single substance. The polysemy of 'globule' — a biological cell (such as a blood cell), a spherical geometric shape, and, historically, an elementary particle (the most basic constituent of matter and light) — sees the human body, the Earth, and the Universe in its entirety, amalgamated in a single word. Elsewhere, in the line 'Elle est une grande, et belle, et vaste, et très nue', the series of adjectives lead to a notably absent nominal phrase, reinforced by the full stop. Here, Tarkos creates a blank space which might be filled with any number of possible metaphors. The missing noun, and the accumulation of adjectives, could be read as a movement away from the desire to name and delineate forms within a substance, putting the emphasis instead on sets of attributes, properties, and features, and reinforcing the idea of a monistic conception of matter. If Tarkos performs the collapse of several typically differentiated phenomena into a single substance, then from this point of collapse, the language of the poem thus carries with it reality, the world, and the subject, immersing the reader in the continuous substance that the passage evokes.

Death and the Everyday

Elsewhere this poetics of immersion manifests itself in a different form. Many of Tarkos's texts, most notably the last book he published, *Anachronisme*, are filled with vivid descriptions of the day-to-day world that he inhabits. As Prigent concedes in his analysis of the emptying of meaning in Tarkos's work: 'les poèmes de Tarkos ne disent pas rien [...], ils montrent effectivement un monde. Ils posent un décor trivial qui est notre vrai monde' [Tarkos's poems don't say nothing [...], they do indeed depict a world. They are furnished with the mundane scenery of our real world].[61] As seen in the previous discussion of lists, this 'décor trivial' is found in descriptions of the abundant paraphernalia of everyday life, elsewhere it involves the transcription of day-to-day events. Enacting the desire to 'décrire le défilement continu' (*EP*, 150), these transcriptions often appear in the present tense, and involve a form of running commentary, as in the following example:

> Je traverse la pont [sic], le pont traverse la Seine, je traverse la Seine, je marche le long du pont je ne m'arrête pas, je regarde en marchant la Seine, l'eau, je suis sur un pont, je marche au-dessus de l'eau, le pont passe au-dessus de l'eau, le pont est long, je marche longuement. (*A*, 11)

> [I cross the bridge, the bridge crosses the Seine, I cross the Seine, I walk along the bridge I don't stop, I look at the Seine, the water, while walking, I am on a bridge, I walk above the water, the bridge crosses above the water, the bridge is long, I walk slowly.]

Often these passages give referential markers — temporal or geographical — that, alongside adverbial phrases such as 'maintenant' and 'réellement', serve to ground the text:

> Cet après-midi vers dix-huit heures j'étais réellement sur un banc dans un parc. Il est maintenant vingt et une heures, je suis allongé dans mon lit. J'y fumais une cigarette, habillé de mon imper noir et de mon chapeau, je croisais et décroisais les jambes, je restais assis sur le banc, le ciel était menaçant. (*S*, 127)

> [This afternoon around six I was really on a bench in a park. It is now nine, I am lying in my bed. I was smoking a cigarette, wearing my black raincoat and my hat, I crossed and uncrossed my legs, I stayed sitting on the bench, the sky looked ominous.]

There is, especially in *Anachronisme*, an autobiographical dimension to this practice, where Tarkos makes reference to places and people that we know to be real: descriptions of his work at the BnF (*A*, 218), encounters with colleagues and friends such as Charles Pennequin (*A*, 54) or Jean-Marie Gleize (*A*, 106). In *Oui*, Tarkos writes:

> Je vais à l'usine
> Aujourd'hui Je vis
> Je vais travailler aujourd'hui [...]
> Je vais Je sais Je suis heureux. (*EP*, 206)

> [I go to the factory | Today I am living | I am going to work today [...] | I go I know I am happy.]

The triplet in the final phrase captures three components of experience: action or event, knowledge or consciousness, and emotional or psychological response. The repetition of 'je' is significant; it affirms the presence of the subject, and grounds the everyday in subjective experience.

Throughout his *œuvre*, Tarkos includes the most prosaic elements from his day-to-day life: a list of the contents of his cupboards (*A*, 155–56), intricate descriptions of his old white socks (*A*, 17) and Adidas trainers (*EP*, 70). The elements Tarkos chooses to focus on are so markedly banal that emphasis is placed precisely on their ordinariness. In *Ma langue* he addresses this point explicitly:

> J'attends dans la file
> d'attente d'un guichet de poste. Cela sans sous-entendre qu'il y a là
> quelque chose d'extraordinaire que d'attendre à l'intérieur d'une file
> d'attente d'un
> bureau de poste. Je le fais régulièrement, normalement, ce n'est pas la
> première
> fois, il n'y a là rien d'extraordinaire. (*ML*, 34)

> [I wait in the queue | at a post office counter. Which is not to say that there's | anything extraordinary about waiting in a queue | at a | post office. I do it regularly, habitually, it's not the | first | time, there is nothing extraordinary about it.]

The inclusion of these details in the poem is neither an attempt to tease out the extraordinary from the everyday, nor a desire to render the ordinary extraordinary through poetic language. Instead, Tarkos's poetry presents the ordinary precisely as ordinary which, as a marked practice in itself, results in a heightened awareness for the reader of the usually backgrounded texture of everyday experience. In this sense, Tarkos's engagement with the everyday involves a reworking of other ways in which it has been represented in poetry. *Anachronisme*, for example, seems to gesture towards Baudelaire's *Les Fleurs du mal* and *Le Spleen de Paris*, in the emphasis it places on the encounter, often situated in the streets of Paris. In the text, Tarkos enumerates various events that represent 'un moment, un instant, un croisement' (*A*, 9), however these encounters are not the charged encounters of 'À une passante' [To a Passerby], but altogether more mundane meetings.[62] He meets an Englishman named Nigel, and then spots him again on the metro (57); a woman stops him at a café to ask if he's German, and then looks disappointed to hear he isn't (72). Earlier on in the book he describes crossing paths with a stranger on the way to an exhibition: 'j'ai rigolé, je me suis retourné, lui aussi s'est retourné, tout en continuant à marcher, il rigolait, j'allais voir les nuages des tableaux chinois dans le Petit Palais' [I laughed, I turned around, he also turned around, while still walking, he laughed, I went to see the Chinese paintings in the Petit Palais] (8). Here, there is a resistance to aestheticising the everyday, or to selecting only the most exceptional or notable details to depict. Later in *Anachronisme*, Tarkos expands on the significance of the 'rencontre' in the text:

> Un élément qui s'est passé. Un élément réel. Ce que fait l'élément quand il est réel. Sa façon de se refaire, de revenir, de dire je suis une rencontre, oui cela a eu lieu [...], je sais que cela a eu lieu, je peux le remonter quand je veux, je ne peux pas le remanier, il est fait, il est solide, j'aurais pu le toucher de la main, je pouvais le toucher parce qu'il est réel, parce qu'il est là en chair et en os, probablement que je l'ai touché, que sa proximité a touché ma proximité. (*A*, 196–97)

> [An element that happened. A real element. What the element does when it is real. Its way of reconstructing itself, of coming back, of saying I am an encounter, yes that took place [...], I know that it took place, I can recreate it when I want, I can't rework it, it is done, it is solid, I could have touched it

with my hand, I could touch it because it is real, because it is there in flesh and blood, I probably touched it, its proximity probably touched my proximity.]

The encounter thus represents a prototypical manifestation of an event, one that affirms both internal subjectivity and external reality, and brings the world and subject into proximity, rendering the exterior immanent to the interior. Later on in *Anachronisme*, Tarkos considers the 'rencontre' again, this time tracing its rhythms, which punctuate the everyday, and extending the conceptualisation of the encounter as a locus of touch and proximity:

> Une fréquence, une autre rupture, par la fréquence, le rythme des rencontres, est-ce qu'il y a un rythme, est-ce que ça bat, les pieds touchent terre, les pieds ne touchent pas terre, la terre vient toucher la plante des pieds, par fréquences, par battement, aléatoirement, régulièrement la terre vient toucher la plante des pieds, quelle est la fréquence, une fréquence rapide, un battement, une régularité, ce qui vient comme une régularité, comme un hiver qui a un pouls, comme le battement au milieu de l'hiver monotone qui ne change pas, qui est toujours la même masse de brouillard. (*A*, 113)

> [A frequency, another rupture, by the frequency, the rhythm of encounters, is there a rhythm, does it beat, feet touch the ground, feet don't touch the ground, the ground touches the soles of the feet, through frequencies, through the beat, randomly, regularly the ground touches the soles of the feet, what is the frequency, a fast frequency, a beat, a regularity, what appears like a regularity, like a winter with a pulse, like a beat in the middle of a monotone, unchanging winter, which is always the same foggy mass.]

Here the encounter takes the form of the meeting point between the ground and the soles of the feet, which provides a fitting image for the point of juncture between world and subject. As we saw in 'Quelle belle terre', metaphors prompt a blending of forms, so that winter is described as having a pulse, and it is the earth that comes to meet the soles of the feet, as opposed to the other way around. The 'rencontre', as both event and a spatio-temporal manifestation of 'relation', sees Tarkos's philosophical reflections crystallised in the everyday. This is true throughout *Anachronisme*, where we find a number of the concepts he has explored in abstract terms elsewhere situated in ordinary, everyday experience. Previous considerations of, for example, consciousness or materiality manifest themselves here in the narrative and descriptive dimensions of the text.

Reading *Anachronisme*, one is struck by the poet's sense of metaphysical anguish, compounded by the depression of a seemingly endless winter and the day-to-day experience of illness. With its autobiographical inflection and its notably present *je*, the book thus presents the existential concerns discussed elsewhere in a more personal guise. My discussion of Tarkos's poetry began with a citation from 'Je m'agite':

> je ne sais pas sur quoi je vais m'appuyer pour savoir.
> pour dire.
> pour appuyer ce que je suis. (*EP*, 315)

Returning to this text, Tarkos makes clear the sense of urgency that underpins his poetic project, an urgency that is generated by an all-consuming 'agitation' and 'nervosité' (*EP*, 307). 'Je m'agite' juxtaposes the poet's desire 'pour savoir' with his current state of restless anxiety produced by *not* knowing: 'je ne sais plus où je suis' [I no longer know where I am], 'je ne sais plus où tourner mon regard' [I no longer know where to look] (*EP*, 307). Not knowing, an idea that is reinforced in the poem by the theme of sight and blindness (*EP*, 310), in turn provokes a sensation of a loss of control ('je ne me contrôle plus', 307) and a loss of familiar reference points ('il n'y a plus de guide', 307).[63] Tarkos's characteristic humour, his lightness of touch in approaching otherwise serious subject matter, is noticeably absent in 'Je m'agite'.[64] The second stanza sets out the stakes of this 'agitation':

> je peux tout arrêter.
> je peux me faire mourir.
> je peux me suicider.
> je vais me faire arrêter.
> je vais me faire disparaître.
> j'arrête.
> je coupe.
> je cesse.
> je meurs.
> je me tue.
> je me suicide. (*EP*, 308)

[I can stop everything. | I can make myself die. | I can kill myself. | I'm going to make myself stop. | I'm going to make myself disappear. | I'm stopping. | I'm cutting. | I'm quitting. | I'm dying. | I'm killing myself. | I'm committing suicide.]

The repetition of the first-person pronoun is striking. The project that Tarkos evokes at the end of 'Je m'agite' — the tripartite desire 'pour savoir', 'pour dire', 'pour dire que je suis' — is thus not merely an abstract, intellectual pastime, but is altogether more personal and immediate. The compulsion to know and to say is also a desire to make sense of the self, 'dire *ce que* je suis', and a desire to affirm the presence of the self in writing, 'dire *que* je suis' (my emphasis). Again, this marks a point of departure from a widespread posture in contemporary poetry, typified by Game's statement in the introduction to *Poetic Becomings*, where he refers to a 'heterogeneity of thought' on the 'subject's intrinsic hollowness'.[65] Unlike, for example, Fourcade's account of poetic voice, where writing is described as 'une affaire très absentuée' (*EJP*, 10) with the poet asleep at the wheel (*CD*, 14), for Tarkos, particularly in these later texts, the lyric *je* returns in full force. By rejecting a Saussurean conception of language in favour of his theory of the 'pâte-mot', and supplanting abstract signification with material, embodied sense, Tarkos, the poet, and the *je* of his poetry, are not irrevocably divorced from one another. In this respect, his approach is pragmatic in both senses of the word. Firstly, it is pragmatic in so far as his theory of language focuses on the 'relation', on the contextual configuration of meaning that shifts between one event and the next, but which allows for the construction, albeit temporary and unstable, of a relationship between poet and first-person pronoun. Secondly, it is pragmatic in so far as, driven by the urgency of existential anguish and his approaching illness, his compulsion to affirm the self in lyric voice overrides a theoretical posture that would otherwise render poetry immobile and intransitive.

It is significant that Tarkos's reinstatement of the *je* is most apparent in texts such as *Anachronisme* and 'Je m'agite', where the themes of illness are prevalent.[66] As Caillé points out, death appears as an omnipresent figure throughout Tarkos's *œuvre*; like Arlette Albert-Birot, she reads this as a product of Tarkos's awareness of his own deteriorating health.[67] Long before his diagnosis in November 1999, Tarkos lived with chronic illness, both mental and physical, and references are pervasive in his poetry to the way this shaped his day-to-day life. In *Anachronisme*, we read about life in medical institutions (*A*, 26), trips to the pharmacy (51), and letters from the hospital (143). Death appears in abstract reflections ('La mort n'est pas rien faire, la mort est organiser la mort du mort' [Death isn't doing nothing, death is organising the death of the dead], *C*, 40), in flippant, humorous passages ('Heureusement qu'il est mort, ça fait du bien. Il a disparu. [...] Merci d'être mort' [Fortunately he is dead, it feels good. He died. [...] Thanks for being dead], *C*, 16), and in reflections on writing ('J'écris de la mort. Ce qui est écrit est mort. [...] Je suis mort' [I write death. What is written is dead. [...] I am dead], *ML*, 85). In *Caisses*, Tarkos presents a distressing address to the reader 'Tue-moi tue-moi ne me laisse pas crever de rien ne me laisse pas | mourir sans que personne ne me touche' [Kill me kill me don't let me snuff it for no reason don't let me | die without anyone touching me] (*C*, 6); in his 'autoprésentations', death pervades even the most factual descriptions: *Vit à Marseille et Paris. Né en 1964. N'est pas près de mourir. R. R. riste*' [Lives in Marseille and Paris. Born in 1964. Isn't close to death. R.R.-ist] (*E*, 7).[68] In a passage in *Ma langue*, he writes:

> Je vais faire celui qui meurt. Je suis fragile. Doucement, je meurs. Je vais faire celui qui est mourant sans douleur. Je vis dans la vie, je ne vais pas vivre comme les autres, je suis mourant quand les autres vivent vraiment, je sais que je suis mourant, [...] je fais la vie plus lentement, je vais faire celui qui meurt lentement (pour que cela se remarque), l'année prochaine je ne serai plus, je vais ralentir et parler lentement, je vais me voûter, je serai fatigué, il ne reste qu'une année ou deux, je vais faire celui qui est en train de mourir. (*ML*, 51)

> [I'm going to act as if I'm dying. I am fragile. Slowly, I am dying. I'm going to act as if I'm dying without pain. I live in life, I'm not going to live like the others, I am dying when the others are really living, I know that I am dying, [...] I am taking life slower, I am going to act as if I'm dying slowly (so that it is noticeable), next year I will no longer be, I will slow down and speak slowly, I will start stooping, I will be tired, there's only a year or two left, I will act as if I'm in the process of dying.]

Here the phrase 'il ne reste qu'une année ou deux' evokes, as he describes in *Le Baroque*, how illness shortens 'le temps d'écrire dans ma vie avant qu'elle ne soit finie' [the time to write in my life before it ends] (*B*, 9), compounding the sense of urgency described in 'Je m'agite'. The syntax of the repeated phrase 'celui qui meurt', 'celui qui est mourant', 'celui qui est en train de mourir', places emphasis on the pronoun 'celui' instead of the various verbal forms of 'mourir'. This locates death in a nominal subject, instead of in the action itself, which reinforces the observation in the passage that death becomes a constitutive part of the identity of 'celui qui meurt', marking the subject, setting him apart from 'les autres'. This same idea also appears in *La Cage* (1999), a poem that was set to music and performed as an opera, where the alternating phrases 'je suis moi, j'ai mal | je suis moi, j'ai mal' [I am me, I am in pain | I am me, I am in pain] suggest an inextricability of illness and identity.[69]

When asked by David Christoffel about the theme of illness in his work, Tarkos replied, 'La maladie, c'est le contraire de ce qui est vital, mais la maladie, ça nous appartient. Ça fait partie de notre mode de fonctionnement, de notre pensée' [Illness is the opposite of what is vital, but illness belongs to us. It is part of our way of functioning, of our thought].[70] In the interview, Tarkos goes on to extend this analysis of illness as a constitutive part of lived experience, to death itself: 'ce n'est pas extrême que de mourir. C'est à côté de nous. Juste à côté de nous. Juste avec nous. Tout le temps avec nous. C'est mélangé avec notre matière' [Dying is not extreme. It's beside us. Just beside us. Just with us. All the time with us. It's mixed in with our matter] (*EP*, 380). These remarks suggest how Tarkos conceptualises death and illness as part of the broader substance of life, not as an outside or other to it. They recall Tarkos's reflections in *Oui* on 'la fermeture', where he writes: 'La fermeture n'est pas à l'extérieur. La fermeture n'est pas extérieure' [The closing is not on the outside. The closing is not external] (*EP*, 170), 'La fermeture est une longue surface' [The closing is a long surface] (*EP*, 179). Death, for Tarkos, might be understood not as a transcendental beyond or outside of life, but rather part of a broader continuity, situated on the same plane of immanence. In turn, as Tarkos suggests in the interview with Christoffel, death is what gives meaning to the world, and helps us to make sense of our existence (*EP*, 382). We might see these same ideas reflected in the closing pages of *Anachronisme*, where the final paragraphs describe a project Tarkos is working on — a novel about being in a waiting room before death. The last paragraph ends: 'Quelques mois plus tard je fis une crise d'appendicite et je démissionnai de la bibliothèque nationale' [A few months later I had an outbreak of appendicitis and I resigned from the national library], and is then followed by the enumeration of pi, as described above. Given the prevalence of death as a thematic motif in *Anachronisme*, the enumeration of pi gains an additional significance. On the one hand, pi is a symbol of continuity and infinitude. On the other, its artificial termination in the text (where just three pages of the number are listed), represents a contrastive discontinuity. As an unknowable, indeterminate entity, pi is also a figure of uncertainty, which reflects, perhaps, the conflicting ways in which Tarkos conceives of death. Alongside his reflections on death as contiguous with life, in *Ma langue* he represents 'la mort' as a figure of immobility and fixity, a binary counterpart to the characteristic movement of life:

> c'est mort, ça
> résiste, c'est résistant, c'est immobile. Cela
> ne bouge plus, c'est mort. Cela ne peut plus
> bouger. Ce qui ne bouge plus est mort. (*ML*, 85)

[it's dead, it | resists, it's resistant, it's immobile. It | no longer moves, it's dead. It can no longer | move. What no longer moves is dead.]

In such a way, death appears in Tarkos's work as a highly ambiguous presence, one that, as we shall see, provides an important backdrop to his reflections on poetry.

Poetry and its Cure

Throughout his *œuvre*, Tarkos depicts a pervasive sense of *étouffement*, or suffocation. In *Anachronisme*, it is a product of mental illness, embodied in the figure of winter; in *Le Signe =*, it is 'le réel' itself that is stifling (S, 122).[71] In the following lines, which echo sentiments found throughout Tarkos's work, poetry appears to offer a form of liberation from this sense of *étouffement*:

> Je suis libre. J'écris ce que je
> veux écrire, je suis libre d'écrire
> ce que je veux écrire. (*ML*, 70)

[I am free. I write what I | want to write, I am free to write | what I want to write.]

This theme is reworked throughout *Ma langue*, for example in the following poem in 'Carrés':

> Je ne suis pas bloqué. Je ne suis pas
> encerclé. Je n'ai pas casé. Je ne suis
> pas encastré dans le trou. Je ne suis
> pas serré contre la grille. Je ne suis
> pas mort. Je ne suis pas enterré. Je ne
> suis pas écrasé et étouffé. Je ne passe
> pas mon temps entre quatre murs.
> Je ne suis pas enfermé. Je n'ai pas
> le mutisme. Je n'ai pas le silence.
> Je ne suis pas emprisonné, prisonnier.
> Je n'étouffe pas. Je ne m'étouffe pas.
> Je ne suis pas écrasé. Je suis libre. (*ML*, 81)

[I am not stuck. I am not | surrounded. I am not in a box. I am not | slotted in a hole. I am not | squashed against the bars. I am not | dead. I am not buried. I am not | crushed and suffocated. I don't spend | my time trapped between four walls. | I am not locked in. I am not | mute. I am not silent. | I am not imprisoned, prisoner. | I am not suffocating. I am not choking. | I am not crushed. I am free.]

There is a simplicity or minimalism to the formal properties of the poem: typographically, the 'carré' forms a regular square on the page; the fifteen negated clauses that constitute the bulk of the poem then offer a neat syntactic contrast to the affirmative final clause: 'Je suis libre'. Echoing this formal simplicity, the poet sets up a binary opposition between freedom and restriction, where the adjectival phrases ('bloqué', 'encerclé', 'casé' etc.) represent a cognate set, diametrically opposed to the final adjective 'libre'. As the poem continues, a number of ideas are thus conflated; 'la mort', 'le mutisme' and 'le silence' gain a semantic equivalence, all being manifestations of *l'étouffement*. Following this binary logic, freedom, by being contrasted with the confinement of death and silence, is therefore aligned with vitality and with language. There is a juxtaposition in the poem of the rigidity of its formal properties and the freedom that is expressed. Compared to many of Tarkos's other texts, the 'Carrés' have a relatively restrictive form: the language of the poem is quite literally 'casé' and 'encastré'. The central metapoetic image, 'entre quatre murs', evokes the four sides of the typographic square, drawing attention to the form of the poem itself.[72] However, poetic form is represented in the poem as only an artificial type of restriction. Indeed, the choice of a comparatively rigid formal framework for a text that gestures towards the liberation of poetic language appears significant.[73]

As the following analysis suggests, for Tarkos, it is the heightened emphasis on form that makes poetry our greatest resource, 'le plus grand moyen face à la grande substance' (*EP*, 163). Poetry is therefore conceptualised as a mode of resistance against the sense of suffocation which, as we have seen, is a product of the poet's ontological conception of reality, as well as the more pressing concern of his illness and impending death. In *Processe*, Tarkos writes:

> Pas d'autre méthode pour comprendre. Que cette langue. Continuer. [...] Il faut continuer à construire. La substance visqueuse menace, essouffle, paralyse, donne envie de ne plus parler, fatigue, endort, donne envie de dormir. [...] La seule méthode est de te parler. (*EP*, 143)
>
> [No other way to understand. But this language. Go on. [...] We must go on building. The viscous substance threatens, leaves us breathless, paralyses us, makes us want to stop talking, tires us out, puts us to sleep, makes us want to sleep. [...] The only way is to speak to you.]

Echoing the same binary contrasts found in the poem above between movement and paralysis, language and silence, here Tarkos suggests how a 'méthode' is required to fend off the threat of 'la grande substance'.[74] 'La grande substance', we will recall, is the sum of all that exists, taken in its entirety, and, necessarily, therefore, the formless mass of language itself. In such a way, language is both the problem and the cure, as Tarkos suggests in *Anachronisme*:

> Ma maladie est de parler, et le guérissement de ma maladie est de parler, parler forme un tout qui est la maladie et qui est le soignement de la maladie, il n'y a rien d'autre, il n'y a rien de plus. (*A*, 48)
>
> [My illness is speaking, and the cure for my illness is speaking, speaking forms a whole that is the illness and that is the treating of the illness, there's nothing else, there's nothing more.]

A 'méthode' is required, a means of continuation must be found within language itself, because there is nothing else at our disposal: 'Il n'y pas d'autre langue que la langue, il faudra entrer à l'intérieur, on a toujours été à l'intérieur, il n'y pas à entrer à l'intérieur, on est dedans' [There is no other language than language, we have to enter inside, we've always been inside, there's no entering inside, we are inside] (*S*, 45). Although 'patmo' is a substance that provokes a certain 'vertige' or 'maladie', its potential lies in its elasticity. We see this in Tarkos's improvised poem 'J'ai un problème voilà', with its very literal manifestation of Deleuzian stutter. The poem describes the sensation or experience of 'patmo', of words being stuck together and inseparable: 'j'ai remarqué que tout était complètement collé | j'ai remarqué que que que que tout complètement collé est complètement collé' (*E*, 312). In his performance of the poem, Tarkos stammers, stumbling over his words, repeating phrases and words in quick succession. The symbolism of the gesture is clear: language is always at risk of descending into disorder, the poet can't get his words out, and 'le mutisme', described above in *Ma langue* and *Processe*, threatens. By conceptualising this state as a form of aphasia, poetry then presents itself as a form of 'soignement' or 'guérissement'. If 'le poème est le plus grand moyen face à la grande substance', this is because it combats formlessness by moulding or shaping language within the text. As Tarkos would have it, poetry presents itself as a distinct type of language use, set apart from other linguistic modes in so far as it is predicated on form and allows for a heightened degree of formal innovation.

Throughout his work, Tarkos experiments with a number of typographic arrangements; the wide variety of forms that Tarkos uses draws attention precisely to their significance. In several instances, the appeal of poetry is that it highlights the shape of language on the page, with the poems in *Caisses*, 'Carrés', and *Dix ronds* and the calligrams in *Morceaux choisis* being the most obvious examples.[75] In a passage in *Morceaux choisis*, Tarkos elaborates an enumerated list of the necessary conditions for creating a poem (*MC*, 91). These conditions consist of simple assertions such as, 'Le résultat d'un poème doit être un poème' [The result of a poem must be a poem] (92) and 'Le poème se doit d'être une chose' [The poem must be a thing] (92), which might at first appear tautological or wilfully unhelpful, but which gain relevance in the context of Tarkos's broader project. What becomes clear from the enumerated statements is the primary significance of form, with the majority of the conditions making reference to it: 'Le poème peut prendre toutes les formes' [The poem can take all forms] (92), 'Le poème doit parvenir à une forme concrète' [The poem must achieve a concrete form] (92), and so on. At first glance, phrases such as 'Le poème doit faire remarquer qu'il est un poème. Dans le cas contraire on pourrait le prendre pour autre chose' [The poem must be recognised as a poem. Otherwise it could be mistaken for something else] (92) and 'Un poème doit être distinctement visible. Il faut qu'en le voyant, l'on puisse dire: voilà un poème' [A poem must be distinctly visible. It's essential that, on seeing it, we can say: that is a poem] (92) are frustratingly slight, but they acquire a certain significance in so far as they emphasise the necessity of a visibly recognisable shaping of language in the text (or in the performance). Tarkos's comments are important when read against the backdrop of radical experiments with form in modern poetry, where from the nineteenth century onwards a comparatively narrow set of traditional verse forms were supplanted by an unrestricted range of textual possibilities (free verse, prose poetry, etc.), and expanded further by the extension of poetry into performance and other media. If these experiments saw the depreciation of form as a necessary constituent of poetry, then Tarkos appears to be reasserting its significance in his own poetics.

That said, while Tarkos reaffirms its significance, his conception of form is not confined to a narrow interpretation based on typographic arrangement. For Tarkos, whose performance poetry constitutes a substantial part of his *œuvre*, the shaping of the 'patmo' takes place on a broader level, in the novel patterning of language within the poem, whether written or performed. I have outlined already several of the most striking and prevalent features of Tarkos's work: the way he reworks a central pivotal phrase, creating 'dérives' that advance and modify an idea, expanding and contracting it through repetition, polyptoton, anaphora, and epistrophe. Lucie Bourassa, like Samuel Lequette whom she quotes here, describes how Tarkos creates new linguistic forms in his poetry, which in turn work against the tired clichés and commonplaces that render language immobile.[76] She writes:

> C'est une poésie de l'accumulation, de la retouche et de la variation; une poésie des articulations — des délimitations et des liaisons — qui 'décolle' la pâte en lui imposant de nouvelles découpes et de nouvelles jointures. Comme l'écrit avec justesse Samuel Lequette, 'Le sens [dans les écrits de Tarkos] n'est pas produit par des références, mais par des différences, des phases et des changements de phases'.[77]
>
> [It's a poetry of accumulation, adjustment and variation; a poetry of articulations — of boundaries and connections — that 'unsticks' the dough by imposing new cuts and new joints on it. As Samuel Lequette aptly puts it, 'Meaning [in Tarkos's writing] is not produced by references, but by differences, phases and changes of phases'.]

Bourassa identifies how the 'nouvelles découpes' and 'nouvelles jointures' in Tarkos's poetry involve a remoulding or reworking of set patterns of language. These novel linguistic forms then create new possibilities in thought, as Tarkos himself suggests:

> L'expression langagière peut changer notre pensée
> [...] la langue, le langage est une arme
> qui va assouplir, changer, modifier la pensée. (*E*, 74)[78]
>
> [Linguistic expression can change our thought | [...] language is a weapon | that will make thought more flexible, change it and modify it.]

It is here that we see what Tarkos describes as the revolutionary quality of poetry, and what inspires him to make the claim: 'Le poème va faire la révolution' [The poem will start a revolution] (*EP*, 163) and:

> Faire la révolution
> Devant la grande Substance
> Le monde s'éveillera. (*EP*, 210)
>
> [Start a revolution | Faced with the great Substance | The world will wake up.]

Throughout his work, Tarkos develops a motif that revolves around the revisions of the phrase 'pour la poésie'.[79] He writes:

> Je suis pour
> l'avant-garde [...] Je suis affilié, adhérent,
> je suis pour. [...]
> Je milite.

> Je suis pour
> la participation.
> Je participe.
> Je suis pour.
> Et
> Je travaille pour. (*E*, 416)

[I am for | the avant-garde [...] I am a supporter, an affiliated member, | I am for. [...] | I am campaigning. | I am for | participation. | I am participating. | I am for. | And | I am working for.]

The choice of vocabulary is significant, presenting poetry as a form of political participation or 'engagement'. There are instances in Tarkos's work where this notion of 'engagement' takes an overtly political form, for example in *Ouvriers vivants* (1999), which was based on a project where a number of contemporary poets worked in collaboration with undocumented workers.[80] However, the revolutionary nature of poetry, as Tarkos would have it, is generated by the transformative power of its language. As a locus of linguistic experimentation and formal innovation, poetry remodels the 'déjà tout dit et tout pensé qui sont incrustés dans la pâte', activating new modes of thought or perception.[81] Returning to Deleuze and Guattari's account, it is this property of Tarkos's work which qualifies it as minor literature. In *Kafka*, they write that '"mineur" ne qualifie plus certaines littératures, mais les conditions révolutionnaires de toute littérature' ['minor' no longer designates specific literatures, but the revolutionary conditions for every literature] (*K1*, 33; *K2*, 18). In Gilles Deleuze and Claire Parnet's discussion in *Dialogues*, we read that 'le langage n'est pas fait pour être cru mais pour être obéi' [language is not made to be believed but to be obeyed], thus the form of linguistic disobedience found in Tarkos's work marks a dismantling of the devices of power that are encoded within the language it deforms.[82]

These questions of revolution, language, and literature also recall Barthes's discussion in his inaugural lecture at the Collège de France in 1977. Having established that all language is inextricably bound up with power, and that there is no outside of language, he writes:

> Mais à nous [...], il ne reste, si je puis dire, qu'à tricher avec la langue, qu'à tricher la langue. Cette tricherie salutaire, cette esquive, ce leurre magnifique, qui permet d'entendre la langue hors-pouvoir, dans la splendeur d'une révolution permanente du langage, je l'appelle pour ma part: *littérature*.[83]

> [But for us [...], all that remains, if I may say so, is to cheat with language, to cheat language. This beneficial trickery, this evasion, this magnificent illusion, which enables one to encounter language without power, in the splendour of a permanent revolution of language, I call: *literature*.]

He continues: 'Les forces de liberté qui sont dans la littérature ne dépendent pas de la personne civile, de l'engagement politique de l'écrivain, [...] ni même du contenu doctrinal de son œuvre, mais du travail de déplacement qu'il exerce sur la langue' [The forces of freedom that are in literature depend not on the writer's civil person nor on his political commitment [...] nor on the doctrinal content of his work, but rather on the labour of displacement that he brings to bear upon language].[84] This echoes what he had written earlier in essays such as 'Écriture et révolution' [Writing and Revolution] and 'L'Écriture et le silence' [Writing and Silence] in *Le Degré zéro de l'écriture*, where he draws the same distinction between writing about overtly political subjects, and employing an implicitly political mode of writing, predicated on the subversive nature of its form. Rejecting or revising the codified formal properties of a given literary style serves to disrupt the ideology that is embedded within these conventions.[85] Barthes's comments here reflect a moment in literary history, discussed in Chapter 1, where avant-garde writers wished to assert the importance of literary production in political action and, as Gleize puts it, to 'théoriser la coïncidence entre subversion formelle et désir de révolution politique: changer la langue, trans-former la littérature, changer la vie, agir sur les représentations, change le monde, la société'.[86] It is clear that Tarkos's own poetics owe much to this earlier form of 'langagement'. We see how he inherited from his predecessors that same transgressive approach to language, with the same belief in the impact of such a gesture, but in place of linguistic eccentricity bordering on obscurity, his poetry favours a more accessible mode of engagement.[87] In a more modest reformulation of the phrase 'Le poème va faire la révolution', Tarkos states:

> Comme [la patmo] est un peu élastique, on peut l'élargir un peu dans un sens; c'est tout ce qu'on peut faire. Ce n'est pas grand-chose mais on essaie au départ de s'ouvrir et de danser, de danser... Pour faire bouger un tout petit peu la pâte-mot. (*EP*, 353)
>
> [As patmo is quite elastic, we can stretch it out a bit. It's not much but we're trying initially to open up and to dance, to dance... To make the pâte-mot move a tiny little bit.]

In his own way, Tarkos reprises the conception of poetry as revolution in language, as the making-other of language, as a linguistic utopia or an 'au-delà de la langue'. This is well-trodden territory, rendered idiosyncratic by Tarkos's inflection of language as 'patmo', and poetry as a form of kneading.

Oui

As previously suggested, the word *oui* forms a key motif in Tarkos's work; it is the title of one of his texts, and it reappears throughout his writing. In a passage already quoted, Tarkos describes this 'oui' as a point of departure for the poetic act: 'pour pouvoir avancer [...], pour faire même un geste, pour faire n'importe quoi dans une telle réalité cohérente, et collée, on est obligé, au départ, d'avoir un "oui"'.[88] This 'yes' is multifaceted: it signifies the affirmative gesture of his poetry, which reinstates meaning and points to the material presence of the world. It also represents a 'yes' to poetry itself: an affirmation of its value as a practice. In this respect, the *oui* echoes the sentiment, described above, whereby Tarkos declares himself to be 'pour la poésie' and 'pour la participation' (*E*, 416). Talking about the *oui* as it relates to 'pâte-mot', Tarkos says: 'Oui, je vais le faire, oui il y a une volonté, de l'extraire, de le dire, de le transformer, de ... Sinon, on se retrouve dans une vaste hypocrisie très poétique d'ailleurs, qui est le "non" désespéré' [Yes, I'm going to do it, yes there is a desire, to extract it, to say it, to transform it, to… Otherwise, we find ourselves in a vast hypocrisy, that is incidentally very poetic, which is the despairing 'no'] (*E*, 244–45). In this sense, Tarkos outlines how this inaugural gesture of the *oui* sets his project apart from a disillusioned 'poésie négative'. We see here a further correspondence with Ponge, who describes a similar embrace of language and gesture of consent:

> C'est le ton affirmatif du Verbe, tout à fait nécessaire pour qu'il 'porte'. C'est le OUI du Soleil, le OUI de Racine, le OUI de Mallarmé […]. C'est enfin la seule justification de la Parole (prose ou poésie), une fois franchies toutes les raisons de se taire. C'est la décision de parler.[89]
>
> [It is the affirmative tone of the Word, entirely necessarily for it to be effective. It is the Sun's YES, Racine's YES, Mallarmé's YES […]. It is ultimately the only justification of Speech (prose or poetry), once all the reasons to be silent have been overcome. It is the decision to speak.]

In contrast to figures such as Rimbaud and Roche, or Cadiot and his conclusion that 'Il fallait abandonner le bateau', Tarkos's work asserts a renewed commitment to poetry.[90] This commitment and the affirmation of the value of poetry is most apparent in the text *Ma langue est poétique*. Pivoting around the repeated nominal phrase 'ma langue', Tarkos qualifies the language of his poetry through a series of revisions:

> Ma langue est poétique et musicale, ma langue est imagée et musicale, ma langue est souple, étincelante et merveilleuse, ma langue aime jouer de la musique, elle vibre et fait vibrer chacun de ses mots qui rayonnent de leurs contours. (*EP*, 48)
>
> [My language is poetic and musical, my language is musical and full of imagery, my language is subtle, radiant and wondrous, my language loves to play music, it vibrates and makes every word that radiates from its contours vibrate.]

The refrain 'Ma langue est poétique' alternates with the anaphora 'Ma langue est [X]' which accumulates a series of adjectives of the sort: 'sonore' [sonorous], 'féconde' [fertile], 'douce' [gentle], 'inondée de soleil' [sun-drenched] (*EP*, 50). This creates a structural parallelism, where the logical inference is that the poet's language is rendered 'poétique' precisely through the qualities of the adjectives it is attributed. If his language is poetic, it is *because* it is rich or sonorous or supple. Poetic language in *Ma langue est poétique* is thus presented as having a number of distinctive features. It involves a desire for language: 'ma langue est poétique, […] c'est un désir de langue, un désir de langue poétique, […] ma langue est un désir de langue' [my language is poetic, […] it's a desire for language, a desire for poetic language, […] my language is a desire for language] (52). It is thus marked by this initial gesture of a *oui*, an active impulse which contrasts with the passive fatigue that might be provoked by 'patmo' ('la substance visqueuse […] fatigue, endort, donne envie de dormir'). In contrast to the stasis of death or the untouched 'substance visqueuse', poetic language is vital and alive: 'Ma langue vit, est vivante, est poétique, est pleine de mots' [My language is alive, is living, is poetic, is full of words] (48). Its vivacity is a product of the fact that it is characterised by movement, an idea which is expressed in a stanza that enumerates a long series of verbs of motion: 'Ma langue abonde accélère accorde accumule additionne agresse ajoute alterne amalgame amorce amplifie' [My language abounds accelerates accords accumulates adds attacks alternates amalgamates amplifies] (51). Poetry sets language in motion; the poet's quest, after all, is to make the word-dough move, even if just a little bit (353).

This alphabetical list of verbs describing the movements of poetic language recalls a list found in *Anachronisme* where Tarkos enumerates the processes involved in modelling 'patmo' in poetry (*A*, 192). One of these verbs, *malaxer*, reappears throughout Tarkos's work, and encapsulates the handling, moulding, or kneading of language that the poetic act involves. In these descriptions, the etymology of the word 'poetry' itself is never far away, with its original sense of making and shaping being restored in Tarkos's project. Indeed, Tarkos tended to substitute the term *poète* with 'poem maker': 'je suis fabricant de poèmes, j'essaye de fabriquer des poèmes' (*EP*, 36). Here, we are reminded of Cadiot's description of poetry as a form of 'travail plastique', as well as the conception of the poet as craftsman in Alferi and Cadiot's essay 'La Mécanique lyrique' in the *Revue de littérature générale* (to which Tarkos contributed).[91] For Tarkos, a performance poet as well as a published author, the emphasis is always on the process or act of poetry, not on the resulting poetic object. This idea is conveyed in the emphasis on verbal forms in the lists evoked above, and more overtly in a document entitled 'Acte', dating from June 1999, where Tarkos writes the following:

> la poésie est un acte
> le poème est un acte
> [...]
> quels sont les actes les actes sont variés les actes sont ceux
> qui appellent de nous, s'appellent de nous, nous appellent
> pour faire un acte, ce qui se rapproche de nous
> il y a une proximité
> tout ce qui est le plus proche est alors un acte
> rougir, être en colère, descendre vertigineusement, esca-
> lader vertigineusement, avoir une dépression, désespérer de
> tout, ne plus avoir de goût pour rien, péter,
> un acte est ce qui pour le faire demande à soi une trans-
> formation
> il y a une transformation de soi
> [...]
> le passage à l'acte est la pénétration. (*E*, 373–74)

[poetry is an action | the poem is an action | [...] | what are actions actions are varied actions are those that | summon us, that are named by us, that summon us | to carry out an action, that which gets closer to us | there is a proximity | everything that's closest is an action then | to blush, to be angry, to descend vertiginously, | to climb vertiginously, to be depressed, to despair | at everything, to lose interest in everything, to snap, | an action requires a transformation of the self | there is a transformation of self | [...] | taking action is penetration.]

In this text, poetry is presented as one type of act among many, and it is notable that, among the various acts that Tarkos enumerates, 'avoir une dépression, désespérer de tout, ne plus avoir de goût pour rien' reappear. As Tarkos suggests, these acts involve a change of internal states, a 'transformation de soi', and a form of 'pénétration' that connects to a proximate external world.[92] This definition can then be traced in the poetic act; Castellin writes:

> La poésie est acte [...]. Que l'on 'écrive' ou que l'on lise en public, on agit-réagit: on réagit à ce qui nous entoure, on l'éprouve et en éprouve 'la poussée', on la prolonge, la transmet *via* un corps singulier, et cette transmission est nécessairement une action à laquelle autrui réagit. (*E*, 75)
>
> [Poetry is an action [...]. Whether we 'write' it or read it in public, we act-react: we react to what is around us, we feel it and feel the 'thrust' from it, we extend it, transmit it *via* a singular body, and this transmission is inevitably an action to which others respond.]

The poetic act is thus understood as mobile and transitive; it connects outwards to the world, affirms its presence, and inaugurates a relation between poet and reader.[93] While clearly loaded with sexual connotations, the phrase 'le passage à l'acte est la pénétration' also recalls a passage from 'Le texte est expressif' [The Text Is Expressive], Tarkos's first public performance poem, given at the Centre International de Poésie Marseille in 1993. In the performance, an initial silence is pierced by four loud howls. Playing on the contrast between silent pauses and the interjection of his reading, Tarkos announces the following: 'Le texte est bon. Court et frappant, il sort sonore et intense. [...] Le texte est surprenant. Sort, fort, exprimé. Le texte exprime intensément. Ample et beau, il sonne et perce' [The text is good. Short and striking, it comes out sonorous and intense. [...] The text is surprising. Comes out, loud, expressed. The text is intensely expressive. Ample and beautiful, it sounds and pierces] (*E*, 107). These verbs, *percer* and *pénétrer*, are significant; they evoke the 'engagement' of the poem, which enters into the world, transforming silence into sound, blank space into text, absence into presence.

We have seen then, how poetry offers a way of being inside the amorphous mass of language, creating new forms, and in so doing, constituting a form of 'pénétration'. Albert-Birot suggests that poetry, for Tarkos, is therefore a way to participate in the world. She writes:

> Modeler la langue, la plier à ses obsessions, fabriquer des poèmes — au sens latin de *faber* — créer dans une prolifération déstabilisante pour lui, pour son lecteur ou son auditeur. Tarkos explore le verbe et le monde, c'est sa façon d'être au monde, de faire partie du monde, d'y laisser sa trace météorique.[94]
>
> [Shape language, bend it according to his obsessions, make or fabricate poems — in the Latin sense of *faber* — create in a proliferation that destablises him, his reader or his listener. Tarkos explores the word and the world, it's his way of being in the world, of being part of the world, of leaving his meteoric mark on it.]

These verbs 'être au monde', 'faire partie du monde', are reminiscent of Jean-Claude Pinson's reflections on what he calls a 'poéthique'. As discussed in Chapter

1, Pinson, following Heidegger, draws on the etymology of the word *ethos* [dwelling], to evoke how poetry involves a particular way of being in the world. In his collection of essays on contemporary poetry, *Sentimentale et naïve*, Pinson writes:

> La poésie n'est pas seulement création de feux d'artifice verbaux, production de textes qui ne seraient que des objets esthétiques sans incidence sur nos existences. 'Morale de la forme', l'écriture poétique est aussi mise en forme de l'*éthos*, de l'être au monde. Elle est aussi, pour reprendre encore une fois l'expression de Deleuze, 'créatrice de vie'.[95]

> [Poetry is not just the creation of verbal fireworks, the production of texts that would otherwise be mere aesthetic objects with no bearing on our existence. 'An ethics of form', poetic writing is also the shaping of *ethos*, of being in the world. It is also, to use Deleuze's expression again, 'creative of life'.]

He continues, describing how every great poetic work is a:

> *Proposition de monde* — et notamment proposition, une ou plurielle, quant à telle ou telle modalité possible de son habitation. [...] elle pose, plus ou moins obliquement, la question 'poéthique' du comment vivre, la question de la 'vraie vie' toujours absente et toujours recherchée.[96]

> [*World proposition* — and notably a proposition, singular or plural, for a given possible modality of its dwelling. [...] it poses, more or less obliquely, the 'poethical' question of how to live, the question of the 'real life' that is still absent and still sought-after.]

This analysis holds true for Tarkos's *œuvre* which, in its own way, addresses this same 'poethical' question. For Tarkos, the stakes of the question are grounded in his analysis of 'la grande substance', and the answers will be found, ultimately, in language. If his work explores a possible 'modalité de son habitation du monde' then the question is first and foremost a linguistic one: 'Comment écrire,' he asks, 'dans la proximité, pâte-mot contre pâte-monde?' [How can one write in this proximity, word-dough against world-dough?] (*E*, 216). The response, then, begins with a commitment to language: 'pour pouvoir avancer [...], pour faire même un geste, pour faire n'importe quoi dans une telle réalité cohérente, et collée, on est obligé, au départ, d'avoir un "oui"' (*E*, 244). This gesture, reminiscent of the final lines of Beckett's *L'Innommable*, is thus one of continuation: 'Pas d'autre méthode pour comprendre. Que cette langue. Continuer' (*EP*, 143).[97] The question is then to find ways to continue within language, which is the only means at our disposal, and for Tarkos, this involves the shaping or moulding of the 'patmo' into new forms. We have seen then how this practice subsequently represents 'un exercice [...] pour l'acceptation du monde' (*E*, 245), whereby Tarkos, in response to a 'poésie négative', reinstates meaning, and affirms the presence of the world within the poem. This 'poetics of presence' also involves a restoration of poetic voice, and in this very immediate sense, Bakhtin's analysis of poetic monoglossia holds true in Tarkos's work. The combination of direct, authorial voice, and the unity of style that traverses Tarkos's work, lends itself to Bakhtin's reading. However, Bakhtin's proposition that monoglossia necessarily involves submitting to the 'homogenizing power of myth over language' (*DI*, 60), the myth of a language that purports to be the only language, is clearly not supported in Tarkos's poetry. For Tarkos, the function of the formal properties that, conversely, lend his poetry a stylistic or, as Bakhtin would have it, 'monoglottic' unity, is to 'faire bouger un tout petit peu la pâte-mot' (*EP*, 353), to find new forms and new variations that deterritorialise ordinary language within the poem.

In this sense, revisiting the hypothesis advanced in Chapter 1, Tarkos's poetry seems to be not so much monoglottic as internally diglottic, with its syntactic and rhythmic effects offering variations on an absent but implicit norm. Returning to a second idea already outlined, Tarkos's poetry flags up a tension between Bakhtin's and Deleuze and Guattari's accounts of the role of style in an author's work. The same features of his work that, for Bakhtin, would represent the maintenance of power structures within language, are precisely the features that Deleuze and Guattari would argue constitute its status as a power-disrupting 'littérature mineure'. It is obviously with the latter of these two accounts that I wish to agree. Within the 'patmo' (which might be read as a 'langue majeure'), the *malaxage* of Tarkos's poetry mobilises difference, rendering language strange or other, and pointing to new possibilities in the process.

Notes to Chapter 4

1. Thomas Clerc, 'La Mite', in *Dossier Christophe Tarkos, Cahier Critique de Poésie*, 30 (2015), 73–75 (p. 73). In this short piece, Clerc asks 'Est-ce qu'il existe un mythe Tarkos?' [Is there a Tarkos myth?] before answering 'Oui, sans doute' [Yes, without a doubt], and expanding upon the reception of Tarkos's work since his death in 2004.
2. For some examples, see Tarkos, *EP*, 31, or *Morceaux choisis* (Arras: Les Contemporains, 1995), p. 110 (henceforth abbreviated to *MC*).
3. Anne-Renée Caillé, 'Théorie du langage et esthétique totalisante dans l'œuvre poétique de Christophe Tarkos' (unpublished doctoral thesis, Université de Montréal, 2014), p. 14.
4. Clerc, 'La Mite', p. 73.
5. Prigent, 'Sokrat à Patmo', p. 12.
6. Jocelyn Bonnerave, 'Le Narratif chez le dernier Tarkos', in *Dossier Christophe Tarkos*, 64–65 (p. 65).
7. Prigent, *Salut les anciens*, p. 9. See Prigent, 'Sokrat à Patmo', p. 11, for further discussion.
8. Tarkos insists on this point with characteristic enthusiasm: 'Je suis l'avant-garde en 1997' (*E*, 20). See Farah, 'Christophe Tarkos: situation de l'écrivain en 1997', in 'La Possibilité du choc', pp. 28–36, for a more detailed discussion of the significance of Tarkos's claim.
9. Gleize, *Sorties*, p. 58.
10. Gleize, 'La Post-poésie', p. 129. We recall here the opening lines of Gleize's *A noir*, which evoke how the investigative mode of poetry is also a self-reflexive one: 'Reste pour nous: la poésie. L'ignorance de ce qu'elle est. La faire, l'écrire, "pour savoir"' (p. 11).
11. Christophe Tarkos, *Le Baroque* (Limoges: Al Dante, 2009), pp. 33, 44 (henceforth abbreviated to *B*).
12. Bertrand Verdier, 'Entretiens de Bertrand Verdier avec Christophe Tarkos', in *EP*, 353–60 (p. 356). The types of truth that poetry and philosophy seek are not necessarily the same, as Caillé points out in 'Théorie du langage et esthétique totalisante dans l'œuvre poétique de Christophe Tarkos', p. 274.
13. For a useful survey of Tarkos's eclectic interests, see Castellin, 'Christophe Tarkos', p. 22.
14. For a detailed discussion of 'poésie pensante' or indeed 'philopoésie' as he often refers to it, see Pinson, *Habiter en poète*, especially the second part: 'II: Éléments (Pour une philosophie de la poésie contemporaine)', pp. 61–134.

15. Christophe Tarkos, *Anachronisme* (Paris: P.O.L., 2001), p. 39 (henceforth abbreviated to *A*).
16. Christophe Tarkos, *Le Signe =* (Paris: P.O.L., 1999), p. 29 (henceforth abbreviated to *S*).
17. For a further elaboration of this motif, see Castellin's discussion of the 'boule' in 'Christophe Tarkos', p. 46.
18. Prigent, *Salut les anciens*, p. 88.
19. In an interview with Bertrand Verdier, for example, Tarkos says, 'pour moi, la langue, [...] c'est hormonal. [...] C'est vraiment hormonal; la vérité corporelle' [for me, language [...] is hormonal. [...] It's really hormonal; the corporeal truth] (*EP*, 358–59).
20. Examples of this can be found throughout Tarkos's œuvre, but the poem 'Gonfle', performed at the Centre Pompidou in January 1999, is a prime instance of the attentiveness to breathing, the inflation and deflation of the lungs, and the movement of air in the respiratory passage. For a transcription of this poem see *E*, 330–69.
21. For a detailed account of consciousness in Tarkos's work, see Kate Lermitte Campbell, 'Thought, Perception and the Creative Act. A Study of the Work of Four Contemporary French Poets: Pierre Alferi, Anne Portugal, Valère Novarina and Christophe Tarkos' (unpublished doctoral thesis, University of Oxford, 2008).
22. Ibid., p. 187.
23. Lucie Bourassa discusses some of the paradoxes and contradictions that can be found in relation to language in Tarkos's work in '"Il n'y a pas de mots" et "Ma langue est pleine de mots": continu et articulations dans la théorie du langage de Christophe Tarkos', *Etudes françaises*, 49.3 (2013), 143–66 (p. 156).
24. Verdier, 'Entretiens de Bertrand Verdier avec Christophe Tarkos', p. 354.
25. Alongside tautologies, assertions such as 'Ce qui est est dangereux' are contrasted, precisely through their less immediately self-evident truth conditions. Enhanced by their similar rhetorical framing as declarative assertions, the juxtaposition of such declarations with tautological phrases, creates a contrast between subjective truths and communally-established ones. Again, phrases of this type tie into this broader practice of advancing a hypothesis, which will soon be revisited, to test its truth within the space of the poem itself (and, indeed, as the poem continues we will glean a further understanding of why this assertion 'Ce qui est est dangereux' might be true for Tarkos).
26. Hocquard, *Tout le monde se ressemble*, p. 232.
27. Philippe Castellin and Jérôme Mauche, 'Entretien. Tout-se-tient', in *Dossier Christophe Tarkos*, p. 10.
28. Elsewhere in Tarkos's poetry, this generativity is extended to its extremes in sequences that are motivated by phonological similarities. In '3 ronds du 19 mai', for example, we read: 'Gros haut | pot mot pot mot gros | haut haut mot pot hou hou poux | mou helo glo plot mlot helo gno mno' (*E*, 180). Likewise, in *Le Train*, complete sentences disintegrate into agrammatical phrases which serve to simulate the sound of a moving train: 'Je ne. Je ne le. Je ne le. Je je je. Ne ne ne. Le le le. Je et me. Je est me. Est je me. Je me est. Je ne meule'. Christophe Tarkos, *Le Train* (Berguette: Station Underground d'Emerveillement Littéraire, 1996), unpaginated (henceforth abbreviated to *T*).
29. Prigent, 'Sokrat à Patmo', p. 17.
30. Laurent Jenny, 'La Langue, le même et l'autre', *Fabula-LhT* (2005) <http://www.fabula.org/lht/0/jenny.html> [accessed 16 May 2018]
31. Prigent, *A quoi bon*, p. 10.
32. This distinction between meaning grounded in things versus meaning as movement and event is in keeping with his broader philosophical reflections. See, for example, the project description he sent to the Collège international de Philosophie, where he outlined his position on movement, time, objects, and materialism (*E*, 483–88).
33. Jeff Barda, 'Boules de sensations-pensées-formes in Christophe Tarkos's Poetry', *Nottingham French Studies*, 57.1 (2018), 18–32 (p. 21).
34. '[On n'a pas] des petits fragments pour — parler — mais on a que des — choses qui sont collées les unes avec les autres [...] c'est une pâte c'est complètement collé [...] c'est un tout [...] on peut pas séparer les éléments mais de l'autre on peut le prendre en entier' [[We don't have] little

fragments to — speak — we only have — thing that are all stuck together [...] it's a dough it's completely stuck [...] it's a whole [...] we can't separate the elements but we can take it as a whole] (E, 231).
35. Hocquard, *Tout le monde se ressemble*, p. 12.
36. In a highly metapoetic text in *Anachronisme*, Tarkos describes 'le bloc', which serves as an apt description of the typographic arrangement of his poems (A, 192).
37. 'Patmo ressemble à la langue selon Saussure'. Castellin, 'Christophe Tarkos', p. 52.
38. For a brief summary of Deleuze and Guattari's critique of Saussure, see Young, Genosko and Watson, *The Deleuze and Guattari Dictionary*, pp. 283–85.
39. Saussure also used the idea of the constellation to describe the relational identity of parts to whole in language. Ferdinand de Saussure, *Cours de linguistique générale*, ed. by Tullio de Mauro (Paris: Payot, 1995), p. 174.
40. The 'equals' sign is significant here in so far as it ties into the 'levelling effect' described above and Tarkos's broader emphasis on equivalence and continuism.
41. Castellin, 'Christophe Tarkos', p. 55.
42. Verdier, 'Entretiens de Bertrand Verdier avec Christophe Tarkos', p. 357.
43. Castellin, 'Christophe Tarkos', p. 36.
44. Verdier, 'Entretiens de Bertrand Verdier avec Christophe Tarkos', p. 354.
45. Prigent, *Salut les anciens*, pp. 86–87.
46. Despite many initial similarities between Tarkos and Ponge — their focus on everyday objects, the simplicity of their language, their exploration of the subject-language-world relationship — this is one significant way in which their poetry differs.
47. Castellin, 'Christophe Tarkos', p. 36.
48. Ibid., p. 58.
49. Christophe Tarkos, *Caisses* (Paris: P.O.L., 1998), 32 (henceforth abbreviated to *C*).
50. Espitallier, *Caisse à outils*, p. 183.
51. Deleuze wrote about the trope of exhaustion in Beckett's work in *L'Épuisé*, in Samuel Beckett and Gilles Deleuze, *Quad; et Trio du Fantôme; ...que nuages...; Nacht und Träume. Traduit de l'anglais par Edith Fournier. Suivi de L'Épuisé par Gilles Deleuze* (Paris: Minuit, 1992).
52. Indeed, Deleuze and Guattari write that 'le rhizome a pour tissu la conjonction "et... et... et..."' [the fabric of the rhizome is the conjunction, 'and... and... and...'] (*MP*, 36; *ATP*, 26).
53. Noland, 'Poetic Experimentation', p. 176.
54. Francis Ponge, 'Berges de la Loire', in *La Rage de l'expression. Tome I* (Paris: Gallimard, 1965), p. 257.
55. Ponge, *Entretiens de Francis Ponge avec Philippe Sollers*, p. 19.
56. Campbell, 'Thought, Perception and the Creative Act', p. 177.
57. Prigent, 'Sokrat à Patmo', p. 20. For a detailed criticism of Prigent's analysis of the supposed 'évidement de sens' in Tarkos's work, see Caillé, 'Théorie du langage et esthétique totalisante dans l'œuvre poétique de Christophe Tarkos', p. 73.
58. Prigent identifies the recurring motif of 'blanc' in Tarkos's collection *Caisses*. However, the argument could easily be made that the colour black constitutes an equally significant motif. The long poem 'Noir' at the end of *Le Signe* = (S, 128–57), collates themes found throughout his poetry, exploring the properties of blackness (S, 128). In *Anachronisme*, the 'noir' reappears, interwoven with themes of depression, bad weather, winter, and the constant presence of death.
59. John T. Naughton, 'The Notion of *presence* in the Poetics of Yves Bonnefoy', *Studies in 20th Century Literature*, 13 (1989), 43–60 (p. 56).
60. Castellin, 'Christophe Tarkos', p. 33.
61. Prigent, 'Sokrat à Patmo', p. 19.
62. Charles Baudelaire, 'À une passante', in *Les Fleurs du mal* (Paris: Flammarion, 1991), p. 137.
63. The theme of blindness reappears in *Anachronisme* where it is linked to the motif of mist and fog of an endless winter (A, 29).
64. The theme of suicide also appears in *Anachronisme*, in a passage beginning 'c'est un jour pour se suicider' (A, 28).
65. Game, *Poetic Becomings*, p. 10.

66. Caillé observes how, in *Anachronisme*, first-person voice is compounded by seven 'reprises' of Tarkos's name ('Tark.', 'Christophe' etc.). Caillé, 'Théorie du langage et esthétique totalisante dans l'œuvre poétique de Christophe Tarkos', p. 362.
67. Ibid., pp. 352–89. Arlette Albert-Birot, 'Découvrir C. Tarkos', in *Arlette Albert-Birot et Traverses* (Mandres-les-Roses: Traverses, 2011), pp. 129–38 (p. 137).
68. The same phrase occurs in a different 'autoprésentation' in *MC*, 110.
69. Christophe Tarkos, *La Cage* (Marseille: Al Dante, 1999), p. 27.
70. David Christoffel, 'Entretiens de David Christoffel avec Christophe Tarkos', in *EP*, 361–89 (p. 378).
71. Caillé describes winter as an allegorical figure representing 'la "maladie" du temps et de la parole' [the 'illness' of time and speech] in 'Théorie du langage et esthétique totalisante dans l'œuvre poétique de Christophe Tarkos', pp. 354–55.
72. We might also read the sixteen sentences of the poem (4 x 4, or four-squared) as a further expression of the significance of the number four in the text.
73. Caillé expands upon the significance of these 'formes carrées' in Tarkos's work. She suggests that Tarkos's predilection for these particular typographic arrangements is because they offer a heightened restrictive form in which to model the 'patmo'. This certainly seems to be the case in this instance in *Ma langue*. See Caillé, 'Théorie du langage et esthétique totalisante dans l'œuvre poétique de Christophe Tarkos', p. 337.
74. This idea of the menacing 'substance visqueuse' recalls both Francis Ponge's poetry, where language offers a means of bridling the infinitude of things, and the 'nausée' of external phenomena freed from their linguistic frames of reference in Sartre's *La Nausée*. In a passage that describes his bookshelves in *Anachronisme*, Tarkos echoes Sartre's terminology, describing 'la nausée' provoked by disorder (*A*, 217–18).
75. A preoccupation with form, taken in its broadest sense, is manifested in the prevalent inclusion of tables and diagrams in Tarkos's work. They represent an exaggerated form of typographic organisation, for example, in *Morceaux choisis* which includes an eclectic combination of tables of words (*MC*, 43), letters (58), and quantities, arranged by year, of 'Imports of Goods and Services' (111).
76. Bourassa, '"Il n'y a pas de mots"', p. 165.
77. Ibid., p. 165.
78. Tarkos expresses the same idea in an interview with Verdier: 'c'est vrai que tu changes la langue, ça change tout, probablement que ça change tout' [it's true that when you change language, it changes everything, it probably changes everything] (*EP*, 358).
79. In Tarkos's various 'autoprésentations' the phrase reappears in different configurations: in one he writes that he is 'Pour les poèmes' (*MC*, 110), in another he states: 'Je participe. Je suis pour. Je travaille pour' (*EP*, 32).
80. Resisting the administrative and legal erasure of 'ouvriers sans papiers', the project attempts to reaffirm the identity of the eponymous workers. It reprises the questions of identity and of affirmation and presence found throughout Tarkos's work in a more immediate way. In turn it demonstrates in practice the idea of a 'littérature mineure', which resists the dominant 'langue majeure'. See Philippe Beck and others, *Ouvriers vivants* (Romainville: Al Dante, 1999). Likewise, Tarkos contributed a number of texts to the review *Action poétique*, a review established precisely for poetry that was engaged in the socio-political realities of contemporary society. See Pascal Boulanger, *Une "Action poétique": de 1950 à aujourd'hui* (Paris: Flammarion, 1998) for a history of the aims and scope of the review.
81. Bourassa, '"Il n'y a pas de mots"', p. 165.
82. Gilles Deleuze and Claire Parnet, *Dialogues* (Paris: Flammarion, 1977), p. 30.
83. Roland Barthes, *Leçon* (Paris: Seuil, 1978), p. 16.
84. Ibid., p. 17.
85. In his discussion, Barthes explores the formal conventions of realist and naturalist literature, which he reads as markers of bourgeois 'literariness', opposing this to the 'neutre' style or non-style of Camus (*Le Degré zéro de l'écriture*, pp. 53–61).
86. Gleize, 'La Post-poésie', p. 124. Julia Kristeva's *La Révolution du langage poétique* (Paris: Seuil, 1974) is a further notable example of this.

87. Gleize uses these terms to describe 'langagement' of the 1960s-1980s in 'La Post-poésie', p. 126.
88. Jacques Derrida also evokes this inaugural gesture of the 'yes' in 'Ulysse gramophone: ouï-dire de Joyce', in *Ulysse gramophone: deux mots pour Joyce* (Paris: Galilée, 1987), pp. 57–143.
89. Francis Ponge, *Pour un Malherbe* (Paris: Gallimard, 1965), p. 216.
90. Cadiot, Mangeot and Zaoui, 'Cap au mieux', p. 12.
91. Ibid., p. 12.
92. In Tarkos's discussion of, among other things, proximity, experience, rhythm, and relations, we see the influence of Deleuze, whom the poet read and commented on. In his description of his unrealised project, 'La Terre', Tarkos evokes this influence directly, describing how he will draw on 'une vision deleuzienne de la proximité à l'objet' [a Deleuzian vision of the proximity to the object] (*E*, 504).
93. Tarkos insists, throughout his work, on the presence of the reader. In *Le Signe =*, he writes: 'On écrit pour le monde | Notre écrit est adressé au monde entier' [We write for the world | Our writing is addressed to the whole world] (*S*, 56).
94. Albert-Birot, 'Découvrir C. Tarkos', p. 137.
95. Pinson, *Sentimentale et naïve*, p. 24. See also Pinson, 'Poéthique de Gilles Deleuze', in *Deleuze et les écrivains*, ed. by Gelas and Micolet, pp. 187–200.
96. Pinson, *Sentimentale et naïve*, p. 186.
97. 'Il faut continuer, je ne peux pas continuer, il faut continuer, [...] il faut continuer, je ne peux pas continuer, je vais continuer' [You must go on, I can't go on, you must go on, [...] you must go on, I can't go on, I'll go on]. Samuel Beckett, *L'Innommable* (Paris: Minuit, 1953), p. 213.

CONCLUSION

One of the primary objectives of this book was to pursue the notion of a 'poésie mineure', an idea to which I wish to return in these concluding remarks. The previous chapters have considered how the language of Fourcade's, Cadiot's, and Tarkos's poetry relates to other forms of language, such as 'ordinary language' or traditional modes of poetic discourse, while mapping this onto the paradigm of the 'major' and the 'minor' that Deleuze and Guattari elaborate. In this discussion, we have seen some of the stylistic features of these poets' work that act as tensors for the deterritorialisation of language within the poem. From Fourcade's use of truncated, agrammatical clauses to Tarkos's vertiginous *ritournelles*, these features lend their work a foreign or strange quality. They highlight the rule-governed, variation-suppressing operation of the major language they diverge from, while at the same time pointing towards new linguistic possibilities, characterised by heteroglossia and multiplicity. Following Deleuze and Guattari's account, whereby major languages are intricately bound up in systems of power and minor literature involves the destabilising or deterritorialising of such systems, I have argued that the use of language in these poets' work lends it an implicitly political dimension. As we have seen, the centrality of linguistic experimentation in their work plays a constitutional role in its status as 'poésie mineure'. By definition, experimentation involves deviation and difference from a normal or established linguistic code. The various forms of linguistic experimentation found in the poetry of Fourcade, Cadiot, and Tarkos deviate from two principal forms of major language: on the one hand, 'ordinary language', understood in its broadest, loosest sense; on the other hand, traditional poetic discourses crystallised over time and still firmly established in the reader's mind. With regard to the first, poetry has long since been characterised by its difference from normal modes of communication, often more so than other literary genres. Historically, this difference has been seen as residing in its formal properties, its rhythmic or prosodic effects, and/or its self-reflexivity. Roman Jakobson's notion of the 'poetic function' is emblematic of how this divergence might be understood, and its popularity as a theoretical approach reflects the convergence of opinion on poetry's essential difference to other linguistic modes. The impulse towards linguistic experimentation that has gone hand-in-hand with the development of modern French poetry has extended this difference further. For example, experiments with non-semantic or non-signifying language, where the usual referential function of language is subverted and emphasis placed on the materiality of the signifier, have widened the gulf between poetic language and the 'mots de la tribu' [words of the tribe].[1] The work of Fourcade, Cadiot, and

Tarkos is situated within this tradition, and its legacy is apparent in what might be described, in somewhat paradoxical terms, as the more conventional forms of experimentation in their poetry. To give just one example, the glossolalia of earlier Dada experiments returns, albeit configured in novel ways according to the various concerns of their particular projects, in the infantile babbling of Fourcade's *Est-ce que j'peux placer un mot?*, in the segmented sampling of minority-language speakers in Cadiot's *Welche*, and in the agrammatical, onomatopoeic play of Tarkos's *Le Train*. A further dimension of their work that again has been a defining feature of modern French poetry is a self-reflexive tendency, where experiments target not only ordinary language in its broadest sense, but more specifically the conventions of traditional poetic discourses. We have seen how Fourcade, Cadiot, and Tarkos return to some of the dominant preoccupations of poetry over the last 150 years, experimenting, for example, with voice, subjecthood, and the relationship between poetry, prose, and other media. Written at the turn of the twenty-first century, Christian Prigent's survey of contemporary poetry, *Salut les anciens; Salut les modernes*, opens with the following address: 'Chers amis, voici le siècle nouveau. Tout a changé. Rien n'a changé' [Dear friends, here is the new century. Everything has changed. Nothing has changed].[2] Prigent raises the same question as Carrie Noland who, in her study of linguistic experimentation in modern French poetry, asks: 'Are the "chercheurs" (researchers) of today radically distinct from the poets of yesteryear? Or can we discern profound continuities between poets as distinctive as Heidsieck and Rimbaud, Roche and Mallarmé?'[3] Both critics pose the questions that lie behind any consideration of experimental or innovative literature: where is the new today? What makes it new? And what is its relationship with the innovative practices of the past?

So beyond the more familiar experimental practices, I hope also to have identified some of the idiosyncratic forms of experimentation that appear in these poets' work, either in the elaboration of novel devices, or in the reprise of pre-existing ones, reconfigured innovatively in each writer's particular poetics. In Fourcade's poetry, we saw how multilingual play intersects with the anthropomorphisation of language in such a way that, although neither property is unique to his work, they are put to new ends within his wider exploration of the mother tongue/foreign language paradigm. Likewise, Cadiot develops a novel use for the otherwise well-rehearsed technique of the cut-up; by using prescriptive grammar books in *L'Art poétic'* and samples from minority languages in *Welche* and *Hôtel Robinson*, he introduces an additional dimension that explores the interplay of power, authority, and language, and the possibilities for its destabilisation within the poem. The innovative quality of Tarkos's poetry stems from the theoretical underpinnings of his project and his experiments with the 'patmo', which challenge a dominant, Saussurean conception of language, and generate a cohesive and idiosyncratic style that, although reprising some of the more traditional features of poetic discourse, is altogether more subversive. Crucially, the centrality of experimentation in these poets' work lends it to a Deleuzo-Guattarian reading because the experiment does not seek simply to supplant the major language it deforms, but remains minor in its contingent relationship, where it is constituted precisely by its divergence.

The experiment thus involves the same contingency and impermanence of minor literature more generally; both are simultaneously bound to their past, to the existing forms they deterritorialise, and, as Deleuze and Guattari's emphasis on the 'becoming-minor' of minor literature would suggest, to the possible but fragile futures they potentialise.

In exploring the notion of 'poésie mineure', as opposed to 'littérature mineure' more broadly, this book has also aimed to address whether there is value in such a distinction. Beyond simply identifying the minor quality of certain poets' work, I have asked whether there is something specific to poetry, or, indeed to this experimental strand of contemporary poetry, that might lend it a particular place in a Deleuzo-Guattarian analysis. In light of Deleuze and Guattari's own discussion, distinguishing 'poésie mineure' from 'littérature mineure' might seem a somewhat contradictory gesture, as it works against their rhizomatic conception of artistic production, their emphasis on multiplicity and heterogeneity, and their resistance to the arborescent structure of genealogically motivated taxonomies. As discussed in Chapter 1, when they refer to the 'poetic' it is often used synonymously with the 'literary', with both ultimately being subsumed into broader notions of creative stuttering, deterritorialisation, and lines of flight. Likewise, the gesture might seem at odds with the post-genre approaches to literature that have recently gathered momentum in contemporary poetry and its criticism. In Chapter 3, we saw how Alferi and Cadiot's concept of the OVNI represents one such example. In their editorial essays in the *Revue de littérature générale*, they asked whether doing away with generic distinctions altogether, to focus instead on the properties of literature that transcend such distinctions, might not be a better line of approach.[4] In an interview with Nathalie Wourm, when asked whether 'La Mécanique lyrique' was a 'projet deleuzien', Alferi replied yes, stating: 'Nous étions tous les deux viscéralement du côté de la multiplicité et de l'horizontalité, au sens au moins de la déhiérarchisation, plutôt que du côté des systèmes de pensée hiérarchisés, exclusifs et autoritaires' [We were both viscerally on the side of multiplicity and horizontality, at least in the sense of dehierarchisation, rather than on the side of exclusive, authoritarian and hierarchised systems of thought].[5] In her introduction to the collection of interviews from which this comment is drawn, Wourm argues convincingly that the post-structuralist philosophy of figures such as Deleuze and Guattari and Derrida has shaped the field of contemporary poetry in significant ways. Evoking the *Revue de littérature générale* and critical approaches such as Jean-Marie Gleize's 'post-poésie', she suggests that the generic status of poetry is one area where Deleuze and Guattari's influence has been particularly great. On this same subject, in an article in *L'Esprit Créateur*, Wourm asks whether a post-generic approach spells the death of poetry, responding:

> No, simply the death of poetry as one single, narrowly defined category of the writing activity. [...] poetry enters the rhizome of artistic activity, leaving behind its elevated status in a fabricated literary hierarchy, as part of a process very much like Deleuze and Guattari's deterritorialization.[6]

Wourm then returns to this idea of the deterritorialisation of poetry in the introduction to *Poètes français du 21ème siècle*, where she cites her interview with the poet Jean-Michel Espitallier:

> 'Je pense qu'on a tous lu Deleuze' affirme Jean-Michel Espitallier dans les entretiens, évoquant une bibliothèque commune, des repères partagés et — reprenant un concept deleuzien — une même *déterritorialisation*. Et il précise: 'Nous sommes tous dans une impureté de la poésie, une impureté générique'. Selon lui, cette 'déterritorialisation' de la poésie passe par son hybridation, son croisement avec d'autres disciplines, telles les arts plastiques ou la musique. En s'hybridant, la 'poésie' est dépossédée d'un territoire, perd sa pureté. Cette interprétation deleuzienne de l'interdisciplinarité de la poésie contemporaine mène implicitement à l'idée d'une remise en question du concept de 'poésie'. Et étant génériquement impure, celle-ci est moins facilement reconnaissable, définissable.[7]

> ['I think we have all read Deleuze' Jean-Michel Espitallier says in the interviews, evoking their shared reading, their shared references, and — reprising a Deleuzian concept — a same *deterritorialisation*. He explains: 'We are all in this impurity of poetry, this generic impurity'. For him, this 'deterritorialisation' of poetry occurs in its hybridisation, its intersection with other disciplines, such as the visual arts or music. By hybridising, 'poetry' is stripped of a territory, it loses its purity. This Deleuzian interpretation of the interdisciplinary nature of contemporary poetry implicitly leads to the idea of a questioning of the concept of 'poetry'. By being generically impure, it is less easily recognisable or definable.]

Wourm goes on to evoke the same 'crise de poésie' that Gleize identified in *A noir* fifteen years earlier. She describes, in similar terms, how this identity crisis, this deterritorialisation of the very notion of poetry, becomes a defining feature of what constitutes its specificity as a practice: 'C'est donc cette absence d'identification, cette propension à être méconnaissable, cette désintégration d'un concept, qui font de la poésie ce qu'elle est aujourd'hui [It is therefore this absence of identification, this inclination to being unrecognisable, this disintegration of a concept, that makes poetry what it is today].[8] Contemporary poetry finds itself at a crossroads, where poets and critics will either continue to uphold a notion of the poetic, of poetry's specificity and its distinction from other forms, or will abandon it altogether in search of post-generic, all-encompassing notions of literary or artistic work. But we might also note how in these accounts that gesture towards a post-generic stance, there is often a paradox, where at the same time as wishing to leave poetry behind, they simultaneously sustain its centrality. Gleize's concept of 'post-poésie' typifies this paradox: the innovative, a-generic forms of artistic practice that he promotes are nonetheless contingent, as the prefix 'post-' would suggest, on a historical or genealogical relationship with poetry. Likewise, in Wourm's account, the deterritorialisation of poetry into other media, into a rhizomatic relationship with other forms, requires that this post-genre literature diverges from a territory that is poetry. Thus, in both accounts, even in the very gesture of rejecting it, genre returns to centre stage. In light of this, far from negating the utility of distinguishing minor poetry from minor literature, here we see how the term 'poésie mineure' takes on a particular significance. The term captures how, posed at a threshold in its own history, this strand of contemporary poetry grapples with its own generic identity, simultaneously deterritorialising established conceptions of poetry on which it is contingent, and becoming-other in the process.

What will be clear from the preceding chapters is that each of the three poets considered, while experimenting with its generic features, nonetheless maintains the specificity of poetry, in one form of another. In each poet's work, there is some notion of poetry that is either maintained, rejected, or fought for, and in this regard, each poet reflects something of their generation and the broader movements to which they belong. Fourcade, no doubt influenced by both the 'lyrisme critique' and 'modernité négative' movements of the 1980s, depicts simultaneously a compulsion towards poetry, a sense that he *must* write, but that he must do so in the knowledge of its inevitable failure to 'toucher le monde' (*EJP*, 80). Inscribed in a lineage of 'poésie pensante', he presents the particular linguistic experience of poetry as a unique way of being in the world, one that is both essential and, as he puts it, terrifying (*EJP*, 79). Conversely, Cadiot typifies the ludic and altogether more cynical approach of the following generation. In his work, we find both a Rochean rejection of poetry, despite, as he says, his preference for it, and a quest, manifested in his consideration of the OVNI in 'La Mécanique lyrique', to explore how poetry might continue by other means. As we have seen, the *Revue de littérature générale* (1995, 1996), alongside other notable works such as Gleize's *A noir* (1992), represents a post-poetic, sometimes anti-poetic posture that formed the zeitgeist in the 1990s. A number of figures who began publishing in the mid-1990s — Tarkos, but also Pennequin, Quintane, and Beck — rejected this posture strongly. Tarkos's insistence on the necessity to militate 'pour la poésie' reflects a compulsion to reassert its value and to ensure its continuation.

Amidst these various postures, the question remains as to what precisely constitutes poetry's specificity, or what precisely poetry *is*. Over the course of the previous chapters a number of ways of approaching these questions have been advanced. For example, in the last chapter we saw how, for Tarkos, a rudimentary notion of form, based on the shaping of language within the poem, might offer one such account. Various critical approaches have also been evoked: some more traditional (poetry as rhythmic variation), others more innovative (poetry as the tension between different linguistic codes, replacing a traditional tension between its metrical or syntactic features). One approach that I have returned to intermittently, and which carries some weight in light of the theoretical framework elaborated, derives from Pinson's notion of a 'poéthique', where poetry is seen as a particular linguistic way of inhabiting the world. At first glance, Pinson's analysis might lend itself more readily to poets such as Bonnefoy or Du Bouchet, who are more immediately concerned with ethical and philosophical notions of being. However, I think it also offers a useful framework to approach the work of Fourcade, Cadiot, and Tarkos. Although their poetry is, to varying degrees, often ludic, ironic, or humorous, it nonetheless poses broader questions of the place of the real, the subject, voice, and affect in poetry, and converges on the insistence that poetry serves an important function. This is particularly apparent in Tarkos's *œuvre*, where the autobiographical themes of death, illness, and existential anguish lend his work a sense of urgency, and where he affirms in no uncertain terms the propriety of poetry as the medium in which to explore such topics. A similar sense is conveyed in Fourcade's work, and is again most apparent in texts that engage with autobiographical themes, such as the death of loved ones in *Manque*, or overtly political subjects, such as the treatment of Iraqi prisoners by American troops in *En laisse*. While these examples illustrate how poetry might address, thematically, particular ethical or sociopolitical concerns, this is not, to my eyes, the principal expression of the 'poethical' dimension of their work, which is to be located, rather, in their conception of poetic language.

As we have seen, Fourcade, Cadiot, and Tarkos are all interested in the relationship between language and power, and in language understood as a sociopolitical phenomenon. This amounts, ultimately, to an exploration of the various linguistic ways in which we inhabit the world, and to an interrogation of the place of poetry, as a distinct 'expérience' of language, within that. Indeed, a recurring motif in the previous chapters has been the idea that experimenting with new linguistic modes might engender new ways of seeing, representing, or being in the world. This is clearly present in Deleuze and Guattari's notion of 'littérature mineure', and Chapter 1 cited a number of critical approaches that convey the same possibility. The notion that poetic language offers a space for resisting or changing the current state of language reappears in various ways in each of our three poets' work, most brazenly in Tarkos's, where his claim 'Le poème va faire la révolution' rests on his belief that 'tu changes la langue, ça change tout, probablement que ça change tout'. For Cadiot and Fourcade, such a claim would have to be attenuated. For example, for Fourcade, poetic language works against an intransitivity, an inevitable absence of the world in the poem, that is a product of the semiotic structure of the language system. To use the terms of Prigent, whose theoretical stance is similar to Fourcade's, poetry is thus involved in the pursuit of more accurate ('justes') ways of representing the world and its 'écart' than those of the conventional 'contrat verbal socialisé'.[9] Although with a greater wariness than the others, Cadiot also has, as he puts it, 'important things to say'; experimenting with various literary techniques and artistic forms, a driving ambition of his project is to find a way in which language can say these things.[10] While Tarkos might be an outlier, the following description by Dominique Rabaté conveys rather aptly the posture of many contemporary poets who take a more tentative and critical approach to the transformative potential of poetic language, while nonetheless sustaining its centrality to poetic practice. In his introduction to *Gestes lyriques*, he traces how, across the history of modern poetry, the idea of what poetry can do or accomplish in the real world, has shifted:

> À l'ère du soupçon, la croyance que les mots peuvent changer le monde a sans doute reculé, et les ambitions du dire poétique ont reflué d'autant. La tâche du poème est rendue plus modeste; elle s'accomplit avec scepticisme ou ironie, avec une nécessaire lucidité contre les puissances de l'auto-illusion. Mais l'interrogation reste bien celle des pouvoirs des mots, contre la mort, et pour décrire la réalité. Pour chercher des voies de sortie, des modes de contact, pour inventer une manière de se tenir ensemble.[11]

[In the age of suspicion, the belief that words could change the world undoubtedly declined, and the ambitions of poetic speech equally receded. The poem's task became more modest; it was accomplished with scepticism or irony, with a required lucidity to counter the powers of self-delusion. But the question remains that of the power of language, against death, and to describe reality. To seek the escape routes, the forms of contact, to invent a way to stand together.]

This book began with Prigent's hypothesis that deterritorialisation might offer a possible definition for poetry. For the strand of linguistically experimental contemporary poetry to which Fourcade, Cadiot, and Tarkos belong, it does indeed appear that the deterritorialisation of various forms of major language within the poem constitutes a significant and central dimension of their practice. A unifying property of their poetic language is its difference from, and relationship to, other forms of discourse. In such a way, Michael G. Kelly's observation, evoked in Chapter 1, that poetry is a permanently othered discourse, whose minority is bound to, and contingent on, the majority of the discourses that it deterritorialises, also appears to be true.[12] Furthermore, where minor literature deterritorialises the power structures of a major language, then one of the first discourses that it will tackle is likely to be that of its own generic conventions. This is all the more true for our three contemporary poets, working in a generic form that has historically been more self-reflexive and inward-looking than other literary forms, and in a contemporary field that is undergoing a so-called 'identity crisis', radically determined by its relationship with its past, and in a perpetual quest to define its current specificity. While Deleuze and Guattari do not extend their discussion of minor literature and its relationship to generic conventions in any great depth, in *Kafka*, they gesture towards it. They evoke how minor literature takes place within the framework of a major literary form, and their subsequent analysis of the metaphor-less language of Kafka's prose points to one way in which a minor author will deterritorialise the conventions of that major literary language. In Bakhtin's analysis we have found a further framework in which to approach the relationship between major literary modes and their counterparts. In Chapter 3 we saw how Bakhtin's account of parodic-travestying forms might apply to Cadiot's work, particularly *Futur, ancien, fugitif*, which parodies the conventions of a number of different major literary genres and modes. More broadly, we have seen how the poetry of Fourcade, Cadiot, and Tarkos might be read as a form of internally dialogic poetry, which evokes an absent but implicit mode that it deforms or deterritorialises. As opposed to Bakhtin's account of poetic monoglossia, far from upholding the myth of a single and unitary language, embodied in the major languages they minorise, their poetry presents heteroglottic forms, either implicitly (for example in Tarkos's 'lyric' poems) or explicitly (in Cadiot's polyphonous, hybrid texts).

Significantly, in the form of 'poésie mineure' that I am arguing for, the discourses that correspond with the categories of the 'major' and the 'minor' will constantly be in shift. As once-experimental practices crystallise as major forms, so too will the minor forms that are contingent on them adjust. Given the generational differences between the three poets considered, we can trace this shift across their work. For example, the focus on linguistic materiality and the absent referent in Fourcade's

Son blanc du un (1986), or the experiments with voice in the grammar book cut-ups of Cadiot's *L'Art poétic'* (1988) dismantle a major language that takes the form of traditional lyricism. A decade or so later, when Tarkos published *Ma langue* (2000) and *Anachronisme* (2001), his reinstatement of the lyric *je*, his emphasis on presence and his affirmation of the value of poetry, responds in turn to what he conceives of as a newly established major poetic mode. Indeed, one of the starting points for this book was Emmanuel Hocquard's description, in 1988, of the poetry associated with 'modernité négative' as 'poésie mineure (au sens deleuzien du terme)'.[13] In Tarkos's œuvre, we see how this had already become an established set of literary conventions, from which his poetry diverges. In this sense, reprising Fourcade's term that has had some currency in recent criticism, 'poésie mineure' will always inhabit the 'extrême contemporain' (*OU*, 20). It will always be 'avant-garde', to use Tarkos's own self-designation (*E*, 20). Defined by experimentation, by a dialogue with its past, by the perpetual renovation of traditional and pre-existing forms, literary, poetic, and otherwise, I think there is value in arguing that the work of Fourcade, Cadiot, and Tarkos might be read as a form of 'poésie mineure'. While this book has offered these three poets as examples, readers will no doubt already have figures in mind to whom such an analysis might apply, and new centres of poetic activity that extend or transform the concept further. This book has attempted to delineate the contours of what minor poetry might look like; further applications and understandings of this term will, I hope, offer fruitful avenues of future research.

Notes to the Conclusion

1. Stéphane Mallarmé, 'Le Tombeau d'Edgar Poe', in *Œuvres complètes*, p. 70.
2. Prigent, *Salut les anciens*, p. 13.
3. Noland, 'Poetic Experimentation', p. 171.
4. Alferi and Cadiot, 'Digest'.
5. Wourm, *Poètes français du 21ème siècle*, p. 43.
6. Wourm, 'Anticapitalism and the Poetic Function of Language', p. 129.
7. Wourm, *Poètes français du 21ème siècle*, p. 3.
8. Ibid. In a passage already cited, Gleize writes: 'la poésie vit son état de crise, sans doute *de* son état de crise, un état critique et autocritique permanent qui est certainement sa seule définition possible aujourd'hui'.
9. Prigent, 'Deleuze / "Poésie"'.
10. As Cadiot says in his interview with Person, 'Le lyrisme, c'est bien ça, l'expression des affects importants. Il y a des affects importants. Il y a des choses importantes qui se passent dans la vie. Comment les dire?' Person, 'Olivier Cadiot', p. 23.
11. Rabaté, *Gestes lyriques*, pp. 23–24.
12. Kelly, *Strands of Utopia*, p. 6.
13. His comment comes from 'La Bibliothèque de Trieste' which was published originally in 1988 by Editions Royaumont. Note that, in this essay, Hocquard actually pre-empts this codification of practice, describing how once-innovative themes and forms soon become rhetorical clichés, before concluding, 'sans une vigilance extrême, le vieil accent revient toujours au galop, [...] la machine poétique tend à s'encrasser rapidement' [without extreme vigilance, the old accent always comes galloping back, the poetic machine tends to get rusty quickly] (p. 27).

BIBLIOGRAPHY

Primary Texts

BURGER, RODOLPHE, and OLIVIER CADIOT, *Welche; On n'est pas indiens c'est dommage* (Dernière bande, 2000) [CD]
—— *Hôtel Robinson* (Dernière bande, 2002) [CD]
—— *Psychopharmaka* (Dernière bande, 2013) [CD]
CADIOT, OLIVIER, *L'Art poétic'* (Paris: P.O.L., 1988)
—— *Art Poétic'*, trans. by Cole Swensen (Copenhagen: Green Integer, 1999)
—— *Le Colonel des Zouaves* (Paris: P.O.L., 1997)
—— *Fairy Queen* (Paris: P.O.L., 2002)
—— *Futur, ancien, fugitif* (Paris: P.O.L., 1993)
—— *Histoire de la littérature récente*, 2 vols (Paris: P.O.L., 2016–17)
—— *Providence* (Paris: P.O.L., 2015)
—— *Retour définitif et durable de l'être aimé* (Paris: P.O.L., 2002)
—— *Roméo & Juliette I* (Paris: P.O.L., 1989)
—— *Un mage en été* (Paris: P.O.L., 2010)
—— *Un nid pour quoi faire* (Paris: P.O.L., 2007)
FOURCADE, DOMINIQUE, 'après les attentats' (Paris: Chandeigne, 2015)
—— *Le Ciel pas d'angle* (Paris: P.O.L., 1983)
—— *Citizen Do* (Paris: P.O.L., 2008)
—— *En laisse* (Paris: P.O.L., 2005)
—— *Éponges modèle 2003* (Paris: P.O.L., 2005)
—— *Épreuves du pouvoir* (Paris: José Corti, 1961)
—— *Est-ce que j'peux placer un mot?* (Paris: P.O.L., 2001)
—— *IL* (Paris: P.O.L., 1994)
—— *Lessive du loup* (Paris: GLM, 1966)
—— *Manque* (Paris: P.O.L., 2012)
—— *Outrance utterance* (Paris: P.O.L., 1990)
—— *Rose-déclic* (Paris: P.O.L., 1984)
—— *Sans lasso et sans flash* (Paris: P.O.L., 2005)
—— *Son blanc du un* (Paris: P.O.L., 1986)
—— *Le Sujet monotype* (Paris: P.O.L., 1997)
—— *Xbo* (Paris: P.O.L., 1988)
TARKOS, CHRISTOPHE, *Anachronisme* (Paris: P.O.L., 2001)
—— *L'Argent* (Romainville: Al Dante, 1999)
—— *Bang!* (Auvers-sur-Oise: Carte blanche, 2000)
—— *Le Baroque* (Limoges: Al Dante, 2009)
—— *Le Bâton* (Marseille: Al Dante, 1998)
—— *La Cage* (Marseille: Al Dante, 1999)
—— *Caisses* (Paris: P.O.L., 1998)
—— *Dix ronds* (Martigues: Contre-Pied, 1999)

———— *Écrits poétiques* (Paris, P.O.L., 2008)
———— *L'Enregistré* (Paris: P.O.L., 2014)
———— *L'Hypnotiseur soigne* (Bageux: Secrètes, 1998)
———— *Ma langue* (Marseille: Al Dante, 2000)
———— *Morceaux choisis* (Arras: Les Contemporains, 1995)
———— *L'Oiseau vole* (Fontenay-sous-Bois: L'Evidence, 1995)
———— *Oui* (Marseille: Al Dante, 1996)
———— *Processe* (Dijon: Ulysse Fin de Siècle, 1997)
———— *Le Signe =* (Paris: P.O.L., 1999)
———— *PAN* (Paris: P.O.L., 1999)
———— *Le Train* (Berguette: Station Underground d'Emerveillement Littéraire, 1996)
———— *La Valeur sublime* (Toulouse: Le Grand Os, 1998)

Secondary Texts

'Cours 12 du 17/03/1981', *La Voix de Gilles Deleuze en ligne* <http://www2.univ-paris8.fr/deleuze/article.php3?id_article=151> [accessed 27 June 2020]

'Cours 58 du 20/03/1984', *La Voix de Gilles Deleuze en ligne* <http://www2.univ-paris8.fr/deleuze/article.php3?id_article=337> [accessed 27 June 2020]

'Biographie', in *Ici d'ailleurs* <http://www.icidailleurs.com/index.php?route=product/category&path=68> [accessed 26 June 2020]

'Olivier Cadiot et Rodolphe Burger: nouvelle géographie sonore', *L'Atelier du son*, France Culture (2012), 26:00 <https://www.franceculture.fr/emissions/latelier-du-son/olivier-cadiot-et-rodolphe-burger-nouvelle-geographie-sonore> [accessed 26 June 2020]

AGAMBEN, GIORGIO, *Infancy and History: The Destruction of Experience*, trans. by Liz Heron (London: Verso, 1993)

AGER, DENNIS ERNEST, *Sociolinguistics and Contemporary French* (Cambridge: Cambridge University Press, 1990)

ALBERT-BIROT, ARLETTE, 'Découvrir C. Tarkos', in *Arlette Albert-Birot et Traverses* (Mandres-les-Roses: Traverses, 2011), pp. 129–38

ALEXANDRE, DIDIER, 'Le Blanc, le brut, le transparent: sur Dominique Fourcade, Emmanuel Hocquard, James Sacré', in *Ecritures blanches*, ed. by Dominique Rabaté and Dominique Viart (Saint-Etienne: Publications de l'Université de Saint-Etienne, 2009), pp. 255–67

ALFERI, PIERRE, *Chercher une phrase* (Paris: Bourgois, 1991)
———— *Cinépoèmes & films parlants* (Aubervilliers: Laboratoires d'Aubervilliers, 2003)
———— *Sentimentale journée* (Paris: P.O.L., 1997)

ALFERI, PIERRE, and OLIVIER CADIOT (eds), *Revue de littérature générale 95/1* (Paris: P.O.L., 1995)
———— *Revue de littérature générale 96/2* (Paris: P.O.L., 1996)

ALIZART, MARK, 'Les Trois Ages du sample', *Critique*, 677 (2003), 776–84

ANELOK, IRINA, 'Les écrits sur l'art de Dominique Fourcade: la naissance d'une poétique' (unpublished doctoral thesis, Université Paris Ouest Nanterre, 2013)

APOLLINAIRE, GUILLAUME, *Œuvres en prose*, 2 vols (Paris: Gallimard, 1991)

BAKHTIN, MIKHAIL, *The Dialogic Imagination* (Austin: University of Texas Press, 1981)
———— *Problems of Dostoevsky's Poetics* (Minneapolis: University of Minnesota Press, 1984)
———— *Rabelais and His World*, trans. by Hélène Iswolsky (Bloomington: Indiana University Press, 1984)

BARDA, JEFF, 'Boules de sensations-pensées-formes in Christophe Tarkos's Poetry', *Nottingham French Studies*, 57.1 (2018), 18–32

BARTHES, ROLAND, *Le Bruissement de la langue: essais critiques IV* (Paris: Seuil, 1984)

―― *Le Degré zéro de l'écriture* (Paris: Seuil, 1953)
―― *Writing Degree Zero*, trans. by Annette Lavers and Colin Smith (New York: Hill and Wang, 2012)
―― *Leçon* (Paris: Seuil, 1978)
BAUDELAIRE, CHARLES, *Les Fleurs du mal* (Paris: Flammarion, 1991)
BECKETT, SAMUEL, *I Can't Go On, I'll Go On: A Selection from Samuel Beckett's Work*, ed. by Richard W. Seaver (New York: Grove Press, 1976)
―― *L'Innommable* (Paris: Minuit, 1953)
BECK, PHILIPPE and OTHERS, *Ouvriers vivants* (Romainville: Al Dante, 1999)
BECKETT, SAMUEL, and GILLES DELEUZE, *Quad; et Trio du Fantôme; ...que nuages...; Nacht und Träume. Traduit de l'anglais par Edith Fournier. Suivi de L'Épuisé par Gilles Deleuze* (Paris: Minuit, 1992)
BIDEAU, ALAIN, 'Cadiot: une aventure extraordinaire / une extraordinaire aventure', *TXT*, 24 (1989), 66–67
BOGUE, RONALD, 'The Minor', in *Gilles Deleuze: Key Concepts*, ed. by Charles J. Stivale (Abingdon & New York: Routledge, 2011), pp. 131–41
BONNERAVE, JOCELYN, 'Le Narratif chez le dernier Tarkos', in *Dossier Christophe Tarkos, Cahier Critique de Poésie*, 30 (2015), 64–65
BOSCHETTI, ANNA, 'Le Formalisme réaliste d'Olivier Cadiot: une réponse à la question des possibles et du rôle de la recherche littéraire aujourd'hui', in *L'Ecrivain, le savant et le philosophe*, ed. by Eveline Pinto (Paris: Sorbonne, 2003), pp. 236–50
BOULANGER, PASCAL, *Une "Action poétique": de 1950 à aujourd'hui* (Paris: Flammarion, 1998)
BOURASSA, LUCIE, '"Il n'y a pas de mots" et "Ma langue est pleine de mots": continu et articulations dans la théorie du langage de Christophe Tarkos', *Etudes françaises*, 49.3 (2013), 143–66
BRETON, ANDRÉ, 'Les Mots sans rides', *Littérature*, 7 (1922), 12–14
BROPHY, MICHAEL, and MARY GALLAGHER (eds), *Sens et présence du sujet poétique: la poésie de la France et du monde francophone depuis 1980* (Amsterdam: Rodopi, 2006)
BURGER, RODOLPHE, and OLIVIER CADIOT, 'Une petite guérilla intérieure', *Vacarme*, 52 (2010), 54–58
BURROUGHS, WILLIAM, and BRION GYSIN, *The Third Mind* (New York: Viking Press, 1978)
CADIOT, OLIVIER, 'Bé-bégayer', *Java*, 17 (1998), 39–40
CADIOT, OLIVIER, LUDOVIC LAGARDE and LAURENT POITRENAUX, *Un mage en été: dossier pédagogique* (Paris: Centre Pompidou, 2010)
CADIOT, OLIVIER, PHILIPPE MANGEOT and PIERRE ZAOUI, 'Cap au mieux: *entretien avec Olivier Cadiot*', *Vacarme*, 45 (2008), 4–12
CAILLÉ, ANNE-RENÉE, 'Théorie du langage et esthétique totalisante dans l'oeuvre poétique de Christophe Tarkos' (unpublished doctoral thesis, Université de Montréal, 2014)
CAMPBELL, KATE LERMITTE, 'Thought, Perception and the Creative Act. A Study of the Work of Four Contemporary French Poets: Pierre Alferi, Anne Portugal, Valère Novarina and Christophe Tarkos' (unpublished doctoral thesis, University of Oxford, 2008)
CASTELLIN, PHILIPPE, 'Christophe Tarkos: "Poète de la lecture"', in Christophe Tarkos, *L'Enregistré* (Paris: P.O.L., 2014), pp. 13–93
CASTELLIN, PHILIPPE, and JÉRÔME MAUCHE, 'Entretien. Tout-se-tient', in *Dossier Christophe Tarkos, Cahier Critique de Poésie*, 30 (2015), 5–12
CENDRARS, BLAISE, *Kodak: (documentaire)* (Paris: Stock, 1924)
CERTEAU, MICHEL DE, 'Utopies vocales: glossolalies', *Traverses*, 20 (1980), 26–37
CHATON, ANNE-JAMES, *Autoportraits* (Paris: Al Dante, 2003)
CHRISTOFFEL, DAVID, 'Entretiens de David Christoffel avec Christophe Tarkos', in Christophe Tarkos, *Écrits poétiques* (Paris: P.O.L., 2008), pp. 361–89

CLERC, THOMAS, 'La Mite', in *Dossier Christophe Tarkos, Cahier Critique de Poésie*, 30 (2015), 73–75
COHEN, JEAN, *Structure du langage poétique* (Paris: Flammarion, 1966)
COLLOT, MICHEL, 'Lyrisme et littéralité', *Lendemains*, 34 (2009), 14–24
—— *La matière-émotion* (Paris: PUF, 1997)
COMBE, DOMINIQUE, 'Derrida et Khatibi — autour du *Monolinguisme de l'autre*', *Carnets*, 7 (2016), pp. 1–6 <https://carnets.revues.org/897> [accessed 10 May 2020]
CONNOR, STEVEN, *Beyond Words: Sobs, Hums, Stutters and Other Vocalizations* (London: Reaktion Books, 2014)
CONSENSTEIN, PETER, 'Le Présent immédiat dans la poésie de Dominique Fourcade', *Contemporary French and Francophone Studies*, 10 (2006), 447–62
CUSSET, FRANÇOIS, 'politique de Cadiot', *Vacarme*, 40 (2007) <http://www.vacarme.org/article1341.html> [accessed 23 June 2020]
DELEUZE, GILLES, *Critique et clinique* (Paris: Minuit, 1993)
—— *Essays Critical and Clinical*, trans. by Daniel W. Smith and Michael A. Greco (London: Verso, 1998)
—— *Logique du sens* (Paris: Minuit, 1969)
—— 'Schizologie' in Louis Wolfson, *Le Schizo et les langues* (Paris: Minuit, 1970), pp. 5–23
DELEUZE, GILLES, and FÉLIX GUATTARI, *Kafka: pour une littérature mineure* (Paris: Minuit, 1975)
—— *Kafka: Toward a Minor Literature*, trans. by Dana Polan (Minneapolis: University of Minnesota Press, 1986)
—— *Mille plateaux* (Paris: Minuit, 1980)
—— *A Thousand Plateaus: Capitalism and Schizophrenia*, trans. by Brian Massumi (London: Bloomsbury, 2013)
DELEUZE, GILLES, and CLAIRE PARNET, *Dialogues* (Paris: Flammarion, 1977)
DENTITH, SIMON, *Parody* (London & New York: Routledge, 2000)
DERRIDA, JACQUES, *Le Monolinguisme de l'autre, ou, La Prothèse d'origine* (Paris: Galilée, 1996)
—— *Ulysse gramophone: deux mots pour Joyce* (Paris: Galilée, 1987)
DIMITROVA, ZORNITSA, *Literary Worlds and Deleuze: Expression as Mimesis and Event* (Lanham, MD: Lexington Books, 2016)
DISSON, AGNÈS, 'Poésie années 90: les enfants de Gertrude Stein et de Jacques Roubaud', *French Studies Bulletin*, 22.79 (2001), 13–17
ESKIN, MICHAEL, 'Bakhtin on Poetry', *Poetics Today*, 21.2 (2000), 379–91
ESPITALLIER, JEAN-MICHEL, *Caisse à outils* (Paris: Pocket, 2006)
—— *En guerre* (Paris: Inventaire-invention, 2004)
ESPITALLIER, JEAN-MICHEL, and JACQUES SIVAN (eds), *Olivier Cadiot*, special issue of *Java*, 13 (1995)
FARAH, ALAIN, *Le Gala des incomparables: invention et résistance chez Olivier Cadiot et Nathalie Quintane* (Paris: Garnier, 2013)
—— 'La Possibilité du choc: invention littéraire et résistance politique dans les œuvres d'Olivier Cadiot et de Nathalie Quintane' (doctoral thesis, Ecole Normale Supérieure; Université du Québec à Montréal, 2009)
FIAT, CHRISTOPHE, *New York 2001* (Romainville: Al Dante, 2002)
FOURCADE, DOMINIQUE, 'Entretien avec Frédéric Valabrègue', in *Dossier Dominique Fourcade, Cahier Critique de Poésie*, 11 (2006), 5–18
—— 'Entretien avec Hervé Bauer', *Java*, 17 (1998), 57–70
—— 'Entretien avec Mathias Lavin', *Action Restreinte*, 7 (2006), 81–95
—— '"La langue en crue": Entretien avec Emmanuel Laugier', *Le Matricule des Anges*, 22 (1998), 46

—— 'Xbo', *P.O.L. Website Catalogue* (2013) <http://www.pol-editeur.com/index.php?spec=livre&ISBN=2-86744-136-6> [accessed 26 June 2020]

GAME, JÉRÔME, 'La Répétition différenciante dans la poétique deleuzienne: bégaiement et ritournelle', in *Deleuze et les écrivains: littérature et philosophie*, ed. by Bruno Gelas and Hervé Micolet (Nantes: Cécile Defaut, 2007), pp. 401–20

—— *Poetic Becomings: Studies in Contemporary French Literature* (Oxford & New York: Peter Lang, 2011)

GAME, JÉRÔME (ed.), *Porous Boundaries: Texts and Images in Twentieth-century French Culture* (Oxford: Peter Lang, 2007)

GAUTHIER, MICHEL, *Olivier Cadiot, le facteur vitesse* (Dijon: Presses du réel, 2004)

GAVRONSKY, SERGE, *Toward a New Poetics: Contemporary Writing in France* (Berkeley: University of California Press, 1994)

GELAS, BRUNO, and HERVÉ MICOLET (eds), *Deleuze et les écrivains: littérature et philosophie* (Nantes: Cécile Defaut, 2007)

GLEIZE, JEAN-MARIE, *A noir: poésie et littéralité, essai* (Paris: Seuil, 1992)

—— *Néon, actes et légendes* (Paris: Seuil, 2004)

—— 'Le Poème est l'afflux de cela', *Java*, 17 (1998), 47–51

—— 'La Post-poésie: un travail d'investigation-élucidation', *matraga*, 17.27 (2010), 121–33

—— *Sorties* (Paris: Questions théoriques, 2009)

GOLDSMITH, KENNETH, *Uncreative Writing: Managing Language in the Digital Age* (New York: Columbia University Press, 2011)

GYSIN, BRION, *Back in No Time: The Brion Gysin Reader*, ed. by Jason Weiss (Middletown, CT: Wesleyan University Press, 2001)

HALADJIAN, MARGUERITE, and JEAN-BAPTISTE PARA, 'Une partie qu'on ne gagne jamais: entretien avec Dominique Fourcade', *Europe*, 744 (1991), 136–46

HANNA, CHRISTOPHE, *Poésie action directe* (Paris: Al Dante, 2003)

HEIDSIECK, BERNARD, *Biopsies: 1965–1969* (Al Dante, 2009) [CD]

—— *Derviche/Le Robert* (Roumainville: Al Dante, 2004)

HOCQUARD, EMMANUEL, *Ma haie* (Paris: P.O.L., 2001)

—— *Tout le monde se ressemble* (Paris: P.O.L., 2001)

—— *Un privé à Tanger* (Paris: P.O.L., 1987)

JENNY, LAURENT, 'La Langue, le même et l'autre', *Fabula-LhT* (2005) <http://www.fabula.org/lht/0/jenny.html> [accessed 16 May 2018]

JORDAN, SHIRLEY ANN, *The Art Criticism of Francis Ponge* (London: W. S. Maney, 1994)

JOYCE, ELISABETH W., *'The Small Space of a Pause': Susan Howe's Poetry and the Spaces Between* (Lewisburg, PA: Bucknell University Press, 2010)

KELLY, MICHAEL G., 'Poetry as a Foreign Language: Unhoused Writing Subjects in the *extrême contemporain*', *Forum for Modern Language Studies*, 47.4 (2011), 393–407

—— *Strands of Utopia: Spaces of Poetic Work in Twentieth-century France* (London: Legenda, 2008)

KHALFA, JEAN, 'Ontologie et subjectivité chez Césaire', in *Sens et présence du sujet poétique: la poésie de la France et du monde francophone depuis 1980*, ed. by Michael Brophy and Mary Gallagher (Amsterdam: Rodopi, 2006), pp. 191–201

KHATIBI, ABDELKEBIR, *Essais* (Paris: La Différence, 2008)

KRISTEVA, JULIA, *La Révolution du langage poétique* (Paris: Seuil, 1974)

KURTS, LIA, 'Olivier Cadiot, ou La Poétique des objets trouvés', in *Formes et normes en poésie moderne et contemporaine*, ed. by Laurence Bougault and Judith Wulf (2011), pp. 31–58 <https://www.academia.edu/4461615/FORMES_ET_NORMES_EN_POÉSIE_MODERNE_ET_CONTEMPORAINEPréface> [accessed 22 June 2020]

LAMIOT, CHRISTOPHE, *Eau sur eau: les dictionnaires de Mallarmé, Flaubert, Bataille, Michaux, Leiris et Ponge* (Amsterdam: Rodopi, 1997)

LANG, ABIGAIL, 'What's in a Bird?', in *Dossier Dominique Fourcade, Cahier Critique de Poésie*, 11 (2006), 31–48

LEIRIS, MICHEL, *Mots sans mémoire: Simulacre; Le Point cardinal; Glossaire, j'y serre mes gloses; Bagatelles végétales; Marrons sculptés pour Miró* (Paris: Gallimard, 1998)

LEQUETTE, SAMUEL, 'Écrits poétiques de Christophe Tarkos', *Sitaudis* (2009) <http://www.sitaudis.fr/Parutions/ecrits-poetiques-de-christophe-tarkos.php> [accessed 30 October 2016]

LEUWERS, DANIEL, 'Dominique Fourcade: une question de cordes vocales', in *Sens et présence du sujet poétique: la poésie de la France et du monde francophone depuis 1980*, ed. by Michael Brophy and Mary Gallagher (Amsterdam: Rodopi, 2006), pp. 203–08

LYNCH, ERIC, 'Olivier Cadiot's Robinson, or A Portrait of the Artist as "Auto-usine"', *L'Esprit Créateur*, 54.1 (2014), 86–99

—— 'Unidentified Verbal Objects: Contemporary French Poetry, Intermedia, and Narrative' (unpublished doctoral thesis, City University of New York, 2016)

MALLARMÉ, STÉPHANE, *Œuvres complètes* (Paris: Gallimard, 1945)

MAULPOIX, JEAN-MICHEL, *La Poésie comme l'amour* (Paris: Mercure de France, 1998)

NAUGHTON, JOHN T., 'The Notion of *presence* in the Poetics of Yves Bonnefoy', *Studies in 20th Century Literature*, 13 (1989), 43–60

NOËL, BERNARD, 'Où va la poésie?', in *The New French Poetry*, ed. by David Kelley and Jean Khalfa (Newcastle upon Tyne: Bloodaxe, 1996), pp. 212–21

NOLAND, CARRIE, 'Poetic Experimentation', *The Cambridge Companion to French Literature*, ed. by John D. Lyons (Cambridge: Cambridge University Press, 2016), pp. 168–86

NOWELL SMITH, DAVID, *On Voice in Poetry: The Work of Animation* (Basingstoke: Palgrave Macmillan, 2015)

PARISH, NINA, 'From Book to Page to Screen: Poetry and New Media', *French Studies: Writing and the Image Today*, 114 (2008), 51–66

PERLOFF, MARJORIE, 'Language in Migration: Multilingualism and Exophonic Writing in the New Poetics', *Textual Practice*, 24.4 (2010), 725–48

—— *Unoriginal Genius: Poetry by Other Means in the New Century* (Chicago: University of Chicago Press, 2010)

—— *Wittgenstein's Ladder: Poetic Language and the Strangeness of the Ordinary* (Chicago & London: University of Chicago Press, 1996)

PERSON, XAVIER, 'Olivier Cadiot', *Le Matricule des Anges*, 41 (2002), 14–23

PINSON, JEAN-CLAUDE, 'Citizen Do de Dominique Fourcade' (2008) <http://www.sitaudis.fr/Parutions/citizen-do-de-dominique-fourcade.php> [accessed 29 May 2020]

—— *Habiter en poète: essai sur la poésie contemporaine* (Seyssel: Champ Vallon, 1995)

—— 'Poéthique de Gilles Deleuze', in *Deleuze et les écrivains: littérature et philosophie*, ed. by Bruno Gelas and Hervé Micolet (Nantes: Cécile Defaut, 2007), pp. 187–200

—— *Sentimentale et naïve: nouveaux essais sur la poésie contemporaine* (Seyssel: Champ Vallon, 2002)

PONGE, FRANCIS, *Entretiens de Francis Ponge avec Philippe Sollers* (Paris: Gallimard, 1970)

—— *La Fabrique du Pré* (Genève: Albert Skira, 1971)

—— *Le Grand Recueil: Lyres* (Paris: Gallimard, 1961)

—— *Le Grand Recueil: Méthodes* (Paris: Gallimard, 1961)

—— *Le Grand Recueil: Pièces* (Paris: Gallimard, 1961)

—— *Œuvres complètes*, 2 vols (Paris: Gallimard, 1999–2002)

—— *Le Parti pris des choses* (Paris: Gallimard, 1942)

—— *Pour un Malherbe* (Paris: Gallimard, 1965)

—— *La Rage de l'expression. Tome I* (Paris: Gallimard, 1965)

—— *Le Savon* (Paris: Gallimard, 1967)

PRIGENT, CHRISTIAN, *A quoi bon encore des poètes?* (Valence: ERBA, 1994)
—— *Ceux qui merdRent* (Paris: P.O.L., 1991)
—— 'Deleuze / "Poésie"', *Sitaudis* (2015) <http://www.sitaudis.fr/Incitations/deleuze-poesie.php> [accessed 26 June 2020]
—— *La Langue et ses monstres* (Paris: P.O.L., 2014)
—— 'On ne fait pas de poésie sans casser d'œufs: note sur la poésie, en parcourant Deleuze', in *Deleuze et les écrivains: littérature et philosophie*, ed. by Bruno Gelas and Hervé Micolet (Nantes: Cécile Defaut, 2007), pp. 429–42
—— *Salut les anciens: lectures; Salut les modernes: sur ce qui apparaît* (Paris: P.O.L., 2000)
—— 'Sokrat à Patmo', in Christophe Tarkos, *Écrits poétiques* (Paris, P.O.L., 2008), pp. 9–23
RABATÉ, DOMINIQUE, *Gestes lyriques* (Paris: José Corti, 2013)
—— 'Polyphonie du solitaire: le Robinson d'Olivier Cadiot', in *Nuove solitudini: mutamenti delle relazioni nell'ultima narrativa francese*, ed. by Matteo Majorano (Macerata: Quodlibet, 2012), pp. 83–97
RABATÉ, DOMINIQUE (ed.), *Figures du sujet lyrique* (Paris: PuF, 1996)
RABATÉ, DOMINIQUE, and DOMINIQUE VIART (eds), *Ecritures blanches* (Saint-Etienne: Publications de l'Université de Saint-Etienne, 2009)
RENAUD, JEAN, 'Le Monologue extérieur d'Olivier Cadiot', *Critique*, 677 (2003), 763–75
ROBERTSON, ERIC, 'Writing in Tongues: Multilingual Poetry and Self-translation in France from Dada to the Present', *Nottingham French Studies*, 56.2 (2017), 119–38
ROCHE, DENIS, *La Poésie est inadmissible: œuvres poétiques complètes* (Paris: Seuil, 1995)
ROUBAUD, JACQUES, *Poésie, etcetera: ménage* (Paris: Stock, 1995)
ROYET-JOURNOUD, CLAUDE, 'Entretien avec Dominique Fourcade', *Banana Split*, 11 (1983), 18–29
SADIN, ERIC, *Poésie atomique* (Lentigny: éc/artS, 2004)
SAINSBURY, DAISY, 'Language and Statelessness in the Poetry of Olivier Cadiot', *Modern Languages Open*, 1, (2019), 1–13
—— 'Towards a Minor Poetry: Reading Twentieth-Century French Poetry with Deleuze-Guattari and Bakhtin', *Paragraph*, 42.2 (2019), 135–53
SARTRE, JEAN-PAUL, *Les Mots et autres écrits autobiographiques* (Paris: Gallimard, 2010)
SAUSSURE, FERDINAND DE, *Cours de linguistique générale*, ed. by Tullio de Mauro (Paris: Payot, 1995)
SAXTON, MATTHEW, *Child Language: Acquisition and Development* (Los Angeles & London: SAGE, 2010)
SHKLOVSKY, VICTOR, 'Art as Technique', in *Modern Criticism and Theory: A Reader*, ed. by David Lodge (London: Longman, 1988), pp. 15–30
STEIN, GERTRUDE, *Autobiographie de tout le monde*, trans. by Marie-France de Paloméra (Paris: Seuil, 1989)
THÉVAL, GAËLLE, 'Poésies ready-made, XXe-XXIe siècles' (doctoral thesis, Université Paris-Diderot-Paris VII, 2011)
—— *Poésies ready-made, XXe-XXIe siècles* (Paris: L'Harmattan, 2015)
THOMAS, JEAN-JACQUES, and STEVEN WINSPUR, *Poeticized Language: The Foundations of Contemporary French Poetry* (University Park: Pennsylvania State University Press, 1999)
VALABRÈGUE, FRÉDÉRIC, 'Dominique Fourcade: "La page langue monde"', *Critique*, 8 (2008), 710–18
—— 'Une chose fuitive', *Java*, 17 (1998), 21–25
VERDIER, BERTRAND, 'Entretiens de Bertrand Verdier avec Christophe Tarkos', in Christophe Tarkos, *Écrits poétiques* (Paris, P.O.L., 2008), pp. 353–60
WALL-ROMANA, CHRISTOPHE, *Cinepoetry: Imaginary Cinemas in French Poetry* (New York: Fordham University Press, 2013)

——'Is "postpoetry" still Poetry? Jean-Marie Gleize's *dispositif*-writing', *Forum for Modern Language Studies*, 47.4 (2011), 442–53
WILLIAMS, WILLIAM CARLOS, *The Wedge* (Cummington, MA: Cummington Press, 1944)
WITTGENSTEIN, LUDWIG, *Zettel*, trans. by G. E. M. Anscombe (Oxford: Blackwell, 1967)
WOELFEL, ANNE, 'Le Système Cadiot: l'hétérogène dans le champ de l'expérience' (unpublished doctoral thesis, Université de Pau et des Pays de l'Adour, 2014)
WOURM, NATHALIE, 'Anticapitalism and the Poetic Function of Language', *L'Esprit Créateur*, 49.2 (2009), 119–31
——'Non-readings, Misreadings, Unreadings: Deleuze and Cadiot on Robinson Crusoe and Capitalism', in *Stealing the Fire: Adaptation, Appropriation, Plagiarism, Hoax in French and Francophone Literature and Film*, ed. by James T. Day (Amsterdam: Rodopi, 2010), pp. 177–90
——*Poètes français du 21ème siècle: entretiens* (Leiden: Rodopi, 2017)
——'Poetry in Moving Image: The French Avant-Garde', in *Porous Boundaries, Texts and Images in Twentieth-century French Culture*, ed. by Jérôme Game (Oxford: Peter Lang, 2007), pp. 101–19
YOUNG, EUGENE B., with GARY GENOSKO and JANELL WATSON, *The Deleuze and Guattari Dictionary* (London & New York: Bloomsbury Academic, 2013)

INDEX

Agamben, Giorgio 123 f. 42
Albert-Birot, Arlette 154, 164
Albiach, Anne-Marie 4, 6, 22
Alferi, Pierre 9–11, 14, 22, 25, 39 f. 43, 70–71, 78 f. 23,
 81, 83, 84, 89, 100–01, 120–21, 163, 173
 see also Revue de littérature générale
Alizart, Mark 119
American Objectivism 6, 12, 43, 68, 83
Apollinaire, Guillaume 9–10, 36
Artaud, Antonin 2, 19, 49, 92, 128
Austin, John L. 140

Bakhtin, Mikhail:
 Carnivalesque 117–18, 121, 125 f. 87
 The Dialogic Imagination 33–37, 89, 91, 104–05,
  116–18, 121, 128, 165, 177
 Monologism 4, 34–37, 71, 76, 89, 104–05, 118, 128,
  165–66, 177
Baquey, Stéphane 22
Barda, Jeff 139
Barthes, Roland 6, 19–20, 29, 68, 109–10, 117, 121,
 135, 160–61
Bataille, Georges 107
Baudelaire, Charles 4, 73, 86, 151
Beck, Philippe 127–28, 175
Beckett, Samuel 2, 18–19, 24, 55, 115, 128, 145, 165,
 168 f. 51, 170 f. 97
Bérard, Stéphane 127
Bergvall, Caroline 26
Blake, William 114
Bobillot, Jean-Pierre 14
Bogue, Ronald 28
Boileau, Nicolas 115
Bonnefoy, Yves 5, 128, 130, 147, 175
Bonnerave, Jocelyn 127
Boschetti, Anna 88, 116
Bourassa, Lucie 159
Braque, Georges 76
Breton, André 55
Buffon, Georges-Louis Leclerc de 64
Burger, Rodolphe see Olivier Cadiot
Burroughs, William 82–83, 109

Cadiot, Olivier:
 L'Art poétic' 13, 23, 36, 81–92, 98, 101–03, 105,
  107–16, 118–20, 172, 178
 Le Colonel des Zouaves 13, 81

Fairy Queen 13, 81, 120
Futur, ancien, fugitif 13, 27, 81–82, 90–99, 102–03, 105,
 107–08, 111, 113, 115–16, 119–20, 123 f. 39, 177
Histoire de la littérature récente 13, 81
Musical collaborations with Rodolphe Burger
 13–14, 105, 116, 119
 Welche; On n'est pas indiens c'est dommage 81, 89,
  91, 98–102, 119, 172
 Hôtel Robinson 81, 89, 91–92, 102–03, 119, 172
 Psychopharmaka 81, 89, 91–93, 103–04, 119
Providence 13, 81
Retour définitif et durable de l'être aimé 13, 81
 see also Revue de littérature générale
Roméo & Juliette I: 13, 119
Un mage en été 13, 81
Un nid pour quoi faire 13, 81
Caillé, Anne-Renée 127, 154, 169 f. 73
Campbell, Kate 134, 147
Camus, Albert 19, 169 f. 85
Casanova, Pascale 140
Castellin, Philippe 136, 139–42, 148, 164
Celan, Paul 104
Certeau, Michel de 123 f. 41
Cézanne, Paul 63–65, 72–73
Char, René 12, 72, 130
Chaton, Anne-James 11, 14, 39 f. 43
Chomsky, Noam 20–21
Chopin, Henri 4
Christoffel, David 155
Cinepoetry 10–11, 68–69, 100–01
Clerc, Thomas 127
Cohen, Jean 31
Collot, Michel 5, 10, 14, 43
Consenstein, Peter 49, 70, 76
Cubism 65, 76
Cummings, E. E. 1–2, 17, 19, 20–22, 35

Dada 49, 83, 93, 103–04, 172
Daive, Jean 4, 6, 22
Defoe, Daniel 82, 90
Degas, Edgar 63, 73
Deguy, Michel 130
Deleuze, Gilles:
 Agrammaticality 1, 20–23, 28, 50–51, 59, 70, 76, 96,
  102, 106, 112–13, 137
 Critique et clinique 1, 17–18, 20, 24–25, 27, 32, 46,
  53, 146

Deterritorialisation 1, 3, 13, 16–20, 26, 28, 32–36, 51, 53, 63, 76, 92, 96–97, 100–02, 113, 118, 137, 171, 173–74, 177
Logique du sens 82
Major language 15–16, 21, 24–25, 32, 46, 51–52, 98–99, 106–07, 111–12, 121, 166, 171–72, 177
Minor language 13–14, 16, 19–20, 46, 82, 91–92, 98–102, 106, 111, 172, 177
Minor literature 1, 15–16, 20–22, 24–25, 27–29, 31–36, 46, 56–57, 70, 82, 91, 98, 100, 110, 114, 118, 121, 126, 137, 160, 166, 171, 173–74, 176–77
Rhizome 13, 60–61, 69, 72, 75–76, 81, 121, 131, 168 f. 52, 121, 131, 145, 173
Stutter 14, 27–28, 32, 57–59, 82, 96, 100, 118, 158, 173
works with Claire Parnet:
    Dialogues 1, 160
works with Félix Guattari:
    Kafka: pour une littérature mineure 1, 16, 24, 160, 177
    Mille plateaux 1, 15–16, 20–21, 24, 27, 59–60, 72, 100–01, 111
Derrida, Jacques 14, 25–26, 44, 56, 77 f. 6, 170 f. 88, 173
Desnos, Robert 75
Dickinson, Emily 73
dictionaries and grammar books 13, 21, 23, 82–92, 101–02, 107–13, 172
Dimitrova, Zornitsa 19
Disson, Agnès 9, 22, 61–62, 70, 79 f. 49
Doury, Pascal 127
Dubois, Jean 82, 107
Du Bouchet, André 5, 128, 175
Duchamp, Marcel 63, 75
Dusapin, Pascal 119

Eskin, Michael 36
Espitallier, Jean-Michel 10, 30, 41 n. 94, 144, 174

Farah, Alain 82, 114
Fiat, Christophe 31, 41 f. 94
Flaubert, Gustave 107
Fourcade, Dominique:
    'après les attentats' 56
    Le Ciel pas d'angle 12, 63–65, 72–73
    Citizen Do 12, 64, 67, 69, 72–74, 77, 153
    En laisse 12, 55–56, 176
    Éponges modèle 2003: 12
    Épreuves du pouvoir 12
    Est-ce que j'peux placer un mot? 12, 43–46, 49, 51–52, 54–58, 62, 66–69, 153, 172, 175
    IL 12, 48–49, 54, 56–59, 62, 65–66, 71–72, 74
    Lessive du loup 12
    Manque 12, 54, 65–66, 72, 176
    Outrance utterance 12, 47, 53, 55, 66, 68, 74, 178
    Rose-déclic 12, 49, 53, 65–68, 71–76
    Sans lasso et sans flash 12
    Son blanc du un 12, 51–52, 65, 68, 72, 74, 76, 178
    Le Sujet monotype 12, 57, 62–63
    Xbo 12, 46–51, 54–57, 60–63, 68, 72, 74, 76
French *chanson* 11, 103–04, 116

Game, Jérôme 2, 13–14, 17, 27, 38 f. 6, 153
    On Fourcade 48, 60–62, 71, 75
    On Cadiot 81–82, 92, 96–97, 125 f. 99
Gelas, Bruno 2
Gleize, Jean-Marie 5–13, 29–31, 38 f. 17 & 24, 78 f. 36, 121, 128–29, 150, 161, 174–75
Godard, Jean-Luc 24
Goethe, Johann Wolfgang von 64, 104
Goldsmith, Kenneth 10, 39 f. 42
grammar books, *see* dictionaries and grammar books
Grice, Paul 140
Guattari, Félix, *see* Gilles Deleuze and Félix Guattari
Gysin, Brion 9, 83

Hanna, Christophe 30–31, 131
Hantaï, Simon 63–64, 73
Heidegger, Martin 73, 165
Hiedsieck, Bernard 4, 14, 94, 107, 123 f. 27, 128, 172
Hocquard, Emmanuel 4, 11, 17, 68–69, 71, 89–90, 114
    'La Bibliothèque de Trieste' 3, 6–7, 20, 178
    Tout le monde se ressemble 22–23, 28, 122 f. 11, 135, 139
Horace 115
Howe, Susan 54, 58, 73, 78 f. 41
Hugo, Victor 114

Jaccottet, Philippe 5, 130
Jakobson, Roman 125 f. 99, 171
Jenny, Laurent 137
Joyce, James 55

Kafka, Franz 2, 19, 24, 177
Kelly, Michael G. 2–3, 32, 35, 53, 71, 177
Khalfa, Jean 57
Khatibi, Abdelkebir 26, 44
Kristeva, Julia 29, 123 f. 42
Kurts, Lia 86–87, 110

Labov, William 140
La Fontaine, Jean de 73
Lamartine, Alphonse de 11, 115
Lamiot, Christophe 107
L=A=N=G=U=A=G=E poets 12
Laugier, Emmanuel 53, 69
Lautréamont, Comte de 1, 4, 114–15
Lavin, Mathias 65
Leiris, Michel 107–08
Lequette, Samuel 159
Leuwers, Daniel 45, 71

Index

Lipschitz, Rudolph 144
Liron, Yannick 70
Littéralité 5–7, 9, 12–13, 38 f. 17, 43, 102
Luca, Gherasim 2, 19–22, 24, 27–28, 32, 35
Lucot, Hubert 2
Lynch, Eric 10, 39 f. 43, 82, 92, 120–21

Maestri, Vannina 31, 39 f. 45
Mallarmé, Stéphane 1, 4, 6, 10, 25, 48, 65, 68–69, 71–73, 75, 78 f. 46, 91, 107, 110, 147, 162, 171–72
Manet, Edouard 63, 69–70
Manno, Yves di 147
Matisse, Henri 63–65, 73
Maulpoix, Jean-Michel 5
Michaux, Henri 107
Michelet, Jules 114
Micolet, Hervé 2
Miller, Henry 89, 102
Molnàr, Katalin 2, 127
Mother tongue:
    in Cadiot 95–96, 105–06
    in Deleuze 24–26
    in Fourcade 43–46, 51–53, 71, 76, 172
    in Tarkos 137

Naughton, John T. 147
Néo-lyrisme 5, 8–10, 12, 128
Nietzsche, Friedrich 104
Noël, Bernard 18, 32, 35
Noland, Carrie 11, 146, 172
Novarina, Valère 128
Nowell Smith, David 4

Onoma, Kat 119
Oulipo 4, 107, 128
Ovid 114

Palmer, Michael 73
Parish, Nina 11
Parnet, Claire, *see* Gilles Deleuze
Pennequin, Charles 14, 30, 39 f. 45, 127–28, 150, 175
Perec, Georges 107, 128, 143, 145
Perloff, Marjorie 10, 17, 35–36, 59
Person, Xavier 89–90
Pinson, Jean-Claude 2, 5–6, 8, 65
    on Fourcade 43, 63, 65, 71, 73–74
    on poethics 8, 129, 164–65, 175–76
Ponge, Francis 4, 22, 49, 55, 76, 78 f. 20, 107, 128, 142, 145–46, 162, 168 f. 46, 169 f. 74
Portugal, Anne 14
Post-poetry 13, 121, 173–75
Pound, Ezra 36
Prigent, Christian 8, 11, 17, 25, 53, 84, 89, 138, 172, 176
    on Cadiot 87–88, 115–17, 119
    on Deleuze 2–3, 19, 25, 28–29, 33, 35, 177
    on Tarkos 41 f. 86, 127–28, 136–37, 142–43, 147, 149–50
Proust, Marcel 2, 17–18, 25, 27, 44, 73, 79 f. 72, 114

Queneau, Raymond 115
Quintane, Nathalie 14, 30, 39 f. 45, 127–28, 175

Rabaté, Dominique 5, 17, 36, 45, 91, 118, 120, 176–77
Réda, Jacques 5, 128
Renaud, Jean 81, 97
Revue de littérature générale 9–10, 13, 22, 61–62, 70–71, 81, 127, 173, 175
    'Digest' 9, 36, 121
    'La mécanique lyrique' 9–10, 22, 70–71, 83–84, 89–90, 117, 120–21, 163, 173, 175
Reznikoff, Charles 13, 83, 122
Rilke, Rainer Maria 75
Rimbaud, Arthur 1, 4, 6, 25, 35–36, 138, 162, 172
Roche, Denis 7, 39, 91, 97, 162, 172, 175
Romanticism 4–5, 36, 75, 104, 115
Ronsard, Pierre de 72, 75
Roubaud, Jacques 83, 123 f. 23
Roux, Paul de 5, 128
Rouzeau, Valérie 30
Royet-Journoud, Claude 4, 6, 22
Russell, Bertrand 129–30

Sadin, Eric 11, 31, 36, 39 f. 45
Sartre, Jean-Paul 25, 29, 169 f. 74
Saussure, Ferdinand de 4, 14, 53, 139–40, 153, 168 f. 39, 172
Schwitters, Kurt 82, 93, 104, 128
Searle, John 140
Sekiguchi, Ryoko 26
Shakespeare, William 114
Shklovsky, Victor 25–26
Sollers, Philippe 146
Sound poetry 4, 10, 14, 107, 116, 118
Spicer, Jack 98–99
Spinoza, Baruch 15, 82, 102
Stein, Gertrude 13, 17, 73, 75, 81–83, 93, 116–17, 123, 128
Surrealism 4–5, 36, 38 f. 17, 40 f. 76, 82–83

Tardos, Anne 26
Tarkos, Christophe:
    Anachronisme 14, 127, 130–32, 136, 141–45, 147, 149–52, 154–57, 163, 178
    L'Argent 135
    Le Baroque 129, 143, 154
    Le Bâton 14, 127
    La Cage 155
    Caisses 14, 127, 142–43, 154, 158
    Dix ronds 158
    Écrits poétiques 14, 127, 129–37, 147, 150, 152–55, 157, 159, 161–63, 165–66

L'Enregistré 14, 126–27, 131, 136, 139–41, 144, 148–49, 154, 158–65, 178
Ma langue 127, 129–30, 151, 154–58, 178
Morceaux choisis 13, 127, 131, 143–45, 158
L'Oiseau vole 13
Oui 13, 127, 134–36, 150, 155
Processe 13, 127, 129, 132–34, 144, 157–58
Le Signe = 14, 127, 133–35, 138–40, 150, 156
PAN 14, 127
Le Train 13, 127, 137, 172
Tel Quel 4, 29, 128
Théval, Gaëlle 102, 122 f. 7 & 12
Tholomé, Vincent 127
Thomas, Henri 5, 128
Thomas, Jean-Jacques 56

Tournier, Michel 82

Valabrègue, Frédéric 48, 53, 56, 61, 63, 71, 74–75, 78 f. 46
Verdier, Bertrand 129

Wall-Romana, Christophe 38 f. 24, 68
Whitehead, Alfred North 129–30
Williams, William Carlos 9
Winspur, Steven 56
Wittgenstein, Ludwig 17, 22, 40 f. 61
Wolfson, Louis 41 f. 85, 46, 53, 78 f. 23, 96, 124 f. 47
Wourm, Nathalie 11, 14, 30–31, 39 f. 43, 82–83, 118, 173–74

www.ingramcontent.com/pod-product-compliance
Lightning Source LLC
LaVergne TN
LVHW061251060426
835507LV00017B/2016